T0290499

THE WHO
ON THE WHO
INTERVIEWS AND ENCOUNTERS

EDITED BY SEAN EGAN

CHICAGO
REVIEW
PRESS

An A Cappella Book

Published by Chicago Review Press Incorporated
814 North Franklin Street
Chicago, Illinois 60610

ISBN 978-1-61373-613-5

A list of credits and copyright notices for the individual pieces in this collection can be found on pages 391–392.

Library of Congress Cataloging-In-Publication Data
Names: Egan, Sean.
Title: The Who on the Who : interviews and encounters / [edited by] Sean Egan.
Description: Chicago, Illinois : Chicago Review Press, [2017] | Series:
   Musicians in their own words | Includes bibliographical references and
   index.
Identifiers: LCCN 2017013436 | ISBN 9781613736135 (hardcover)
Subjects: LCSH: Who (Musical group)--Interviews. | Rock
   musicians--England--Interviews. | Who (Musical group)
Classification: LCC ML421.W5 W53 2017 | DDC 782.42166092/2--dc23 LC
record available at https://lccn.loc.gov/2017013436

Interior layout: Nord Compo

Printed in the United States of America
5 4 3 2 1

CONTENTS

Introduction   v

The Making of The Who | JOHN HEILPERN

    March 20, 1966 | *Observer Colour Magazine* (UK)   1

Miles Interviews Pete Townshend | BARRY MILES

    February 13–26, 1967 | *International Times* (UK)   12

Pete Talks About Tommy | BARRY MILES

    May 23–June 5 and June 13–28, 1969 |

    International Times (UK)   19

A Talk with Pete Townshend | JONATHAN COTT

    May 14, 1970 | *Rolling Stone* (US)   38

The Who Puts the Bomp or They Won't Get Fooled Again | JOHN SWENSON

    December 5, 1971 | *Crawdaddy* (US)   58

Chatting with Pete Townshend | CONNOR McKNIGHT AND JOHN TOBLER

    February 1972–August 1974 | *Zigzag* (UK)   95

Who's Still Who | JOHN LAWLESS

    March 19, 1972 | *Observer Colour Magazine* (UK)   151

Four-Way Pete/Who's Jimmy? | CHARLES SHAAR MURRAY

    October 27 and November 3, 1973 | *New Musical Express* (UK)   160

Pete Townshend | ROY CARR

    May 24, 1975 | *New Musical Express* (UK)   174

Who's Last? | TONY STEWART

    August 9, 1975 | *New Musical Express* (UK)   190

John Entwistle: The Who's Great Bass Guitarist | STEVE ROSEN

November 1975 | *Guitar Player* (US)............................ 203

Who Said That! The 1978 Pete Townshend Interview | TONY STEWART

August 12, 1978 | *New Musical Express* (UK) 214

The Keith Moon Exclusive | EAMONN PERCIVAL

September 1978 | *International Musician
and Recording World* (UK)...................................... 235

The *Rolling Stone* Interview: Pete Townshend | GREIL MARCUS

June 26, 1980 | *Rolling Stone* (US) 244

The *Guitar Greats*: Pete Townshend | JOHN TOBLER AND STUART GRUNDY

1983 | *The Guitar Greats* (UK) 263

Who's Back | CHARLES M. YOUNG

July 1989 | *Musician* (US)...................................... 290

"It's Like Climbing Mount Everest": Roger Daltrey | SEAN EGAN

2002 | Previously unpublished in this form 319

"Any Cunt Can Be an Entertainer": Pete Townshend | SEAN EGAN

2003 | Previously unpublished in this form 326

Generation Terrorists | SIMON GARFIELD

September 2006 | *Observer Music Monthly* (UK)................. 345

Amazing Journey: Roger Daltrey | SEAN EGAN

2007 | Previously unpublished in this form 359

**Kenney Jones, Drummer of Small Faces, Faces with Rod Stewart
and the Who, Looks Back (and Forward)** | BINKY PHILIPS

January 17, 2014, and March 19, 2014 | *Huffington Post* (US)...... 365

Look Who's Talking! | ADRIAN DEEVOY

October 26, 2014 | *The Mail on Sunday/Event* (UK) 380

Credits 391

About the Contributors 393

Index....................... 397

INTRODUCTION

When the Who announced that their 2014–2015 tour was "the beginning of the long goodbye," they served notice that popular music was losing one of its titans.

The Who were a mass of contradictions. They created the anthem of their generation but were loved by audiences not even born when they started. They brought intellect to rock but were the darlings of snotty punks. They were the quintessential studio act yet were also the greatest live attraction in the world. The most striking of the dichotomies underpinning their story, however, is the contrast between the way they meshed on stage and their lack of personal chemistry offstage. Aside from primarily hailing from West London, they had nothing in common. As their lead singer Roger Daltrey once observed, "I don't want to be in a group with anybody else, although if I could choose three friends to go about with it wouldn't be those three."

Drummer Keith Moon was a clown whose buffoonery often tipped over into wanton acts of demolition, even self-destruction. When he was behind his giant kit, though, his disturbing desperation for attention was channeled in a benign direction: Moon's blurred virtuosity was astounding.

Moon's partner in the rhythm section could not have been more of a contrast. Nor could John Entwistle's brutal, belligerent bass style be more sharply juxtaposed with the person purveying it. Having said that, his reputation as the Quiet One was overplayed: he was a hedonist literally until the moment he died.

Guitarist Pete Townshend's prominent nose gave him a very peculiar look for a pop idol of the era. Behind that odd exterior was a ferocious intellect and an extraordinary talent. Although initially hesitant about songwriting, by the end of the sixties his compositional gifts had—banal phrase, but true—changed the world.

Fronting all of this was Daltrey. Roger Daltrey was—to use a Britishism—stroppy. He was overconfident in the manner of many men who are both good looking and able to handle themselves in a fight. He was also, however, a vocalist of exquisite sensitivity, interpreting Townshend's visions in alternately roaring and tremulous fashion. Moreover, as Townshend's concepts became ever more cerebral, it was Daltrey who sustained a working-class grit within the ensemble.

Despite being bound together only by the knowledge that they needed each others' skills, the Who weaved a magical collective spell.

Even when in the early seventies they abandoned their auto-destruction, they remained the most exciting spectacle in rock. Moon mugged, grimaced, tossed his sticks, and affected posh voices even as he played both ferociously and professionally. Entwistle stood looking like he was waiting for a bus as he peeled off bass lines whose qualities few alive could hope to match. Townshend leapt, flailed, and dramatically windmilled his playing arm. Daltrey—increasingly resembling Michelangelo's *David*—strutted the stage with his blond locks tumbling to the shoulders of his buckskin jacket as he twirled his microphone lead like a cowboy's lasso.

Release-wise, the Who were neither prolific nor consistent. When on form, though, their genius was indisputable. Their 1965 single "My Generation" was a rampaging, galvanizing call to arms that perfectly summed up the feelings of the young at a point when an unprecedented chasm lay between the values of the age groups. The string of singles that followed "My Generation" brought to the UK charts with wit and melodicism subjects no one else dared to essay, including self-loathing ("Substitute"), enforced transvestitism ("I'm a Boy"), and image-assisted masturbation ("Pictures of Lily").

In May 1969, the Who unleashed an album underpinned by a concept the depth of which popular music had never seen. Their previous two LPs had ended with mini-operas, but *Tommy*—a double set when they were still rare—was an album-long narrative centered around disability, child abuse, and messianic cults, with a little whimsy thrown in in the form of a pinball strand. "I always felt sick that rock was looked upon as a kind of second best to other art forms," Townshend later said, "that there was some dispute as to whether rock was art." Townshend changed all that. *Tommy* not only raced up the charts but also garnered coverage in conservative areas of the media that were amazed to find that rock could be something more than incoherent and primitive.

The band's follow-up was a complete contrast. *Live at Leeds* (1970) was an in-concert recording whose abrasive virtuosity made it as influential on the development of the nascent heavy metal medium as the LP debuts of Led Zeppelin and Black Sabbath.

Who's Next (1971) was the remains of Townshend's next intended opus, a double concept album called *Lifehouse.* Following a torturous development, producer Glyn Johns persuaded Townshend to cut it down to a single LP consisting of what Johns considered to be the best *Lifehouse* songs, sequenced with complete disregard for original narrative purpose. The result was, quite unforeseeably, one of the dozen greatest albums ever made, then or now. The highlight was "Won't Get Fooled Again," an eight-and-a-half-minute barnstorming epic that provided a disillusioned bookend to the defiance of "My Generation." It struck a profound chord in lamenting of the "sixties hangover": "Nothing in the street looks any different to me."

If *Who's Next* was the last long-playing Who masterpiece, it could never be said that their subsequent releases were not well-crafted and thoughtful, particularly the lavish tribute to their original mod fanbase *Quadrophenia* (1973) and the self-doubting *Who by Numbers* (1975). Moreover, on individual tracks they periodically proved they still had it: the beautiful "Love, Reign o'er Me," the saucy, infectious "Squeeze Box," and the sweaty, self-loathing "Who Are You" were patently neo-Who classics.

As well as proffering great spectacle and supreme audio experiences, the Who provided great copy. During the sixties and seventies, Townshend was a de facto spokesman for rock royalty. Messianic about contemporary popular music and its central importance in the lives of young people, especially those young people determined to change the world, he was in the habit of giving to the music press sprawling interviews in which he alternately celebrated and deplored what he saw in the "scene." Several of these interviews have come to be considered classic documents of the age.

Moreover, the chalk-and-cheese Daltrey and Townshend seemed to feel more comfortable conducting dialogues in the press than face to face. It was fascinating to follow the back-and-forth as the guitarist's comments on the Who's career were repudiated or contradicted in print by his colleague, using the kind of blunt phraseology for which Daltrey is known. Moon and Entwistle joined in, in their respective inimitable styles—lunatic and lugubrious. Even when the Who were nonoperational or past their peak, their interviews continued to be as (or even more) compelling: changes in allegiances and social mores left the band members freer to talk about sex, drug-taking, business, and in-fighting, while changes in individual perspectives saw them discuss past behavior, stances, and recordings in a different light.

By collecting interviews with Who members from across five decades, *The Who on the Who* provides the full, fractious story of a band that veered wildly between art and barbarism, academia and anti-intellectualism, and effortless artistic highs and artistic depths plumbed through no lack of trying. The articles herein—mined from such prestigious outlets as *Crawdaddy*, the *International Times*, *New Musical Express*, the *Observer*, *Rolling Stone*, *Zigzag*, and others—provide an insight into not just a great rock group but the tumultuous times in which they reigned.

—SEAN EGAN

THE MAKING OF THE WHO

John Heilpern | March 20, 1966 | *Observer Colour Magazine* (UK)

Pete Townshend felt that this cover feature from the magazine section of British broadsheet newspaper the *Observer* misrepresented the Who on two counts.

As John Heilpern now says, "The *Observer* magazine was edited then by Anthony Sampson and he wanted to know who was *behind* a new rock group weirdly named the Who. His wife Sally had known Kit Lambert since they were both at Oxford together, which is how this novice reporter first came to meet Kit and Chris. I was so struck by their unlikely, fun partnership that we went ahead with the story on them.

"Out of the 'The Making of the Who' came a very happy thing: Chris Stamp and I became life-long friends. I was honored—and greatly saddened—to speak at his 2012 Memorial Service that Roger Daltrey attended. Pete Townshend was otherwise engaged.

"And what does Townshend personally leave me with? See his autobiography *Who I Am*, where he writes, 'The *Observer* story itself was a puff for Kit and Chris, but the rest of us were represented as braggarts, spendthrifts, dandies and scumbags.' In fact, the rest of them were scarcely mentioned, apart from a pro forma list of who was who. That was the point.

"But Townshend truly excels himself when he complains that the photographer deliberately made his nose 'look enormous' during the shoot for the magazine cover. I ask you in all fairness, how on earth can one make Pete Townshend's shnozzola look any bigger than it already is?"

Nonetheless, "The Making of the Who" was an important feature. The Colin Jones picture that graced the magazine's cover was instantly iconic, featuring the band swathed in, and backed by, the Union Jack, a future Who motif. The article being inordinately business-oriented was less important than the fact that a "posh" paper had published a serious piece of journalism about the practitioners of what was then widely dismissed as low culture.

1

Notes: for "The Highnumbers" read "The High Numbers"
for "Townsend" read "Townshend" —Ed.

On November 5, 1965, The Who released a stammering song called "My Generation". It sold more than 300,000 records, won a Silver Disc, became an international hit throughout Europe, and assured the group a gross income over £1,000 a week.

Fourteen months ago The Who were unknown. This is the story how they made their fame.

They are managed by two extraordinary young entrepreneurs, Kit Lambert and Chris Stamp. It's an odd combination. Lambert, son of the composer Constant Lambert, was educated at Lancing and Trinity College, Oxford. He talks very fast, posh: "When I did National Service, I was the worst officer in the British Army."

Stamp, 23 years old, is the son of an East End tugboatman and brother of Terence Stamp, the film-star. Dressed in Carnaby Street, he speaks in a broad Cockney accent. "I like the blatantness of pop, the speed, the urgency. There's either success or failure—no use bollockin' about."

Two years ago Lambert and Stamp were both successful assistant film directors earning £5,000 a year. They decided to make a documentary about pop, and most nights of the week they'd go out in their cars looking for pop groups suitable for the film. After several weeks' search, Lambert came across the Railway Tavern, Harrow and Wealdstone. In a crowded back room were a group called The Highnumbers. "As soon as I saw them I felt a total conviction that this was it. It's as simple as that—this was it! Bingo!" They were The Who.

The next day, Lambert was already thinking in terms of taking them over. He persuaded Stamp to come and see the group. They drove together to the Watford Trade Hall—still one of The Who's most popular venues—and caught the last 20 minutes of their act. "I was knocked out," says Stamp. "But the excitement I felt wasn't coming from the group. I couldn't get near enough. It was coming from the people blocking my way."

For £2 Stamp and Lambert hired the Youth Club in Notting Hill Gate and auditioned the group in the morning. Four days later, Lambert and Stamp were their managers.

The contract guaranteed each member of the group £1,000 a year, irrespective of whether they got another booking. "Pop appealed to us," says Lambert, "because it's a field where it's possible to make a great deal of money very quickly. We've subsequently been proved dead wrong." Within three months, personal savings of £6,000 were eaten up, fine apartments made way for digs, and gold watches were pawned (they still are).

They changed the name of the group to The Who. "The High-numbers was a nothing name," explains Stamp. "It implied the Top Twenty, but The Who seemed so perfect for them. It was impersonal, it couldn't be dated." Lambert: "It's a gimmick name—journalists could write articles called THE WHY OF THE WHO, and people had to go through a boring ritual of question and answer. 'Have you heard The Who? The Who? The Who.' It was an invitation to corniness, and we were in a corny world."

The group began to have their hair styled by Gordon at Robert James Hairdressers in the Charing Cross Road. Three-hour sessions every two weeks: "Long hair is glamorous, distinctive." They listened to hundreds of records. Pete Townsend, the lead guitarist, experimented with sound, perfecting a deafening system called "feedback" which became The Who's trademark and was later used by the Beatles. In 10 months £6,000 was spent on electronic equipment.

"Appearance is the most immediate association with the kids," says Lambert. "The clothes just had to be right." They had them specially designed. They went to Carnaby Street, spending as much as £150 a week. They searched for military outfits, period costumes, shopping in women's stores where the colours are brighter and the sweaters distinctive. They held countless photo sessions, four hours at a time. "We didn't want any boy-next-door image," says Stamp. "We hated those grinning gits on other pictures." Even now, £1,000 a year is spent on photographs.

Working alternately on films, Lambert and Stamp went out on the road. They wined and dined promoters, worked 17 hours a day, and buttonholed anyone who'd listen. But it was no use.

The pop boom, which began with the Liverpool sound, was on the decline: record sales were falling off, promoters going bankrupt, and groups which had once gone out for £300 a night were lucky to get £50. After three months, The Who were getting nowhere.

"We realised that if the group were to build up any national following, we must take the West End." They chose the Marquee Club in Soho, a famous haven of mod teenagers, putting enormous pressure on the promoter, Ziggy Jackson. For five weeks they nattered him silly until Jackson finally caved in and let them promote their own show on Tuesdays, a dead night.

"Our primary concern was to get an audience. Money didn't matter." They rushed out 1,500 posters for a London-wide campaign, dealing with The Fly Posters' Association.

They printed 2,500 handouts, distributing them at dances, clubs, coffee bars, Saturday-morning markets—anywhere. And the campaign was particularly intensive in the group's home town, Shepherd's Bush: The Who had to acquire a clear, geographical tag. Every street was covered, and 30 key fans from the area were given free tickets. More tickets were at half-price, particularly to a club called The 100 Faces, formed for the occasion. The promotion costs were £300.

But on the night it was raining cats and dogs. The Marquee has a capacity of 1,200. 147 turned up. 69 paid. They turned off the lights and Lambert quietly doled out whisky to the faithful Shepherd's Bush mods. The Who did the rest: Keith Moon attacked his drums with a sound and fury, breaking four drumsticks, until his clothes stuck to him and his jaw sagged with exhaustion. Roger Daltrey, the singer, dripping with sweat, shouted himself hoarse, smashing his mike onto the floor. Pete Townsend, nicknamed "The Birdman", went berserk, ramming the neck of his guitar into the amplifier until it smashed to bits. And John Entwistle, former french horn player in the Middlesex Youth Orchestra, just stood there, all in black, legs apart. "Without him,'" says Stamp, "they'd fly, they'd fly away." The Who were booked for another 16 weeks.

"To my mind," says Stamp, "their act creates emotions of anger and violence, and a thousand other things I don't really understand myself." Lambert agrees: "Their rootlessness appeals to the kids. They're really a new form of crime—armed against the bourgeois." (Keith Moon's father is an engineer.) "The point is, we're not saying, Here are four nice, cleancut lads come to entertain you. We're saying, Here is something outrageous—go wild!"

But records are the essence of the business. The group had already failed a recording audition with the biggest British record company, E.M.I. They decided to cut their own demonstration disc at Studio 2,000 behind the Marquee: the number was to be their first hit, "I Can't Explain", composed by Pete Townsend.

Shel Talmy, an American independent record producer, heard the record, immediately auditioned The Who in the basement of The 2 I's Coffee Bar and moved in with a recording contract.

"The kind of success we hope for," explains Lambert, "could only come from America." Talmy leased the contract to American Decca, and through them to Decca in England. Lambert and Stamp signed for five years. Within weeks, they were to have a blazing row with Talmy and beg American Decca to free them.

On January 15, 1965, they released "I Can't Explain" in Britain. At the same time, Lambert and Stamp moved into an apartment in Eaton Place: "It was the only slum in Belgravia," says Lambert, "but it got us credit." In the smallest bedroom they set up an office consisting of a two-line switchboard and a kitchen table, and hired the first of 20 successive secretaries. With Stamp's wages from filming, Lambert threw a champagne party to launch the record. The world's disc jockeys were invited, but only Dave Dennis of Radio London turned up.

The celebration was premature. Decca printed little more than 1,000 copies of the record, giving it minimum plugging time on their own Luxembourg record shows.

Lambert decided to promote the record virtually single-handed. He went all out: jukebox firms, ballrooms, coffee bars, handing out hundreds of posters, talking personally to every D.J. in sight. He went for the pirate radio stations, where Dave Dennis turned up trumps and plugged the disc as a "climber" on Radio London.

But most of all, he plugged for television—the key to sales promotion. Lambert had an introduction to Bob Bickford, a former *Daily Mail* journalist who was now editor of "Ready Steady Go". Fortunately, Bickford knew of The Who's reputation at The Marquee and booked the group. Lambert could hardly believe his luck.

In the week that The Who were due on the air, "Ready Steady Go" unexpectedly needed 150 extra dancers at four days' notice. Lambert innocently suggested they went down to The Marquee, where The Who were performing: and a TV official unknowingly handed out 150 free tickets to the Shepherd's Bush mods and members of Lambert's own club, The 100 Faces. The result was a managerial triumph: on the night, half the studio was filled with key fans of The Who. The show was a smash.

On the following Monday Decca swung behind Lambert. Lambert succeeded in getting the group on to Southern TV through an Oxford contemporary, producer Angus Wright. On February 14 the record began to show at number 47 in the *Music Echo,* a newspaper then in its infancy. It went up gradually, reaching number 25 in the *New Musical Express,* a key chart. And then, the following week, it dropped out completely.

Then Lambert and Stamp gambled heavily: they directed a film of "The Who", hoping to persuade a TV programme, "That's For Me", to use it. They worked day and night for three days. The cost was £350, but "That's For Me" took the film for their next show—at a price of £25.

Within a week the record was back at number 23 in the *New Musical Express.* And then, a lucky break: "Top of the Pops", a programme networked into 5½ million homes, was let down at the last moment by a group with managerial difficulties. They gave The Who their "Tip for the Top" spot. One week later, the disc shot into the Top Twenty—selling 10,000 a day—and finally ended up at number 8 with a sale of 104,000. Lambert went wild, running through Belgravia screaming, "We've cracked it! We've cracked it, you bastards!"

But the next morning was like a hangover. Record royalties amounted to almost £35,000, but the publicity campaign wiped out any managerial profit. The shops would make £10,000, songwriter Pete Townsend and his publisher, David Platz, would make £2,000, and the taxman, £4,700—everyone would make money except Lambert and Stamp. The Who ended up with £250 each. Decca grossed roughly £16,000. For the first time, they made strong objections to the actual terms of the contract. After three weeks of frantic argument, Decca agreed to raise the percentage deal retrospectively to 4 per cent in England and Europe.

"It's known as The Myth of Pop," says Lambert. "We began to realize that the first record was only a start." In debt up to their eyes, they refused to give in, and instead abandoned making films entirely. They were going for the jackpot, for America.

They went all out for a second, crucial hit. "If we didn't make it, we'd had it," says Stamp. "We had to bring through the image of the group on record. After all, they were creating something, they're not just four geezers in a suit." There was one encouraging sign: the Press was at last beginning to take an interest. Richard Green wrote a feature called A DISTURBING GROUP in *Record Mirror,* describing Lambert as "a very loquacious young gentleman who takes great pains to put his points across". And *Boyfriend* wrote: "Love them or loathe them, The Who have made themselves something that other groups have longed for—a new image."

But the image was about to change. Singer Roger Daltrey had a gimmick of sticking black Sellotape onto a white sweater—changing the designs from night to night. The trick spread, almost by accident, to the rest of the group. Entwistle bought up dozens of medals, pinning them onto a diamond-check jacket. Moon wore a white T-shirt with a coloured target, a picture of Elvis, and the word "Pow!" And a Union Jack, until now draped over Townsend's speaker cabinet, became his jacket. Only in the world of pop could the sacred symbol of British royalty come to be identified by thousands of teenagers as the symbol of The Who. But it was the turning point: The Who were first in the field with Pop Art.

Lambert didn't waste a second: "We never intended to go for a quick profit with the group—we wanted a whole new scene going. We knew Pop Art could swing it." Rather dubiously, they claimed The Pop Art *Sound,* rushing out thousands of specially designed handouts, re-taking hundreds of pictures, contacting every journalist they could lay their hands on. On May 21, the release date of the record, The Who had a live appearance on "Ready Steady Go", shambling nervously into the studio dressed in Pop Art gear. They were an overnight sensation.

"D.J.s love a new sound," says Stamp. "It gives them something to say, gives them spiel between records." The record itself went out with a Pop Art cover in bright orange and yellow: *Pow! Don't walk, run to your nearest record player.* The national Press were now doing full-scale features, fashion houses turned to Pop Art, and Carnaby Street began to rake in a fortune. Within a week, "Anyway, Anyhow, Anywhere", composed by Pete Townsend in a day, made the charts. After three more television shows, it went to number 12, selling 88,000.

Suddenly the established figures in the industry began to sit up. A surprise lunch date arrived from Rolling Stones' manager, Andrew Old-ham. At the Ad Lib discothèque, where the hierarchy of the pop world were seated with all the snobbery of a church wedding, the humblest table became vacant.

With the success of their second record, The Who went out on a gruelling three-month nationwide tour. Either Lambert or Stamp went with them, attending to the thousand and one crises that can arise with four teenagers travelling as much as 750 miles a week. They stuck with them for another reason: to protect the group and themselves from takeover bids.

Touring expenses were high—£150 a week—but, at least, the money was beginning to pour in. At the Astoria Ballroom, Rawtenstall, Lancs, the Dungeon Club, Nottingham, Trentham Gardens, Stoke on Trent—£150 a night.

"My Generation" rocketed into the charts:

> *People try to put us down,*
> *Talkin' 'bout my generation*
> *Just because we get around,*
> *Talkin' 'bout my generation.*

The success of "Generation" meant that The Who now averaged £300 a night. But they have to pay for clothes, instruments, travel (£7,000 a year), and two road managers. Lambert and Stamp took 40 per cent and the agent, Robert Stigwood, took 10 per cent of this. It left them with about £300 a week, set off against royalties. But they didn't keep a penny. Promotional films averaged £15 a week, travel costs another £50, office rental £10, picture sessions another £20, American and overseas promotional budget £60 a week, entertainment £20. And more—telephone and cables £30 a week, office stationery and fan club £20, secretary (Anya Butler) and publicist (Patricia Locke) another £45. They even hired a tour manager: £40 a week.

"My Generation" just squeezed into the American charts at number 97. Stamp decided to go over to America for two weeks to whip up the promotional campaign, and to confront Sir Edward Lewis, the head of British Decca, who happened to be there at the same time. He took to a stifling New York like lean men to a steam bath. "What a scene," he kept on saying. "What an unbelievable scene!"

He went to see his agent in America, Lloyd Greenfield, on the fifteenth floor of the Rockefeller Plaza. Greenfield is 38 years old, wears monogrammed shirts, and smiles mischievously. He is the man who discovered Buddy Holly, who is to pop what James Dean was to films: "I had his teeth capped, changed his glasses—and the rest was history." And then, "Listen, shmock, I'm gonna break my neck to get The Who a hit record here," said Greenfield. "I don't just take on anybody—I was the man who made Buddy Holly."

Greenfield reassured Stamp of his faith in The Who: "The only way to sustain yourself in this business is by visual performance. That's where The Who have it. There's only one group so punchy—Cannonball and the Head Hunters." Stamp smiled, and Greenfield grabbed the phone. "Listen, baby, twenty thousand dollars and that's it. That's it!"

Greenfield spent $4,000 promoting "My Generation". "And it's not going to make it," he said. "It's just not gonna go." The money went on mailing more than 500 records to disc jockeys all over America, together with a personal letter to each one. Promotion men—hired to cover the east and west coasts—talked non-stop to D.J.s and programme managers.

the hard sell

The next day, Stamp got down to business. A girl called Gale, who seemed to turn up from nowhere, spent the day typing out 400 letters to D.J.s. Stamp tore round to the producers of "Hullabaloo", America's top pop show, giving them a promotional film of The Who, hoping to secure a booking. And on to W.M.C.A., the biggest pop station in New York, to meet any disc jockey who would see him.

Stamp went to see his publisher, Happy Goday, Vice-President of the Richmond Organisation, in an office packed with demonstration records, sheet music, a piano, and a stereogram that played non-stop. "'Generation' is in the charts by hard graft. If it's got it in the grooves, it'll go. From there we can't control it." On his desk was the sheet music for a song called "God is My Mother". "Everything is chance. I can hear 8 bars of a song and say no."

But, like Greenfield, Goday was confident of The Who's success in America; "It's a matter of time, the right record." He handed Stamp a personal list of 500 D.J.s. "It's a tough business. I'm 48 and work an 18-hour day, every day of the week. I try not to hurt anyone."

Stamp was fixed up with an interview on W.N.E.W., a radio show broadcast from "The Dudes and Dolls" discothèque, where girls in tights dance on tables. The interview was a farce: *"Hi there, everybody! And welcome to Dudes and Dolls where tonight we have Chris Stamp all the way from merrie England. Nice to have you on the show, Chris."* "Nice to be here, Tony." *"Chris, I believe you're the brother of film star Terence Stamp?"* "That's right, Tony. As a matter of fact, Tony, he's mad on the pop group I manage called The Who." *"Who's this, Chris?"* "The Who, a new Pop Art group with a Pop Art sound. Paul McCartney said The Who were the biggest musical influence on the Beatles in '65."

Stamp started to work hard again at the D.J.s and programme managers, perhaps the most powerful men in American pop. Even now nobody asks any questions if a crate of whisky arrives on a D.J.'s doorstep. Stamp didn't get very far: they only wanted to know about a hit record. "My Generation" was still getting nowhere, and Stamp despaired of his record company.

The next day he telephoned Marty Salkin, Vice-President of American Decca, almost crying with anger. He phoned Lambert for advice and they decided; once and for all, to break the contract with American Decca, whatever the cost. Stamp consulted his American solicitor, Joe Vigoda, who thought there was a legal loophole, and immediately arranged a meeting with Sir Edward Lewis of Decca the next morning.

That night, unable to sleep, Stamp went the round of the discothèques. He went to Arthur's with Kay King, a fashion editor of top-selling *Glamour Magazine*. She agreed to arrange a spread on The Who with pictures by David Bailey. Stamp controlled his delight: to swing the feature he had to agree to a separate picture story of himself modelling clothes: "They'll think I'm a fairy, a fairy!"

The meeting with Sir Edward Lewis, aged 65, and the most important man in the record industry, went well. Stamp took Greenfield along: the meeting was cordial, friendly. Sir Edward agreed to see American Decca, his former company, that same afternoon, to see if The Who could change their American label. (Stamp had already received an offer from a rival company offering an inducement fee of £10,000 together with an astonishing 10 per cent of the American retail price.) But at 5.30 p.m. the next day, Sir Edward telephoned to say that nothing could be done. Stamp telephoned Lambert, and said, "Break the contract."

Stamp came back from America quite hopeful of the next move. His agent, Lloyd Greenfield, said: "In Britain The Who are today—today. Well, in America, they may be tomorrow."

the myth of pop

So, 14 months after they were originally discovered at the Railway Tavern, The Who wait anxiously for the last breakthrough. Their managers have seen a great deal of their first hunch borne out: they have made an unknown group break into the headlines, the hit parades and the hysteria-belt. But they have discovered, too, "the Myth of Pop", and have seen big money sliced up into small parcels, and the constant warning of groups who hit the top for a moment, and then disappear.

And they have realised how, in the bigger and bigger business of the pop world, the stakes get constantly higher, and the risks of failure get greater: scarcely 12 groups, it is said, out of the thousands performing all over Britain, are making "real money"—and that's the only kind of money The Who want.

MILES INTERVIEWS PETE TOWNSHEND

Barry Miles | February 13–26, 1967 | *International Times* **(UK)**

In early 1967, the Who had released just two albums (*My Generation* and *A Quick One*, December 1965 and December 1966 respectively), journalist Barry Miles went only by his surname, and music journalism was still largely mired in gushing banality. The latter fact makes the audacious, articulate philosophizing in this interview, drawn from UK underground newspaper the *International Times,* all the more astonishing.

Miles was as interested in the Who's famous instruments-wrecking stage act as he was their music. The nature is not known of the Who's forthcoming "blatantly commercial move" Townshend mentions herein, but it was almost certainly partly designed to compensate for their onstage auto-destruction which—while it had contributed to their reputation—was causing the Who to bleed money.

If Miles's reference to the group as "oft number-oned" was meant to refer to singles, it was as inaccurate then as now: despite their success and longevity, the Who, perplexingly, never had a recognized chart-topper either side of the Atlantic.

As with many counterculture publications, the *IT* had a louche attitude toward copyediting, something reflected in the reproduced text.

Notes: for "Shel Telmey" read "Shel Talmy"
    for "Edgar Allen Poe" read "Edgar Allan Poe" —Ed.

WHO? Pete Townshend, that's Who. Lead guitarist, song-writer, destructivist for this oft-number–oned-pop group. He walks, he talks, he smashes. The WHO is the most popular among many

auto-destructive groups on the scene at the moment. They are in the forefront of the smoke-bomb generation and are raping the boredom and expectation of the pop music world. WHO speaks.

Miles: Is your music an extension of anything you did at Art College?

Pete: Some fantastic things were done there. People were doing things which are now recognised as psychedelic images, and slides with liquid in them and things like that. Some great things were being produced but I got the feeling it was all to no good in the end and I got fantastically interested in auto-destruction because this was my answer to the problem which I had at the time. I didn't understand what was happening so I needed an answer and auto-destruction was the answer. This was apart from the rhythm and blues which we were playing in a group that I was in.

M: How do you see auto-destructive art?

P: When I was at Art College Gustav Metzger did a couple of lectures and he was my big hero. He comes to see us occasionally and rubs his hands and says, "How are you?" He wanted us to go to his symposium and give lectures and perhaps play and smash all our equipment for him. I got very deeply involved in auto-destruction but I wasn't too impressed by the practical side of it. When it actually came to being done it was always presented so badly: people would half-wittedly smash something and it would always turn round so the people who were against it would always be more powerful than the people that were doing it. Someone would come up and say, "Well WHY did you do it?" and the thing about auto-destruction is that it has no purpose, no reason at all. There is no reason why you allow these things to happen, why you set things off to happen or why you build a building that will fall down. The people who knock it can be so sarcastic, they're in such a powerful position.

M: Don't you see it as a creative act—creation through destruction?

P: Nobody knew what it was all about. Before the Who got big I wanted them to get bigger and bigger and bigger and bigger until a number one record and then wrap dynamite round their heads and blow themselves up on TV. It's just been one of those things. Well presented destruction is what I call a joy to watch, just like well presented pornography or obscenity. Although destruction is not as strong as obscenity, it's not so vulgar but it's rare, you don't see destruction so often, not malicious destruction just for the sake of it, and so when you do you normally stop and watch. I'd always thought that high class, high powered auto-destructive art, glossy destruction, glossy pop destruction, was far, far better than the terrible, messy, dirty, disorganised destruction that other people were involved in.

M: So you have only practiced it through music?

P: On the stage, yes. I have really done it, on a couple of occasions, glossily and flashily.

M: And it needs an audience?

P: When you've got an audience there it is one of the most exhilarating experiences you can have, like dropping your trousers in front of an audience. It's THE exhibitionist's delight, to do something really big in front of people. OK they know you're going to go out there and sing and play so that becomes nothing. For the next couple of years that's great but then you want more. You want people to tear their hair out when you appear and when they don't you feel you've got to extend your end a bit, you've really got to make them spew up. I think a lot of groups are just now finding out what audiences want. This is probably why acid's popular, because it makes you part of the audience. You take it, you sit back, there's no work, and off you go. It's 24 hours of touring. I think everyone is a member of an audience, everyone wants to sit back and watch. I do.

M: You have obviously evolved your own type of destruction as an art form.

P: I'm not afraid of calling anything I do an art form, I've just never thought of it further than it being something that personally I got pleasure out of, and which made me money. And cost me money. I've smashed up 28 guitars now which all cost about £200 each; let alone the amount of equipment that I've set fire to. But people just don't care anymore.

I go on and smash a £200 guitar and they go home and say "Yes, they were quite good tonight!" When I first did it people used to come up to me and say, "You Bastard! I've been saving all my life for a guitar a tenth of that price, and there you are smashing it up on stage. Give me the bits!" and I have to say, "Calm down, it's all in the cause." But nowadays people just come up and say "Like your LP." Yet there I am still getting the same kicks, it's the ultimate end to the act; along we go, we play through our LP tracks and we do our joke announcements and we do our commercial numbers and we do our movements. And then it comes to the end, we do **My Generation** and we fucking smash everything up.

M: How is this aimed at the audience? Do you do it to break through their materialism?

P: In a way. Unfortunately I've never really regarded my audiences high enough to say this. The materialism that I'm trying to break through is mine. It's my own. I'm probably the biggest most stupid materialist in existence. All the time I need to be fairly near to security. Money is great because it's just fucking paper.

M: Is "A Quick One" a reflection of your current direction in music?

P: Not really, I call it our first LP. It's our most important record but it's also weak because the group haven't really got together yet. It's good because the group have admitted that as the chief song writer I'm not a person to be scared of and that they can write songs and I'll play them and they'll be successful. The fact is that people haven't admitted that the group is still the basic vehicle. This is a problem but then it's a beginner. This is our first LP. Our first LP in reality was crap. It was all my songs of which I had 1000's and still have 1000's and we just sifted through the bunch for ones which were fairly commercial and knocked them off in a studio with Shel Telmey. And then we came out with our shit LP. With this one, if someone came and started pushing me around because my first LP was shit, I'd walk away. But if someone started pushing me around with this one I'd stay and take it or if I didn't agree I'd defend it.

This is something I was involved in and something which I'm willing to stand for.

M: I found "Run, run, run" the most interesting track because it gets away from conventional chords and into feedback and things like that which I've always thought was the direction which pop music was going in. But then I may be wrong . . .

P: Yes you may be wrong. Electronics take a lot of skill and good luck to control and feedback is a difficult thing. When I first started I could make a guitar feedback on any note for any length of time and I had such control I could do anything I liked. At the Marquee when we first started I used to have a guitar going on a chord and stop certain strings with my feet while I was playing something else on another guitar. In the end I was standing with one foot on a guitar which was feeding back and playing something else with one hand while turning a knob up here and I thought: "What am I doing? Why Bother?" The thing is to create the same dramatic effect musically. You could lean on electronic music if you think it's really valid as part of what you are doing musically. There is a place for electronic music and there is probably a place for it in pop. I think that someone should take it up but I don't think that it should be a course of development for **any** group to take. We're going to take a blatantly commercial move which will be very, very big but it will be blatant and commercial at the same time. And it will probably upset a few people that thought we were making progressive moves. What is more important is that record sales were going down.

M: **My Generation** was one of your biggest hits and that was progressive.

P: Yes, but that wasn't what sold the record. It was the sitter that turned it over. It's a very big social comment **My Generation**, it's the only really successful social comment I've ever made. Some pilled-up mod dancing around trying to explain to you why he's such a groovy guy, but he can't because he's so stoned he can hardly talk. People saw different aspects of the record, it was repetitive, there were lots of effective key changes in it so it didn't bore you too much. And there was a bit of feedback at the end to keep people happy. It was our biggest seller and we never hope or want to produce anything like it again.

M: There seems to be a bigger and bigger difference between your recorded music and your live performances.

P: This commercial move answers every problem we've ever had. The idea which we've got, the idea which our managers have got, will answer all these problems. The group will be able to do what they like. I can bring out an opera a day if I want to, or conduct at the Opera House, and they would all be tremendous successes because of this little secret, which even I'm not very clear about at the moment. All I know, is that there's this beautiful land ahead where all the problems are answered, and I believe in it. Just like some people believe in heaven, because I believe anything. I think that this is inevitable, this must happen to someone. British pop, although it's not so much on the decline as some morbid miserable groups say, is generally taking a drop.

M: How do you fit into the world on a general level?

P: I don't see myself in a position of power or anything. I see it as quite convenient because it means I can lead a quiet uneventful life other than the fact that people point. I get away with murder, because for instance to be one of the Small Faces is sheer hell because they're so approachable. You can go up to them and you can poke them, they're little and cuddly and you can poke your finger in their eye and steal their buttons, and you can take their shoelaces off when you're talking to them, and you can scratch big screwdrivers into their cars because they're the Small Faces and you can kick them and they're cuddly and you can get in their car and you can stand outside their house throwing pennies up at their window. But you can't do that to Pete Townshend. Thank God!

M: Do you have a philosophical standpoint?

P: No. I don't think I have. I understand life now I think, and I understand work and I think understanding work is far bigger than understanding life because work is really what keeps one living. You see it's so easy to deteriorate off into a twilight sub-culture pot-smoking world, where you sit there smoking, and work only so that you can get enough bread together to buy some more pot, so that you can sit in your red light and play Jimmy Reed records. Oh I did that for years! Fine, so you are in a position of great understanding but you are one of the people who watches and that's the drag. The best thing it so be involved in something that's moving, rather than saying, "Well that's moving. Dig It! That's moving. Dig That! Look at that! Look at that plane!" It's far better to be on the plane, it's far better to have painted that picture, it's far better to have done something. I'm not saying that everyone that somes pot is part of the sub-culture, it's just this thing I've got.

M: Do you like Stockhausen?

P: I like his music, but I always tend to do something else with it. It's good to play it through stereo earphones so you get all those funny little noises running all over your face and read Edgar Allen Poe while it's going on, and end up in a screaming frenzy. Once I did this and I had cans on earphones in stereo with Stockhausen playing through them and I was speaking in stereo. I had two microphones, one with re-verb on and one without. So that if I went near this microphone I was miles away and if I suddenly leapt over to this one I'd be speaking very close into this ear. I had all the windows open and there was a storm going on outside, and Stockhausen was playing and I was reading Edgar Allen Poe. In the end I put the book down and I was saying my own terrible, revolting things into the microphones. Suddenly there was a big clap of thunder and it came in through the cans and the rain was falling and Stockhausen was wailing and I was screaming and I thought "God, this is going to be fantastic! I'll play it backwards, with Stockhausen, stereo recording of thunderstorm, me doing this fantastic narrative, jumping up and down screaming." In the end I got this guitar and jumped up and down on it. Then the record ended and everything subsided after the scene. There was the tape recorder going round and round with the knob clearly on 'play'. I just collapsed. It was one of those terrible things.

PETE TALKS ABOUT TOMMY

Barry Miles | May 23–June 5 [part one] and June 13–28 [part two], 1969 |
International Times (UK)

"I don't think that we'll attempt another opera as such, not unless this one really does get people at it!"

So says Pete Townshend herein about *Tommy*, the Who's May 1969 double album, which had just been released. Their December 1967 offering *The Who Sell Out* had been a concept album in the sense that it was made to sound like a radio show, but *Tommy* was an actual narrative. Although not the first narrative rock record, it was easily the most influential. Its story of a deaf, dumb, and blind boy who masters pinball on his way to setting up a messianic cult proved—at a point in history when it was felt it needed proving—that post-Elvis popular music was not limited in its intellectual potential. It certainly did get people "at it": *Tommy* made the Who superstars while simultaneously conferring respectability on the entire rock medium.

This interview was published across two issues of the *International Times*. It sees Townshend explain the not-always-straightforward *Tommy* storyline while offering his thoughts on a few of the Who's contemporaries. It's astonishing to realize when reading his cultured and articulate comments that Townshend was a man from a working-class background who had only just turned twenty-five.

Notes: for "Raoel" read "Rael"

      for "Eyesight for the blind" read "Eyesight to the Blind"

      for "John Entwhistle" read "John Entwistle"

      for "Procul Harum" read "Procol Harum"

      for "Odyssey and Oracle" read "Odessey and Oracle" —Ed.

THIS INTERVIEW is the edited result of a two hour tape recorded Sunday May 4 at Miles's house. The story of The Who's two volume opera

'Tommy' and a description of each track was included in my review of the album in the last issue.

I begin by asking Pete how the opera changed as work progressed on it . . .

[PART ONE]

Pete: THE WHOLE PROCESS HAS CHANGED so much through the working that it's ridiculous. I mean the ideas that I started off with: it was a different plot. It was a different story with a different theme music. The whole thing has evolved to an incredible degree. The writing of Kit's (Lambert) film script made a lot of difference too. He wrote a film script for the opera and that changed my ideas towards the plot a lot because he put forward some very groovy ideas, with a groovy kind of scenario which I liked and which added to the atmosphere of some of the songs which I'd already written. I wanted to let that atmosphere leak in more . . .

Miles: Did you write all the music out or did you work it out with the group?

P: I wrote projected arrangements for bits which we never used. As for the stuff which we've got, I was writing arrangements but I was against the idea because I didn't want to use any outside musicians at all. I felt that the American audiences and particularly the American critics seem to think of it as a very good thing that we don't use outside musicians so we thought that, rather than detract from all the work that we've put in, it would be better to just leave that aside. I was afraid of jarring people too much, or sidetracking the actual input of the thing, and people thinking that the whole strength of the thing lies in the orchestra or something because it would have been the first time we'd ever used orchestra. I wanted it to be a big step in terms of Rock & Roll and in terms of WHO history and in terms of just what we've been doing and not a big step using any other . . . I didn't really want it to be incredibly produced or anything so I'm kind of glad that the sound is very simple and that the basic idea's strength as whole came over as being the important thing.

M: Now you've got it as an opera, do you see it as a stepping off point for your stage act? Or do you want your stage act to always be a version of the opera?

P: Far less a stepping off point than I imagined, I always imagined it was going to be a sort of big thing, all that happened was that when we actually got to do all the numbers, to rehearse them all they all came out just so, sort of normal WHO funky, that it was just like doing a basic stage act you know. I felt that a lot of the numbers were very anti-WHO music for the stage but in fact it came out quite easy to do, in fact none of them were rehearsed more than once, we just played them through once and that was it.

M: How do you think they'll develop, the musical/emotional qualities in some of these tracks are very much the qualities determined by the story line in the opera, yet if you do them on stage you're not necessarily going to be in that frame of mind.

P: True . . . Yes, like the mini-opera has changed in character an incredible amount in the act. I've got very high hopes for it, I think the stage version is more concise as a section of numbers, it's much nearer that original demo tape I gave you, in structure, less padding and less fills and less bullshit and so it tends to be more concise and more effective lyrically. We're hoping that with a little bit of explanation before it, it should hit quite hard, probably harder than the album does, but you won't have that time to live with it that you do get with an album.

M: On the stage act you do a lot more improvisation than you do on the album. You did extended guitar solos for instance and Keith did a lot more on drums.

P: It was very hard to get him to play like he does on the album anyway. But on stage, there's no holding him so there's very little we could do about that. We were delighted that all the numbers were so kind of WHOesque, I was worried that they weren't going to be. I was very worried that we were just going to have to say, 'Bollocks we're just going to have to play "Summertime Blues" over again' you know! And to be quite honest, it's getting to be a bit of a drag because like 'Summertime Blues' is written by someone else and composition has always been a very big aspect of our strength.

M: How long did it take you to work on this album?

P: Well I've been working on the basic idea for this for about 18 months and the complete plot as it stands now, I started writing the plot and the songs in the States on our last tour which was last July or August and we started recording in September. A lot of studio hours, in all it was about 10 weeks of evenings, five evenings a week, so about 50 evenings. There's a lot of re-recording though because the structure of the thing seemed to change as tracks were backed up against tracks so their natures changed in reference to each other and so on and so on. No re-writing though had to be done which surprised me but a lot of tracks had to be re-recorded because the earlier tracks were bad in reference to the newer tracks.

M: The initial piece in the opera where it's explained how he becomes deaf dumb and blind is very hard to figure out, did you make that purposely difficult . . .?

P: Yes yes, it would have been quite easy to do it straightforwardly, you know, I felt that there was no way really of covering over the basic acceptance of it as a, a kind of a hype way of getting the boy deaf, dumb and blind. And I tried about six or seven ways of doing it and each one worked lyrically well and scanned well and all that bollocks, and none were exactly a brilliant piece of architecture. So I felt it would be much better to indicate it in a very loose way with just a switch of events. It's meant to be something that's not too direct, because it's a very delicate part of thing, it's very brusque. The thing about him witnessing a murder in order to become deaf dumb and blind, it makes the thing start off like an excerpt from a detective story and I wanted to avoid that, I would have preferred it if he could have been born deaf dumb and blind but this made the cure so much more difficult to accept in terms of normal entrainment. You see apart from the spiritual connotations I wanted it to have normal entertainment connotations as a plot and . . .

M: You were concerned with plausibility?

P: Right, yes, so that people who couldn't get into the spiritual end of it could see it as a huge cartoon strip if they wanted to. And I think that this is necessary in order for it to be successful. Rock. . . . As far as plausibility goes, the point where he becomes like, a Saint figure is meant to be plausible in anybody's terms. He gets this consciousness rush and becomes a famous kind of figure and sings inside his head. You've already heard him speaking inside his head. And in order to get the plausibility of the fact that he's giving sermons and everything after being dumb, there would be another assumed time lapse there. I did actually want to date the things in order to give people the idea of this time thing as well. That will be implicated far more in the film script.

M: The first Dream Sequence sounds very arranged, as if you'd worked on it an awful lot . . .

P: It's a theme that we've lived with for like, hundreds of years, which we've done a lot in the past. We've done it a lot on the stage, fallen into it a lot on the stage as a riff and stuff. We also used it once before on "Rael". The full "Underture" dream sequence is something which I've had in my possession as a demo for about three years, which the group have had copies of and have lived with it for various purposes, in the past. Always with some sort of opera in mind. I've always had my eyes set on it as a positive musical piece which I would use, no matter what the things was about, whether it was like the "Raoel" thing, about population explosion, or what, I wanted to use the theme in that and also in the original "Amazing Journey" idea of a series of converging dream sequences. It would be usable for that. Then came the point on this album where we wanted a really strong musical theme to indicate the timeless sea of consciousness that he was going through. The solidarity of his evolution underneath all the trauma of all the events that were going on in the outside world. For the feeling that everything was going very smoothly for him, this bit of music just fitted perfectly. That's the reason it sounds so arranged but actually it's ad lib. It's bits layed on top of it, it's tracking over that makes it sound arranged.

M: How much do you see the album as a peak in WHO music? It seems that it's all the WHO's previous themes and, not only musical themes but subject themes, crystallised into one massive undertaking. As if it's a cumulation point rather than a starting off point, and that the next thing you do will be something completely different.

P: This is one of those things that I'm kind of glad that we've got together because I think you need this kind of cumulation point. I know what you mean and I think that you're right. But on the other hand the thing came together with great ease as a composition and I think that, although the recording process was arduous, as a composer of the lyrics, which is essentially what I am, I feel that I could do much better on the same project again with as much enthusiasm. So I feel that I'm ready to do another one. If only I can get . . . You see I've got to be very enthusiastic about the ideal behind the thing. Songs like 'Sally Simpson' just rolled off the pen. And then their implications in the script came later, with a few alterings of words they fitted in far better. I am also very good at problematical writing, like writing films, like writing songs which last exactly 4 minutes and 33.9 recurring seconds, writing a soap ad and that sort of thing. And that also comes easy to me so I've got flexibility for this sort of thing which I feel I'd like to follow through. I don't feel hundred percent successful because I feel that, as a Rock thing it's good but the plausibility factor is something which is annoying me a little bit. One of the things which always annoyed me about old-fashioned opera were the completely bullshit scripts. I really feel that the whole thing should be able to tie up perfectly. I don't think that we'll attempt another opera as such, not unless this one really does get people at it!

M: The Sonny Boy Williamson number seems to stick out a bit, probably because it's by someone else. How does this fit into the theme?

P: Originally there were a lot of old blues songs I wanted to run in it because there were a lot of blues songs about things like cripples and blindness and all this sort of thing, like "I'm gonna get me some kind of companion even if she's dumb deaf crippled and blind, I'm so lonely" all this sort of thing and I wanted to get all those in because I thought they were great blues comments, which fitted in really well to the structure of the opera as I saw it then. It wasn't half as pop and cosmic cartoony as it is now. 'The Hawker' was one of the ones which I arranged fully on an old Sonny Boy Williamson number called 'Eyesight for the blind' and I did this arrangement on it which I really liked and so decided to keep it in because it was musically good. It was meant to go before 'The Acid Queen' but in its present context it feels slightly awkward . . .

M: It's its position really, coming before the 'Cousin' & 'Christmas' tracks it indicates that Tommy's about seven years old and the possibility of it meaning that he has a chick is rather remote . . .

P: Yes right! But it does say 'The Hawker' and this is what I'm relying on, this little note. There's no direct relationship between these two now, which is a drag, still never mind. It's nice to have mysteries to a degree, but this one, as you say, is a bit disrupting so early in the thing.

M: With 'Cousin Kevin' do you think that children are inherently cruel and evil to each other or is it a comment on upbringing . . .

P: Yes I think they are . . . It's meant to be a comment on upbringing but not that much of a heavy one. The reason it was put in there was because we needed to get over to people that Tommy was going through this incredible kind of surface abuse, that he was having a hard time superficially, so that we could imply that on the inside he was getting very good results from all this. He was getting spiritual pushes from all these events because of the extreme nature of all of them. It was written by John [Entwhistle], I told him to write a song about the cousin and this is how it came out. I think that all sorts of things came out of the general theme like political things and sexual ones. None of which was intentional, but which were all rather groovy. I think it's very successful. The group actually didn't agree, they thought it was a very down feeling, too successfully menacing to have on a Rock album but I thought we had to be that menacing. I feel that 'Fiddle About' is like a sick song but 'Cousin Kevin' is a kind of menacing song so that the sick potential of it goes by the board, what really gets you is the fact that it's menacing.

M: The overall comment extends into the rest of the album.

P: The degree of menace and violence in the album is there so that we can draw the line, show the degree of Tommy's attitude and reactions to good and bad . . . good experience, bad experience. And to accelerate his experience so that it's acceptable that he becomes God-realised in a period in which normally a man just about gets it together to make a living. His remoteness made it easier to get away with all this because he was safe inside his affliction. We could really be that much more cruel to him on the outside. Drum home to the listener the feeling that there were really incredible traumatic events happening to him. They're meant to capture periods of his life. 'Cousin Kevin's' not really meant to be an event but really what happen to him when he was a kid, from other kids. And 'Pinball Wizard''s supposed to be a much nicer time when kids were being much more groovy to him because he had something going for him. If you're a good football player everybody digs you, if you're deaf dumb and blind, nobody does, nobody digs a fat kid. Also the disregard of the family for him and his remoteness from personal affection and everything. From 'Fiddle About' and the parents getting angry with him in the 'Smash the Mirror' song and 'Tommy Can You Hear Me' and the father's remoteness. This feeling of the family accepting him as a burden and the mother and the father being even more unsympathetic because they know it's a block whereas no one else does because they obviously can't mention it. But they know and so they're harder on him than everyone else. But the immediate family and everyone around him are all out to exploit his disability.

M: How much were you concerned with building him as a character?

P: Not at all. As little as possible. I wanted to build up the characters of everyone around him. Uncle Ernie becomes a very lovable figure because he's so human. I wanted Tommy to be very remote up to the point where he actually first gets a buzz, and then he becomes a very remote spiritual figure, kind of Saintly.

M: I got the feeling you were purposely withholding information about him.

P: Yes. Mike (McInnerney) & I made a decision in the art work too that we must be very careful not to represent him visually. I shied away from songs in which he spoke. Originally 'Sensation' ran, 'He overwhelms as he approaches' but I felt that he really needed to assert himself even if he was abstractly in his own head, in his own excitement. He has to assert himself as himself, 'You'll feel me coming' because he was going to play such a powerful role later on and things were happening so quickly towards the end that he really had to be established fairly ruthlessly as a character, however remote.

M: The overall speed is important. The last side goes at incredible speed.

P: This is another thing that I ruthlessly planned. There's so much obvious planning and obvious processing gone into it because it had to be exploited over such a long period. We've actually seen where the mistakes were and corrected them.

[PART TWO]

M: Is there any musical influence in this album at all? Outside of the WHO itself I suppose the nearest thing is The Mothers, except they're really in a different area.

P: I really like the Mothers, I really like 'Uncle Meat'. But then I really think Zappa's a master of the very same technique that the Beatles are a master of, and I think it was you that pinpointed it, a master of editing. And their isolated compositions are always very strange. The Beatles album as such would have been, the Double Beatles album, would have been far more acceptable for example if all the tracks had been of the production quality of 'Get Back' but at the same time, it was still good as it was because it had the Beatles stamp of musical and lyrical production, it was a good documentation. Here they document their influences so openly and without affectation and the same thing I get from Zappa with forward moving, the feeling that he doesn't mind using what is apparently a very kind of freaky way-out effect. But if it's freaky and way out, he wouldn't let that stop him. For example he wouldn't NOT use the Albert Hall organ because someone would say 'well that's just flash piece of moody', he'd get right up and use it you know. And HAS done (laughter). He also wouldn't NOT use, and he did this as well, use the London Symphony orchestra, he'd use it for the right reason, not the wrong reason. The Bee Gees would use it for the wrong reason, Zappa would use it for the right reason. I'm always afraid of using things like that for the wrong reason, so in a way although I'm influenced by both those parties, I'm not half as influenced by them as I am by straight forward groups like the Stones and straight forward musicians like Bo Diddley and Chuck Berry, and people like that, who affect me far more and straight forward lyricists like Brian Wilson. And I find these people effect me far more as a composer. And straight forward musicians you know like Hendrix & Clapton affect me a lot.

M: Clapton? I don't see much trace of blues in your playing?

P: No. But then at the same time, his style is something which . . . you know it's such an indirect thing. I mean it's quite a BIG indirect thing! Whereas I listen far more to Zappa, than I do to anyone else really.

M: I would have thought his guitar style was probably nearer to yours than Clapton, Zappa's actually a damn good guitarist.

P: Right, he's damn good at everything. I piddle about on a lot of instruments and do a lot of things you know. But I feel that he really follows through, if he does an orchestration he does an orchestration and uses it and its good. If he does anything he does it with complete mastery, he even . . . he really is a modern composer. A modern composer's got a lot at his disposal you know, particularly media-wise and he uses everything that is available in 1969. I think Uncle Meat is an incredible album. I heard an incredible thing, that he really doesn't spend that much time in the recording studio, that when he does go in, he arrives, Zoops through the evening in record time and does the most incredible amounts of work in that time. That whenever they go in they really work in a business-like manner, and that engineers really dread him coming because he really makes them work. I wouldn't say that 'Uncle Meat' was in any way ahead of its time. It's just very successful. I don't think you really can isolate his feeling of time, you really can't put a general date to the atmosphere of Zappa music, because as you say, it covers such a ready defined spectrum anyway. I really think that despite anything else it still falls under one major category called 'Rock'. To me Zappa is essentially Rock. In his direct orchestration, his composition for orchestra, you get a very formidable Zappa style musically coming through which you can recognise from album to album, it's always very similar. I personally really like his style as composer for orchestra. I find it very elating. I really find it very pleasant.

M: Zappa's one of the few people working with themes which were in existence before he started writing whereas you, everything you work with you created yourselves, there are traces of Diddley, Berry, etc . . .

P: These themes are very interesting because sometimes they're right . . . one of the strongest things which came across was suddenly locating where I got that 'Pinball Wizard' theme from. It's a very recent influence from that Strauss music in '2001'. I just built up a similar Rock structure on it. The same sort of thing, and it works in exactly the same way. I suddenly realized the other day that that's what I'd done. I'd satisfied that need. I do this with such a lot of music . . . I hear something I dig and I always write my own little thing of it.

M: Did you consciously use the greek chorus form?

P: I think that during the working on the thing we thought that these things had some sort of operatic significance, so we were playing operas to a degree, like the 'A Son, A Son, A Son . . .' bit.

M: You didn't analyse normal operatic before you started?

P: No. I had to keep away from that. I like a lot of opera, I like Purcell, and I like a lot of Wagner, and Mahler, but Italian opera completely pisses me off. And that's basically what everybody thinks of as 'opera'. Mahler and Wagner are much nearer opera to me. The way the music surges and makes time and events and cities and battles and life and death, just by the very nature of the music. I felt that with Rock we had some basic ingredients, although not as much potential. The points which sound the most operatic in this are the ones which are nearest to Italian opera which I think is a drag, most of it anyway—I mean there are exceptions.

M: How does the final reprise work, it's very classical . . .

P: I think the reason for that is we start to get into ideals, spiritual ideals, which can't be explained in rock terms. Things like this lend themselves a lot. I mean asserting something like 'I'm Free' lend themselves well to the basic WHO Brag form. Stuff like 'We're Not Gonna Take It' is good in the revolutionary bit but when it goes out into a triumphant bit, it has to become more . . . I had the same trouble with that "Odorono" thing, where I'm singing triumphant . . . if I did it any other way it would tend to sound jazzy. So I had to do it pounding.

M: How did you achieve the symphonic ending? It really goes out on a high level!

P: I dunno. Its really very simple chords, it's a A B C and then G D B, and then A B C G D B, ABC GDB just like that repeated over and over again and they've got a built-in rise.

M: Sally Simpson is the only completely separate story . . . almost a mini-opera within an opera.

P: It was very difficult to get a theme which explained the kind of aura which would be around the boy at that particular time. That's why I resorted to that "Extra Extra Read All About' stuff. I had to really resort to 1930's newspaper headlines flopping back and I thought the best thing to do was completely leap out of the story and go into a new objective: the little girl and her family, focused on him. It's a technique which I really dig and I'll probably use it a lot more actually.

M: It's very effective because it doesn't tell you a lot about Tommy . . . but tells a lot about the pop business and the feelings . . . Was it supposed to relate to pop?

P: No, it's just that it uses images which I'm familiar with. The event actually was taken from the Doors in a concert where I did actually see a kid rush up and try and touch God Jim Morrison and get hurled off by a policeman and a metal chairleg go right through her cheek. She went off, the gash wide open, crying 'Jim!' and they just carried her off. That story seemed to lend itself very much . . . also the point of Sally Simpson is that the kid has really missed the point about Tommy. She's built him into the wrong thing. She hasn't realized why it's good, for example, to go and hear him speak, because of what she can gain from it. She is not religiously selfish enough, as it were. She's built him into too much. Whereas what he's trying to do is give . . . even to a degree he's not even trying to do that. He's slightly confused by the whole thing.

M: Was there any thought of Maharishi or Billy Graham in this?

P: Billy Graham yes but definitely not Maharishi, I've got a mental block to that cat. I mean Billy Graham very much so, because I really felt that the feeling of this particular 'Sally Simpson' bit was very evangelistic. Also the 'Welcome' song. But it's really meant to build up a relationship between people and their existing Messianic and Avatoric figures like Jesus and Meher Baba. Re-instate their importance, rather than build up evangelistic figures, like Yogis and such.

M: Why does the end of 'Welcome' have the fades at the end? It sounds like an ending to a section!

P: There's a couple of reasons for that. That flowing ending thing has to to do with a, I was kind of side-tracked by your idea of it (laughter). It's where the institution of these vague beginnings of the church, or beginnings of the holiday camp thing, the beginnings of a formalised religion occurs. He feels that people just want to be in his presence so he welcomes them into his presence because they benefit by being in his presence. He wants them to enjoy themselves, drink, have fun and generally just 'the more the merrier' you know! But towards the end it starts to get very obsessional and this is why there are a number of false starts in the thing: 'There's more at the door' and 'We need more room', 'Extention' and then this obsessional ending to indicate the growing dissent and unrest in his house, in the circle of companions. They're beginning to demand more action and its at this point that Uncle Ernie re-appears to establish the holiday camp.

M: It's not really clear whether the holiday camp grows out of his house or whether it's a separate institution.

P: You're supposed to be able to gather that it's a separate institution by the fact that Uncle Ernie is running it. That's supposed to be enough! Again its one of those bits where it does tend, I agree, to go generally, just vaguely uphill.

M: The ending?

P: What actually emerged is that the holiday camp starts and he starts to feel that the thing has got out of hand. He still has an incredible love for everyone and its because of this that he takes upon himself this . . . it's a kind of crucifixion representation, that he takes on, he invites this revolution. In other words he realizes that he is going to have to be rejected and abused in order for people to get back to their world, their own path. He realizes that he's instrumental in all these people thinking that if they become deaf, dumb and blind and play pinball and so on and so on that they're going to be like him and that they're going to get

God-Realisation. And he sees that people like Uncle Ernie are cashing in and the whole thing's getting very concentration camp like. So Tommy decides to use some of his real power and become incredibly tough. He starts to really lay down some very unpleasant laws which are still fairly straightforward. He welcomes to the camp but he says like 'You got to do it this way. You've got to do it the way you asked to do it. If you're going to do it the way I did it, you've got to put the fucking eyeshades on and put the cork in the mouth and play pinball and no shit! And you getting drunk—that's out! And you smoking pot—that's out! and there's no good trying to look conventional either because that's out too! You've got to do it my way!' And then the dissent starts and he suppresses it in the early days with more laying down of the law, saying 'You can't speak, you can't see, or anything' and like 'Here comes Uncle Ernie with stage four' and eventually the revolution does completely break out where they completely reject him. They say 'We don't want the religion, we don't want you, we forsake you, we rape you, we forget you!' Then afterwards he makes his reprise. He establishes the fact that he's still the same Tommy. Still more or less deaf, dumb and blind only in a completely different way. He's still very far from them, as far away as he was in the beginning, just to emphasise that nothing ever really changes. Then we go out on this devotional music, worshiping music which just means to be like your heavenly chorus! Or really it's meant to be him, it's meant to be him worshipping.

M: How much of the opera is an embodiment of Meher Baba's thought?

P: Well it's all directly influenced by things that I've learned from Baba but I don't really know how much of it is representative of his teaching.

M: I see you've put an acknowledgement on the sleeve.

P: That was partly a joke. The idea of Avatar being like a function which in fact it is, very much a function. Just like being the Messiah, it's a job of work which somebody has to do. The general theme of the album is a direct result of me getting involved with Baba, getting involved in a powerful spiritual move forward. I think the thing is more powerful because of that very reason, because the project has got a very high ideal to it. And also there's been a lot of Baba's basic teaching which has kept me from getting spiritually proud, you know what I mean? Sticking to the basic formulas of Rock and the basic formulas of lyricism and not to be religiously snobbish about the whole thing. To build up Tommy as a sort of Human being and a Saint figure at the same time and in a funny sort of way, by isolating him, to make him more endearing, so that people would be more endearing to him. That people would actually identify themselves with people like Cousin Kevin, the Acid Queen and people like Uncle Ernie and Sally Simpson, but never with Tommy! They would assume that they weren't where Tommy is, they'd never been where Tommy is, but they were like other people. They wanted to be like Tommy. I'm taking this as a basic assumption. Tommy in the position, not so much as teacher or master (as Baba is, a perfect master), but of a God-realised person. Someone who's evolved up through the stages and reached it. I think every other character other than Tommy in it and that every other event in it is supposed to be something to which people can directly identify in some way. Particularly open-ended people as it were. I thought it would be nice musically to make the thing so obviously successful that it looked like a parallel or it became parallel with the success of Tommy's life. That if it was possible musically, then it was possibly actually. To actually bring in an element of fact. Then it is possible to live a life as he did and end up as he did. As anything is possible it obviously is possible. It's still very much a fairy story, but one with a lot of latent meaning and relevance. I think that in a way we're on the crest of a wave at the moment, and that there are a few things which are going to tip the scales one way or the other. I prefer it tipped toward religious fairy stories than very heavy drug trips. What I really want to put emphasis on is that it was a project. What I want to be very careful to avoid is people reading things into it which aren't there. Because we've gone to such lengths to make the thing crude as it were, we've wanted certain connotations, for the first time ever, we've deliberately written connotations in. Normally we've allowed people to get their own connotations from the music, say like Procul Harum. 'Shine On Brightly' I really think is an incredible album. I don't know if you like how they are. I really like them, really like the music and everything. And that will be from this point on a very heavy influence for me. I think that album probably has influenced a lot of people. I know Procul Harum influenced The Band, and all that. But they're such an unsung band, because their music is totally connotations, really is.

M: I always thought they were weak musically, compositionally.

P: Yes, but they've strengthened that up now. I think that their musical thing now is far more basically strong. I know it had its roots in such a vague era of music, that's why. Days of cantatas and God knows what, was a very very boring one, and there was only about 4 or 5 pieces of music which lifted their heads above the rest in that era, and so that's all that Procul Harum have got to draw on.

M: They are masters of ornation and build-up, all the professional qualities, the equivalent painterly qualities, but their basic themes I never thought were strong enough . . .

P: I know what you mean, Yes! Oh, I get this too but I'm carried along by the . . .

M: I prefer the Fudge because although they're too serious at times, they have very strong themes . . .

P: Yes, I find the Fudge unlistenable at times. I find I can't get through their characters and personalities to the music. This is what I find upsetting, that they are a good band and that its wasted in a way. They're using the music as a vehicle for character and personality building. I don't think they're half as much a musical ego-trip as people imagine, I think they're sincere communicators as it were. Because they're city people I think they essentially feel that they're definately like 'The Rock City people', they feel they've got to communicate with fists clenched. So the dynamics are always like angry/soft and angry/loud and triumphant/very loud! Whereas with Procul Harum I feel they're the exact opposite, they're like country communication, you know, they never really expect . . . I think that thing about the tunes not being quite there is because they never really expect to totally communicate from the first instance. So their music always meanders and its got a relaxed quality about it. It's got a really cosmic feeling of being cyclic in itself which the Fudge are always like forging ahead to me. I think the Fudge are a very underestimated group, particularly in the States, by all the critics. I think its basically because they make very obsessive public appearances.

M: People didn't like the 'History of recorded sound' on 'The Beat goes on'.

P: Yes, people were pissed off by that.

M: I quite liked it.

P: Yes, well, I like 'Yummy yummy yummy', man (laughter). I like 'You got me dizzy', you know, there's all sorts of things I dig and I like a lot of the bad things about the Fudge. I like a lot of the bad things about the Four Seasons. Because the Americans have lived with it all they can't dig it you know. I think to a great degree this applies to a lot of things which they dig from here. A lot of kids in the States kept on at me about the Zombies, the Zombies, the Zombies . . . and I really couldn't see what they were going on about. I knew they were a good band and all that, pop group, but I really couldn't see and yet when they brought out an album called 'Odyssey and Oracle', I really enjoyed that. I thought it was very straight English nicely laid out music. It wasn't so much pop as like music. Like you could imagine music was made like in Elizabethan times, only today. I think we can get a clearer perspective of American music. I think you'll find a lot of people in the States underestimate a lot of good American music. But I think that if you live in Europe you get a far better perspective of both camps than you do from the States because it differs so much from coast to coast and from paper to paper, and from station to station and so on. And personal prejudices and personal opinions over there get so much more room for expansion. I mean in this country they go just about as far as the Record Mirror and that's it. I mean there's so little discussion goes on between parties about music over here. Whereas in the States a lot goes on.

M: Is this really your record and The Who have helped you a lot with it?

P: That's basically it. It started off a long time ago when the group wasn't too amicable 'as my egg' and has ended up compositionally today as my thing. What started to emerge was the shock of knowing just how much they could help me. Which I've never had before, I've always regarded them as like: I'm going to make a demo, and then they're going to come along and its going to be fucked up say 10% by them, then its going to be fucked up 10% by Kit Lambert learning to produce records on it, and then its going to be fucked up 10% by some cunt in some recording studio cutting it with too much treble, so it's going to be 50% as good as the demo right! And this is what I used to feel. But with this, everything was added to, at every stage. There was a lot of preening went on. A lot of things were taken away from it but nothing was ever detracted from in quality. I mean the effort that went into the singing performances on it for example and the musical performance of Keith and John. Like the bass-line in 'Pinball Wizard' is John's bass line—I think its really instrumental in the way it rolls along. A lot of this sort of thing has really amazed me. A lot of ideas came directly from the group like the idea of using a Holiday camp at the end was Keith's.

M: I get the feeling that the group's at a stage where no one could ever sit in with it.

P: You're so right!

A TALK WITH PETE TOWNSHEND

Jonathan Cott | May 14, 1970 | *Rolling Stone* (US)

As a new decade dawned, the Who were left with the formidable task of following up *Tommy*. Their first solution was the May 1970 in-concert set *Live at Leeds*, a stopgap that unexpectedly proved worthy and highly influential in its own right.

Townshend discusses this and other subjects in this interview from *Rolling Stone*, then the bible of the generation who saw rock music as the soundtrack of a new progressive global mentality. Townshend's comments herein indicate he shares that point of view, while at the same time emphasising that he himself is far more in thrall to a different philosophy: the teachings of Indian-Persian mystic Meher Baba. —Ed.

Pete Townshend's quiet and unassuming 18th Century house stands on the Thames Embankment in Twickenham facing Eel Pie Island where, eight years ago, the Stones, Aynsley Dunbar, Acker Bilk, *et al,*. first used to blast music out of the island's club where the floors bounced in all directions. "Free were on the other night," Townshend told us. "I opened the double frame windows and listened and they sounded good."

The gardener was pruning the roses in front of the house when Jan Hodenfield and I arrived. Boats were grounded in the low tide riverbed, scores of gulls resting on them. "When spring comes, the birds fly to the sea," he told us as we waited for Townshend to return home. It was one of those lazy afternoons when spring promises and river scents set you in the mood for an 18th Century English gardener to say something like "Sir, I for my part shall almost answer your hopes, but for this gentleman that you desire to see has stretched his legs up to town."

Pete Townshend soon stretched his legs back down to the house, invited us into the living room where, hanging just above scores of little wooden animal figurines on the mantel, Meher Baba's smile floated off the wall out through the windows across the river and into the island. Townshend made tea and then we talked about his plans and ideas since exhausting the performance possibilities of *Tommy*.

Afterwards, we went down the hall to Townshend's home studio where he played us tapes: "A Normal Day for Brian, A Man Who Died Everyday," which Townshend wrote and recorded just after Brian Jones' death:

> *I used to play my guitar as a kid*
> *Wishing that I could be like him*
> *But today I changed my mind*
> *I decided that I don't want to die*
> *But it was a normal day for Brian*
> *Rock and roll's that way*
> *It was a normal day for Brian*
> *A man who died every day*

"Accidents," a song from the forthcoming Thunderclap Newman album which Townshend produced and on which he plays bass, about "little kids having terrible accidents, falling down holes and being run over by cars"; "There's a Fortune in Those Hills," a slow wailing country song; "I Don't Even Know Myself," a dazzling song which begins with riffs out of "Gimmie Shelter," shifting into a gentle mountain music chorus and brilliant instrumental solos. These last two songs will appear, re-orchestrated and including the other members of the Who, on the second of the Who's forthcoming two LPs, the first one being *The Who Live at Leeds*.

Townshend explained how he recorded these songs in his studio: "This is just a two-track tape recorder, but it's got self-synching on it. I can put something on one track and then put something on the other directly parallel to it. Then I can get those two tracks, which were in this case voice and acoustic on one track and drums on the other, mix them together adding a bass guitar and put it onto one track of another tape recorder. Then on the other recorder I've got guitar, voice, drums, and bass together and I put a piano on the next track of that recorder. And then I mix those two tracks down onto the *other* recorder again in stereo, adding a guitar." Which is how Townshend becomes his own one man band.

When we left, Townshend presented us with a privately released Meher Baba birthday LP featuring Allen Cohen, Ron Geesin, and Pete Townshend singing solo: "The Seeker," "Day of Silence," "The Love Man," and, if you can believe it, Cole Porter's "Begin the Beguine."

What are your next plans?

Pretty complicated, actually. We kicked *Tommy* out of the stage act. We're doing rehearsals and recordings for the next two months to get some new numbers into the stage act and record them for a new album at the same time. We'll probably keep some of our numbers from *Tommy* like "Pinball Wizard" and stuff like that. We're doing some shows in England during this period, the next couple of months, to try it all out. And then we've got a fairly short tour, which'll be the first one we're promoting ourselves, in the States for four weeks, and we're going to try following some of the success that the Stones had in playing theaters, play some bigger theaters, you know, because we've always shied away from them in the past, because we felt we just couldn't get the contact, you know. Also we want something to put ourselves on the spot, so that we don't get in the position where we're just going through the motions.

You're not going to do any free concerts?

There are some considered, but only concerts for causes. When we were last over there, there was a Bust Fund for the Berkeley Park thing, which we considered doing if it came at the right time. All kinds of bust funds. Good way to give Abbie Hoffman another punch in the stomach would be to give him the returns from a bust fund. I think I'd do it for him if he asked me. We think we might do one or two—we've got to be really careful, that's the only thing, I mean after that Altamont thing, I'm a little bit worried.

Can you give an idea specifically of the songs you're going to be playing?

Well, I'm still on a kind of a Self with a capital S trip, you know. It's a bit difficult, writing heavy when you really want to write light or when you really want to write devotional, you know? It's like a period which I know lots of other people have already gone through. I know the Beatles went through it, and quite possibly the Stones for a while. I've just done a thing of getting out of that trip, *Tommy* got it out of my system. I'm getting a balance now between "straight head" and "clear head," getting back to the point now where I realize that if you want to get anything done you've got to actually do it, you know, with a capital D, and not wait. So the kind of stuff we're doing at the moment—have you heard "The Seeker"? It's a bit like back-to-the-womb Who, not particularly very good, but it's a nice side, it's good because it's probably the only kind of thing we could do after something like *Tommy*, something which talks a little bit about spiritual ethics, blah blah blah, but at the same time is recapturing the basic gist of the thing.

The first thing I associate with self and quiet in terms of rock are groups like the Incredible String Band or Donovan. That's where the tone of the thing equals the content, right? Whereas the Who is a rock and roll sound basically.

Yeah, but it's roughly the same thing, it's just that I'm saying it in a different way. I've written something quite similar called "I Don't Know Myself," which is kind of blaming the world because you're fucked up. It's very much like "The Seeker" in a way. I kind of dig that, I think that, you know, the world *is* responsible. You can blame a lot on society, and you can blame a lot on yourself in society, and that's good, but I rather think of myself as something tender which has got to be sorted out and be found. I think that the self is an enemy that's got to be kicked out the fucking way so that you can really get down to it. Most of the songs that I'm writing now are a bit like that—"Don't pretend that you know me because I don't even know myself." Things like, "don't send me to war because I'm too busy fighting a battle with me," that kind of thing.

Well, that can be an excuse too. It's a half put-down of yourself, isn't it?

Well, it's a half put-down, but it's only a half put-down of one bit.

There are some people who think you really can get what you're after. The idea of asking the Beatles and Timothy Leary for guidance because they're "stars" might seem to some people just like reading a lot of newspapers. How do you feel about that guy in the "Seeker" song?

He's just like a whirling dervish. It started off as being very much me, and then stopped being very much me. It's very personal, but then the whole thing is that, as soon as you discover that songs are personal, you reject them. It's what happened with "I Can See for Miles." I wrote it as a personal song at first, and as soon as I sussed out that that was what was going on, I completely pushed it away.

Quite loosely, "The Seeker" was just a thing about what I call Divine Desperation, or just Desperation. And what it does to people. It just kind of covers a whole area where the guy's being fantastically tough and ruthless and nasty and he's being incredibly selfish and he's hurting people, wrecking people's homes, abusing his heroes, he's accusing everyone of doing nothing for him and yet at the same time he's making a fairly valid statement, he's getting nowhere, he's doing nothing and the only thing he really can't be sure of is his death, and that at least dead, he's going to get what he wants. He thinks!

I wrote it when I was drunk in Florida. We were in the middle of an American tour and me and the production manager went out to Tom Wright's father's pad in the middle of the jungle to get some sun, and because we were only there for like five days, this guy was a very good friend of mine, he got in lots of steaks and lots of booze, and he like to overdid everything and it ended up with us, him and the production manager getting completely stoned every night and me being the only person that could stand up, playing, and we were just standing amid the sand spurs one day, I was just covered in sand spurs, I kept on falling and they stick in your skin and you can't get them out, screaming with pain and singing this song and it just came out, "I'm looking for me, you're looking for you, we're looking at each other and we don't know what to do."

Sometimes there's three of you in a room, it happens very rarely, three or four people maybe, and you get to a certain state, you might all be on completely different trips but what you really want to do is like hug one another. But you know it wouldn't do any good, all you want to say is, "You know, I think you're really a great guy." You know that drunken thing that you might go through when it makes that come out. Makes a stranger your friend. It just was a good way of expressing it. Tom Wright was going, "It's gotta be your next single." It is. And they carried on to do the rest of the verses. By some miracle I remembered it all.

Was "The Seeker" done here or in—?

I did a version of "The Seeker" which appears on an album which we did for Meher Baba's birthday celebrations, which I still dig more than the version done by the Who. But I normally do, in an egotistical way I always prefer my demos to what the Who does. But, this is just my own trip. Usually you find that when the Who does it, it's completely heavier, whereas with "The Seeker," I felt that the group was just being whipped into shape, and that what I really want to do when we record in the future is to allow the song to emerge as we're actually recording it, something which I've threatened for years and years and years.

You see, recording is really, it's the recording of a process of discovery. It's shifted, it shouldn't be just a performance going down on the tape, it should also be people discovering lyrics for the first time or maybe a song evolving. It's like when I listen to something like, say, the very first demo of "My Generation," the second demo of "My Generation," the third demo of "My Generation," the group's first try at it, the group's second try at it, and then the final try, you know. Then the reduction of that try and then the cut of that try, and then the pressed recording of that try, and you listen to the two things together and they're worlds apart. One has class; it's ridiculous, but I mean the finished thing is kind of polished and slick and it hasn't got too many bum notes in it, that kind of thing. But the demo, it's scruffy, it's hissy, it's lousy, it's distorted, and nobody would be able to listen to it; but none the less, it's got something which the finished one hasn't, and vice versa. The thing is to bridge that gap.

And I mean, no matter what people say about the Band—I know a lot of people really think they're kind of frigid—but I think the reason why so many people dig them is because they've done that. I mean, while they're making sounds they're discovering things, they're practically writing as they're going along, and it's all being recorded as they're doing it. It's like someone picking up a guitar in a room and playing something. Well no, it's not like someone picking up a guitar in a room at all, I mean they're conscious of a heavy performance trip.

Have you ever thought of putting out one side of a record with all the takes of a particular song? You'd put it in free as a bonus record.

Yeah, I tried it once. I did this thing with a friend of mine who's a lecturer, at an art college, he said come down and play some tapes. And everyone was on holiday. I took a system down and I took a load of tapes, and I was going on about the thing that I've been going on about, the difference between the finished thing and the demo, and trying to bridge the gap, just talking about the difference in generations, as it were, in copy dullness that you get between an artist having his work printed and a musician having his work recorded and then fucked about with and perhaps copied and then buggered about with in other countries and so on. And I was playing them this song that's on the Thunderclap Newman album, it's called "Accidents." The original demo's just a guy with a twelve-string going and someone was hitting a cardboard box in the background. But I mean, the first time I heard it, it completely blew my mind. I just knew it was incredible. Then it went into another phase and then into another phase and then a kind of a crisp recording, and I played them all three. And they flipped for the finished thing. Nobody even mentioned the early one.

It sounds like they're brainwashed to me—terrible. Maybe you're right: Maybe if you did allow people the time to digest—no, that's wrong, it's wrong, it's not true. The thing is, if you give them three versions, they're going to make a choice. If you give them the one version, let's face it, I was lucky, because first I heard the first version, got hip to that; then I heard the second version, got hip to that; then I heard the final version, so now I'm hip to them all. You play them all bang-bang-bang—like that—and it doesn't happen. There's no evolution there, because you're not working towards anything, it's all finished material. I don't think it would work. Young musicians would find it interesting, maybe, to see how songs evolved.

How much interested are you in the effect your songs have? Like the effect of 'Tommy' on people listening to it?

I'm very worried about the effect of *Tommy* because we wanted to avoid so many of the things that actually happened with people. I don't mind, for example, a kid coming up and saying, "Something very incredible happened to me while I was listening to *Tommy* and I felt a spiritual awakening" or anything—I mean, that's cool, because if I could have got at someone like Dylan or the Beatles in the past, or in my case it would probably have been the Stones, I probably would have said similar things to them, particularly to Brian Jones, whom I used to see a lot, who used to come and look at me with boss eyes and wonder what I was talking about. I don't mind that, but what I do mind is a situation when people hear about that kind of thing and expect it to happen part and parcel with the music. I don't think kids take that kind of journalism seriously, but you've got to admit that most of the stuff that was written about *Tommy* was fantastically unbalanced, without exception, it was all unbalanced. I think the thing is that there was nothing real about the criticism of it, but there was something very real about what we were trying to do; we were trying to fuck the criticism from the word go, so that the whole thing was watertight.

But because the structure was loose, a lot of things could be read into it, too.

Exactly, I mean, this is what I suddenly realized. The thing was we wanted it to work on lots of levels. We said, well, you know, we want to turn on the spiritually hip, we want to turn on the fuckers and the streetfighters and everyone, we just want to turn on the whole gang. We want to turn on the opera lovers but also we want to turn on other people as well. And we succeeded in turning on a lot of people that weren't included before, but what we also succeeded in doing was confusing a lot of people. Let's face it, the Who were the Who before they did that, and that's the key, that's where the thing clearly went out of balance. It's very strange to be talking about something like *Tommy* as a kind of a failure, but I think the thing itself, everything we intended to do, we did.

I believe rock can do anything, it's the ultimate vehicle for everything. It's the ultimate vehicle for saying anything, for putting down anything, for building up anything, for killing and creating. It's the absolute ultimate vehicle for self-destruction, which is the most incredible thing, because there's nothing as effective as that, not in terms of art, anyway, or what we call art. You just can't be as effectively self-destructive if you're a writer, for example, or a painter, you just can't make sure that you're never going to fucking raise your head again; whereas if you're a rock star you really can. And of course, all this choice is always there. There's always musicians who say, "Well, I've had enough." There's always somebody there saying, "Really?"

How do you control the situation, then, if you don't want that?

Well, it's not a matter of being able to control it because it's a matter of it being always a situation where you're aware of the possibilities and you make a rough choice. Let's put it this way; I suppose it is controllable. The thing is, you can look at something like a song like "My Generation" and say that the intentions of that were quite obvious, it worked all the way down the line. It repulsed those it was supposed to repulse, and it drew a very thick line between the people who dug it and the people who wouldn't dig it. Well, what if we say we want to make that line disappear, and we don't want to repulse anyone, but what we do want to do is fuck everyone, as it were, what we want to do is to stimulate everyone and take away their preconceptions about us. We say, we're the Who, and we've been blah blah blah up to now, we've been guitar specialists, we've been people that wrote such and such type rock lyrics. But we want to get to a position where we want to break down people's conceptions of what we're doing by doing something like *Tommy*, right? This wasn't the original plan, it wasn't to do something like this, it was more of a heavy kind of neo-classical thing that I was into, thinking, just go from the sublime to the ridiculous, just completely twist.

And then just when everybody's like trotting up behind you, turn 'round and get out the whip, and say, "Right, now we've got you, now listen to this, because this is what's really happening." The only thing that happens is that you break down people's preconceptions, but as soon as their preconceptions are gone, it opens a door, and the thing which broke down their fucking preconceptions instigates a new lot. It really did escape me that in fact the first thing people are going to hear after listening to *Tommy* is, of course, *Tommy* again. So as soon as it breaks down what they know the Who to be, the Who take their next big step—what's next? Obviously we're not going to be able to make the record change immediately in nature and then present ourselves—ha *ha!*—out of the cupboard.

Well, maybe the best thing for the Who is just to embody what's going on, because that's apparently the way people finally take it.

Well, absolutely, I mean, the whole trick really of rock is to be a reflection of what's happening anyway.

Of course if what's happening is just chaotic, then you can't do much to change it, can you?

No, not really. But I mean, the thing is this: You can make an order out of chaos by calling it chaos—do you know what I mean? Say, well OK, everybody's fucked up, right, we're fucked up again—you know, that's it, and then everybody's quite happy to be fucked up. It's when you don't know what you are and when you don't know what situation you're in that you can't bear it, or when you're pretending to be something that you're not or pretending to be the other thing.

I really got very heavy over *Tommy*, I really thought I was doing the world a service at one stage. The thing that hit me about *Tommy* looking back on it, is that it wasn't very Who, you know. Let's face it, I could have walked up to any group, even a group like the Kinks or the Stones or the Beatles and said, "Look, here's *Tommy* with all the songs and the demos, just sort it out, Ringo sing this" and blah blah—you know what I mean?

But the harmonies and the phrasing was all the Who?

Yeah, but I still resented slightly the way it came out, because I feel that the Who have got to be on top of it, otherwise they don't shine. You can't accept our recorded sound unless the group is really on top of what it's doing, because our recorded sound isn't good enough. We're getting on top of it slowly, but it's like so miserable waiting, like it was miserable waiting for the Stones to get on top of their recordings. But they did it, I think, with *Beggars Banquet*, they were on top of it then, like when Charlie hit the deep tom-tom it sounded like a fucking deep tom-tom, and not like a cardboard box.

The production of our records has got nothing to do with sound. It's got to do with trying to keep Keith Moon on his fucking drum stool and keep him away from the booze. And through that period it was to do with keeping me from fucking out on some kind of other dope. I'm very good now, I sit there waiting for each tape, but there was a whole period when Kit Lambert was just keeping us from really fighting. We're a dreadful group to record.

How does Meher Baba come to be involved with your music?

It's getting to the point where the whole thing is relaxing quite a lot because I'm beginning to see something quite simple. If you want to get your head together, right, or your soul together, or whatever it is you're trying to get together, there is no necessity to go 'round changing the color of the walls and changing the carpet that you've got on the floor, and cutting your hair off, and stopping smoking or any of those trips, there's no need for that. It's the translation of what's happening and the way you get into what's happening that is the thing. And so I've just got to the point now when I've suddenly realized after a long time that writing and things like that shouldn't change; and subsequently this is why musically I feel I'm moving a little bit back to the position we were in before *Tommy*, which wasn't very healthy, actually.

It's kind of peculiar, in other words it's like going back into a position where we were in a decline. And I prefer that alternative rather than following up *Tommy*. I'm sure the Beatles were faced with it after the height that went on after *Sergeant Pepper*. I just feel that that's the best thing to do, you've just got to own up to what's happening, you can't fuck around. It would be very very difficult to follow up *Tommy*, and I don't want to do it, and I don't think people really want it anyway.

What's on your new live album?

This was incredibly lucky. On our last tour of the States we recorded every night on a stereo machine taking feeds from the guitars and the drum kit and the P.A. onto a rough stereo picture (the road manager was doing the balance), with the theory that in 80 performances, or whatever it was we had, we must get a good show. We go over there, we do like 80 fucking good shows, you know, some shows incredible shows. We come back, some of the tapes are bad, some of them are good, some of them sound all right. Suddenly someone realizes there are 240 hours of tape to be listened to. You know, now who's going to do this? So I said, well, fuck that, I'm not gonna sit through and listen, you'd get brainwashed, let's face it! So we just fucking scrapped the lot, and to reduce the risk of pirating we put the lot on a bonfire and just watched it all go and we said, right, let's get an eight track.

So we got a Pye eight track and we said take it to Leeds, and we went to Leeds and it just happened to be a good show and it just happened to be like one of the greatest audiences we've ever played to in our whole career, just by chance. They were incredible and although you can't hear a lot of kind of shouting and screaming in the background, they're civilized but they're crazy, you know, they're fantastic. And we played it in their own hall. And the sound is all right, it's a good atmosphere.

Do you know what songs are on it?

Yeah, we've just gone for the hard stuff. The first number in the show, which was "Heaven and Hell," was something written by John Entwistle which was something I was very keen to get on, but it didn't come out well enough. So it starts off with "I Can't Explain," then it's got "Young Man Blues" and it might have "Fortune Teller" on it as well; "Young Man Blues," then "Substitute," "Summertime Blues," and "Shaking all Over" on one side. Then on the other side it's got a long version of "My Generation" and then an encore with "Magic Bus." It's kinda groovy actually. I like it. It's where we are today musically, and when you listen to it, it ain't very far, quite honestly!

What hits you when you listen to it is you realize how much you need to see the Who. You know, I've never seen the Who, but it makes me realize how much you need to. Because I know that people wouldn't rave about us so much if they could just hear that tape, but I'm sure what happens is that the kids that'll buy the live album will probably be kids that will be able to remember us when they've seen us and they'll compensate. But there's all kinds of bits where sticks are obviously in the air when they're supposed to be on the drums and arms are spinning when they're supposed to be playing solos. And there's a bit like when we are all doing "Dooby de doo doo" like scissor kicks and you can hear halfway through, where, although I'm playing in time, I'm landing in the middle of the beat. A kind of weird lumpy noise. They did a terrible job on the recording. They fucked it up incredibly. It's the Pye Mobile set up. They did Air Force and Delaney and Bonnie and they did alright with them but they fucked up on ours, they got crackles all the way through, horrible crackles. But I'm just going to put it out anyway.

Can you say anything about the record Brian Jones made in Morocco that Track is supposed to release?

I haven't heard it, but I remember when he was making it. He's done a lot of film music as well you know, which I heard tracks of, for some French guy or some Dutch guy, which he did with all these weird instruments which he used to play. You know there's something really escapes people now, and I miss it when I hear Mick Jagger play the harmonica, and that's Brian Jones' harmonica playing. Brian really was a good harmonica player. He was into quite a lot of ethnic stuff. I wrote a song about Brian Jones dying. A lot of people on the day he died rang 'round and said, "What have you got to say 'bout it?" And I got one from Peter Cole of the Daily Express and it was about ten o'clock in the morning and I didn't really think about what I was saying, it was the first I'd heard of it and it just seemed very normal you know—well, Brian Jones has died, rock singer's death, good stuff, you know, he had to go and like he was dead already kind of thing, so I just said "Oh, it's a normal day for Brian, like he died every day, you know," and he said, "Thank you very much," put down the phone and I thought, "Fucking hell," then I got a phone call from the Rolling Stones' publicity man, Les Perrin, saying, "This is terrible," so on and so on. And I got all upset about it and to back up my words I wrote this song, "A Normal Day for Brian, the Man who Died Every Day," and it really came out very good.

You're not going to release it are you?

I don't think I will, but I think it might not be too late. I did it and recorded it so I could put it out that day.

Maybe it's too soon.

Yeah, perhaps. I used to know him quite well. Fairly well. I know a lot about the vibes that were about. The Stones have always been a group that I really dug very much. Dug all the dodgy aspects of them as well, and Brian Jones has always been what I've regarded as one of the dodgy aspects. The way he fitted in there and the way he didn't fit in, I always felt was one of the strong dynamics of the group. And I felt that when he stopped playing with them that dynamic was going to be missing, but somehow it seems to be still there. I credited him with a lot. I think the thing is that the Stones have just managed by some miracle to kind of replace him somehow. Not with Mick Taylor, I mean, he's like a musician, but they've kind of filled the hole. Either that or the fact that he's dead has made that dynamic that was there when he was alive kind of permanent. I don't know.

What about the Keith Moon episode, the chauffeur business?

Keith is going to come back from his holiday to a bit of a shock, because he's been charged with drunken driving and being in charge of a vehicle without a license. His solicitor says that the police did it so he gets the chance to clear his name, which sounds very suspicious. But they kind of did the inquest or whatever it is, and it made him feel better because nobody actually pointed a finger at him and said, "You killed your best friend." But that was the thing that went through his head, and it took a lot of heavy thinking on his part to straighten himself out. Because what basically he must have felt like is that there was trouble and he ran away, which is the exact opposite of what was true. I mean, he thought in fact that this guy had run ahead and he was actually driving ahead to get him. But it was just pointless, the whole thing was pointless.

Especially coming after Altamont.

Yeah, it was probably some kind of moon thing going on.

How do you feel about Altamont and Woodstock now?

Well, the Woodstock thing I'm still very unhappy about. Altamont I don't know about, because I wasn't there. At first I was a bit repulsed by the way ROLLING STONE wrote about it, because I felt like it was written by a whole batch of writers who seemed to be unanimous in the decision that it was the fault of rock and roll or the fault of the Stones. But what I really felt was wrong with the whole thing was the fact that there were murderers in there. And I mean I know there's murderers everywhere. I think it's just as silly for Keith Richard to say it wouldn't happen in this country, because, let's face it, it did happen to Keith Moon's chauffeur. Somebody killed him; somebody kicked him under the fucking car. They arrested what, like four 14-year-old boys? There are reasons why kids do things and there are reasons why grown men do things, and they've all got a lot more to do with rock and roll than they've got to do with anything else. But at the same time I felt that with a little bit of care, a little bit of thought in advance, you can avoid things like that.

What didn't you like about Woodstock?

Quite honestly, I mean knock for knock everything Abbie Hoffman said was very fair. Because I did hit him, he must have felt it for a couple of months after. I didn't like Woodstock for one reason because I took my wife and the baby, and you know when women are pregnant they go through a whole thing where if they get in a crowd they freak out. Well, I was kind of like that, paternally, people coming up to me—"You're going to Woodstock? You're crazy. Turn back, go home, there's millions of people there, the food's poisonous and the water . . ." Well, I imme-diately got into an incredible state and I rejected everyone, I wouldn't talk to anyone. And I was telling really nice people like Richie Havens to fuck off and things like that. And it just got to a point where when we finally did get out of the helicopter and the helicopter never arrived and we eventually got in a queue of cars it took about six hours to get there. Well, we got there and then we waited another ten hours in the mud; the first cup of coffee I had had acid in it. I could fucking taste it. I took one sip and threw it away because I really can't play if I'm tripping. Can't trip if I'm playing, as it happens. Like I thought I was going to be up by the time the trip had gone through, it was only a little trip, you know, a very bad one incidentally, but I mean it's just a little thing, went up/down in the space of say three or four hours. But there was another six hours to wait before we got on the stage and we got there at eight o'clock at night.

And people came up and said "It's alright for you fucking rock groups, flying in by helicopter," but we had to walk a mile through the mud from the car, then we got there and just started to pick up vibes that were just great. I must admit if you went out of the section where the musicians were, forgot that you were there to work, it was great, but every now and then you'd think, "I'm part of the sideshow, I'm selling the soft drinks here"—No one else was doing his fucking job—no one was supplying water, no one was cleaning the lavatories, no one was supplying food. But the groups played. I know that's what people were there for, but it's a whole trip.

People picked on the Who as the group to criticize because you demanded money, is that right?

That was because we were leaving the morning after, you see. I expected this as we were fucking asking for it. They were giving us such a lot of bullshit. This geezer said, "I invited you to play as a friend and now all this distrust," and we said, "Look, man, we've come from England to play your shows specially. We want our fucking money. Want to take it back and spend it. You know, we're in debt." And they said, "Well it's very difficult." They had to get a bank manager in the middle of the night to sign a check. So we did it, and then everyone else started to do it. They said, "What's the trouble?" So we said, "We just got our money, it's all cool." So Creedence did it, Grateful Dead did it, Santana did it, all the bands that were on the night we were tried it on. We went and the Jefferson Airplane came up and said, "Did you get your money in advance?" So we said, "Yeah and you should," so they said, "We already have. Paid six months ago."

Everyone felt it wasn't the spirit of the thing to ask for money.

Oh yeah, I mean in a way it wasn't the thing. Oh fucking hell, Woodstock wasn't what rock's about, not as far as I'm concerned. When the sun came up I just didn't believe it. I was giving a little prayer, you know, I was saying, "Look this is a disaster, we're playing and Abbie Hoffman and company are spreading their peculiar vibes about and I've done the wrong thing," and the vibes were well down. *Tommy* wasn't getting to anyone. Sly and the Family Stone had just whipped everyone into a frenzy and then kind of walked off. Everyone was just silent and then we went on and all the bad vibes, and all the photographers all over the stage. I had to kick about ten photographers off the stage to get on.

By this time I was just about awake. We were just listening to the music and all of a sudden, bang! The fucking sun comes up! It was just incredible. I really felt we didn't deserve it, in a way. We put out such bad vibes. But like it started for that bit and then we went into "Summertime Blues," "Shaking All Over," "My Generation," and as we finished it was daytime. And it was just incredible. We just walked off, got in the car and went back to the hotel. It was fucking fantastic. Still, if people offer us festivals now, we say no before we say yes.

What are you doing with the opera tours now? It that all over?

We pulled out of that really because it was we were going and playing in fucking opera houses, you know like thousands and thousands of kids were coming to see us and then only about a hundredth of the kids who wanted to see us could. And we'd go in and play and like the first 20 rows would be Polydor people. Or Prince Rainier and his royal family, and honestly it was such a bad scene. We were going to play the opera houses in Vienna, Moscow and the New York Metropolitan, but I just thought that was the biggest hype bullshit I'd ever heard of. We blew it out.

The thing I didn't dig about it is that we didn't play big enough places. The opera houses over there are very small. There are 1,500 people usually and you could see every face. But you can't win them over. Say there's an old guy in a bow tie out there, he's come to write up a review in some opera paper or some serious music paper and most of the night he sits there with his fingers in his ears. It's just impossible to work when someone's doing that.

You were talking about the next step for the Who.

Well, I was talking about it then in terms of a film and I think a film would be the ideal thing. A film, a bit in nature like the Stones' Rock and Roll Circus thing. Only a feature. Something which was about rock but was about a lot of people in rock. The Stones scooped, as far as England was concerned, Taj Mahal and Jethro Tull and people like that and at the same time gave a good reflection of the kind of music they dug, gave a good performance of their own and had some oldies but goodies like the Who on, and had some fun at the same time. If this could be done—but where the balance was one where you were actually filming something turning on its axis or doing a spiral upwards or doing something incredible, say a whole picture including a whole lot of groups, filmed from the viewpoint of the Who maybe or just using it as an excuse. I think this is yet to be done. It's very vague, but there are people, and I am one of them, who have got a lot of ideas in that direction, and I am one of them, who have got a lot of ideas in that direction, for a rock film which is not a documentary and not a story and not a comedy either but a fucking Rock Film. A film which is the equivalent of a rock song, only lasting an hour or longer.

Why did you write to The Sunday Telegraph about drugs?

Because the guy that wrote the article, Lionel Birch, who's a friend of mine, asked me to write a letter backing up saying that Meher Baba had caused some people to stop taking drugs, and I got into the letter and got carried away and wrote a lot of other stuff as well. I just feel that the whole thing is that if there is such a thing as a drug problem and if there are people who get fucked up because of drugs and there are many who don't but quite a lot who do take drugs get fucked up—it's because they're looking for something and they're desperate and even if they don't know they're desperate themselves, they are. I mean even if you're not taking drugs, you're still fucking desperate.

The first thing that hit me about stopping . . . you see the first thing Meher Baba says, which is logical, is that drugs like acid and STP, the psychedelic drugs, right, are harmful mentally, physically, and spiritually. Fair enough. Who am I to say they are not? In fact it was probably the harm they did that I dug. But then he says that it is all right for a sincere seeker to have been stimulated by them but not to continue use of them in the light of that. In other words if you get a buzz from something and then you dwell on it, it's the equivalent of like getting in a mood. It's like seeing something fucking incredible like a daffodil and then just looking at it till it wilts and dies. Do you see what I mean? He just put it in a way which got to me.

And I just stopped using acid straight away, just the words got me. But I went on smoking pot, and coke, and I started to get heavily into coke and other things and then all of a sudden when I did that long ROLLING STONE interview, I was very hyped up on coke because we went round to the Jefferson Airplane pad in the middle of the interview, which was a silly thing to do. The day after I did that interview, a Baba lover came to see me in San Francisco and he was talking about drugs and things and what Baba says about it, and he says, "Of course you're not still smoking dope, are you?" So I said, "Yes, sure. What's Baba said about dope?" "Didn't you know that it's been proved now that pot's an hallucinogenic drug, so it falls into Baba's teachings?" he said. So I just stopped. Just because I felt more keen about getting into Meher Baba than I felt about being stoned all my life.

And then as it started to go down I started to realize how much I credited to drugs. I used to think, "Well, man, I can't play the guitar unless I'm stoned, I can't write a song unless I'm stoned, I can't be happy unless I'm stoned, I can't listen to records unless I'm stoned, I can't do anything unless I'm stoned. Because if I'm not stoned it's not as good." Well, I've just kind of got out of that, and I get just as much now out of everything perpetually 24 hours a day as I used to out of that high. It's like that thing in the hearing, they call it A.G.C., like if you hear a very loud sound, very quiet sounds are inaudible, but if you play a very quiet sound, other sounds become audible. In other words if you've got the loudspeaker on, you don't hear the doorbell ring, but if you've got it on quietly then you do hear the doorbell ring. I think it's a lot like that with dope. When you're on dope, it's so extreme it dulls a lot of other aspects. You dig what you're focused on, but you miss what you're not focused on.

Well, your music works the other way, doesn't it?

What do you mean?

You go to a Who concert and couldn't hear the doorbell ring if you wanted to.

That is of course an old pre-dope thing, where in fact we used to be a mod group and we'd go on the fucking stage and we'd literally get heckled. You go and play a really tough town like Glasgow and you get bottle thrown at you, so the thing was you just turn up your amplifier. It's good, it's good, I still like it loud. We're not as loud as we were on the guitars, it's going down, but the P.A.'s going up. I mean, English groups just discovered the P.A. system.

THE WHO PUTS THE BOMP
OR THEY WON'T GET FOOLED AGAIN

John Swenson | December 5, 1971 | *Crawdaddy* (US)

The Who did prove up to the difficult task of following up *Tommy*. It was a rocky road, involving an abandoned film and a savagely cut-down double set, but they got there in the end: their August 1971 studio album *Who's Next* is considered one of the greatest albums ever released.

This marathon feature consults all four members of the band for their memories of how the new album came together and their perspectives on their "comeback" (a year out of the limelight—nothing today but extraordinary then).

For at least the third time in this book so far, Townshend is claiming that the Who's latest effort is uncharacteristic of the band.

The album *Happy Jack* referred to is the American version of what fans in the Who's home country know as *A Quick One*.

Notes: for "Entwhistle" read "Entwistle"

       for "Viv Standshell" read "Viv Stanshall"

       for "Mrs Peal" read "Mrs. Peel"

       for "The Bonzo Dog Doo-Da Band" read "The Bonzo Dog Doo-Dah Band" —Ed.

Who night. The crowd waits reverently, attention vaguely focused on the massive half-ton fortress of amplifiers looming in the shadows of the dimly lit stage. The house lights go down . . . two guitars are brought out to Peter Townshend's side of the stage, amplifiers are switched on and the stage lights turned full up. The theatre becomes deadly silent, everyone focusing intently on the stage, charging it with a palpable energy. The Who walk out into the warm glow of cheering adulation, and the show begins . . .

Largely due to the efforts of bands like The Who, no one questions the power of rock anymore. Rock's power involves magic. There's magic every time a group steps on stage and an audience responds with that strange exalting welcome, the kind of love reserved for nothing less than gods. When the first chord sounds to begin a concert, when the show reaches a high point fusing the group and the audience through the music, the magic is working well.

Every band shares a piece of that magic at one time or another, but The Who are that magic. It's in them as if it were a part of the act, along with the WEM PA and the cooler of beer and soda behind Entwhistle's amps. They use the magic like the Stones use it, like the Beatles used to use it, the way only a real Rock band knows how. And they've been doing it steadily for years.

Peter Townshend calls the Who stage a sacred place. He's serious about that, just as much as the people that come to the concerts are—they believe in Rock. It's all part of the magic. Townshend doesn't have to play anymore if he doesn't want to. Ever since the popularity of Tommy, The Who could have gone for the big bank roll and split—lots of bands do that. They could have played Madison Square Garden a dozen times. They haven't because they believe in Rock and in themselves as one of the music's prime forces. They are exacting and uncompromising as performers, idols and musicians, and what's more, they know what they want in terms of what's best for Rock, and are never satisfied with less.

In England, The Who have always been mammoth. Their fans there claim them to be the greatest band in the world, even greater than the Stones. In America, there's been a more dreamlike quality to their rise. They came here in 1965 through the back door, playing the Murray the K Easter Show.

They didn't leave without making converts, and each successive time more and more people went to see them on the strength of word of mouth. Thus The Who built up an American audience without the aid of the standard media myth makers. Their initial following consisted of the first rock underground, the kids who were looking for something more than what was offered on the AM radio.

Their strength was in their performance, a vibrancy that made a lasting impression on audiences, made them come back to see the group again and again, made them want to get as close as possible. Here was power—partly in the music itself, which was overwhelmingly loud and irresistibly driving, and partly in the genius of the group, in the sensitivity of Townshend's compositions primarily, but also the theatricality of the group on stage. The Who were always the ideal image of a rock band, each member contributing his unique part that added up to a strangely complementary image—Townshend's schizophrenic awareness, Daltrey's arrogance, Moon's clownishness and Entwhistle's cool made up a self contained unit, perfectly balanced.

But the best thing about The Who was that they never deserted their audience, they always came back. No English band can claim the distinction of being on the road as long and as consistently as The Who. They realized the primary importance of Rock wasn't in records, but in live performance, and they followed their instincts.

Finally, with the release of Tommy the publicity machine caught up with them and the rest of the world found out about The Who, "the group that did the rock opera". In America, Tommy was the best and worst friend The Who ever had, putting them at once in the limelight (when they would perform it) and on the spot (when they wouldn't). Before they could move on to their next goal, they had to make people forget Tommy. So the summer before last they played Tommy for the last time on the last night of the tour, telling the audience they wouldn't be back for a year.

They came back with a new act and a new album, appropriately entitled Who's Next. We interviewed them at their hotel in Chicago on the final day of their tour. The first interview, with John Entwhistle, had been arranged the night before, so Entwhistle had been expecting us. We found him quietly watching television in the outer room of his suite while he toyed with several plastic skeletons.

JOHN ENTWISTLE

I'll ask you a really obvious question first: How did you get the nickname "The Ox"?

Ent: Ah, since I was the biggest in the group. We all have sort of appropriate nicknames . . . Roger's nickname is "The Dip", which comes from Dippity Do, which he used to use on his hair to straighten it. Pete's nickname is "Bone" cause he's so tall and skinny. Keith's is "Sponge", or "Barney", like Barney Rubble of the Flintstones, he's always got a five o'clock shadow.

Are these long standing names?

Ent: Oh yeah, about three or four years.

How did you get together the people that you were going to use on your solo album "Smash Your Head Against the Wall"? Was it a conscious decision that you needed this kind of a drummer, or . . .

Ent: I'd been puttin' off bookin' time for the album for quite some time cause I didn't feel that I had enough numbers to complete the album, so I kept hanging back and waiting to compose the rest of the material. And I went down to the office and Cyrano, the guitarist, works at Track because he's too lazy to join a group, and he decided to give me a push to do the album while I was there. We were looking for a drummer but we just couldn't find one and he was pretty friendly with Jerry Shirley so we got hold of Jerry. He sounds a bit like Townshend. He plays that way because he's seen him so many times.

How long had you been planning to do an album? Had this been a long time idea of yours?

Ent: Yeah, since *Tommy,* really, before we started recording *Tommy* we were thinking about doing solo albums . . . I'd never accumulated enough compositions 'cause I hadn't composed seriously until like six months before I started the album I suddenly got into composing a lot more stuff.

So you don't consider the stuff on the Happy Jack *album serious?*

Ent: No, not really. It was just the first attempt at composing. "Whiskey Man" was like about six different numbers all rolled into one that I sort of joined together. "Boris the Spider" took me about ten minutes to write, you know it was just a sort of a brainstorm I had—it just all came at once, the tune and the words.

The themes of those two songs were more or less carried onto your album.

Ent: Yeah. There's another drinking song, "Pick Me Up (Big Chicken)." It's only got that "Big Chicken" there because right, I think it's about the second verse the guitar goes ba-bppmh [he trumpets a chicken noise through his nose].

When you did decide to finally do the album, did you have to write a whole bunch of stuff to do it or did you finally come up with it . . .

Ent: No, I had about ten numbers of which I only sort of attempted to do about six, and, we were still short two numbers. During the time we recorded the backing tracks, I did quick demos, just wrote out the music for these two other songs I had in me head, but just never decided to sort of get them out. Another one, "My Size," was just written in the studio, we wrote the chord progressions and then I went home and composed the tune and the words.

There was a lot of death imagery in the album. People have accused you of being morbid in the past, though I'm not sure if that's quite what it is . . .

Ent: I've always been obsessed with the idea of Heaven and Hell. Not obsessed that it's true, but just obsessed that it's sort of a legend, there's such a person as the devil. My family's not the sort of family to be serious about death anyway, we've got rather a sick sense of humor, the whole family, that is, my father, my grandfather before him . . .

It's hereditary.

Ent: Yeah, it's hereditary, right. So I don't mind jokin' about death at all. I'd written this number quite a time ago called "Teddy's Funeral" which I retitled "Ted End" and changed a few of the words. That's about four years old, and I wrote "Heaven and Hell" about the same time, those two numbers were connected. They were written in the same sort of spirit, I was writing horror songs at that time, "Boris the Spider" etc.

Was "Ted End" inspired by someone you actually knew?

Ent: "Ted End" came from a conversation that my grandmother had with a neighbor. I changed the name, but all those things were more or less said, that his children had immigrated to Australia, they wouldn't come back 'cause they didn't have the money, and his wife got married again and wouldn't come either. He wasn't a very popular bloke 'cause he was pretty miserable.

There's a whole section on the album that's connected one part to another, it starts off with "Heaven and Hell", then we've got the funeral section, then "You're Mine", which is like the devil saying "there's no such place as heaven anyway."

Isn't that song also saying that as long as you're human, "You're Mine", I mean as long as you have human failings?

Ent: There just . . . isn't anybody that hasn't sinned in some way, I mean, everyone's trod on an ant before, and things like that, and that means you've broken one of the commandments, so you go to the devil. The end of it, it's like the devil sayin' "Everybody's mine at some time . . . you'll enjoy your stay 'till you're reborn someday," s'like going to the devil . . .

"You're Mine" ties into "Number 29 (External Youth)" too—is there a relationship between the two songs other than just that rhythmic passage?

Ent: The only connection is that that's sort of an interval number, it's talkin' about tryin' to look young while you're alive, bringing it back to earth for awhile.

Bein' deceitful, more or less? . . . not being truthful about what you really are?

Ent: Ah, yes. Having plastic surgery and all things like that, putting a false thing over to the public.

What about things like "What Kind of People Are They" and "What Are We Doing Here"? They don't seem to fit in.

Ent: Well, the actual shape of the album, when the numbers are associated with each other, that doesn't begin until "Heaven and Hell". The rest are just some of the recent things I wrote. On "What Are We Doing Here" the words were written in the States, they're very homesick words, we were stuck in Houston, Texas, the television had finished, there was no booze, we'd done a terrible show and I'd been away for four weeks and was startin' to get a bit homesick so I wrote those words. I wrote part of the tune when I got back, then I finally finished it when we were actually recording the album. On "What Kind of People Are They", the first thing I wrote was the brass section, the beginning, and then I'd written this song about people in uniforms, which I hate, I hate people in uniforms because they always get so officious. Waiters and policemen, you know, I've been turned out of so many restaurants 'cause I didn't have a tie on. I've got so many parking tickets, I could wallpaper a room with 'em . . . traffic wardens. In every traffic jam in England, when you get to the front of it there's a policeman sort of directing things but he ends up causing a backup himself. So I had those three things in mind and I joined them together in different verses.

So the album is actually three or four more or less throw on cuts and then from "Heaven and Hell", on, one unified idea? How does that last song "I Believe in Everything" fit? It's a bit of a ringer, it throws you off.

Ent: I'd been saying a lot of stuff that I didn't really believe in. I sort of wrote it for the heads, really, the people thinking, "ah, so that's where Entwistle's brain's at, he really sort of believes in the devil and hell and all that sort of business". So I wrote a number that touches on reincarnation, then goes into the absurd, with Father Christmas and the whole bit and right at the end just to prevent the heads from thinking that I did believe in everything like I was saying, 'cause they always seem to believe that you actually believe in your own words. I believe in some of them but not all of them, so I just wrote the joke in to throw them off, and it's done it.

Yes, (laughing), it has! I think the overall image of the album, aside from "Heaven and Hell" and all that is like a description of middle class sensibility. There's something about the whole album that reeks of that—the idea of guys that can't go home because they're too drunk, which ties into that song "My Wife" from the new Who album. How do you relate to that whole thing now that you're sort of removed from it, you've finished the album.

Ent: I don't really . . . my circle of friends isn't within the pop world, you know, when I'm not working I strictly divorce myself from the pop business unless there's something I wanted to go and see or if I want to go out to a club or something. But I try to stay away from it, just to give my head a rest. I do enough in my own studio at home to cater to my outside tastes.

You do what you would consider serious composing alone, at home, that you don't really intend to use for albums and stuff?

Ent: Yeah, I've written a couple of classical things on manuscript.

You must have felt awfully frustrated at times with The Who.

Ent: That's how it became, because I've got the two numbers on *Tommy* and I started to do a lot of writing during that year and I liked a lot of the numbers when I'd written them, but then they suddenly seemed like rubbish to me. I got these all mounted up and cut them as demos in my own studio and then *Tommy* came along and I had to scrap all that stuff to do the two numbers for *Tommy*. Then we had that live album which gave me time to start composing again. Well, I just really started to get frustrated, if I hadn't done the solo album, which was the easiest way out for me, I might have left the band. It was getting that bad . . .

It was the only thing for me to do because I had the reputation of being the quiet member, which I am on stage, visually.

Why?

Ent: It was the only way out for me, to let people know that I was an entity, I was a composer as well, I had my own musical brain. I wasn't a robot, I wasn't a cardboard cutout on stage. I had a mind there as well. . . .

It was a boredom. I could never . . . the only time I ever really enjoyed myself on stage was when I was allowed to do something free form. I didn't like playing set arrangements, I couldn't really get off of the other stuff. *Tommy* I grew to like. We played it so many times . . . the group always accused me of falling asleep on stage and carrying on playing, they'd look and they'd see my eyes closed, and I'm leaning against the amplifiers. I must admit, some gigs I just don't remember doing, I'd just sort of get up there and play and then it's finished.

You didn't like Tommy *at first?*

Ent: I think it's just an association of ideas really. It took us eight months altogether, six months recording and two months mixing. We had to do so many of the tracks again, because it took so long we had to keep on going back and rejuvenating the numbers, that it just started to drive us mad, we were getting brainwashed by the whole thing, and I started to hate it. In fact I only ever played the record twice—ever. I don't think what *Tommy* was all about was on the record—I think it's on the stage. The message is much stronger on stage than on record.

The Who have always seemed to work that way. Recorded versions of songs don't take shape until played on stage for awhile.

Ent: Yes, like on "Cobwebs and Strange", the brass band sort of thing really makes me crack up. Our manager at that time was completely nuts—he had us marching around in band formation around the studio because he wanted that going away and coming back sound. And like we were marching around this monitor speaker at one end of the studio, which already had the bass guitar, drums and guitar track on it, we'd done that already and were playing it back on the monitor speaker and marching around with Pete leading, playing a recorder, me playing a tuba, Roger was playing bum notes on a trombone behind me and Keith had two straps on two cymbals, doing that while marching around the studio. And every time we got to the monitor speaker we realized we were out of time because by the time we got to the other end of the studio we couldn't hear the backing track. If we'd worn cans we could have gotten tangled up, so we had to finally track it standing still but every time we play it live I'm reminded of that time marching around the studio.

When you were gonna do Tommy, *how did your two songs fit into the larger concept of the thing, is it that Pete came to you and said "I have holes to be filled here" or something?*

Ent: No, Pete said that there were two characters that he thought he himself couldn't do as good a job as me in describing. One was a homosexual uncle and the other was the cruel cousin, which were supposed to be two of Tommy's traumatic experiences, that and the acid queen.

I found it so easy that I'd written "Fiddle About", with the character of Uncle Ernie, by the time I'd got back to the room. If I've got a subject, an idea for a song, then it comes almost immediately.

What about the brass on your album? You originally played brass, so it's not just something you decided to pick up to add to the sound.

Ent: Right. The Who had always wanted to use whole brass sections on albums, played by me, but The Who had also always prided themselves on being able to play songs from the albums on stage.

It is important, though, because the group would have busted up if we hadn't played on stage. Cause that's the only time we really had anything to do with each other, the only time we were really ever together. That's the only time we fit together because we're so completely different from each other. We don't socialize. In the studio we're always sort of grumpy, everyone pissed off and going in all sorts of opposite directions 'cause everyone's been to the pubs before the session. And it seems to me to be a hell of an existence, just going into the studio recording your latest album, then sitting back and wondering how it's gonna do. Instead of getting out and playing it for people, which is the only thing to do or else you get eaten away.

And, the album in front of you adds so much credibility to the new act, which must be important?

Ent: Tommy had just been released when we played it quite a few times a while back during a tour of the states. At first, people were going "Yeah, too much," mostly because it was such a mammoth. But as we got on with the tour, it started to mean something to everybody, it started to work . . . (At this point the telephone rings, and Entwistle picks it up. "Hello? Yes . . . ah, hello Mr. Fox (he's talking to the drummer for the James Gang, Jim Fox). An *Army* problem? . . . Really? . . . Oh, Jesus Christ, ha! Yeah . . . I've got this fantastic knife if you want to cut your toe off, heh, heh." Entwistle hung up and explained to me that Jim Fox had just been drafted.)

I'm gonna try and keep guitar off my next album, if I can . . . There's quite a few numbers on this album where I haven't used electric guitar at all, like "What Are We Doing Here" just has acoustic guitar, "You're Mine" has just got acoustic on it . . . On my numbers I prefer a piano texture, rather than a guitar. Mainly because I either write on bass guitar or in my head, just transfer it to manuscript paper, or piano. I write mainly on piano now, and I can't play lead guitar, so there just isn't a guitar part on the demo and the whole number takes shape around piano, brass, and whatever other instruments I'm using, so the guitar just doesn't matter. If you play the same figures as on the demo, then you don't need the guitar. You can just stick an acoustic on the thicken it out a bit, jangle wise.

What's your next album going to be like?

Ent: It'll still be black humor but it won't be about death and funerals so much. There might be a couple of numbers about old age. It's the sort of instruments to be used that I'm looking forward to and the way it's going to be recorded, 'cause we've got our own engineer now. Glyn Johns. He's sort of signed to us, we don't need a producer, we need a sort of producer-engineer who can just sit in the box and give us the sound we want while we're outside, since we can't sit in the control booth and play at the same time.

But as I said, on the next album I want to try to get rid of the guitar almost completely. I bought some new instruments on this tour. I bought a new French horn because my old one seized up, that's why I didn't use it on the album. I've bought a mellophonium which is like a French horn only it's much easier to play—it's like a French horn only it's straightened out. I bought a piccolo trumpet so I can get some sort of high range, and a bass trombone so I can get lower trombone sounds.

You're gonna have to do a lot of tracking over.

Ent: Oh, I did on this one too. On "No. 29" we used four tracks with the stereo drums, bass guitar and rhythm guitar, then there were two electric piano tracks, four trombones, four trumpets and four voices. So on a 16-track we still had to mix down to get it all down. Oh yeah, also on all the vocal tracks we stuck on a percussion track as well.

That's getting a bit complex.

Ent: Yeah. It took me three weeks to record.

It's amazing that it can keep so much life to it, doing that much overdubbing.

Ent: If you get enough energy in the backing track, and if you don't relax when you're overdubbing, if you really sort of play with a lot more energy all the way through—I mean, I must have drank about fifty bottles of brandy doing that album . . . I'm gonna do a bass solo on the next album—it's about time I did another bass solo . . .

———————————

I was struck by Entwistle's essential urbanity. Notwithstanding his notoriously morbid sense of humor, he behaved with the exacting intent of a rough Scottish nobleman. It seemed that of the four members of the group, Entwistle would be the one most approaching sanity.

I left John with a hearty handshake and walked down to Pete Townshend's suite. He answered the door with a smile and led us into the outside room, where a few friends were sitting. He gave one a guitar pick as they left, and after gazing intently at the color TV which had been silently presenting a film of people on horseback chasing each other through the snow, he reached over to switch it off and settled down on his couch.

PETER TOWNSHEND

You're about to finish your first tour of America in a year, and the first tour after Tommy. *Looking back on it, what do you think of your comeback?*

Town: We came back with a very weird stand on things. The first part of the year we really spent trying to put together a film, which was basically gonna be the output of our troubles. In actual fact we spent a lot of the time doing other things involved in music, stage act, hardware and things like that. Trying to improve ourselves so that when we finally did get to the point of making the film there would be a new, better Who, as it were, encased in that to give the film an added impact as well. And this proved to be probably the biggest waste of time the group's ever got into since the very beginning. Basically because it was kind of an aimless thing that we were involved in.

You mean too vague?

Town: Yeah. With this backlog of effort we feel now that we've worked probably harder in the last year than we ever have. Not only did we have to . . . I mean I've worked myself on something which you'll never see to the point of like nervous breakdown—I've never 'ad one, but I came close. I've never come across something like this before—I've always felt an abundance of energy, particularly if it's one of my projects, I've always thought "well, fuck it, it's my thing, I've got to push it through, convince everyone that it's good and so on" and put more energy into it than other people. But in this particular case it went on and on and on and on and the time limit, after about six months with no product, only problems, and only me involved in it and the rest of the group gettin' bored, John gettin' involved in makin' his own album, Roger ringing me up every day tryin' to dissuade me from doing the project, y'know, saying what we really need to do is to work on the road. Ah, we eventually gave up, and to put it quite frankly we just went back into the old mold. We went into the studio, I picked out a few of the numbers I'd had for the film project, recorded them . . .

Which ones?

Town: Eh, "Pure and Easy", "Gettin' in Tune", "Won't Get Fooled Again", "Love Ain't For Keeping" and "Behind Blue Eyes". We did a very straight album and then it naturally followed that we would do a very straight tour, for some reason, so we just came over and we toured, really having nothing to do except promote a new album.

Do you really think that Who's Next *is that straight?*

Town: Yeah.

But the addition of the synthesizers brings about a huge change from The Who's former dynamic form.

Town: I like to think so. When we produce ourselves we might be a little bit embarrassed by our musical identities on record—we might not like particular things, idiosyncracies that make us more The Who. So this one's kind of like an un-Who record, in a lot of places on stuff like "Baba O'Riley" the lyrics mean fuck-all, you know, but it's probably one of the best vocal performances I've ever heard Roger do, and yet he's singin' about nothin—that's very unfortunate, I think (laughter).

What do you mean, he's singing about nothing?

Town: He's singing . . . about nothing! . . . how's it go- "Out here in the fields I fight for my meals . . .", I mean, it's a bit o' the script . . . it's a bit of the script of the movie which never 'appened.

Unless it's just me putting what I think about the group onto this, but I know I'm not alone in thinking this . . . I don't know what you were doing with that film, but the feeling of it translates itself to the album.

Town: That's good. We hoped it would do that because we figured . . . at first we were gonna do a double album . . . I'm gettin' around to the way we felt comin' back to the states (laughter] . . . we were gonna do a double album because we thought, well, this is eight months of our lives, right? for better or worse let's put it down . . . 'cause I've got a whole roomful of these really weird sounds and stuff, a lot of it in quadrophonics, which we want to use on the stage, special collage tape effects and everything.

The stuff on the album is quite unadventurous, and I mean they're not pure electronic sounds, they're musical sound, they're rock sounds which celestially work on you. We were gonna do a whole thing, then we figured it would be far better, much more solid to just pick the best stuff out and make it a good, hard, rock solid album 'cause we were very very afraid of doin' what The Beatles did, just layn' ourselves wide open like they did with their double album and making it so that it was too much, too many unlinked ideas which to the public would look like untogetherness, despite the fact that it's always there in the background.

We decided on a single album because, really it was the straightest thing to do, basically every angle, every tangent that we went off on we eventually arrived back, if you like, to where the group used to be. The more times this happened the more times it reinforced Roger's stand which was that the group was perfectly allright as it was and that, basically I shouldn't tamper with it.

Were you tampering with the group itself?

Town: Oh yeah, I was actually . . . yeah, in a way. But if we want to go into that it's better to go into that as a separate thing.

So really what my position is at the moment is . . . obviously very, very happy that the group got over the hump and that I had the guts to back down, if you like. It's a lot harder to back down sometimes than it is to back up. We're here and we're working and we've got an album out that is the culmination of all that effort. But comin' over to the states is worth the same thing. It's nice because we're here, because we're doin' it, but I still have the same needs inside of me, I still have the same . . .

Frustrations?

Town: Frustrations, if you like, but more than that—ambitions for rock and roll and for the group. It makes me impatient to have to go through the tour and have to go through *Who's Next* and everything in order to arrive at where we're gonna have to arrive at if rock and roll is gonna continue and if The Who is gonna keep climbing. 'Cause you can't stop just because somebody's decided that that's a pinnacle.

Lots of groups do that. Lots of groups just say "this is where we are" and leave it at that. Tommy *would have been—must have been at at least one point a really inviting peak to ride along on.*

Town: Not really, 'cause . . . it just made me feel that maybe if we could do something like *that*, then we could do something with public performance, which is really what it's all about. I always used to imagine how potent something like *Tommy* would be if it never was a record, if it always was a stage performance. And I started to think in that sort of way, that recordings first and performances afterwards were somehow getting to be upside down. I still very much feel that.

Who albums always have seemed like blueprints for what the group was going to do on stage, and the stage versions of the stuff are usually so much better, but I don't know about Who's Next, *'cause now that you're putting synthesizers and stuff on it you're putting a great dividing line between the album material and the material on stage.*

Town: One of the points about that is that we've always regarded albums as being jumping off points for the stage act . . . in actual fact the way we've gone around arriving at a stage act from *Who's Next* is very much the way we used do—we've taken the numbers that are practically possible on the stage and—the best and most adventurous being "Won't Get Fooled Again" and that, really, is the feather in my cap at the moment, that's what I'm really relying on because that was the basis, that was the first number that we did. But it has to be transcended, though, right? "Won't Get Fooled Again" is great because it's the kind of stabbing rhythm that you can play to. Some of them are more subtle, but we'll learn them and we'll do 'em, because . . .

Do you eventually see that as . . .

Town: As, absolutely. Not only that but I definitely want to start using cartridge tapes on stage. You hit a foot button and you get the sound. And also processing the voice through the synthesizer and also settin' up synthesizers to play rhythms. They have these things called sequences on 'em. You do all the work before the show, you set the thing up then you start it going and play on top of that. Once the group establishes a way of monitoring the effects of the tapes or whatever, we're OK. The big problem of this first eight months of work, in a way, was that every technical bridge we came to was very hard to cross because we were trying to do everything all at once, trying to make the film, invent the new Who, make incredibly big strides in music, write a whole load of new numbers, I was tryin' to write a film script, we were trying to service a quadrophonic PA, we were up to our ears in it and getting really nowhere very fast.

And you came out of it with "Won't Get Fooled Again".

Town: Yeah (laughter all around).

So you see the new Who—I hesitate to use that phrase—Who prime, perhaps—as a sort of electronic bath.

Town: We are electric musicians, after all. The guitar is a stepping off point . . . the guitar has become if you like the violin of the rock orchestra. It's the instrument through which identities and personalities are established. You can much more identify a guitarist, even, than a violinist . . . it's become the instrument which is almost like a voice, there are different sort of sounds that are made from different ways of playing and it's like . . . you can recognize guitarists.

So there's always that bit of humanness, if you like, but it's only a breaking off point because a guitar is not that much just a guitar, but once it becomes electrified it's turned into a giant instrument which can play to 60,000 people. It can also do a lot of other things, a guitar can be the control center for a synthesizer. A guitar can go into a synthesizer and have its sound taken apart and put back together again in a different form, so that you're playing the guitar, but the actual sound that's comin' out is a completely different thing. On the album, on *Who's Next*, there's a very simple one which we use with the ARP synthesizer caller an envelope follower, where you plug the guitar in and you get a sort of fuzzy wah-wah sound.

That's on "Going Mobile". So that's how you got that incredible sound.

Town: But the guitar itself was controlling the amount of filter sweep. When you hit the note the filter went Bwaaumm! and when the string stopped the filter closed so you got nothing.

The synthesizer part on "Baba O'Riley" is supposed to be your personality chart or something, isn't it?

Town: Yeah. It's really difficult to explain because the intentions were good but the way it all came out was a bit cockeyed. I was trying to do what is really, I suppose, a very John Cage type thing which was to take . . . it was my "to make rock more reflective" crusade. We bypass all the bullshit and go straight down to the "soul" as it were, and get the music from there. In "Baba O'Riley" that's about as near as I ever got to it.

The effect of "Baba O'Riley" is really really strange. There's another song on the album that's strange too, and that's "Song is Over". Why is that, or, how did you come by that?

Town: That was the very last song in the film. Basically what happens in the film script . . . It's an age when overpopulation and pollution and all that kind of stuff has forced man into a totally artificial existence. He lives out his experience in his life in a cocoon—it's a very stock science fiction idea called an experience suit. You put on a suit and you live programs, if you like, for your experience. Everyone's in tubes on the ground because up on top . . . there's an elite—it costs a lot for an experience suit but it's regarded as the best thing to do for your kids—get them an experience suit and they grow in it and they're away from the trouble of the surface. And on the surface, that's where all the bad things go down, that's where all the scum are, that's where all the hippies are, and the farmers. The heroes of the thing are the scum of the surface which is meant to be the lower classes and the people in the experience suits.

The Festival Hall in London is taken over and various experiences take place like . . . orgies and football matches and everything you can conceive of. But this has become a kind of a theatre—like an art form in itself—to provide good experiences for people on the experience suits. Art is taken way, way beyond what it is now, that is, something to be appreciated, for it *is* life, it's what you *get.*

And on the other hand is this guy who I called "Bobby", for a gag, who decides that it's all bullshit and that only one thing is gonna put everything right and that's rock and roll. And he's an old rock and roll musician, and he talks a lot about his memories of the old days which is basically just me, rapping. He was gonna put on a six month concert event which people came to and they put up a force field so that no one could get in, and then they just did it—indulged in a good old fashioned rock and roll concert. The people who come are regular people, but they're the scum off the surface, there's a few farmers there, that's where the thing from "Baba O'Riley" comes in.

What eventually happens is that the whole thing gets really big, the government decides that the concerts have to be stopped because they see it as a developing thing taking things out of their control, 'cause once people are in experience suits, they're under the government's control.

It ends up, basically, with an amazing day. Bobby gets everybody's pieces of music together and it turns into basically what was gonna be . . . I was gonna use "Baba O'Riley" for this which like started everybody going, started everybody dancing around, and the thing at the end . . . "Baba O'Riley" was originally thirty minutes long and the way you hear it now is all the high points just shoved together and there's lots and lots of passages in between which were just supposed to be shots of the dancing. The pitch gets bigger and bigger and bigger and bigger . . . the force field goes down at a given moment, the government troops come in and as they walk in, Bobby is up on the platform and he gets shot by the government official and he falls off the balcony. As he hits the ground, all the kids rush in to catch him and as he hits the ground they all disappear, and that was just gonna to the end of it, right? But the way it's written is that everybody that was taking part in the rock concert disappears but nobody else does and they're just standing there, looking, and they don't know what has happened to the people, right? They've gone. And that's when "Song is Over" starts. We had it played by the Bonzo Dog Doo-Da Band.

The whole point is that all the hardware that is used, that they use in the theatre, is the hardware that was used to program the experience suits, so everyone in the experience suits is dead because they've had no experience, no food, no nothing. The kids have disappeared, and the only people left are the farmers and the government official and a few scattered individuals, and it's just like a wasteland sort of thing. That's like a rough synopsis of what it's all about, and "Song is Over" was like the last song. That's why it's kind of weird, it's like a mixture of being sad and wistful but at the same time there's a high point.

There's a happiness to it. It's a feeling of release.

Town: Because you know basically that the kids have gone somewhere . . .

Writing it was good for me just to sort of say "well, really this is what I wanna see happen, this is what rock is capable of doing". But not in such an obvious science fiction-y sort of way, I mean, science fiction is today, if you like but I mean it's . . . it was the vehicle I chose to write around because I read mostly science fiction and I felt it enabled me to get away with preposterous statements . . .

Basically what you keep saying about rock is, "the magic is gone. Rock and Roll can go up to a new point and what we're trying to do is get it there." You're trying to do what Bobby was trying to do in the story . . .

Town: Yeah, yeah. What we really feel is that . . . we have a big responsibility because we're capable of doing *it*. Or moving towards it, I mean, I obviously don't care if anything quite as sensational as what happens in the script actually happens, but I do care about having an audience to play to, and I do care about them loving me and me loving them, I mean I do care about the experiences that I've had on the stage being very precious ones, and that, in America in particular I've known the deepest experiences on the stage, and I feel that slipping away because of the fact that rock is an accelerating medium. It's always accelerating, it's always moving faster and faster and faster and faster. As soon as it starts to level off and plane off, it might not decrease in speed, it might remain, alright so rock still does what it was doing last year, there's another rock opera, there's another this, there's another that, there's another superstar era and so on and so on and so on. But if it doesn't keep accelerating, it's not reflecting the changes in kids, because the kids are still accelerating, life accelerates, you know wha' I mean? It doesn't ever stop going faster and faster and faster and faster. Evolution doesn't, evolution is on a logarithmically increasing sort of plan, and so is everything else, science does it, and Rock has to do it. And when Rock levels off and starts to rest on its laurels, that's when I start to feel pain, y'know . . .

We're in a dry period.

Town: Well, I don't mind the dry periods, they're very necessary . . .

Well it happens every now and then.

Town: A lot of people have accused me of probably what's a very real accusation is that I can't wait for the next big thing to happen, and that also I'm afraid that it might not be The Who that is it. Both those are very true, but mostly the fact remains that we won't exist anywhere else other than in rock. And the only place where we *can* exist, now, is in front. For us, and for the audience and for everyone. We've pushed ourselves into this position, and there's only one way to go and that's further up. It's not really an upness, though, that I'm talking about, it's not a one-upsmanship over the next man but it's like—let's call it deeper, which is a better word.

What do you feel now in relation to this? It's been a year and you came back. A year is a long time to be gone, almost too long, but you came back I think in time, you know, to keep it going.

Town: Well, I think in some cases we came back in time but in others it wouldn't really matter if we hadn't, because, quite honestly I don't think there was anything to miss.

You just said that things keep accelerating...

Town: Well, right, but the group has to do what it's capable of. When we try to do what we're not capable of, we quite simply don't succeed. I think it's unfortunate, for example, that the Stones missed out two years of American history, but it doesn't really matter...

To them?

Town: I dunno, I mean I don't think it really matters in the whole scheme of things. I don't think it really matters if The Who drop dead tomorrow. But I mean...

To The Who it matters.

Town: In a sense it does, but I mean the people it should really matter to is, y'know, the rock nation if y'like, because we stand to lose most by their loss. I think, basically, because we're the ones that take the somewhat flippant and sometimes very careless instabilities and insecurities of young people and live them out. And that can be very tough, you know what I mean? You're taking on a lot of frustrations of the people, but when the people are very, very frustrated the group becomes very, very, very frustrated. It's like one of those situations... you're not just reflecting, as such, you're also living out a very extreme case—this is when you're on the road, obviously... this is why it's so great to be a fucking English band, because you can go home and you can look, and you can remember, and you can think and you can pull yourself back together again and get more strength.

There was something you said before that I wanted to jump on, but I forgot what it was . . . It has to do with your relation to the audience . . . your commitment . . .

Town: We understand it but it's really hard to talk about it, it's one of those things you have to do. We definitely developed a sixth sense about where the audience's heads are at a certain time, but we're gettin' turned around a bit at the moment because our sixth senses suddenly seem to be working in different ways. In other words, I might get up on stage and decide the audience are a bummer, and I might decide to use commando tactics on 'em. Roger might decide that this is a very pleasant evening and that he feels very much at home and that it's a nice, easy, friendly audience and that he's gonna play this one straight. Keith might decide that he feels a bit of lunacy is in order and so everybody decides to do different sort of tactics. I think that indicates that the group are facing audiences much more as individuals at the moment, and much less as a group. That again brings us back to the point that to be a group, really, you have to be more fully intimidated by the audience, you have to be more fully pigeonholed by the audience. To be a group you have to be a group because the audience say you are a group. When the group gets bigger than the audience then they start findin' out about you as people and start watching for certain expressions and this and that—they don't see you as a mass, they see you as four people that, that . . . are oversized . . . it's like having four great big . . . like having a man and a woman on stage that call themselves man and wife. Taking a tab of acid, if you like, right? and lookin' at them and seein' that there's no way these two people are really connected (laughing). No way, whatsoever, that the whole thing is a complete and total joke, and that the connection which they're aiming at is way, way, way ahead in their future. But for the moment they're very separate but they happen to be walking in the same direction together . . . some of the time. And I feel very much under that kind of rock analysis, and one which is very very drug oriented. You're strongest when you're a group, and when you're working together, and when you're very sure of yourself, than in the state we are now. We know we're not gonna break up . . . ah . . . but we want to.

You want to break up.

Town: Yeah. I think there's that sort of thing with the band, y'know.

I thought that was alleviated when John put out his own album.

Town: No, I mean that . . . it's not that kind of breakin' up, like "we want to break up", we don't sit around and say I wish we could break up . . . d'y'know wha' I mean, we want to fly apart. Holding four guys together is like . . . it's three people that each member of the group has got to deal with and all the time on an everyday working basis and it just gets, it gets to be that you spend so much energy in holdin' a group together that you don't have that much left for facin' up to an audience on a positive basis. It's not like . . .

Do you feel now that you're in command, that you can dictate exactly to the audiences?

Town: You were right the first time, I really get that—the feeling that we're strongest now, we do the best performances when we walk onstage and don't stand for any nonsense—"This is a rock and roll concert you mother-fuckers so shut up and listen to the music", which is hardly rock and roll but it gets the best effect.

Let me take an example, and one that I know best, New York. Every time you've played there, it seems, something disastrous has happened, the first night. I mean, someone was killed last time. And then the Fillmore fire, Martin Luther King's assassination, something really disastrous happens each time. Can this just be coincidence?

Town: Ah . . . well, let's put it this way: I don't think that The Who playin' in New York had anything to do with Martin Luther King. But I think it definitely had a lot to do with the death of the kid because, he was tryin' to get into the concert, or so I understand. So that obviously is on our shoulders. It's one of those things which happens at rock concerts.

The fire, in a way, was a weird thing, but then . . . there's a lot of rumors about that too, see, some say it was a firebomb that was aimed at the Fillmore, whereas Bill Graham says without a doubt, he knows the history of the whole thing, that it was a protection thing for the store, there was a store next door, a betting firm or something—the guy was liquidating and he refused to pay the protection money and he let 'em blow the place up and collect on the insurance, right? Basically (laughing) that's the story of that one.

But it's so strange that this kind of stuff always happens in conjunction with The Who opening in New York.

Town: Well, a lot 'appens, I mean . . . when I'm an old grandad I'll 'ave a lot of stories to tell people—I mean rock and roll does tend to go around, like . . . speeding up events a lot. If you're in a rock and roll group, right? particularly if you're in The Who, it seems that you're tryin' to live 80 years of your life in a very short period, right? at the time when you've got the most energy to do that and you reach maturity very very very early but you're still very very young and it sort of balances out into a situation which is like almost an ideal of utopian existence which is to be a successful rock star who is happy, right? and without croonin' on and on for hours, The Who are very much in that position. In the light of that extreme of experience which you're going through, y'know with life flashing by so incredibly fast, meetin' lots and lots of people and dealin' with an incredible weight of karma all the time, tryin' to avoid relationships and make relationships and so on, tryin' to sort out relationships and deal with incredibly large numbers of people, you . . . a death of a politician seems very innocuous, seems like the sort of thing that should happen, it's like dropping a cap or a plane crash or . . . I mean on the Herman's Hermit's tour the fucking plane crashed, and nobody whimpered, nobody said a word. Nobody. Nobody *cared.* Crash landed . . . that was in the days of the Herman's Hermit's tour but it's still insanity . . . you go in and you wait for the explosion and it comes—BANG! Keith's blown up his laboratory again, every day. And yet they still welcome us with open arms at Holiday Inns! This is the kind of thing—I mean everybody said tragic things about the deaths of Hendrix and Joplin, but they had both lived at such an incredibly accelerated rate that their time had come. They were both very old and very very wise people.

The feeling I get from the new album is . . . there is a new goal and this is the first step. How much of a step is it?

Town: It's as big a step, if you like, as *Happy Jack* ever was. It's hard to tell. I don't really know even, yet, what we're stepping toward. I decided on a title though, which I ain't gonna tell you, 'cause it's like the best title I've ever come up with for anything, ever. It's for the whole—what we're gonna do . . . It came in Cleveland—I had this flash, so I kind of know the direction I want to go in. A title is a reflection of a flash, if y'know wha' I mean. You have an idea and you get a conception of something and the title is merely an affirmation.

This title is positive?

Town: Yeah. I think we know where we're going.

You're not gonna do the movie now, the movie was bombed, right?

Town: Yeah. I tell you one of the problems, in fact, our biggest problem, is that our managers desperately want to make that movie, and they're very disorganized people. They started with The Who for the sole purpose of makin' a movie. And it's something that I think Kit Lambert desperately wants to do before he's ready to die, I think this is probably what keeps him alive. When I suggested to him that we might have another bash at talking about a movie of *Tommy,* I mean he literally jumped for joy and leapt around the room and kissed me and hugged me and took me out to dinner and started talkin' to me again, y'know (laughter). I mean, when I said that it might be good if he directed it, he gave up everything he owned and gave it to me, brought it 'round in a big truck and dumped it on me doorstep and said that he'd be me servant for life. That's how much Kit wants to make a movie.

The Who really feel that too, I mean we want to make a fucking movie incredibly badly and it's just simply a movie—one of the reasons why I feel it's important is because it's still the only medium which can capture the largeness of rock, the bigness of it. *Woodstock* for example, you felt the bigness of the event. There's no other way you could have felt it, not through people talkin' about it or photographs or anything—the movie did it, and the movie can capture the bigness of rock and get the bigness of the sound, too. That's important, big speakers all 'round the theatre. And also it can capture the silliness—the stuff that a lot of the kids don't see. You know, the reality, if you like, that lies behind but which is like all part of it. It's hard to talk about it without soundin' like were gonna make a documentary.

You want to make a movie about The Who?

Town: We wanna make a movie *about* what The Who are going to do—what The Who do. We figure in terms of like changing rock performance, y'know, from our point of view, that we're gonna have to do it.

The whole essence of it is gonna be that rock can no longer service all the people that wanna see it. People are gonna have to *be* rock, if y'like, and that rock is gonna have to be a different type of event, it's gonna have to be something where you go and live with it. I mean there's a lot of impractical things about it, but, there are things that have to be done. Whatever happens, whatever needs to be done we'll do, and we'll prove that we did it and we'll prove that it happened by the movie. And then no one will ever accept the way that rock has to work, in the confines of what has been laid down by other types of music, other types of entertainment, by the ballet, by the opera, by the circus, by the football match, by other types of entertainment, 'cause rock is its own, it needs its own framework for working.

In a sense it becomes only a matter of personal scholarship whether you're there or not. As long as you can see it, and want to be it, you are it.

Town: Right. The other thing of course is that records are great because you can live with 'em. Video is gonna be great, too. There's too many preconceptions about the television shaped box, as it were. I don't like it at all . . . people are gonna want to project it, I think instead of watching it on the television. In which case, it means that then rock can really do amazing things in terms of people makin' their own movies and musicians making movies for the people, and both getting their feedback through that means.

The one question I have to ask you, though, is this: this is obviously your trip, and Kit Lambert's. Where does this leave the other members of The Who? I mean, where does John Entwistle fit into a movie?

Town: I dunno, really. I've never really, ever sat down with John and discussed where he fitted in. I've always just either written the music and asked him to play it, or . . . been his friend, really. With someone, for example, like Keith, you can get a certain level of enthusiasm from, I mean Keith's a real enthusiastic person. If you rap and you talk to him about a project he gets very excited and he wants to do it. Roger, again has got an incredible amount of energy—it's reserved, right? in the same way that John is reserved, but it's different, he's . . . less ambitious, I think, more contented with wherever he happens to be. But John is just . . . we learned more about John from him making an album than we did in all the years he'd ever played bass with us. Really, because he *did* it, and it spoke to us, it's like I was saying about feedback. I got a lot of feedback from John's record.

The reason I asked that is that when you talk about going into film, when you talk about extending the kind of sensory impression that you're gonna have on people, not just live but in a recorded way so it becomes, like, history, you change the definition of the group in a sense that's very far reaching. It's no longer just The Who, but a historical entity.

Town: I don't think it should be just The Who at all. I think that whatever we do is gonna have to solve a lot of problems, in order to move forward from where we are now we've got to learn a lot of things about one another. I'll obviously have to give up a fantastic amount, but then so will the group, in terms of image and credit and stuff like this. But we'll gain a fantastic amount in the shape of audience, in the shape of feedback. Whether or not it will solidly bond together the group as more of a group, or whether it'll make us more individuals, I don't know, but we are becoming more individuals now and so in a way, whatever we do, I think if it is positive it will make The Who more The Who.

I see John's album to be very much a Who album, just like I feel that Keith's odd nights with Bonzo Dog, or, he's done this radio show with Viv Standshell in England and all this, and he'll probably make comedy albums and stuff and I feel that to be very much within the framework of The Who. I feel my Meher Baba record to be The Who in a lot of cases. I feel that to be The Who. I think all that is great so long as the group can use it. I think "My Wife" is the best rock number on the new album.

One last question. Can you tell me something about what's going to happen in the immediate future in relation to all this, 'cause it's still been kind of vague.

Town: Well, firstly, we're gonna try and give ourselves a break. I don't mean a holiday, I mean give ourselves a break with regard to keeping things solid and moving, and keeping things belonging to The Who rather than becoming my personal fantasies. By going back and doing a lot of work on our stage act, we're gonna try and work on employing more tapes on the stage, more effects . . . we're gonna try to improve the lights, which we're very, very unhappy with. With the amount of manpower involved, they're very tinny. We're gonna try and get the sound straightened out and try to get our heads together in that area, and we're gonna do a TV special which is going to be a documentary about us preparing to make the movie. The reason we want to do this, apart from the fact that we feel it could be incredibly interesting, is that we think it will catalyze a lot of action, it will actually make the thing happen, if you like. Do you know what I mean? Oh, and also an album. . . .

Who's Next leaves too many loose ends if it's not going to be followed up. Just as Happy Jack/A Quick One *was followed up by* Sell Out *which sort of concretized a lot of things which were yashing around in there, it would seem that you'd sort of have to follow* Who's Next *with something a little more definitive of what the Who's next actually is.*

Town: Well, I think natural evolution of the band's sound will do a lot of that—an increasing positivity will also do that. But most of all, what'll do it will be tyin' up the loose ends that are involved in it. Knowing that *Who's Next* is the result of an unsolved problem, when we solve the problem *Who's Next* will take on a different meaning. It will be part of the problem and will be more interesting in a way, once we've done what we want to do, I think.

It's hard to follow an interview with Peter Townshend. He seems completely at home right from the beginning, attempts to be as helpful as he can, and generally controls the interview himself, answering most of your questions before you can even ask them.

By contrast, Roger Daltrey seems very uncomfortable. We found him in his room, sitting with a few friends. He was hoarse, constantly sucking on some mints for his throat and alternating that with nervous puffs on a menthol cigarette. He was incredibly nice, but on alien ground.

ROGER DALTREY

How do you feel, getting back down to touring?

Dalt: Getting too old, man. Too old to do it and play. Just need them days off here and there, these one nighters every night are gettin' to be too much.

Pete was talking about a movie that the group was planning to do in the future as the next step. How do you fit into that—what the group is going to do now?

Dalt: Depends on what it's gonna be . . . I like wha' the group's gonna do now . . . basically an idea . . . I can't really talk about it, I don't wanna talk about it, actually . . . I mean, basically it's just about rock and roll, simple as that. We're gonna try to make the first rock and roll film ever made.

Are you gonna write some material for it?

Dalt: I'm writin' too, but it's not suited to The Who, y'know?

You have been writing things?

Dalt: Yeah, all the time . . . s'just not suited to The Who. And I don't wanna do my own album. Maybe when it's all over and finished, perhaps. As far as I can see the whole thing is to keep it together, so I just devote all of my time just to keep 'em together.

Has it been threatening to fall apart?

Dalt: Oh, we've come nearer to breaking up than ever.

John said that he was ready to leave the group up until the time that he made his album, which made him . . .

Dalt: John's always been leaving the group. Perhaps that's the problem, y'know, perhaps John doesn't wanna be in the group, I dunno (he laughs rather emptily).

Pete said that it's going in so many different directions that it wants to fly apart, but can't because the whole . . . is so important.

Dalt: Eh . . . Me and Pete have been gettin' on better'n ever! I think that's one of the reasons we still are together . . . There's a few things been going on but we can't sort it out here, we'll sort it out when we get back to England.

A lot of people write in analyses of the group on stage, that often you're used as a spokesman for Pete's views or whatever . . .

Dalt: Well, it's obviously true.

How much of you actually goes into it?

Dalt: Oh, quite a lot. Pete's always written songs that I believe in so that gets over 'alf the battle. It's easy to sing about something you believe in. And as long as I keep believin', I can go on singin'. Quite a lot of me does go into it, I assure you.

I think a lot of Pete's songwritin' comes from me anyway. A lot of ideas come from me, but then he can put it to words whereas I can't. Pete's always wanted to be me in some ways, I think.

Do you actually, like, sit down, and . . .

Dalt: Oh, no. He writes the song and I sing it. He makes a tape of it one way and I sing it another way.

His voice has very little power, but . . .

Dalt: Yeah, he uses it in a nice way, usually it works out well. What do you think of the new act, now?

Well, I think the act has a little more maturity now, in the sense that songs like "Won't Get Fooled Again" have gotten down. In the beginning there were some soundups, but now it seems all on the same wavelength.

Dalt: We're gonna experiment more with tapes, actually, they're very good. The only thing is not to get tied to it too much you know, this is where me and Pete are always at loggerheads. But there again Pete's a little more adventurous now, but I would prefer that the group doing its thing, then laying the tape on the top, rather than doing a thing around the tape, which is what happened on "Won't Get Fooled Again"—the whole number's around the tape, which I think is completely wrong. Well, it works very well, it's alright for one number, but . . . no more.

Do you feel that in the time you've been gone from America, the audience has somehow changed?

Dalt: Yeah. It's changed a lot. Seems to be much more teenybopper oriented now.

How do you feel about that?

Dalt: Ah, weird, I haven't thought about it that much. I don't do much thinkin' in hotel rooms—bad for ya . . . It's probably a good thing, y'know, teenyboppers grow up and get better taste, just 'cause you're . . . we've played to teenyboppers before.

What has happened, I think, is that there's a big gap, and an awful lot of really hungry kids are walking around looking for something. But there hasn't been anything—that's why I was enthused about The Who coming back, but now that I actually sit down and talk with you about it, nobody quite knows . . . everyone seems very reserved about the whole thing.

Dalt: This is when we go back home to think about the next project.

It doesn't seem like the consensus from the band was that this was a successful tour. There's something that seems to be bothering everybody.

Dalt: Yeah. I don't think it was very successful—I mean, we didn't gain any ground, I don't feel.

Well, did you set out to gain ground?

Dalt: Not really. We set out just to bloody let people see that we were still alive and thinking about them. So I suppose we've done what we set out to do. But it's still been hard doin' it.

Sure. I've always thought we should never have gone away. We should have built on what we could do best rather than try to send it away, which's what we tried to do. The only problem that annoys me within the band—it's no serious problem, it's just that . . . I feel that I'm singin' better now than ever and I'm really enjoying it and really getting good feelings off audiences, Pete's been playing well . . . I think the size of the group has kind of gotten to their heads a bit. Don't put that in (laughing). It's all right if you say you think it, might do some good. 'Cause I tell him all the time and I get laughed at. Pete's really tried, and I'm really trying 'cause—I don't think we've made it.

What do you mean?

Dalt: Well, the situation's not that desperate, I mean it's just a matter of people ownin' up y'know . . . let's face it, nobody's playin' that bad—most people wouldn't even notice. But we notice, I notice, and what I wanna do is get better, not worse. As far as I'm concerned, I've only been really singing well for like, maybe two years, it's startin' to go my way, now. As far as I'm concerned we just bloody started. That's what's so weird. I mean in England we played the best gigs of our lives right before we came here. When we first went back on the road, after the project, they were the best gigs we've ever played, ever. Everybody really played well. Then, I dunno . . .

Rock and Roll is so basically contradictory. I mean, you're dealing with a . . .

Dalt: That's the fucking trouble with it, it couldn't be.

Well as long as you have a situation wherein people feel that five dollars entitles them to something, which can't always happen—it's goin' to be contradictory, because there's the idea of "Rock as Theatre", and, you know—"Rock as Professional Entertainment", and contrasted with the idea of rock as some really vital force that transcends all that, the contradictions are pointed up on an everyday, mundane, day to day level. Only after a long period of distancing does "only the good things" stand out.

Dalt: They don't stand out any more than the five dollars in your pocket. Really. That's how I look at it, anyway . . . do you understand me? . . . See, I mean . . . that's the trouble with rock, that kids have to pay five dollars to see it and they think they've got to get their five dollars worth. That's the trouble with it, but it's nothin' to do with us. We give all we've got . . . we really do. And you can't give anymore, I mean if that's not enough . . . I mean to me, five dollars . . . I mean I've, we've been poor, we've been poor for fucking years now, we're just startin' to make money. It still means fuck-all to me. When it comes down to that, I mean I'd pay five dollars to see The Beatles back together. I'd pay a hundred dollars to see them back together. (He laughs) I'd pay a thousand dollars, actually. 'Cause the money means fuck-all, it's just to see them. Most kids don't look at it that way today . . . Plus the fact that you get all the phlonzes in the business. I mean the agents and all that crap, boastin' about how much money they're makin', which is bollocks . . .

What do you see in the immediate future?

Dalt: Travel, I dunno. This idea that Pete's got I think is incredible. I'm behind him all the way.

And you think it can be brought off?

Dalt: It's the way he wants to make it work that gives this the advantage over the other one. His other idea was great, too. Unfortunately he tried to run before he could walk. I could see it, and everybody else . . . I get a lot of advice off of our road managers because they . . . they're not musicians and they can see a lot more than we see. They can see the audience because they're not in the lights. They hear the complete sound. I talk to them all the time about things and I get a lot of ideas about the act from them. Even they couldn't figure out this thing of Pete's to work, the way he had it written down. So I wasn't just being dogmatic for the sake of it, I just knew that it wouldn't work and what we should have been doin' is what we're doin' now, but maybe we're doin' it too late. That album should have been out much earlier.

Yeah. The album really should have preceded you a couple of months so that people could get used to it, 'cause the stuff is just too new. There's something out there that you're going after. . . .

Dalt: Yeah. I know what it is . . . we'll get it. I'm not gonna say anything about this idea, I know you're trying to fish it out of me but I'm not gonna . . .

Nobody will say anything about it, it must be really good.

Dalt: It is.

Leaving Roger, we went to visit the suite on the ninth floor where Keith Moon was staying. Now Keith Moon is well known for his antics—he is one of the most famous clown figures in rock. And certainly when we walked into his suite this image was fulfilled. Compared to the neat complacency of the other three suites, Moon's was chaos. A card table sat in the center of the room, covered with bunches of empty and half-empty glasses and assorted debris. The television's sound was very audible from the inside room, providing a constant electronic reminder to all present. Keith himself was grand, greeting us with a flourish and offering a glass of brandy.

But like so many clowns before him Keith was no fool, rather a clever wielder of masks and postures, all the while very sure he was giving you nothing he didn't want to. I found myself gradually posturing back at him until the interview started to dip into the sensibility of a drawing room battle of wits.

KEITH MOON

I'll start with a very direct and straightforward question. How do you see your role within The Who?

Moon: Um . . . sort of drummer, middleman and . . . sort of kept lunatic. (From within the television announces The Avengers theme)—Great Guns, The Avengers have started! Coming, Mrs. Peal . . . Oh, yes, excuse me, I'm sorry, er, ah . . .

Obviously, now you've gotten to the point where you're a big group, and you have success, but . . . do you feel there's something driving you towards new heights?

Moon: More success! Ah, well it's ah . . . I feel that the amount of talent and power in the group, you know, is such that it hasn't really reached its natural conclusion as yet. There's still a lot that we have to do—a lot of things we're doin' now which we could do better.

With Who's Next *I feel that there's something out there that you're just starting to point at . . . .*

Moon: This is true. When we were working on *Happy Jack and* the mini opera thing, we really didn't know anything about *Tommy,* we didn't know it was working out that way until we finished *Tommy.* This is true now, we're using a lot more electronics . . . synthesizers and different instruments.

Well, how do you relate to that as Keith Moon, drummer for The Who?

Moon: Well, that's it, as Keith Moon, drummer for the 'oo. That's how you do it.

You just react to it, totally feelingfully, no thinking about it or anything?

Moon: Thinking about it just gets in the way.

Yeah, I can see that. It's a contrast to, say, Pete, who appears to think about it constantly. You don't seem to think about it, but . . . well, let me put it this way—occasionally, when "Won't Get Fooled Again" starts, you lose the beat.

Moon: Right.

I mean, like it is a strange position. Do you feel weird having to play to an accompaniment of a tape?

Moon: No, it's, ah . . . because it's metronomic, the very rigid time pattern. It doesn't fluctuate at all, you have to think robotically. It lacks interest. It's just adopting a concept and working within that concept, that shape. It's a much more comfortable shape now than it was. I moved in a few pieces of furniture and had the place carpeted. I find it a lot easier to work within it now. In the beginning it was just sort of uncomfortable.

When did you pick up on the headphones?

Moon: 'Bout halfway through the tour. The big problem was not being able to hear the tape. So we've got John and Pete blasting away and this tape, which is important because they take their thing off of me. I get mine off the tape so if I don't get that, we all go and lose it.

Yeah right. Pete says that he plays with your top kit and John plays with your bass.

Moon: Right. And I play with the tape. If the tape isn't there, none of us are there. So we got the earphone idea, we were playin' some theatres where the monitors just couldn't be heard at all. It happened that first night at Forest Hills.

I had a couple of pairs catch fire. I was wearing them and Bob came rushing over halfway through "Won't Get Fooled Again" with a bucket of water. He looked as if he was gonna throw it at me. So I started to move around, turned me head and there was this smoke pouring off me headphones, and the bloody thing was alight.

That's what I call pyrotechnics . . .

How do you like the new act? There is a big difference . . .

Moon: Yeah. It's kinda gettin' nicer now, we've been playin' it a lot—it's much more familiar, we can relax a lot. When you start it off you have to concentrate on gettin' the numbers right, so you can't have fun and relax and the audience can feel this. It's got this newness about it, and, ah, now it's sort of relaxed . . . we can just play the music, sort of subconsciously.

Do you feel that you had to put in so many new numbers to make a significant enough break with the acts of the past, Tommy *etc.?*

Moon: We don't like to drop any numbers of any particular period the group was at—we like to keep them in, but the main material has to be the new stuff.

Do you all sit down before the tour and work out the order of the numbers, etc.?

Moon: Yeah. We just say which ones work on stage and which ones don't work. And then we just sort of get a runnin' order for 'em, this one would work there, this one wouldn't. So we've got quite a storehouse of songs, so we can fairly interchange one song for another.

One thing that really surprised me in talking with the other three is that there seems to be a bit of disappointment with the tour and how it developed, stemming in part from failure of equipment.

Moon: Yeah. It's been a bit of a problem. The audiences . . . were incredible, they've been great so far. It's affected . . . Pete and John . . . and, ah, Roger, more than me (starts laughing). So I'm the only acoustic one in the band . . . well, Roger, but he's got more equipment than anyone else.

You mean the PA.

Moon: Yes, the PA, monster that it is . . . We're doin' an act that we're not totally familiar with, y'know, and we've got this goin' on at the same time, so it's very hard to get off with that sort of thing goin' on. You need to rely on your hardware, but of course it's not always there—in some halls you've got a five amp shaver socket in the dressing room and you have to run ten and a half tons of equipment through it. So at this theatre we had to run in power lines from the street lamps outside . . . Would you like a shot of brandy?

Sure . . . What do you think of this new idea of Pete's to do a movie?

Moon: I don't know, what is his new idea? Play it back, will you? He hasn't told me about it yet . . . I think, ah, we've got to do quite a lot of sitting around and rapping when we get back, 'cause there's a lot of ideas comin' out of this tour that were used, so when we get back, we'll have a couple of weeks off, John will take his dogs out for a walk, then we'll all sort of get together in a boozer, all sort of get drunk and decide absolutely nothing . . . but eventually it'll all get thrown together, that's how we wrote most of *Tommy*, in a pub opposite the recording studio. (then, abruptly) I think I'll have to pack me gear and get down to the Ox's room. . . .

———

We left Moon just in time to get down to the theatre for the show. The Who were in great spirits and played a blistering final set, resounding with the sense of their own ascendency. They had come back successfully, on their own terms, and proved themselves once again.

The high point of the night was the feature number, "Won't Get Fooled Again". Townshend's introduction ran down a history of The Who and finished with a flourish: "We've seen you do this," he gave a clenched fist, "we've seen you do this," a peace sign, "so we just do what's in between . . . This." He raised his outstretched arm in a Nazi salute. "It's a natural development, y'know . . .", he said. Then, in a much louder voice, "This one, the number we're about to play, puts all that rubbish . . . right. This is a rock and roll song." There were cheers from audience. ". . . which is the salvation . . . of our society . . . Today!" Now screaming as loud as he could, "Won't . . . Get . . . Fooled . . . . . . Agaaaiiinnn!"

CHATTING WITH PETE TOWNSHEND

**Connor McKnight and John Tobler | Approx. February 1972 [part one],
July 1974 [part two], August 1974 [part three] | *Zigzag* (UK)**

Zigzag was a lively alternative UK rock magazine whose heyday was the first half of the seventies. As with most alternative ventures, it was free and easy with convention, one example being cover dates. The only way to work out the juncture of the appearance of part one of its epic Pete Townshend interview is from *Zigzag* no. 24's advertisements and editorial references.

It took two and a half years for parts two and three to materialize (there was no part four, despite what is suggested). By that time, *Zigzag* was printing cover dates, asterisking profanities, and asking seven pence more for its product. There had also, of course, been changes in the Who's career and the wider world. Despite being overtaken by events, however, these belated new installments remained—and, like part one, remain—fascinating snapshots of a specific period in the Who's career.

The discursive discussion, which makes little allowance for those who don't know the Who's story, takes in not just the Who but also their contemporaries, Townshend's production work for Thunderclap Newman, and the politics of Track, the record label run by Who managers Lambert and Stamp.

Band-wise, Townshend willingly feeds the legends of excess by publicizing the antics of the man who had become known as "Moon the Loon." Yet he also proves thoughtfully anxious about the Who's role as members of the rock-star set and the responsibility that he feels derives therefrom.

Incidentally, it's almost hilarious the way Townshend dismisses *Who's Next* as a stepping stone best forgotten.

Notes: for "Watt's For A Pig" read "Waltz For A Pig"

for "Entwhistle" read "Entwistle"
for "Keith Alton" read "Keith Altham" —Ed.

[PART ONE]

After almost three years of Zigzag, it was about time that we got round
to doing something on the Who. So, at the end of last year, John and a
Who-freak friend called Connor McKnight, spent a couple of evenings
with Pete Townshend and came away with 7 cassette-fuls of chat. This
was duly transcribed and a pile of handwritten foolscap, about two inches
thick, arrived for perusal and editing. What to do? Well, in the end, we
decided that we would publish selections of the interview in this issue
and number 26 (next issue is solely on the Byrds), and the whole thing
will eventually be coming out as a Who Special (details in 26). Subjects
discussed ranged from Hells Angels, via Thunderclap Newman, to evolving technology in the recording studio, and from Dylan, via Chuck Berry,
to all the Who's albums. . . . and it's all good stuff. So, for this issue, we
chose a random section labelled 'Tape One - second session'.

ZZ: A lot of your earlier songs had a definite Stones feel about them (and
you recorded a couple of their numbers) and you said in The Times that
their re-surgence as a live band owed a lot to your example. It's obviously
a pretty complex relationship, but can you talk about it a bit?

Pete Townshend: Yeah, sure, but first let me say that that thing in The
Times was a bit embarassing, because re-reading it, it seems to be full
of name dropping. To really pin that down . . . I'm writing a piece for
a magazine that Meher Baba lovers put out in India, and one of the
questions they asked was to give an intimate glimpse of three of your
famous contemporaries - and I really couldn't. . . . I can't give an intimate glimpse of anybody really. I could give several intimate glimpses
of Ronnie Lane, but there isn't anybody else. We don't really know the
Stones; we've never spent any time with them socially, and we've never
really spent time with the Beatles - we were around them a lot when

Epstein was their manager because we were hoping to get in that stable. Kit Lambert and Brian Epstein really respected each other very highly - quite rightly I think. We were hoping for some sort of leakage into the Beatles thing, but it fell through when Epstein died, and I don't think I ever saw any of the Beatles again socially.

Hendrix I always admired tremendously but never got to know, and same with Eric Clapton, who I spent a bit of time with. I met Dylan once, but that's all. But Mick (Jagger) is one of those guys who seems to ring up occasionally and say "hello", but everytime he rings up he asks about a gig or a particular venue or working on the road or some particular problem which has to do with touring. I think that the reason he came to us was that we were the only group that lasted; a contemporary of the Stones right from the ground up, and we were working the kind of gigs that they needed to work when they went back on the road last year. It was at a point where the status was similar, the kind of performance was similar, and the dynamics that we were involved in would be similar.

Quite simply, I personally feel that the Stones are the world's best rock and roll band - I think that unqualifiedly. Not that I think their records are always great . . . it's like Glyn Johns says about a Stones session; you can sit and wait for weeks and they'll just churn out a lot of rubbish - and Glyn's very tough like this - but when they do get it together, they're the best in the world. This is why they are often weak live - because you can't wait for three weeks to get it on, but if they did a live tour that came up to the pitch that they get onto some of their albums . . . the presence, the physical excitement, the mental exhilaration, the electricity of the whole occasion, they would be, really, the best in the world. They suffer, I feel, because Jagger's the only one who wants to play.

ZZ: Mick Taylor wants to play . . . Have you seen Altamont?

PT: No. I was too nervous . . . we've had a few experiences with bad vibe audiences and evil audiences here and there.

ZZ: Not in, England presumably.

PT: One was in England . . . we had a few in England actually. I had an argument with a Hell's Angel on the stage at Leicester once, and got bottled. It made the press in a small way, but they treated it like 'Christ, don't let this sort of thing happen again' - that sort of way. A road manager and I had to have eight stitches apiece, but even so, I think that if I had not been quite so pissed and quite so bloody, I would have got stuck in a lot further and probably got a lot more badly hurt. Because I got hit on the head, and it bled a lot, I thought I'd better get to a hospital, but I was really wild; I broke my guitar across some geezer's collar bone, but it didn't seem to do much to him - he had a ring in his nose, I remember.

ZZ: It's a nasty thing to say, but I wasn't sad when they got their's over Weeley.

PT: I know; I must say that I felt the same. I know a lot of Hell's Angels and they always seem, on the surface, to be incredibly innocent, fun-loving people, but there isn't any doubt that when they get involved in a fight, they're willing to go a lot further than other people. This too, I suppose, is the feeling I've always had about skinheads, and it's because they're not interested in anyone as a human being, they're much more interested in themselves as a showpiece. When they're clubbing you with a billiard cue, they must look graceful when they're doing it - and they're not going to hold back, because their chick is there watching. You find that by themselves, they are very ordinary people, and that's what scares me the most in a situation like that - this mindless thing where they're out to get you though they haven't really got any grievance at all . . . it's like facing an army of robots, and the obvious thing is to run.

ZZ: To get back to the Stones/Who thing, I feel that the Stones have come adrift from their audience. I mean, 'Brown sugar' is a long way from 'Goin Home', don't you agree?

PT: (pauses) I dunno . . . it's hard to say.

ZZ: I think they're about dope, basically.

PT: Maybe . . . I suppose they could be . . . it's really hard to say. I know that Mick is an incredibly sharp guy, and if he thought that the Stones would remain a vehicle for him if he wrote songs about dope, then he would. . . . because he wants the Stones to exist and he wants to work within the Stones - he wants the whole thing to keep going, and he might even do it subconsciously, if you like. 'Brown Sugar' might be about a black chick's cunt or about raw cocaine - I mean, I don't really know, but I do know that coke is a huge thing in the rock world at the moment. In the last two years, it's overtaken pot in popularity among musicians, and I feel it's very much something to remark on, because coke is an addictive thing. Whether you snort it or mainline it or take it in your mouth . . . it's addictive, and much more than just psychologically addictive. It's slower to get to you, but it gets you in the end. I've had people here, and they've really amazed me - I won't mention any names, obviously, but I've had people here that I'd never ever thought of as being drug-hungry people, and I've seen them just break down right in front of me and say "I've just got to get some coke. . . . get me some coke, I've just got to have some - where am I going to get it from . . . who do you know?"

ZZ: Do you think that drugs are self-destructive, or destructive of anything?

PT: I think that's such a difficult question . . . . I don't really know. Some drugs, like hallucinogenic ones, actually alter the mind - they don't just cloud it over like alcohol does . . . they actually alter it.

ZZ: On a permanent basis?

PT: No, not on a permanent basis . . .

ZZ: What about acid?

PT: Well, I don't know about acid. I mean, chemically, the only thing they've been able to pin down to acid is the chromosome damage, about which there is no doubt, but apparently, by the time you're 80, you've already lost half your chromosomes anyway - through eating too much vinegar on your fish and chips or something. So I don't really know the relevance of that.

What I'm worried about is the psychological thing about it. When I stopped, and I stopped because of Meher Baba, my whole world suddenly caved in. Mind you, it had got to the point where I found it very repetitive; it was humping everybody's music into the same bag and it was always going to the same place in my head. When I first got into pot, I was involved in the environment more; there was a newness about Art College, having beautiful girls around for the first time in my life, having all that music around me for the first time, and it was such a great period - with the Beatles and all that exploding all over the place. So it was very exciting, but although pot was important to me, it wasn't the biggest thing; the biggest thing, rather, was the fact that pot helped to make incredible things even more incredible.

Later on, say 5 years later, I'd gotten into that rut of listening to every record stoned, and it was just turning to sculpture in my head . . . I was seeing the music rather than hearing it. It's hard to explain but it was like symmetrical towers of sound - that's how I saw it. The last time I ever heard a record stoned on pot was 'Music from Big Pink', the night I first met John Sebastian, at Peter Tork's house - so there!

ZZ: So what happened to you when you stopped smoking?

PT: Well, like I said, my world just sort of caved in, and I suddenly thought 'Christ, what have I been up to?" I found that I couldn't listen to a record unless I was stoned! I've got about 250 albums now, and the only ones I like are the ones that I first heard when I was stoned . . . what I call 'the stoned ones'; the ones that had that 'stonedness' around them, that aura. I've got to learn to listen to music all over again, and I've got to learn how to write all over again. . . . I've got to learn how to enjoy life all over again, without leaning on dope. This wasn't the betrayal though; the betrayal was that I found I could give it up just like that (snaps fingers). When I realised that everything I'd been crediting to pot was nothing at all to do with it . . . . the fact that I could write a song, or play guitar, or have a good time at a party, or enjoy a satisfying sexual relationship. Alright - a lot of people would say that I learnt through pot, but anyway, it was like a betrayal.

It was a very strange thing; I thought "Christ almighty, what have I been doing? I've been giving my whole life to a weed". Previously, I'd been saying "it's only a weed growing out of the ground - what can be harmful about that?" But now I think that pot is possibly the most subtle evil of all, because of its subtlety and because the psychological dependence, which to me is a far more gritty dependence than actual physical dependence, takes over . . . it's more spiritually based, where you can't enjoy the pleasures of the spirit or the soul. I found it very easy to give up tobacco, and I found it very easy to give up pot, and I think that if I decided not to drink any more I'd find that fairly easy - if there wasn't a Keith Moon in the group, that is - but it was the results which were important. I know I'm lucky in that respect, but it was the results which made me take a positive stand on it - and it's not just aping Meher Baba's words and spouting them out in a quasi-religious manner. I really did make that decision for myself, and in some respects I made it before hearing about Baba. I was, as I said, getting bored with these symmetrical visions, though at the same time, I was attached to them. I liked them, yet I was bored by them, so I suppose that in itself shows that something was in decline.

What shook me about acid was when I took what I thought was acid, but turned out to be STP - something that I would never ever ever take. It was after the Monterey Pop Festival, and I spent more time outside of my body looking inside myself than I've ever spent. . . . it was like a hundred years. It was actually a four hour hump, whereas a normal acid hump is about 25–30 minutes. . . . you have a hump and then plane off into a nice trip. Well on this STP trip, the hump was about 4 to 5 hours - and it was on an aeroplane over the Atlantic.

ZZ: What do you think about legalising dope?

PT: Well, even though I'm against drugs, I say pot should be legalised. You see, I spent so much of my time pissing around with pot purely because it is illegal; and I came very close to being involved with far more serious drugs because policemen in police stations told me, with grave looks on their faces, about the terrible things dope does - "do you know what this stuff does?" I mean, do they know what it does? No. One day they get a pot smoker in and give him an incredibly hard time just because the day before they had a heroin addict in - and to them, it's just the same . . . . if you're not one, you're the other, because you're on your way.

ZZ: They say that if pot were made legal, people would find something else that was not.

PT: That's a possibility. The other argument I've had put to me several times is that alcohol, which is legal, is still very dodgy. But then look at prohibition - that never stopped people drinking . . . they made their own and died because it was such poison. This is the point; if we're going to have dope, let's have decent dope - at least that would do away with the corruption, and it would bring the thing into the open. Then you could separate pot from drugs that really do cause physical and mental problems.

ZZ: Let's get onto a lighter subject, shall we? Can you tell us about Keith Moon's epics in American hotel rooms?

PT: They do happen with alarming regularity. Keith feels that he has to be involved in some form of entertainment all the time - even when the rest of the group is asleep, he feels he has to entertain us and wake us, either by causing explosions or by getting us thrown out of the hotel. The first really big thing he ever did was on our first American tour (with Herman's Hermits); we happened to go to Georgia, which is the only place in the States that you can buy fireworks. They sell these things called Cherry Bombs. Anyway, a few days later I was in his room and all the paint round the door knocker was black where he been putting these things in the key-hole. I happened to ask if I could use his bog and he just smiled like this and said "sure". I went in and there was no toilet - just a sort of S bend coming out of the floor! "Christ, what the fuck's happened?" I asked, and he said "well, this Cherry Bomb was about to go off in my hand, so I threw it down the bog to put it out". "Are they that powerful?" I asked, and he nodded. "How many of them have you got?" I said, with fear in my eyes. He said "500", opening up a case which was full to the top with Cherry Bombs.

Of course, from that moment on, we got thrown out of every hotel we ever stayed in. The Holiday Inns were phoning round saying "don't let this group in - they'll blow the place up", and it got to the point where they were asking for 5000 dollars deposit to let us stay in even the shoddiest hotel.

My nerves finally broke in the Goreham, which is like the hotel in New York where all the groups stay. My wife was with me at the time and it was hard enough just to try and keep the hangers-on away from the cosy family situation, but we got ensconced in our room and tried to make it feel a bit like home. A couple of hours or so later, we got to sleep, only to be woken up by police cars outside and a lot of police running about. I thought that Tom, our production manager had been busted, because he was really heavily into dope, so I ran out and got the lift to the seventh floor where his room was. Then I heard this huge great explosion which rocked the lift. Then the lift stopped, the doors opened, and all I could see was thick smoke - so I got back in and pressed the button for the seventh floor again, and just as the doors were closing, I saw Moon walk past. He'd apparently picked the hotel manager's wife's room, and so, of course, we got thrown out of that and every other hotel in New York as a result. We still have difficulty finding a place to stay in New York.

ZZ: Does he still carry on like that?

PT: Well, Moony's got this thing now, where you wake up in the morning and he says "greatest hotel room I've ever done - it was a work of art" . . . and you look in his room and it's just total chaos. He does this a lot now - he actually arranges it artistically . . . . you don't hear any great smashing noises these days - he just arranges it so that you look in and go "Oh Christ, what you done?" - but he hasn't actually broken anything, he's just made it appear wrecked. He unscrews cabinets and prises them apart, takes the television cabinet off and sticks black sticky tape over the screen to make it look shattered. . . . . or, if he's drunk enough, he just smashes the place up. . . . pours tomato ketchup in the bath and puts those plastic leg things sticking out.

When we play English towns, Keith always finds the joke shop; tear gas pellets and smoke bombs, stink bombs and itching powder in the bed, bugs under the pillow, naughty doggie in the sink. . . . .

ZZ: Why do they always nail down that plastic sheet under him on stage?

PT: I don't know. I can't really work that out. . . . it can't have anything to do with the sound.

ZZ: Does he still own the pub?

PT: Yeah - he's got a half share in it. . . they got an Egon Ronay star this year for good cooking - it's a very good hotel.

ZZ: Did he have something to do with that shout of 'I saw ya' on the end of 'Happy Jack'?

PT: Oh yeah. Keith, you see, is very annoyed at not being allowed to sing; he's got an awful voice . . . really terrible. So when we do all the vocals, he feels left out, and being Keith, he pisses about. On that particular session, we kept trying to get the vocals down, but he kept stopping us by talking and so on. In the end, we stuck him in the engineer's booth so that we could do them - but that didn't work because he kept pulling these funny faces at us through the glass, so that we laughed in the middle of the take. To stop him, we made him crouch down under the panel so that we couldn't see him - and just as we were finishing, he lifted his head up to see what was happening. . . . so I yelled out 'I saw ya', and we left it on.

ZZ: Is is right that Roger made all your guitars in the beginning?

PT: He made his own. There was a time when we were all using home made guitars - it was a bit of a weird situation; we used to make our own, rather than put up with shoddy gear. John was the first that I know of; he'd make bass guitars out of one piece of half inch ply. He'd mark out the shape with a pencil, cut it out, divide the neck into frets and get someone to fret it, put a pickup on with the wire hanging out, put a few false knobs on and paint it bright red. He used to get a fairly good sound out of it too. I had a guitar that I made myself, but it wasn't really very good, but Roger had one which he made, and that was alright. He was a bit of a handyman, but he only made his own and told us how to make ours - he was always too busy pulling birds I think.

ZZ: You played on Mike Heron's album, and Keith was on 'Becks Bolero' - what else have you all played on besides the Who?

PT: Sorry to disappoint you, but I think that's it. Keith's played on a few.

ZZ: Like that awful Viv Stanshall record 'Suspicion'.

PT: Well, he produced it didn't he? He was on the Scaffold's 'Do the Albert' and one or two others. The thing is that when Keith did Beck's Bolero, that wasn't just a session - that was a political move. It was at a point when the group was very close to breaking up - Keith was very paranoid and going through a heavy pills thing. He wanted to make the group plead for him because he'd joined Beck.

ZZ: Was Ronnie Lane on that session?

PT: I don't think so.

ZZ: What's the tie-up between you and Ronnie Lane, because you must've been rivals in the old days.

PT: No, we were never rivals . . . I don't think he's got a rival in the world. The tie-up is the fact, I suppose, that the Small Faces and the Who always got on incredibly well. I don't know how it came about though, because Kit Lambert was murderous to the Faces; he accused them of copying us. I always used to get on really well with Steve Marriott too - it was a pity when he and Ronnie split up, because they were cohorts. . . . I looked that word up today, and it said 'Roman legion'. They were the two songwriters and producers, but I think it was natural, in a way, that the Small Faces broke up after 'Ogdens Nut Gone'. . . . there's that 'Tommy' thing. . . . the 'Tommy Test'; you do your classic album and then you really have to use every ounce of stamina and guts to stick together, because it's so tempting to relax.

ZZ: Can I ask you a question that's intrigued me for years, and that is this: The two best bands in Britain today, in terms of sitting in a seat and watching and listening to them, are the Faces and the Who. How much is this that you share the mod thing?

PT: I don't know. They were a damned sight more real mods than we were. . . . at least they were the right size.

ZZ: Shepherds Bush wasn't really a very mod place was it?

PT: It was the sort of place where you'd never wear your mod clothes because you would get them dirty in the bundles. But no . . . Shepherds Bush was a very mod place as it happens; the Goldhawk Club was amazing - I used to spot all the major fashion changes at the Goldhawk Club. . . . nowhere else. Like you'd see one guy wearing a pair of sneakers with buckles and you'd know that next week they'd all be wearing them. . . . . and, sure enough, they were. Maybe it was because I got to know all the leaders and could spot the right things.

But to go back to your question, I don't think the mod thing has much to do with it . . . it might be in a line - Stones, Who, Faces - not that Rod Stewart follows in a line from us. I used to go and watch him when I was in short trousers; the night he started - the Cyril Davis benefit night - was the first night I saw him. I remember saying to my mate "Cor, look at 'im, what a poof, what an 'orrible 'aircut", because he had exactly the same haircut then as he has now, and it was really outrageous.

ZZ: He always used to camp it up on stage.

PT: Yeah. Well, to put it bluntly, I think Rod Stewart was a poove - still is a poove. I've gone from my poovy stage. It's difficult to say whether what you see means anything, or what you hear means anything, because people allow what they want to hear to be heard. In those days it was a really good mystifier if people thought you were queer.

I think the Small Faces were a mod group, and we were a mod group, and in their way, I suppose the Stones were too, although they came from different sources and were quite old. We were a mod group because we picked the situation and went into it; the Stones were picked by the mods and dragged into it, and the Small Faces came out of the mods. We weren't mods but we became mods - we looked at it and said "that's incredible, let's be involved in it". . . . we didn't grow up as mods, but had to learn all the stuff. I was at Art College, had long hair, was smoking pot and going with girls with long red hair, and all that. Painting farty pictures and carrying my portfolio around. . . . and I had to learn how to be a mod.

Like in those days, a scooter was a big status symbol, but I used to have an old American car - that was my symbol. But I used to have to lie to the little mod chicks I pulled, and tell them I had a Vespa GS . . . "Oh yeah, I buzz all over the place". If I'd told them I had a '58 Cadillac, which to me was a dream, they would have thought I was a rocker.

ZZ: Do you want people to think really deeply about your music, or just listen to it?

PT: Oh it's so difficult - I don't want to pin people down to any attitude. I know that people get things out of certain people's music that I just can't relate to. For example, when Dylan first came out, I dug his music - his sound and chords and voice, but I'm only just beginning to get the lyrics of his songs. It's not that I'm thick, it's just that I wasn't listening to them. I think, however, that Dylan made people listen to the lyrics but his genius lay in the fact that he didn't consider his lyrics. The way he used to write and record was to write down the rhyming words and fill in with the first words that came into his head. . . . . or spontaneous titles that came into his head, just sing them off and fill in lines. Let's face it; Dylan is a poet and poets become expert at doing that. Ending up in the same place they started. Allowing their minds to flow freely and yet organising their minds at the same time. I don't suppose for a minute that he was conscious of what he was saying, but when you look at it in retrospect you can really find out an incredible amount about the man - more than you'd ever find out by meeting the fucker. He won't rub two words together for you - and if you mention a song, you've had it.

I suppose he's really got the biggest problem of responsibility of any rock star in the world; his biggest problem of responsibility is that he can't face people - that's why he's so incredible in his music; because everything, everything comes out in his music. But, because of things he said in his early music, now that he's become big and influential his responsibility (if you look at it in the Jean Paul Sartre syndrome) is to get up and do something about the world. . . . . and of course, he's not capable. He's a very ordinary, shy, weak person. This is really where I hope to be a bit more successful . . . . I dunno, to try and relate the group's work to some role in life. It's really hard, but it just has to be done - you can't just walk around in a dream all the time.

ZZ: Well Dylan's got his problems - like Weberman for a start.

PT: Well, Weberman I would've killed by now; I've had Weberman equivalents and they've had hammers bashed over their heads before they got in the door. If someone looked through my dustbin. . . . . Christ, Hoffman got a bat in the neck for less. It's just bull headedness for bull headedness's sake. To go back to the lyrics, if you want to know where Dylan stands, you've got to look there - that's the problem. Weberman is listening to the lyrics and saying "there's the man, there's his words, there's his work - but look at him just sitting there with a lot of money, a wife and family and doing nothing. He isn't using the money for the right purposes - he's a hypocrite". But that isn't true; Dylan is a one way person - from him to you through his music - that's what it's all about, and you can't play the guards-van off against the locomotive. The whole drag is that people really do that. I mean, I can't play the first few years of my musical career off against what I'm doing now. When I started off, the object was to make as much money as possible in the shortest time, don't let any fucker get in the way, be a big star, fuck a load of women, and end up with a mansion in the country. It's taken a lot longer than I thought, and in the meantime I've learnt some sense.

[PART TWO]

I bet you'd given up all hope of seeing the second part of this little epic, eh? How many of you even remember the first part I wonder? Well, just to refresh your memories, in issue 24 (now completely sold out) there appeared a miniscule fraction of an enormous interview with Pete Town-shend conducted by Connor and John. After receiving numerous requests to find out what happened to the rest of it, and seeing the Who give a performance at Charlton that some say was slightly below standard, but which I found unbelievably good, I decided to obtain the interview and see if we could use the rest of it. When I'd finished reading it through, I quite frankly found it difficult to believe that it hadn't been printed before, so here's another instalment (they'll probably be another two after this), and although it's dated, it nevertheless remains absorbing and is still, in my opinion, relevant. It also effectively illustrates Townshend as a refreshingly articulate and intelligent person, as well as a true rock giant.

ZZ: Is there a new 'real' album, or are you going to leave that for a bit?

T: Well at the moment when we made 'Who's Next'—one of the things about that—it's a long story—it isn't my idea of a new Who album, and to a staunch Who fan it's not their idea of a new Who album and so I suppose The Who and a lot of other people are waiting for the next Who album which should really be some event in and around the Who which is a logical next step from Tommy, which 'Who's Next' wasn't. 'Who's Next' wasn't a logical step in anyone's language. 'Who's Next' was a stepping stone, if you like, as Roger says it's like The Who treading water. It was a big step for us as it was our first major break away from Kit Lambert as a producer and it was a big step in sound 'cause Glyn Johns has got a characteristic knack of getting really excellent sounds in the studio and so he made The Who sound a little bit more polished and professional but as an album I was really quite disappointed in it. I quite liked bits of it, like 'Everyone Else'. A week after it was out and in the charts I forgot about it and now the public's forgetting about it and I think it's a good thing.

ZZ: A lot of the songs have musical images. 'Pick Up My Guitar And Play', 'Getting In Tune'. Was this accidental?

T: Well that really stemmed from the project we were involved in at the Lifehouse. The whole thing was based on a combination of fiction—a script that I wrote—called The Lifehouse which was a story—and a projection within that fiction of a possible reality. In other words it was a fiction which was fantasy, parts of which I very much hoped would come true. And the fiction was about a theatre and about a group and about music and about experiments and about concerts and about the day a concert emerges that is so incredible that the whole audience disappears. I started off writing a series of songs about music, about the power of music and the mysticism of music. 'Getting In Tune' is a straight pinch from Imrat Khan's discourse of mysticism of sound where he just says music is one way of individuals getting in tune with one another and I just picked up on that. And there's a couple of others which I don't suppose you've heard, One's called 'Pure And Easy'. You hear the beginning of it at the end of 'Song Is Over'.

> *There once was a note pure and easy*
> *Playing so free like a breath rippling by.*

It's about this note that pervades everything.

ZZ: Is this the same song as 'The Note'?

T: Yeah; it's a song about reflecting creation musically, i.e. there being one infinite consciousness—everything in infinity being the one note and lots of other consciousnesses being us and vaguer consciousnesses being gas and grass and space: I just wrote a lyric about all this—talking about it as music. That is really one of my favourite songs, it really should have been on 'Who's Next' if nothing else was a culmination of the frustration of The Who trying to go somewhere. We didn't get anywhere near where we were going but there are a lot of parts of where we were going on the album. 'Baba O'Riley', 'Won't Get Fooled Again', 'Getting In Tune'. There were a few things in there that had nothing to do with it at all—'Behind Blue Eyes', 'Going Mobile', which were really throwaways. There's a few things in there that are really worthwhile. We could have put together a really tight concept album I think. Roger thought so too at the time but Glyn Johns was very adamant that from his point of view as an observer he couldn't see any concept. And I think maybe he could have been wrong. I don't really know. I think that as a producer he perhaps stands a little too much away from the ethereal concepts that a group gets involved in because it's active, it's working and it's exciting and tends to just listen to what comes out of the speakers and take it at its face value without realising, of course, that a whole lot of people who are interested in The Who are very deeply into everything that we're doing, all of the time.

ZZ: So? he's taking a Steve Miller producer type attitude.

T: I think he's very much a musical producer. He's very much a musician and he's not creative the way that, say, I am. The way I create things is that I blind myself and I go behind for year, come up with something at the end and then I explain it to people in the following year, despite the fact that I didn't know what I was doing or how I came about it. Glyn's much more considered. He would say "What have, you got *now*?" I'd say, "Well nothing, but I never do at this time of the day, and he'd say, "Well unless you've got anything now I think the best thing to do would be to put the album together this way." Of course half way through 'Tommy'—if he'd asked me the same question, I'd have had to say nothing, 'cause we had nothing—a lot of disconnected songs about a deaf, dumb and blind boy.

ZZ: Does this lead you to think that perhaps you shouldn't have split from Kit Lambert as producer?

T: We didn't split with him. Our relationship drifted. It was very much one of those situations where—I think it was 'Tommy' that destroyed the relationship. It was so exhausting. It was incredibly long and drawn out. It took about two years of active involvement. Kit's real contribution will never, ever, ever be known because of course it wasn't production at all, it was far deeper. The word producer is, I think, an absurdly misused word anyway. Kit was much more involved in the overall concept of the thing—much more than people imagine. Not all that much in fact with the overall sound. Although he did produce it and mix it and he did make us work at it—still the main thing was that he thought of the idea of Rock Opera.

ZZ: What, with 'A Quick One'?

T: Yeah and I just did it. He thought of it.

ZZ: Did he suggest 'Live at Leeds'?

T: No, that was pretty much a group idea.

ZZ: You said once that you'd been asked to do a live album.

T: Slip of the tongue I think—maybe I was talking about fans. I mean a lot of kids have asked us to do a live album. They'd often say: "I can't understand it because your live sound is so far removed from your recorded sound—how about a live album?" And of course we'd been trying from the year dot and none of the stuff was any good.

ZZ: What about 'Ready Steady Who'?

T: That wasn't live.

ZZ: Well what's those whooshing noises when you play 'Disguises'?

T: That's just a special cymbal effect dreamed up by Kit. No, that's how we sounded in the studio. We made records to sound tinny—recorded tinny to sound tinny. It's no good recording things to sound hi-fi if they're gonna sound tinny. It was just a real clangy sound. I think Shel Talmy first invented it. But that early clangy Who sound was very much suited to the Dansette record player with the tin speaker and two watt amplifier.

ZZ: You said you went blind for a year and came up with something. Was Thunderclap Newman a product of that?

T: That was really a chain of events. It wasn't any part of my creative process. Let's just say that I'm very organised when it comes to recording. I mean I've got a studio here that I work in and write in. I built myself and run myself and service it myself and I do that because I enjoy it—it's like a hobby but which is an extension of my work—much more fruitful a hobby than playing golf. I get all the exercise I need playing on the stage thanks. Look—it's part of what I'm normally involved in and I think Thunderclap Newman were more a part of that than my own creative processes. In other words they were of their own making. A lot of them would say, if asked now, that we were a figment of Pete Townshend's imagination—but they weren't. It's not true. Independently all three of them came to me, or I got involved with them with a view to helping them and then suddenly I realised—or rather, again, it was Kit Lambert who said to me, "You haven't got time for all of them, why not try them together." I thought, "Impossible, three more unlikely people you couldn't get," but they got in a room together, they played together on some film music for a friend of mine and they were really great and I played them back the tapes and they said "Yeah, seems to work," and they liked it and they were all enthusiastic about it, as a concept, as it were. We recorded, we made 'Somethin' In The Air', it worked out great, it got to number 1 and from then on it was a downhill slide.

ZZ: No! No! The album was fantastic.

T: Well I think so.

ZZ: I saw them at a gig, and they were terrible. Surely the ingredient was yourself?

T: No, no. The ingredient was that I gave them a process to work in, which wasn't the formal process that musicians are usually asked to work in. I mean I'd bloody well like to work in a process that didn't consist of just going on stage and jumping about all over the f**king stage and turning full up, but that's the only way to play live these days. If you play any other way it fails. It fails when Neil Young goes on the stage and strums his f**kin' acoustic guitar for 2½ hours. It fails when a group like Floyd try anything fancy. It really fails because what has gone down before prescribes a new limitation which is the limitation within which you have to work. You're defined by it. And it's a bloody good thing—obviously because if you didn't have limitations you wouldn't know how to judge one group against another. But at the same time, the recorded medium offers another kind of limitation. It offers a limitation that you start the tape knowing, and although you get several stabs, what you get, what you do is proven, you know what I mean, it's on the tape. There's no escape from the fact that what you've done is still there. So what I mean is that Thunderclap Newman did the f**king playing. All I did was play engineers. They played. I came up with the arrangements. Jimmy played every solo on that album straight off. Some of them are fantastic, spontaneous chipped solos, considered solos.

ZZ: So was Andy's piano playing and weird clarinets, yet at the live gigs you couldn't hear them and this is where the loss came.

T: Yeah, I said always, right from the beginning, that they should never play live. But . . . Jimmy desperately wanted to play live. You can imagine, he's a good guitarist and he was brought up in the tradition of loud, young, arm-swinging guitarists and he was into Clapton and Hendrix and The Who—groups of that ilk, guitar groups, and he wanted to play and so I suggested that he got his own group and that Andy got his own group, but Speedy, for a start, should never, ever, ever have got on the stage because he's not constitutionally built for it, he's incredibly nervous. Well, Speedy and I have like parted company for about [pause] a year. And at the end of that year I hope Speedy's going to have enough songs to do a solo album. Because I think Speedy's a genius, I really do. Andy's finished his album—it was finished today.

ZZ: Did you produce that?

T: No, a friend of mine called Dick Seaman did it. I wouldn't have had time, it's taken Dick Seaman 18 months. I've edited it and done some mixing and stuff like that . . . sort of 'creative production'.

ZZ: You say you didn't do much to make Thunderclap Newman gell, but Speedy told us that you used to come out yelling "F**kinggetittogether!"

T: That's not me. Glyn does that to The Who, mate. It's not making a creative contribution. I mean Speedy very much needs me to tell him that he's written a song. He doesn't know until I've told him. That doesn't mean that I've written it. I mean, he will stand in front of me and I'll say "Well, what have you got?" and he'll say, "Well, nothing." So I say, "We can't record then, can we. You must have something—what's on that bit of paper there?" "Oh, that's just a few lines I wrote down the other day." "Well, has it got a tune?" I ask . . . "Yeah—a bit of a tune, but it's not very good." "Well, play us that," and it's a great song like 'Something In The Air'. He wouldn't play me 'Something In The Air' because it was originally called 'Revolution' so Speedy wouldn't play me 'Revolution' which was a number 1 hit. We just changed the title to 'Something In The Air' and it was alright. That's the sort of phobia he has. Like, a lot of the songs he won't play me because I don't take drugs any more and he does and he thinks I'm gonna get all upset if it's a song about drugs. That's the sort of guy he is. There was an incredible amount of misunderstanding because I suppose they did look like a manipulated group, or a dreamed up group. But a lot came out of the top of their heads. Stuff like 'Hollywood Dream'.

ZZ: Who picked 'Open The Door Homer'?

T: I think I chose that, it wasn't one of the more successful songs on the album but . . . it was a song that Speedy and I have always mutually liked and we had the basement tapes before they were released as an album—came from a publisher or something. No, Arthur Brown had 'em, that's right, so they were at Track. There was a good quality version there and we listened to them and liked them. It was the only unreleased one of the basement tapes, so we figured we'd put it out as a single. So it was recorded as a single. It was recorded at I.B.C. but everything else was recorded in my studio up here. Some of it was actually done on stereo recorders, not on 8-track. We got the 8-track half way through the session. 'Accidents', which is the best track on there, was done on two Revox. The other ones—'When I Think' and 'I Don't Know' were done on Revox and 'Old Cornmill' and 'Hollywood 1'. The ones that were done on Revoxes have a sound—I don't know what it was—they have a sort of silky sound. I can't explain it. The ones that were done on the 8-track had that typical rock hardness, but 'Accidents', for example, has got an incredible spacious hi-fi stereo feel about it. I dunno what it is. As an album I feel that my biggest mistake was the way I put the tracks together. I don't think I really did it correctly. I was far too into it—the group; like putting two versions of 'Hollywood' on was daft. I should have made a choice. A few other things like that. It could have been shorter. It's about 22 minutes a side and it could have been shorter and tighter.

ZZ: Well, as it turned out it's the only thing to remember Thunderclap Newman by except the singles and it's nice to have as much as you can. They obviously had something different. They were a novelty band but still musical.

T: Yeah . . . I'm glad you listen to it. I mean a lot of people haven't. The album's sold very badly. Alright in the States.

ZZ: Andy said he wanted to get something acoustic. He obviously wanted to get something quieter so people could hear him play. What's on the new album?

T: No, he's done one track with a friend that's acoustic, but Andy's real talent lies with himself, not with organising, not with playing with other musicians. He wants a band, I suppose, because the human being is a social animal and likes to work in that way. But really, again, and it points right back to the fact that Thunderclap Newman had brilliant potential as far as recording—it's that Andy has always done what I have done, since, before I even knew what tape recording was, he was into it. Multi-tracking—bird songs and locomotive recordings, you know, special effects, echoes. I've got a stack of tapes upstairs that he did as early as 1960—which are all done just on piano, or his version of 'Rock Around The Clock' with Andy Newman's saxophone sixteen times. I think the album he's just done is good because he's done it all himself. There's a couple of things that he's done with other musicians.

ZZ: Does Andy resent the 'freak' image at all?

T: No he doesn't but I do. I mean on his behalf and so does his producer at the moment, Dick. Dick was at school with Andy and was the first guy to play me the first Thunderclap record which I've actually got here, which is absolutely amazing. If you hang on I'll play it for you.

ZZ: We'll bootleg it.

T: It's the right quality for bootlegging. He played me this acetate of tapes. Thunderclap Newman with Richard Cardboard on drums. This was when I was at art school.

ZZ: Who is Richard Cardboard?

T: Co-producer of Stormy Petrel. Well, that's him, Richard Seaman. That record was the beginning of Andy's image as a freak. We all played the tape and it built up an incredible mystique. Is he a jazz musician? Is he dead? Who is this guy? And then suddenly there he was on the Wall, Thunderclap Newman. The people who hadn't heard of him thought he was, like, a jazz sax player come to play in lunch hours at college.

ZZ: Well, a lot of my friends think he's a freak—but in the best sense of the word, a real individualist.

T: Yeah. He's certainly eccentric, but above that, the word 'freak' means different and he is different to other people—he's a darn sight more talented than most people and he's a musical genius. That's what I think and I'm right about a lot of other people and I think I'm right about Andy. I think he's a genius. I think he's better than a lot of other minority geniuses, like John Fahey, for example, who I like, people of that ilk. Andy's new record is like a work of art and that's the end of it. It stands up against 'The Ring' or anything Debussy did. I mean it really is incredibly heavy stuff—fantastic stuff. It's the perfect bridge between the rock educated ear, the trad-jazz educated ear, which is really what I am—I mean I was brought up on a mixture of trad-jazz and the Shadows and the classics. He has an incredibly spontaneous way of putting things down and I suppose he is a freak, but I'm worried that if we get a contract for this record, that the record company will decide "It's another R.R.S.—Hey, some of this sounds humorous—let's just dress him up in a top hat and put an ad in the paper." This is why I don't think Andy should go with Track, because Track have got a bit of a reputation for tasteless ads in the paper and they might be tempted to do that—because this album really does what should have been done, *eventually,* by the group, Thunderclap Newman. It brings Andy out as a musician, 'cause we never really got the time to do that on the first album. I suppose the only section where he got full rein was in that little bit in 'Accidents' where I just surprised him by saying "Why don't you do that bit on your own and multitrack it."

ZZ: You put out a single of 'Tommy' and you withdrew it after about a fortnight and put out an E.P. What was that about?

T: Well that was all company policy. We've always been a group that's said that the singles market and the album market are distinctly separate. I still hold that—in America and England I think it's true. So it's not so much a class thing—lower classes buy singles or that kids buy singles and students buy albums. It's much more that if you're into buying singles and the process of buying singles it's the neatness of the brain. The brain stacks singles on piles and people relate bits of music to bits of their life. You know, they say, "This single here, say—'Surf's Up'—was when I was going out with Tony and it was a lovely sunny day." Not only nostalgia is involved in that. A lot of my albums I can't really listen to now because they are so strongly related to periods of my life, and I can't take the music at face value, even though at the time nothing in particular was happening. Album buyers get into an album buying rut. They collect albums like people collect stamps or coins or banknotes or whatever. They develop into two distinctly different markets for some reason. People who buy the 'Tommy' album would never dream of buying a Who single at all. They would sit back and hope that one day—unless they were avid Who fans—they would hope that one day a Who single would come out. In fact until a Who single came out, was played in the charts, on the radio, they may not have heard of The Who, despite the fact that we might have had an album high in an album chart. In the States they might not listen to FM radio and over here they may not buy the trade papers. And if you don't buy the trade papers you don't know what the latest albums are.

ZZ: Well what about the single that was brought out and pulled back?

T: What single was that?

ZZ: Well the EP had 'Overture', 'See Me, Feel Me', 'Christmas', and something else, but there was a single that was just 'Overture' and 'See Me, Feel Me'.

T: I'm not quite sure what happened there. I think 'Overture' was put out—I think. I'm right here, but 'Overture' was covered in the States by Assembled Multitude, it got to number 2 or something fantastic and so we released our version, right, because naturally we wanted our version— if they were gonna buy someone else's version, they might buy ours as well, 'cause I'd make a fortune out of it as writer, so why shouldn't the rest of the guys have a bash too. So we put out 'Overture' backed with something else in the States and so we thought if it's coming out in the States English people were gonna sort of say "What about us?" so we put it out over here. I think the group and Kit and Chris got together and said "Tommy's been out, done its thing—it was incredibly highly priced in this country—how about releasing everything from Tommy on singles—everything. So that if somebody wanted to buy 'Tommy' as a serial, as it were, they could do it." So we started off with the Overture and we put out another two EPs which contained four tracks—some of which never even reached the shops because there was no record company interested at all, and Track is actually marketed through Polydor and we're dependent on their distribution a lot. It was a nice idea but the public didn't really want to buy 'Tommy' on singles. I suppose they wanted all the trimmings. As far as I can remember, that's what happened. Also Track pioneered the whole concept of really cheap singles. They took no profit whatsoever. They gave away their whole share and forced the distributor to go without a share. On 'Voodoo Chile', for example, a number 1, nobody made any money at all.

ZZ: What about Backtracks or Track tones? There was 6 to start with. Then there was gonna be another 25. We've got 8 of them. Then there was talk of putting out Electric Ladyland at 25/- and presumably 'Tommy' as well. What happened to that idea?

T: I dunno. Backtrack sells very well. Whenever you go to Track offices there's always a lot lying about which is a good sign—that there's turnover.

ZZ: Would you like to see 'Tommy' out now?

T: Maybe, but it's important if you're gonna have 'Tommy' that you have the artwork. The artwork is intrinsic to it in a lot of ways. And the Backtrack stuff has got cheap covers—that's where it saves a lot of money in fact. On 'Electric Ladyland' I could do without the cover quite easily—it's bloody horrible. A lot of Dave King porno rubbish.

ZZ: And what it didn't have was the names of the people playing on it which would have helped.

T: Yeah. That's another incredible thing. Dave King is a genius, I think, but he's got a bit of an obsession with pornography. 'Who's Next' nearly came out with the most revolting pornographic cover you've ever seen. In the end it turned out to be mildly pornographic, but slightly boring at the same time. Dave King was commissioned to do a cover and he came up with one cover with a huge fat lady with her legs apart and where the woman's organ was supposed to be would be a head of The Who, grinning out from underneath the pubics. Anyway I don't really know that much about Track or Track policy or Track history. If you really wanna know that, the guy to talk to is Kit Lambert, but then on the other hand that would be a 50 page article full of history that really nobody is interested in. Track was good not because of the small details but because of the intentions really. It's unfortunate that Kit and Chris weren't able to concentrate only on Track but really had The Who at their most difficult stage which was before 'Tommy', during 'Tommy' and at the time two years after 'Tommy' which proved to be just like a huge hump in The Who's career, which was just where we needed management most crucially and it caused everybody to go through incredible traumatic experiences and Track just got lost along the way because of it. Yet maybe I'm talking out of the top of my head—maybe it's other things. Kit would probably scream with laughter and say that it was him getting screwed by Polydor—aw f**k, I dunno. I think that if Track continues they'll probably continue just for The Who, in which case why should we go with anyone else. Track gave us 75% more than we were ever getting on our original deal with Decca.

ZZ: What about with Reaction, then?

T: That was a stepping off point. That was really Robert Stigwood putting his foot on the legal connection between Track and Shel Talmy. Because Shel Talmy had to be got rid of—and the only guy that was really powerful enough, that was connected with The Who in any way whatsoever at the time and who wouldn't suffer by it was Robert Stigwood. So we were temporarily on his label.

ZZ: It seemed to be a pretty potent label because it had Hendrix, the Cream, the Bee Gees. Started off with a bang and then just sort of disappeared.

T: Well there again I don't know that much about it. 'Substitute' was a bloody amazing session—Keith can't even remember it. That was the first Who-produced session. Kit didn't slide naturally into the seat of producing The Who—he kind of arrived in the position of producing The Who because we desperately needed a producer. It was obviously logical that I should produce The Who—even then. So it was logical that when it came to 'Substitute' and we got out of Shel Talmy's clutches we should enjoy ourselves and go into the studio and work, so we went in and there was a blonde guy. . . Chris. . . the first Olympic Studios in Baker Street. We went in and we played through the thing and we went up and heard the playbacks and they sounded alright, mixed it, and Robert Stigwood came in and listened to the vocals and said "Sounds alright," didn't really know much of what was going on at the time. Keith doesn't remember the session, Roger was gonna leave the group. It was just an amazing time in The Who's career. We were more or less about to break up. Nobody really cared about the group. It was just a political thing. Kit and I used to go for walks in Hyde Park and talk about combining what was gonna be left of The Who with Paddy, Klaus and Gibson. Things like this—strange things. Anyway that's as much as I know about Reaction. I know I've borrowed a few quid off Robert Stigwood at various points—tapped him for a few knicker. I also wrote a song for his artist who was called Oscar who later reappeared in Hair, called 'Join My Gang', which was a f**king good song—[sings]:

> *You can join my gang*
> *Even though you're a girl*

which he did. Unfortunately Robert Stigwood owns the publishing, so I haven't even got a demo of it to listen to—but I really like it.

ZZ: That's an interesting topic—the songs of The Who that have been covered. For example, The Untamed's version of 'It's Not True'—another very good song. Any that we mightn't know about?

T: Yeah, maybe. There's one called 'Lazy Fat People' by that comedy group. . . The Barron Knights [sings]:

> *Lazy and fat they are, they are*
> *And because they are all the same*

They laugh and complain
The young are so ugly.

That song was about Allen Klein. Allen Klein tried to get hold of The Who as being the first of his purge on rock. I mean he shat all over the Beatles and the Stones. F**k knows how we managed to get out of it. But we took along our solicitor, who is still our solicitor today . . . an austere, conservative, almost Edward Heath character called Edward Oldman, who just took two looks at Allen Klein and said, "We're leaving," so we ate his caviar, had a look at the Statue of Liberty from his yacht, shat in his toilet and went back to England. In fact he paid my first-class fare to the States four ways. I went over there to talk to him, came back to England to do a gig—which I missed at Sheffield University, which got us a bad reputation for missing gigs, and then flew back again. That was also when Andrew Oldham was trying to take over our management.

[Unknown question]

T: . . . It was just after Substitute. See, about the time of Substitute we were still having a lot of problems breaking with Shel.

ZZ: Yeah, you had 'A Legal Matter' out on both labels . . . no, 'Circles'.

T: Yeah we did two versions of 'Circles', which were both identical because they were both copies of my demo. Shel put in a high court injunction saying there was a copyright in recording, in other words if you're a record producer and you produce a song with a group and you make a creative contribution then you own that sound—there's a copyright in that sound, that arrangement. I suppose it's so that you can't steal the 'John Barry' sound as it were, or copy 'Apache' exactly, while it's in the Top Ten. Well, he took it to the high court judge and he said things like, "And then on bar 36 I suggested to the lead guitarist that he play a diminuendo, forget the adagio and play 36 bars modulating to the key of E flat," which was all total bullshit—he used to fall asleep at the desk, Glyn Johns used to do everything. Eventually we ended up in court and

Quintin Hogg—he was the attorney for Shel—and we dreamed up an even more preposterous thing. "Shel Talmy certainly did *not* tell us at the 36th bar to play a diminuendo. He told us to do this and we suggested blah, blah, blah." All in incredible, grand, grandiose, musical terms and then we produced the demo which was copyrighted with Essex Music a good year before it was recorded. And it was identical to the record. As far as the judge could tell obviously. I mean, he'd listen to 'Help', 'The Last Time' and 'Respect' and think they were all the same song. I mean probably to him they sounded identical. That was a real triumph, and a very funny day too.

ZZ: But you didn't win it, did you?

T: We won that particular thing, so they weren't able to stop our particular release of 'Circles', but Shel Talmy ended up getting a piece of our recording.

ZZ: Didn't he put out a song called 'Watt's For A Pig', with The Who Orchestra?

T: We had to because the single was out by the time we won it. Obviously we had to take it off the back because . . . .

ZZ: It was only a 'B' side after all.

T: Yeah. Last time I saw Shel he was gloating at our success. 'cause he gets quite a large chunk of our recording royalties—even today.

ZZ: Good lord! . . . He can't see, can he?

T: I don't really know about him. I've seen veiled hints about The Who in interviews he's done, like "Snotty, East End kids would come up to me and ask me to record 'em and I'd make 'em stars and a week later they'd start getting too big for their boots." And it was obviously directed at groups like us because we're the only group ever to have argued with him. The Kinks have never argued with him as far as I know and until quite recently they still used him. I mean, he never said a word to me. On 'I Can't Explain' he brought in the Beverley Sisters to do the backing vocals, and Jimmy Page to play lead guitar. I said to him *"F**k that*, I'm the lead guitarist in this group." It was incredible, it was a typical Love Affair scene—we were the 1965 Love Affair. We were The Who—a few chart successes and then we were gonna be out—we were on, like about half a percent. Because he was The Kinks' record producer we thought he was alright. But he underestimated Kit's venomous intelligence.

ZZ: Did you ever use any of these other musicians? Daddy Rolling Stone' doesn't sound like your guitar.

T: It was.

ZZ: That's an old Muddy Waters' song, isn't it?

T: Probably. Derek Martin. We picked it up from where he was on the Island label. The only song we ever used other musicians on—apart from Nicky Hopkins—was 'Bald-headed Woman' which was on the same session as 'Can't Explain'. Jimmy Page played lead guitar, 'cause he had a fuzz box which went 'urgggg'. . . and three guys on backing vocals on 'Can't Explain' who turned out to be the Ivy League—I was joking about them being the Beverley Sisters.

ZZ: What about these demos? Has it ever occurred to you that you could do one of these, bring it out as The Who and nobody would be any the wiser?

T: Well, that's never occurred to me. That's some thing I'd never wanna do. If I put out a record I'd wanna take the credit. It's occurred to me to put out a solo album and it's also occurred to me to put out an album of demos, because I would find it very interesting and I think a lot of people would. Not because the demos are similar to the finished product but really because of a consistency all along. The group's relationship to me and my relationship within the group, as it were, has always been the same—all the way along. I've always been separate as a writer but very much part of the group as a musician and guitarist. And it's been something that I've never been able to fathom and the group's never been able to work out 'cause it's never really gone wrong up to now and it looks like it's gonna continue. So really—there's not any need to prove it because it's painfully obvious. It works and all putting out an album of demos would do would be to say—"Look, this is amazing because this is the songs that I wrote, the group did and this is the way I suggested the group do them and the group did them in the way I suggested, because the way I suggested it was tailor-made in the first place." It's not that interesting. Far more interesting to me is John's solo album, which is interesting because of the fact, I suppose that there should have been John Entwhistle singles. 'Boris The Spider' should have been a single, and maybe even 'Heaven And Hell'.

[PART THREE]

FINDING THE NEXT BIG THING AFTER TOMMY

ZZ: Is it actually getting to that step that's important? *Or* that there always is a next step beyond? There have been so many things that The Who have been going to do—the Rock Farm, the movie of 'Tommy', the TV spectacular, the Young Vic.

T: Well, in actual fact, these are all the same thing—all part of the same thing. They're all the 'after 'Tommy' thing' that I spent a year on—there's a filing cabinet over there full of it, tapes full of it. Really what we're talking about now is interviews, interviews with me and what I thought the next step was. Previous to that I was in the enviable position of whenever I said anything it came true. I sat down and said I was gonna write a rock opera two years before I did it. A lotta people laughed and said "What you?" And I did it and it made the group into a million-selling act for the first time in its career. I said we're gonna make the best live album that's ever been made and we went ahead and did it—well, at the time it was the best, or came across like it. And also, if we took drugs we said we took drugs, and if we decided we were gonna do this, we did it. We've always been pig-headed to that degree and 'Tommy' was the break in that because for the first time in our lives we were really successful—really taken over by the audience. Up to that point we really had been our own bosses and then we weren't any more. 'Tommy' and America—the great consumer nation—took us over and said "There are 50 million kids that wanna see you perform; what are you gonna do about it—are you gonna stay in Twickenham and work on your next album, or get your arse over there?" So you get your arse over there and you get involved in the standing ovation and the interviews, the 19-page Rolling Stone articles, the presentations of the Gold Albums, you know, blah blah blah, and that all takes two years to get out of the way and then you realise that it's gonna take another two years to work on the thing. And I started and I thought one of the best ways to get it together is to talk about it and maybe there will be some kind of commitment that the group can be involved in. The biggest thing was that what was going on in my brain wasn't going on in the group's brain—the group as a whole—and that includes me as part of the group. I live this sort of dual role—in a managerial position if you like, a creative managerial position, working in conjunction with Kit and Chris and also a guy in the group. It's very funny. I say to myself. . .

"Manager: We need a tour, we definitely need a tour.

"Group: But I don't wanna go.

"Manager: We've got to tour, we've got to tour Japan, otherwise . . . blah blah blah blah.

"Group: But I couldn't go to Japan because I wanna stay at home and be with me family."

It's total schizophrenia.

ZZ: Do you see the way out as technology? Is technology just more roadies and more tons of equipment?

T: Well, unfortunately that's true. This is something we're trying to get over. Technology is often just buying the bigger and bigger synthesiser. I got involved in the Young Vic thing in a fantasy. The script was a fantasy—it was about the future and total control of entertainment to the point where entertainment became experience and that doubled back on the fact that experience is entertainment, and the best way to live is to look at life as entertainment and it's something to be looked at with respect but not gravity. The fantasy that I wrote which was really about The Who, fairly directly, was to do with future technology, and the control of technology and that you can control people's experience to the point where you're very rapidly taking them through thousands and thousands of lifetimes of experience, and take them to the point where they are infinitely away, so that their minds transcend their physical environment, so that they disappear. And in a way it was like saying that we've played at rock concerts and I know damn well that when I've walked off the stage, me and a few of the audience have had to piece themselves back together again, in order to reincarnate who they were. The last time it happened, it was an uncanny experience. We were playing at Newcastle at the Fillmore—it's just the Mayfair Ballroom—and we walked off and I couldn't remember who I was—I swear it. I wandered out into the audience. I didn't go back into the dressing room and I got in a fight. Somebody started making remarks and I didn't know what they were talking about and I got in a fight with this guy and he started to beat the living daylights out of me and I sort of came to get up and I started to do lots of showy things, pieced myself together again, went back to the dressing room and got a drink. And then I drove all the way home at 120 miles per hour. And by the time I got home I was me again. It was an amazing thing. I was out of my body but my ego couldn't stand it. My ego had to say, "You're you," and, really, occasionally, at Hendrix concerts I've had that. I've watched him and gone off—just walked out and walked about London for 17 hours or something. It's not simpleness or anything. I dunno—if you go to a really great film or the theatre you get a taste of that, like you come back from a really great film and you get in the car with whoever is at the film with you and you say nothing for two hours and the film is still with you. It's very hard to explain what happens but that experience—it made me feel that it would be possible to do it permanently, rather than temporarily. Now I've gone back to the point where I think that experience as such is not an end of infinite consciousness—although it's crucial in terms of Karma and the various laws that relate to what we know as reality—it's much more important the flashes of insight that you have. The seemingly temporary flashes that you have into the present are very important. The awareness of the present is the most important part of infinity. The flash that you have of the present is like a taste of infinity. And with a taste of infinity you are eternal. It's very hard to explain and this was part of the problem, I didn't really know what I was talking about. I knew what Meher Baba had said and to me it was very logical, but I wanted to put it into fact somehow, and allow the group to become the tools of an incredible extreme—a fantasy extreme of experience in live performance. I felt that what The Who were doing could be taken several steps forward in a few months, so that when you went to a Who concert you just sat and instead of being subjected to a barrage, you were seduced out of yourself into something else and it became part of the whole thing, and the techniques to be used would be very devious and very, very thought out.

REFLECTIONS ON 'TOMMY'

ZZ: How much of 'Tommy' was preconceived, and how much done on the spot?

T: Those two things—the bit from 'Rael' and 'Glow Girl' aren't connected with 'Tommy' directly, they are utilisations of bits that were lying about. 'Glow Girl' was a separate song. I used that bit from the 'Underture' in 'Rael' because we were doing 'Rael' in New York and Kit was cutting down from several hours to about two minutes and it wasn't working and I thought that was my trump card—because I had to have a trump card. So I thought those chords which I had and loved and played all the time to myself—and handed those over and put a bit of lyric on them—in the studio and felt when we were doing 'Tommy' that I wanted to use them again, that they were under-played. And, fxxk it, if I don't still feel that. I still feel that the 'Sparks' section that we did on stage on 'Live At Leeds' gets close to what's possible for that classical rock thing. [Sings it] I always imagine a classical conductor with his hair flying. The Who and Keith incredibly are capable of those classical flourishes. The expressive Wagnerian dynamics stuff. That's what I really wanted to come across, whereas 'Underture' and 'Rael' were really a bit lilting. They're not really connected at all. It's just that 'Tommy' was long and in the end we were digging about a bit and so we pulled from all sorts of sources. 'Tommy' is a direct illustration of the way I write a lot. I saw something on the television the other day about how Mozart would stop half way through a piece—however good it was—if the guy decided he wasn't gonna commission him any more. He'd get the work that was done for this guy and just tear it up. Whereas other people like Bach would use everything. Every note they wrote they'd fit in somewhere. Like everyone else I come a bit in between, but I do tend to find that I think along a channel. Maybe tomorrow I'll think up an idea that will use up all the ideas that have been lying around for a long, long time. That seemed to be what happened with 'Tommy'. Everything fell together like a jigsaw. I'd sit and think what I wanted was a bit of a vignette like Tommy in the theatre with all the kids screaming, and I had this song called 'Sally Simpson' about this little girl who fell in love with a rock star. It wasn't about Tommy at all. The guy's name was Damon. It was like 'Joker James'—a little thing I'd done years before and never got used. I had a little demo of it, redid the words and there it was, 'Sally Simpson', the perfect thing. That was a classic case. 'I'm Free' was written long before 'Tommy' was ever thought of. What else? 'We're Not Gonna Take It' without 'Listening To You I Get The Music' tacked on the end. That was written in as a suggestion of Kit's. 'See Me Feel Me' was also Kit's idea. You see, he really had a lot to do with it. He was thinking operatically and I was thinking rockatorically. He was suggesting things to me from his deep operatic thing—which I'm beginning to get an inkling of now.

ZZ: His father was something.

T: Yeah, Constant Lambert. He used to be the musical director at Sadler's Wells and Covent Garden.

ZZ: Again I'm quoting you. You said there were bits of 'Tommy' that you didn't identify with. Why was that and what were the bits?

T: I suppose I don't identify with the unglamorous bits.

ZZ: What, Cousin Kevin?

T: Well, obviously I don't identify directly with that—it's not something I wrote. It definitely seemed to be a piece that was out of my control—the whole thing. Kit Lambert never did that much, the group never did that much. I did all the *graft*, but it definitely seemed to be something that was happening outside of me. Something was putting it together. In a way I don't identify with any of it. I identify much more with 'We're Not Gonna Take It' as it was originally written. It was a song about we're not gonna take fascism. It was a song about police brutality. You know—we couldn't take it from Hitler and we're not gonna take it from you. It was a British song, if you like. It was what 'Won't Get Fooled' said but a bit earlier. Applied to that situation it worked well. It was very considered writing, in that respect, but somehow the whole thing as a complete thing, including songs by other people and including all the suggestions by Kit, and including the fact that it took the group ages to do—when it was finished the cover and everything—I looked at it and thought this was my work and this is my expression. I'm taking it and I did take it and express it and talked about it and found out about me and what I was intending subconsciously. But I don't suppose I'll ever work in that way again because I'll never work under the influence of Kit Lambert again.

ZZ: What did you think of all the people who raced round saying it was sick?

T: Well . . . they're just looking at the surface. Tony Blackburn got a drumstick in his eye for saying that on 'Top Of The Pops' on his first night announcing.

ZZ: Shoulda got the fxxking lot.

T: Ha, ha—yeah. But I didn't choose the theme of a deaf, dumb and blind boy for sensational reasons. I wanted to have someone who would dramatically draw sympathy from people, and yet someone who was dramatically remote. I wanted someone who was a cameo of remoteness. And a deaf, dumb and blind boy is ideal. He's cut off and yet still alive. My sort of cameo was at first that Tommy was deaf, dumb and blind and his coming to know what it was like to be normal looks like what it would be for you and I to become infinitely conscious. It was a big step for him which was equivalent to the biggest step that we can take which is to stop living in illusion and see reality—infinite reality for the first time. This is why I originally used it. I had this double story in my mind and then I made him jump. He became a double person so that not only did he become normal like you and I, but he jumped beyond that into what I was paralleling with it, into being a universally conscious person. And then I back wrote the story so that he turned into a Messiah etc. 'Tommy' was very arduously put together, clumsily put together. And it's got a grace that I just can't account for. It's a long time since I talked about it at length. I spent most of my time of the story—talking about it in the States. People over there would say, "Well, why does Cousin Kevin walk in when the mother is under the bed? Blah, blah, blah." So I'd say, "No, Cousin Kevin doesn't walk in then." Because they figured that the whole thing was totally watertight. The American audience thought that it was completely watertight and that a film could be made, and everything hung together. So I suppose I had to find a way of making everything fit, after the act. When we put it out we thought that people were gonna pick holes in the story, because it just doesn't work.

ZZ: It doesn't really have an ending, does it?

T: No. My whole idea was that Tommy was left behind—poignant. You know, 'See Me Feel Me' and you didn't get enough of it. That should be the last thing you hear, whereas the last thing you hear is 'Listening To You'. That's what I felt was one mistake. There were lots and lots of others. We could've gone on for ever and then not got it right.

RANDOM COMMENTS ON CONTEMPORARY LUMINARIES

ZZ: How about the Stones Rock'n'Roll Circus which you were a part of?

T: What? Whatever happened to it? Well I suppose that's a question for the Stones really. It was finished, it was paid for.

ZZ: Was it any good?

T: From what I hear from Glyn the Stones were mad not to put it out because the Stones were alright. "The Stones were as good as they ever are," were his exact words. But they were constantly depressed by it because they'd chosen people for the acts in it who were knock outs. The raves of the time. They chose The Who because we were the natural group down. They chose Jethro Tull and Taj Mahal because they were the two people that they were stuck on at the time. They chose Lennon and Clapton for the supergroup because they offered to come. The circus thing was actually meant to go out on the road after that. Mick had an incredible amount of plans. Arrangements with American circuses. He'd gone into it very deeply. Hired trains and everything and, in the end, I think, it fell apart because the group weren't together. Brian was really ill—what of I don't know. I think a lot of it was really mental. He obviously hadn't seen the rest of the group for a long, long time and he was getting blamed for everything. This is why when he died I was really angry with the group in a way, and said so in the papers. Brian was dead before he died because he was so remote and pushed out.

ZZ: He always did look very ill. Even at the Crawdaddy he looked very emaciated and pale. He never looked healthy.

T: And yet he had quite a lot of stamina. He used to live at night. I think that was it. His face never ever saw daylight. You should see Keith Richard these days. He looks like a fxxkin' walking skull. I really enjoyed his interview in Rolling Stone. All those bits about when they met Brian Jones on the train and on motor coaches. Really incredible. The first time I ever saw the Stones was walking away from the Ealing Club along Ealing Broadway station platform. And I remember thinking that my hair was long—I had a fringe down to my eyebrows, but very short at the sides, 'cause you couldn't get a barber to do anything else and you had to have your hair cut or otherwise you got thrown out of your digs. And there were these long-haired blokes. I mean they had hair slightly over their ears, with dark grey suits. I thought instantly I knew who they were, scruffy, a gang of louts. It was obviously them. When we worked with them, Keith wasn't even in the group then. We were doing a few Jimmy Reed numbers then and the rest was just Beatles' songs. It was a total turnaround. From that moment, the first time we worked with them, which was at St Mary's Ballroom in Putney in 1963, from that day forget it. It was a metamorphosis.

ZZ: What was Arthur Brown like?

T: He's an amazing guy.

ZZ: Is he mad?

T: I always thought he was. But I think underneath he was probably fairly calculating. I always say that because I am. No. No. [laughs]

ZZ: Well, would you set your head alight if you thought it would earn you a fast buck?

T: Well, when I first saw him, the thing that attracted me to his situation, his music, his sound and everything was the amount that he was putting in. It seemed that later on it developed into a thing where instead of putting things into his performance, he seemed to like—I can't explain this linearly—but pouring all of his energies out and bringing them back again, then pouring them onto the ground, the spot where he was stand-ing. So, in fact, although he was giving out a lot, exhausting himself, he was taking it all back again and not giving the audience anything. And he wasn't taking any risks—although he was setting his hair alight—he wasn't taking any risks as far as the audience was concerned. And this is why he failed. Why he always will probably. But then I've read a few interviews with him and he sounds like he's sussing that out for himself, so maybe it'll change.

ZZ: What, you reckon that if he'd burnt himself once they'd have taken him a lot more seriously.

T: I dunno. If he'd just treated an audience an audience. Apart from anything else I think he was incredibly underestimated as a poet. But then thousands of poets are underestimated. Millions of poets are underestimated. Poetry is a whole, underestimated art form. It's also an incredible form of rock'n'roll. There's a lot of poetry about that has far more to do with the streets than rock'n'roll has. But then it's boring reading poetry. Anyway, Vince Crane actually went mad—schizophrenia. I think he's alright how.

ZZ: Talking of poets or that sort of thing—how did Murray Roman get involved in Track?

T: Oh, God knows.

ZZ: Is he a friend of yours?

T: God knows. I don't know whether I like him or not. He's a right devil. He's a friend of Keith's. He's much, much worse than Keith which is really saying something. He hogs the limelight much more viciously and he drinks more and can't hold it as well.

ZZ: He can be very funny, though. That bit about the Baharnarmba Band.

T: I get the feeling that a few of those gags have been handed down from Jewish joke books. Let's put it this way—it terrifies me when I'm in his company. I get paranoid that I'm gonna blow apart. He's one of those people that when you're in a car, you're trying to think if you should get out of the car while it's travelling at 70mph, 'cause you wanna get away from him and yet he's making you laugh. He's good company, he's just too intense as a person. I know that Keith makes a lot of people like that too, so I suppose you can learn to live with it. Murray Roman's happily married, believe it or not. It's quite interesting.

ZZ: 'Can't Explain' has that characteristic Kinks sound and Ray Davies was a big influence on you. Was there anything besides the arrangements?

T: I think there were two things that influenced me, which came from Ray Davies. One thing was 'You Really Got Me' which was the key changes thing in it. He used key changes to build and that was like something I'd never heard—jumping a tone. Normally in popular music you jumped a semi-tone, just tastefully up a bit. It got to be a cliched sound and he rockified it by jumping up a tone. Whether or not he really knew what he was doing I don't know. I've gone through my old rock records and I've not found that anywhere. 'I Can't Explain' didn't manifest it that obviously—it was just a straight lift. 'You Really Got Me' was a number one—we thought "Let's have a go with a similar sounding record". And we got round sounding like The Kinks by me using an electric 12-string which cut the sound a bit. In fact Shel was the one—he booked a whole rhythm section to play for us who we wouldn't let on the record in fact—Jimmy Page was there—

ZZ: Cattini?

T: No, not him, someone else who was supposedly playing tambourine, but I think he was there to play drums but he played the tambourine on the session, and the Ivy League—a really Love Affair scene—I think I mentioned this before. I think what he was trying to do was stop that Kinks copy thing—which he could see was going down—maybe that's what attracted him to us. I dunno. But 'I Can't Explain' was a direct influence, but the chord change thing—the modulation—was picked up in 'My Generation' which was after all only about four months later. And the next big thing that really hit me about the Kinks which really made 'em stand out to me was a track which didn't seem to get anywhere called 'See My Friends'. It was an eastern sort of thing [sings]

See my friends staring cross the way—

and when I heard that I thought, "This sound is gonna be the next thing". It was the exact opposite of the other thing, it was a drone.

THE BEST IN THE BUSINESS

ZZ: Talking about tuning up five guitars, what about Bob Pridden?

T: Well, he couldn't tune up five guitars—I wish he could. He and a couple of other guys.

ZZ: Cyrano?

T: No, not Cyrano. John Woolf is our lighting engineer and production manager, personal manager if you like.

ZZ: Is he the bald guy?

T: Yeah. Well he and Bob really run it. They have people below them. Bob looks after the sound and Wiggy looks after the money and the lights, and keeping the group together. Basically their job—and they, do it better than anyone else in the business—is to make sure that when The Who walk on the stage it is an ideal place to be. They just know our every whim. I've had Bob come into me and say, "The stage is a bit sloping, I'm a bit worried, maybe I should chock up your amp." And what he's really saying is that the stage is two degrees too low at the front and I'm gonna slide and trip over and sure enough I'll go out and slide and trip over and Bob knew I was going to and sprinkled a bit of sawdust down. It's these sort of touches that you come to rely on and depend on and take for granted, until you reach the point where the Who've got where if somebody said, "What would you do without Bob and Wiggy?" and we go, "Oh, Bob and Wiggy are at a group meeting, about having a percentage of the Who's earnings—the matter is in hand, just in case you're worrying." It's very difficult, whether to give a roadie a bit of the earnings. You can't just keep upping his wages. It just gives him a bigger tax problem. It will end up he needs a Bahama bank account. You see, the reason he works well is because he's deeply involved with the group. If we said to him tomorrow that we were gonna give him 50% of the group's earnings he'd be pleased but not bat an eyelid. Or if the group hit hard times and we had to cut his pay in half, he wouldn't bat an eyelid either. He's just that committed a sort of person. Wiggy probably works a little more for money but I suppose he's been forced to. He's the money man in the group. Making promoters pay.

Peter Townshend Esq, Writer

ZZ: Why did you stop doing the Melody Maker column?

T: Well I felt that I was running out of things to say, and secondly it was at a really dodgy time when the Young Vic thing was going badly. Someone said it was an astrological thing on the box the other day. He said, "Of course, all Taureans had a terrible time between blah blah blah," and I shrieked, "Well, that's the fxxking understatement of the year—that is!" In fact, he said "Taureans would come close to insanity at that point in the year"—and I thought if there isn't anything to astrology it must be just coincidence because that was a period when they were ringing us up saying "Your copy's due in" and I had to think up something to write about. And it was reducing me to the level of a workaday journalist who doesn't really enjoy his work. I started off because I was privileged enough to write about what journalists never get a chance to write about. So I knocked it on the head four editions before I was supposed to. I agreed to do a year. The one I liked best was the first one—I was on holiday when I did it. I had bags of time. It had all the nicest things I had to say. I used a lot of friends. When I first conceived it I was very enthusiastic. It was supposed to be a page, not that I wrote but that I edited. It was gonna be the Pete Townshend page—not the thoughts of Chairman Townshend—just my page. I could print anything that didn't get the Melody Maker into trouble. No ads. Bit by bit that arrangement fell apart until in the end Ray Coleman and I got very pissed off with one another. He, because *he's* the editor of the paper and I because I felt he wasn't sticking to his original agreement. And then we found a happy compromise where I'd dream up a fun photograph and dream up some piece—and nobody else would be on the page—just a half page ad or something. I just thought what the fxxk. I mean—what do I want to get hung up on the politics of the Melody

Maker for? I like writing but only when it's on my terms. Rolling Stone is a different story.

ZZ: That thing on Meher Baba, I got the impression it was pretty instinctive and uncontrived.

T: Yeah, I typed it off in one go. Jann Wenner edited it a bit. I wouldn't have the time—it was about 15-20 pages of foolscap typed. I couldn't have done it over and over again. I did a rough copy, then spliced it together with scissors. Cut out bits I didn't want—comes from editing tape. I sent those bits to them—cut out bits that didn't work grammatically and just sent it. It was a very easy piece to write because it was everything I wanted to say at that particular time. I really wanted to say all that—to Baba lovers who came up to me and said, all shocked, "You know, my friend's still smoking pot," what I wanted to say was, "Well, I still would if I had half a chance". What I wanted to say to people who were still smoking pot was why I turned off it not just "I don't smoke pot any more because of Meher Baba". I wanted to say what had gone down before and what went down afterwards. This is what Meher Baba means to me—he isn't just a second-rate Maharishi to me, you or anyone else. To really put the depth, the breadth, the gravity of the situation across, in terms of my life. Just to sort of say, "I'm incredibly committed and if I'm committed then you should be committed and that's how much I think of myself". [Laughs] That's really what I was trying to put across—that it's no good writing about Baba's life or using it to put pictures of Baba in or anything like that. Although they did print some really nice ones. Jann Wenner when he wants to can really do it nicely. He did all that. He re-edited it, reshaped it. He picked that Mike McKinnon thing to put in. It was just very sensitively done. When he wants to he can be incredibly 'correct' about things. I just felt that Baba must have had his thumb right on Jann Wenner's head because when Jann Wenner walked into this house and said, "I want you to do a piece about Meher Baba—I'm gonna put in a section about all the new religious swami, blah blah blah, will you do the piece?" So I thought, "Great, I really fancy it". I did it and he just said the rest of the stuff, against it, was too factual. He wanted more facts.

Actually, when I sent the copy he said there was not enough facts, I had to get more facts. But it wasn't a factual thing. You don't wanna know about Baba as a man, because Baba's life as a man is something which to a lot of people is going to be meaningless. It's the effect of the time—the time that we're in to which you attribute the things that are going on spiritually at the moment. Whether you equate those with Baba's coming and the things that he said—the very point where he said various things, certain specific events happened. Tides of spirituality happened—but to relate that to spurious things like dates, information, height, weight,—it's not really gonna help. So I just wrote a personal piece—it was fantastically easy. An incredible outpouring which still this day is a piece that I'm incredibly proud of. It was certainly my celebration of the typewriter which I think is the next best thing to the guitar. Really, it's an incredible instrument. In fact 'Let's See Action' I wrote on the typewriter. I just wrote it as scat poetry and when I sung it, it all fitted.

ZZ: Have you written anything besides that—is there a Pete Townshend 'Tarantula' somewhere upstairs?

T: No. The really interesting thing which I often take time out to read is the script for the 'Lifehouse' thing, which is a good laugh. One day I'd like to get that published because that would tell more about how 'Who's Next' came together than anything I could say. That again I just wrote in one go. I video-copied 60 copies myself which took months, up a tattooist's office in Greek Street. I distributed them to the lads and they keep turning up with lists on them, or wrapping mike cables, or notes to the mussus. Roger's turned his inside out and uses the blank pages to write all his words on. It's certainly the most abused part of my life—'The Lifehouse'.

MUSICAL COHORTS AND COMPANIONS

ZZ: Who played piano on all your records?

T: Nicky Hopkins stopped working with us on . . . No. I played piano on 'The Who Sell Out' and 'I Can't Reach You'. If there's any piano before that it's probably Nicky Hopkins. We never used anybody else. Now after that we didn't use Nicky Hopkins until 'Who's Next'—so it was all me.

But 'Tommy' was all me—organ and piano. It was all quite laborious—I had to go over things quite often. I'd done the demos so I'd got into things. Things like the overture I did in me sleep because I'd recorded it seventeen times in me sleep. Stuff like 'Amazing Journey' was written on piano so it was no trouble to do that. 'Sally Simpson' was clever work—it was dead simple.

ZZ: Was that Overture/Underture thing taken from that Blood, Sweat and Tears album?

T: No, we did that as a gag. Don't tell me Blood, Sweat and Tears called something 'Underture', did they?

ZZ: Yeah, on the first album—the Al Kooper album, there's an Overture and an Underture.

T: Really? [amazed] Amazing. Well, what happened with me was that I never ever heard the first Blood, Sweat and Tears album. I always listened to a tape that I had of it so I never had any titles. Was the Underture that strange classical thing?

ZZ: It goes into 'So Much Love', then at the end it gets violins, that's the Underture.

T: Well, Al Kooper doesn't give a monkey's because he's never ever mentioned that to me. He's an incredible guy.

ZZ: Very underrated.

T: Underrated, certainly, but a very great listener—[self-mockingly]—a great listener. I was really flattered because I did that thing about getting off on Elton John's first album. And when I went over to the States he was carrying it about in his attache case, which is record player with a pair of cans coming out so that whenever he's on the subway he can listen to a quick dose of his favourite record. He can only get one record in.

He once opened it up and there was 'Who's Next'. I was really pleased. "Best album ever made," he said. "That's what you said about Elton John," I said. So he said, "Well, here's to the next one."

ZZ: Leslie West and Felix Pappalardi told us that they were playing with you.

T: They did some work with us in New York. After 'The Lifehouse', the group was about split. We'd done everything there was to be done, and we'd got nowhere. I wasn't willing go back on the road. It was pointless because we had nothing and it was pointless working for the sake of working, we've got to have something—a film, an event. Nothing was big enough for the Who—for it had to be as big as possible. The group had shown that they had no confidence in the script, but a bit of confidence in the music, which to me was a throwaway—tracks like 'Behind Blue Eyes', Getting In Tune', 'Song Is Over'. They were like teasers for what was to really come. They were saying that this is what it should be about—the music. But that was because that was the way we've always done it—it always has been the music. So in the end it got worse and worse until I was having hallucinations and really going through an incredible thing—I couldn't leave the group but I couldn't do anything with it—we had meetings that were very poor and unproductive. Then suddenly Kit said, "Look, come to America—we'll call at the Record Plant—the sound will turn you on and we'll do it all quadrophonic." So I just thought thank Christ for Kit. He's saved the day as usual—he's taken the whole responsibility for the whole thing. Yet it had nothing to do with him—it wasn't his problem. The group was trying to be free of him and yet he'd come back and made this gesture. We all trooped over to the States—to the Record Plant. We had a lovely, merry week recording with Leslie West playing rhythm guitar, Pappalardi produced 'Won't Get Fooled Again'—a version of it. We did 'Behind Blue Eyes', 'Pure And Easy', 'Getting In Tune', 'Love Ain't For Keeping'—they were all great, like a new Who. We'd found ourselves and Kit was producing again—it was fantastic. By producer I mean he rolled up at half past seven in the evening and started to disrupt the session, but by then we had enough to get it together. But it was his gesture that had achieved it all and it was exhilarating because it was The Who again. Well, we came back and we said what was the weakest track. Kit wasn't there at all, Pappalardi didn't pull it off. So we said, "Let's do it on the Stones' mobile," because we wanted to test it for the Young Vic, because we were gonna go back in again and do it all live. We went down to Mick's place and did 'Won't Get Fooled' again with Glyn Johns and it just incredible. We couldn't believe what was going down. What with the gig at the Record Plant and the gig here the whole recording thing with the group is coming together. We must just have found ourselves. Well, Glyn said, "If you like this, come to Olympic." So we went to Olympic and we suddenly realised that it wasn't Kit or the Record Plant at all, but The Who who had discovered another facet that we could really record like a group of session men when we were up against the wall. And produce a recording with a producer like Glyn that sounds like it was recorded by a group of session men. Halfway through the album we were encouraged. We heard the tapes we'd done in the States and they weren't really very good. If they'd been mixed in the States when we did them they might have been alright. Tapes done in America can never sound right over here and vice versa. The other thing was that Leslie played lead on a few of the tracks and I played rhythm to him, which for a Who record was impossible. We did a version of 'Baby Don't You Do It' where he plays lead all the way through. A lot of his licks I've pinched for the stage. Second hand licks.

SUPPORT ACTS AND OTHER OCCASIONAL PROBLEMS OF THE ROAD

ZZ: Talking about the struggles of a pop star, what was all this with Chuck Berry at the Albert Hall?

T: Well, that really is not such a serious thing as it might seem. We know Chuck Berry quite well. We ran across him quite a few times, at the Saville and a few other places and at the Fillmore where he backed us up, and quite honestly we were fxxking terrible.

ZZ: When was this?

T: Quite a long time ago. All we had then was the mini opera. It was just when Hendrix first started. Three years ago. Anyway, when we got the Albert Hall, he was there and he was just doing his routine. He's got a wife that we know quite well, and we went in and said hello, and he quite likes The Who and he quite likes our records. He's actually listened to them, which is something. And I think he's incredible, and I'm always flattering—which is what I should do—every time I see him. I suppose it was a natural thing for him to do. After all, here's these young punks coming in here, so I don't care whether they are drawing the people, I'm the star. And in a way he's right. For the first show at the Albert Hall, we just said, "Alright, take top billing, and we'll take it in the second house. The house isn't full and if you're a big draw like you say you are, you've failed miserably. You take the blame for the first house. We'll take the blame for the second house." Chuck Berry wasn't the problem anyway. The problem was his audience. Throwing pennies that are sharpened. Luckily none of us got hit. Roger got one on the forehead, caught it on his head. But it was the sharp end that hit him. They sharpen one edge, like a razor, with a file. Or they sharpen them all round and a girl was throwing them with a glove. Of course, if they hit you they just split your skin apart—three or four inches. If they hit you in the eye they just cleave your eyeball in two and that's what they were throwing at us. That was one point where we felt animosity towards an audience and won because the audience was with us and was eventually drawn—after being exhausted from being in the Park for the Stones—into saying "These fxxking rockers are gonna ruin the whole day unless we get up and do something". They didn't really owe us anything directly. They got up and they did what the rockers were doing. They jumped on the chairs and they screamed and they shouted and as soon as somebody did that the rockers stopped—they thought, "Blimey, why are they doing it? I didn't think that sort of thing happened."

ZZ: That was when I most enjoyed 'Tommy'

T: It must have been the time I played it most aggressively.

ZZ: No, Purley. A few feet from the stage.

T: No, the best performance of all was at Croydon, Fairfield Hall. It was the first time we played it including 'Sally Simpson' and a few other things we did specially. The sound in that place—oh. Croydon, I could bloody play there all night. You sound deafeningly loud, yet the voices come over even though they've just got a couple of PA speakers. It's something to do with the fact that the front of the stage is much liver than the back of the stage, so the PA is just miraculously loud, however bad it is. It is just a good acoustic. It's [as] though the whole place was designed so that you could hear the conductor banging on his rostrum and not the orchestra. It's a freak but it's great for rock.

ZZ: Did you play a long time at the Isle of Wight just to get your own back on Sly Stone who'd done what to you at Woodstock?

T: Absolute rubbish. What we did do to Sly Stone to pay him back was pinch his lighting act—with the big lights. Because he used that at Wood-stock, and we pinched it as a gag, and there was a bit of animosity about that. But they never really kept us off the stage—they did a long set, but everybody did a set that they felt was right and that's what we did at the Isle of Wight. We didn't use the lights thing specifically to needle Sly. But it must've needled Sly. It must've done, because our lighting man chose to use it that day, and I'm standing up there thinking, "Fxxkin' hell, Sly are following," and we're doing exactly what they did to us last year—but it wasn't in any way preconceived.

ZZ: That was an incredible gig.

T: We didn't play it quite right, that one. We had trouble with the ending. We ended once and it was perfect. Then for some reason Roger carried on singing. He did it again at the Oval. We ended and then Roger suddenly thought—"Right, it's my turn to be creative"—[sings]

I'm a roadrunner, honey.

Well, the group can't walk off, so we had to go into that. I'd thrown me guitar up and bounced it on the ground, and of course it was grossly out of tune. It took me five minutes to get it into tune, five minutes to get me head together because me adrenaline had gone down, five minutes to get enough energy to get Moon to end. You very much have to play the end of an act right. It's probably far more important for The Who than the rest of it put together. We've got to end right.

ZZ: Did you see any of that night?

T: When we're working a gig I can't bear to watch any of the other acts. It disorientates me completely. The last time it happened was at Monterey. It turned me on so much—I swore I'd never do it again. I saw Ravi Shankar and I just thought "Well, what the hell am I gonna do—I might just as well give up." They were applauding for about two hours, it seemed like. It went on and on and on.

ZZ: Didn't you see the James Gang on the last tour?

T: Oh yeah, I saw them. When we've done tours with lots of groups—like the one we did with The Herd, The Tremeloes, Traffic—that was one where I got very interested in watching Traffic, because that was very early in their career and they had that incredible Mr Fantasy album out. And I thought they were a fantastically interesting group—Stevie Winwood's a fantastic geezer. I suppose I have to watch people who are not competition in a way. I mean, I have trouble watching someone like Ron Geesin who played a couple of gigs with us. He was gonna do the tours with us but got weasled out of it by a bit of politics, unfortunately. Ever seen him?

ZZ: No.

T: He did two test gigs with us and to put it mildly, he wiped the floor with The Who—just him, and his bits of paper and his piano playing. He's so far ahead of his time as a performer that people just can't pick up on it. His biggest problem, I suppose is realising that fact. If you tell him that, it pleases him.

ZZ: You're playing with Quiver at the Rainbow. Ever played with them before?

T: Yeah, the whole tour. I had nothing to do with choosing them. If I'd had a choice it would've been Ron Geesin. If Keith had had a choice it would've been Ron Geesin too.

ZZ: What do you think of them?

T: We:ve played with them a couple of nights and to be quite honest I haven't really looked at them.

ZZ: Well, they're favourites of ours.

T: Are they? From what I've heard, bits and pieces—I've heard them loudest of all at Greens in Glasgow—they seem to pick chords that didn't really appeal to me, but then I've heard them buggering about in the dressing room and really liked them. I'm sure if I went out front I'd really dig them.

AUDIENCES—HIGHS AND LOWS

ZZ: The best gig I ever saw was The Orchid Ballroom, Purley. What was yours?

T: What was my best Who gig? Oh, fxxk, we've worked more than any other band in the world. I just can't remember—we've had so many amazing gigs. The best gigs we ever did were about that time—when we had that long two-hour act with 'Tommy' and somehow we had the stamina to carry it through. It had that ending—towards a smash up, but not quite. The whole of 'Tommy', a good bit of history before it. Occasionally the mini-opera thrown in.

ZZ: Yeah, the Coliseum was a good one.

T: Yeah, I felt that that was the best time the act ever was. At the moment, the act is good. We're at a peak now, definitely of musicianship. On the stage we're approaching the Who's next pinnacle. We've got a few things together to prove that it can be got together, despite the fact that there's absolutely nothing in our heads at all, other than that we're a rock'n'roll band, which is something we desperately needed to prove—that if all else failed we could play. If suddenly Townshend's head was empty we could still play, and we can. And this is what we're doing. We're waiting for the follow-up to 'Tommy', for the follow-up to 'My Generation', for the rock revolution. We're waiting for rock to make a revolution, to indicate a direction, so that we can be part of it. The silly thing about The Who is we've always been followers, not leaders. We really have.

ZZ: I feel very sorry for you never having been to a Who concert—it is quite an experience. Do you get a lot of diverse reactions from the audience? What do you think of audiences?

T: I dunno. I suppose still that thing about The Who is to [pause]—I'll try and choose my words carefully because it's not something I've ever really said properly before. When the group is on the stage it's hard to imagine, after coming off, that you know what it is that you were doing. If I project myself now into being on stage, you go through a metamorphosis. I'm a different person altogether from the one that's talking to you now. I've got more courage. In my own mind I'm a lot better looking. I've got a lot more physical strength. I can do things like break a guitar over my head and not get a bump on my head. I can tune up my guitar in two seconds whereas in the dressing room beforehand it takes me an hour. Keith and I can put one another in and out of moods like that. It works both ways. Keith can say to me "Blah blah blah," and throw me into an incredible mood and then just snap me out of it with another gag, or something. It's a different intensity of experience. It's like being in another world and this is really—this *must* be one of the reasons why The Who have never stopped working, because once you've tasted an experience like that you can't really do without it. It's not the power of being a leader or being in front of an audience. It's rather the power to realise a bit of yourself, of your own being that you never ever thought was there. And you only realise it while you're on the stage. It's temporary. So it becomes like a drug. You just learn how to get at it, to better it, to heighten it when you're on the stage each time. It's temporary because when you come off the stage you've still got the same hang-ups, you're still the same person with the same problems.

ZZ: But that's what it's like for the audience too.

T: Well hopefully. The whole reason we go on the stage in the first place is that part of that realisation is a giving and a receiving. It's a pity that the word is so abused but I suppose it's a sort of loving relationship, my definition of love being happiness. Often it can make an audience happy to see a group take themselves so seriously—like The Who do. Doing such absurd things. But then theatre is great in that way because you see someone pretending to be someone who died 400 years ago, strutting about the stage really pretending to be that person, and being incredibly serious about it. Not only that but throwing themselves into the part, reliving this dead person's life, as though it was important. And, of course, the life itself wasn't important but the reliving of it is—between him and the audience.

ZZ: Is that part of the reason it took so long to develop a stage act that wasn't built around 'Tommy'? The audience just wouldn't let you?

T: It's really hard to say. [Very slowly and deliberately]: We're so wound up in ourselves that we never know sometimes that the audience is manipulating us. We think we're manipulating the audience. Luckily I'm not contradicting something I said earlier because I haven't said "We've got power over an audience." I mean often. I have said that, but I think it would be a lot truer to say that we allow audiences to dictate a lot to us, subconsciously. If you like, we allow ourselves to let audiences make us stay the same. Because when we try to change, audiences are confused and we can't bear that period, however short it might turn out to be, of confusion.

ZZ: If The Who came on and sat on stools and played acoustic guitars, it wouldn't be The Who. It might be artistically valid, but the audience would be pissed off . . . You know the thing by Roy Hollingworth in the run about the Oval concert. Well in a way he was right, the band haven't changed but the audience is stopping you getting into something else which you'd have to if you were a less successful band.

T: My immediate reaction to Hollingworth's thing was, when Keith Alton our publicist read it over to me over the phone and said "What are we gonna do about this?" I said "It sounds like one man's opinion and it sounds alarmingly like how I feel about the group, and I just hope the rest of the world don't think it." And at the time a friend had come round with his sister and they'd seen us at the Oval and this girl quite coldly said, "Of course at the Oval everybody'd come to see The Faces. Half the audience walked out when you came on." So I thought, "Eh, that's the way things are, are they?" But we've had this before—The Creams, The Zeppelins, the Jimi Hendrixs coming along and taking bits of Who and often we've taken back, stolen bits from them. And at the moment we're stealing bits of Faces—not stealing—but being influenced by their presence, because we're involved with them. They respect us and we respect what's happening. But when the feathers stop flying we always seem to be still here. So I laughed at it at first, but then I thought really there has to be a time, and this is what I've been saying since the Lifehouse project—we've got to shake ourselves up, musically, and do something new and we're the only group in a position financially and idealistically to pioneer a new form of performance which, as a microcosm, denies corrupt society—their . . . their backlash. In other words we as a group have a high enough ideal that we can do it for the music and not for the money. We have that high enough ideal and also the power and the consistency and the stamina to put on something which would help rock go on to its next step—even though we obviously couldn't take the credit, because we're not new, but we could set it up in some way and help to make it happen, even if it was just a different way of promoting a concert.

ZZ: You talk about the ultimate as being when the audience disappears. But isn't it that The Who should disappear and the audience just sits there—richer?

T: Well, in a way. I want The Who to disappear as well, but I want that moment that happens in every good Who concert or every good rock concert—to be a bit more generous—where suddenly you're up there and you've forgotten about everything except the music and you're up there and you're riding up there and you look around and when you look around you're not brought down. That's an important moment—when you're high on the event and you look around at people and the group and you check out what's happening and you're not brought down by it. You don't suddenly see some guy thumping someone over the head with a cosh. These, to me, are the sacred moments in rock, and why, I suppose, I worship it. It happens.

ZZ: When you turned the lights on at the Isle of Wight, was this part of focusing on the audience or just a gimmick or what?

T: Sort of a gimmick symbol in a way. We said all those things—it'd be fun, etc. And then I went into the intellectual thing but really it was a gimmick symbol of the audience's importance and the way the audience could get turned on by themselves and also look incredible and have a good time without seeing the group at all. It's like saying The Who are incredibly important but at this moment we've disappeared—we're not here.

WHO'S STILL WHO

John Lawless | March 19, 1972 | *Observer Colour Magazine* (UK)

In March 1972, the *Observer* once again assembled the Who in front of a Union Jack for the purpose of complementing a color-supplement cover feature.

It was almost six years to the day since the previous *Observer* supplement article. In that half-dozen years, the band's contemporaries had almost all split—even if Lawless had to resort to scrubbing the Rolling Stones and the Kinks out of the picture to posit the Who as the last men standing from the sixties beat boom.

Lawless concentrated on the group members. (Lambert and Stamp, focused on to the exclusion of the band by John Heilpern, would be dispensed with by the Who within three years.) His article shows the Who settling into their role of rock gentry. It was accompanied by photographs of the now flowing-locked and bearded band members alongside their families in the sumptuous homes success had bought them.

The reference to "I'm a Boy" being a chart-topper should be clarified: in the sixties there were four competing UK charts and that single reached the summit of the lesser-referenced *Melody Maker* table.

Notes: for "Entwhistle" read "Entwistle"
for "Barbara Anne" read "Barbara Ann." —Ed.

OF ALL the groups that chased along behind The Beatles in the early 1960s, only one can really claim to have kept going: The Who. It kept going to the very top, and that is where it still is.

Six years ago THE OBSERVER COLOUR MAGAZINE chose to feature The Who as being typical of a group of promise. That article left the group poised before what everyone recognised as being the nastiest fence on the obstacle course: breaking into the lucrative American market.

Even in those days, success in this country and on the Continent simply wasn't enough. You either crashed in on the multi-million dollar American industry, or died.

Today, The Who are such a major force in America that one wonders why they had any trouble in the first place. When it came, round about three years ago, success was like the sudden relief from a pain; almost overnight, a double-album entitled 'Tommy' was top of the LP charts, outselling anything that had gone before. Two million dollars' worth of sales were achieved in a matter of days, and the record has gone on to take seven million dollars.

A follow-up album, 'Live at Leeds', was also a tremendous seller. So much so that American teenagers view Leeds with a reverence previously given only to places like Nashville. It is said that on any day last summer half the youngsters thumbing their way up the M1 were on the final stage of a transatlantic pilgrimage.

'Tommy', the inspiration of lead guitarist Peter Townshend, was the first, and since much-imitated, pop opera. It told the story of a young boy, deaf, dumb and blind, and surrounded by the most vicious relatives and acquaintances. Among them are Cousin Kevin, who burns him with cigarettes; the Acid Queen, who offers LSD; and drunken Uncle Ernie, who is homosexual. Amazingly, Tommy goes on to become the world's greatest pinball-machine player, using only his sense of smell for guidance. A truly miraculous cure seems almost an anticlimax, but it happens, and Tommy becomes a preacher and cult hero—and opens a holiday camp. Story ends.

Hardly 'Carmen', but, carried by the album sales, The Who took their work on a world tour of opera houses. In New York, Leonard Bernstein gave it high acclaim; in Amsterdam, the Dutch royal family booked seats; in Cologne, President Heinemann entertained the four musicians at a reception. And so on, to the Theatres des Champs-Elysées in Paris, the Royal Theatre, Copenhagen, the States Opera House, Hamburg, the Berlin Opera House, and the home of Sadler's Wells, the London Coliseum.

THE OBSERVER left The Who 'anxiously waiting for the last breakthrough'. But when it came it was received with mixed delight

Bass guitarist John Entwhistle says: 'The opera was nearly our rise and fall. Everybody wanted to hear it all the time. We played it solidly for two years and were getting cliché'd.

'You have to remember as well that, before anybody else heard it, we had been in the studios making it for eight months. We had terrible trouble with the story; in fact, at first it just didn't make sense. It was only because Pete had to keep adding bits that it became a double album.

'By the time it was released, I for one was sick to death of "Tommy". I have only ever played the record at home about 20 times, and never all the way through. On stage now, we do a selection and that's it.'

For Townshend, of course, it meant much more. Before the opera, he was considered a brilliant guitarist who had a taste for lustful destruction, cleaving the stage with his £300 guitar at the end of every performance, and ramming it into an amplifier until both were shattered. (In those days, such exhibitions of 'musical frustration', otherwise known as gimmicks, were necessary.)

'Tommy' gave Townshend a top rating as a composer. But he says that, after reaching such a peak, The Who find it difficult to regain the kick of the days when they had the best incentive of all, the will to survive. The Who carry the burden of pop respectability—when they stick two fingers in the air these days, everybody smiles.

Being one of the few groups able to command a concert fee in America of £10,000 plus—together with a cut of the gate receipts—they are at last what is known as loaded. But the knowledge that each could retire tomorrow and live on record royalties is truly a recent acquisition. Until three years ago, the whole operation of musicians, management and backstage helpers was just one huge IOU.

Singer Roger Daltrey explains: 'When we got our first hit, "I Can't Explain", we started earning what was then pretty good money, say £300 a night. But after the first year we were £60,000 in debt. The next year, after working our balls off, we were still £40,000 down. And the biggest choke of all came the year after that when we found we were back up to £60,000 again. Every accountant's meeting was ridiculous. We always owed so much money that we ended up rolling around the office laughing ourselves silly.'

Having had other hits in this country, including still-famous numbers like 'Substitute' and 'My Generation'—while their one and only chart-topper, 'I'm a Boy', is among the least remembered—The Who started touring America.

John Entwistle recalls: 'On the first tour in 1967, when we were backing Herman's Hermits, we played 30 concerts and earned $40,000—and I still had to borrow $100 to get home. It was heartbreaking.'

A second trip was also a financial disaster. 'We worked from coast to coast, revisiting all the places we had done well at before,' says Entwistle. 'But the money just went; we even had $5,000 stolen from a bedroom. Then the biggest gig of all was cancelled because Martin Luther King was assassinated, and we came back after 10 weeks with £300 each. There was a load of rubbish talked at the time about the grand job British groups were doing in earning all those dollars. Really, we were being milked dry by the Americans. Why, I even remember one concert where the fellow actually fined us for playing too long.'

Things have changed. Two visits back, Entwistle returned with a black Cadillac costing £10,000 and fitted with a dozen stereo speakers, as one of his perks. On the last visit, Daltrey returned with an immaculate 1929 Studebaker—a present for his wife, who had just passed her driving test.

But there were problems other than money. Daltrey says he had to decide between keeping his place in the group, or staying with his wife, Jackie, who was then expecting a child. 'I knew,' he says, 'that if I didn't move away from her in those early days, I would be a sheet metal worker for ever.' The couple have divorced and Daltrey has remarried a model called Heather.

Townshend was also shifted away from his family, although he wasn't married, and put into a flat in Ealing. His companions were two tape recorders. 'I woke up one morning and said to myself "How come such a successful young man can be so totally out of things?" I really was incredibly lonely.'

There was an undercurrent of insecurity felt by all but drummer Keith Moon, whose madcap activities matched his frantic playing on stage and crowded out worries. Entwhistle, a rocker at heart, was uncomfortable in mod gear. The mod movement swept across the country on scooters, clashing on bank holiday jaunts with the aging rockers, and took on The Who and the Small Faces as its groups.

Entwhistle felt sure he was going the same way as the original drummer Doug Sandon, replaced when The Who was formed. That would have meant a clock-watching return to sorting out the tax fiddles of Slough. He tried 'leaping around a bit', got the girls screaming, but couldn't do that and play his guitar at the same time. He retired to a backstage shell, pinning his backside to the same piece of woodwork and not moving—and so became loved by the fans for being so different to everyone else around at the time, and so serious about his music.

Such images didn't endear The Who to the mass audience, and it would be easy, and lazy, to explain away the difference between them and The Beatles as being a matter of sophistication. The foursome which launched the Liverpool Sound swept along on Beatlemania—a popularity initially so powerful that it even broke Sooty's traditional hold on the fancy soap and tea-towel market.

John, Paul, George and Ringo were the lovable schoolboys, naughty but nice, whose songs were sung on every coach that headed for Margate or Blackpool. Pete, Roger, John and Keith, on the other hand, surged with violence. They bred their own cult, which needed to be seen to be understood; and that is the likeliest explanation why it took them longer than the groups which were little more than reflections of The Beatles to break into the American market. They had to communicate over 3,000 miles, and it took several visits to get themselves started.

The Who also began the idea of groups calling themselves something unusual. Previously, bands had one of two types of title: they were either called So-and-so and the Thingamybobs, which ran the risk of the whole group coming to depend on the personality of the flashy leader staying strong; or they had a name which hinted at a musical style or chart success (e.g. The *Beatles*).

The four boys were originally in the second bracket, being called the High Numbers. Bringing in Keith Moon, they decided on a change of name and sat around making suggestions. One of them put forward an idea; somebody else didn't hear it properly and asked, 'The Who?' And that was it. Since then we have had names like Blind Faith, Family Dogg, and The Plastic Ono Band, all trying to be distinctive instead of catchy.

The tragedy of pop music in the 1960s was its sheer commercialism. Talent will out, everyone assured everyone else. And often it did—straight out. The truth, of course, was that musicians were judged almost entirely by the charts; thus, sounds created by experienced engineers, working with thousands of pounds' worth of studio technology, could shoot otherwise untalented people to stardom. The real 'stars' were often the unseen producers and arrangers.

It is clearly ridiculous to pick up the evening paper on Tuesdays and judge ability and standards from who is in or out of the charts. It is like producing a weekly Sotheby's Top Ten: Matisse is still at number one, but a new Picasso has leapt six places on last week's sales price; Turner has a golden oldie in at number nine, while Constable's maxi-canvas is hovering just outside and likely to push its way in next time round. I question the accepted view which says that The Beatles were far and away the best of the groups.

To make a fair assessment, we have to look back at the way in which the Beatles and The Who have developed. It is widely assumed that the Beatles were 'great' from the start. In commercial terms this is true; although it must be remembered that their first record, 'Love Me Do', only managed to get into the lower half of the Top Twenty. The records that followed sold so many; but I would argue that success in the first place only allowed The Beatles to do exactly what they wanted later. In complete freedom, and eagerly encouraged, their combined talent flowered.

But this, I stress, was as a result of the sales development, and did not begin it.

We are now far enough removed from the overpowering enthusiasm of the day to ask if early lyrics like 'She loves you, Yeah, Yeah, Yeah' were really so sophisticated. The middle period of their career saw the tremendous fusion of talent, culminating in the magnificent 'Sgt Pepper' album. From this period come the seemingly endless number of hits, particularly from the combination of Lennon and McCartney. The other largely-unseen factor in the group's rise was the iron-hand and velvet-glove management of Epstein.

After 'Sgt Pepper', the four developed the strongest of individual personalities and gradually went their own way in music. McCartney, even before splitting away, was softening his tastes; Harrison retained a marked feeling for the sitar music of India; Lennon became strikingly different and, I believe, is only nowadays beginning really to surge forward; while dear old Ringo Starr has reverted to what I suspect was his true inclination all along. As an all-round entertainer, he has proved himself to be a natural. He has even taken to doing sing-along songs, not to mention comedy guest appearances on the all-family Cilla Black television show. I wouldn't be surprised to see him playing Mother Goose in pantomime in 20 years' time.

The Who have taken exactly the opposite course. They started out with a couple of managers, Kit Lambert, son of Constant Lambert, and Chris Stamp, brother of Terence Stamp, who knew nothing about the accepted practices of the pop world. Naturally they broke most of the rules, and were far more prepared to gamble on their instinct and ingenuity. They once took advantage of a television producer, offering to help him get rid of complimentary tickets for a show, and filled up the studio with scarf-waving Who fans.

Having been film directors, they tried to make their young musicians tiptoe through the pop music publicity bit wearing hobnail boots, treading on as many toes as possible in interviews, without actually offending anybody but the journalist. Says Townshend: 'Kit used to brief us before we went into interviews about what to say; sometimes to be as objectionable, arrogant and nasty to reporters as possible. And oh, those outrageous lies we told! I remember telling Jonathan Aitken "I have got four cars, a Lincoln Continental, a Jag XK150, a Cortina GT and a London taxi"—all I had was an old banger.

'Then I said to somebody else that I was spending between £40 and £50 a week on clothes, and had to borrow money to go to Carnaby Street and buy a jacket in order to pose for a picture.'

They did make one early mistake. Conflict over which way they should go musically developed into a niggling situation between Daltrey and Moon. It almost caused a total split up during a Swedish tour in 1965. Roger wanted to base their style on rhythm and blues, while Keith was drawn to the Beach Boys' surfing sound. The result was a compromise, and The Who's repertoire still contains a strange sprinkling of numbers; Eddie Cochrane's 'Summertime Blues' and the Beach Boys' 'Barbara Anne', for example.

Initially, this even helped, giving them an extremely varied stage act. It did, however, tend to suffocate their distinctive musical expression. When that surfaced, it proved pretty weighty. Even McCartney stated that The Who's sound had influenced his group's work at one stage.

The Who were willing to copy others only in things like fashion and stage presentation. Pete Townshend got the nickname 'The Birdman' for windmilling his arm around while striking the guitar strings. He says: 'I took it from Keith Richard of the Rolling Stones. I just saw him do it one night. If he did it now, he would be accused of pinching it from me.'

They watched accepted fashion leaders, known as 'faces', in the trendiest club, The Scene in Soho, and rushed off to model themselves on their styles. (Roger Daltrey often used his mother's sewing machine.) Within two weeks, the mod strongholds in such places as Forest Hill and Catford were all in the same gear—and attributing the innovations to The Who.

Most important of all, they were never afraid of getting close to their audience. While The Beatles were being surrounded by security, The Who made a point of going among the fans. This in itself promoted their music; their songs were about the hopes and frustration of the youngsters of that age.

The Beatles, for all their new sound, were at first only giving an exciting twist to the old turtledove, stars-above lyrics. The Who still get feverish calls for original songs like 'My Generation' at their concerts, where audiences largely sit and listen and hold their adulation until the end; it would be difficult to imagine The Beatles even contemplating a return to 'She Loves You' and 'Please Please Me'.

While The Beatles have divided, The Who have come closer together. 'Even if The Who split up some day,' says Moon, 'we'd still be The Who, if you know what I mean.'

Adds Townshend: 'I just can't imagine The Who not existing now.'

The folk and classical music of tomorrow is being created today. To assume that the efforts of our wild and hairy musicians will leave no trace of their existence is rather like believing that Mozart and Bach were the only musicians striving in their day. No doubt they had stiff competition from men whose music has failed to stand the test of time.

To go on from here is for The Who far more challenging than trying to break into the American market—and it will probably take a lot more than another six years to settle their real worth and destiny.

FOUR-WAY PETE/WHO'S JIMMY?

Charles Shaar Murray | October 27 [part one] and November 3 [part two], 1973 |
***New Musical Express* (UK)**

It was the Who's first manager, Peter Meaden, who made them mods. Although their adoption of sharp modernist fashions was as much a gimmick as smashing their instruments, and although their appearance soon morphed into something more pop-art, the intimacy of the Who's relationship with their mod followers was genuine. In October 1973, Townshend explored it with the double concept album *Quadrophenia*.

In this two-part interview with the *NME*, Townshend explains with his usual preternatural eloquence and honesty why and how the album came about.

Curiously not picked up on by the interviewer is a comment in which Townshend seems to suggest that *Quadrophenia* might be the Who's last album. —Ed.

[PART ONE] FOUR-WAY PETE

TOWNSHEND'S "Quadrophenia" is a rather daunting proposition. Another Who double-album rock opera? About a kid called Jimmy? With a massive booklet of grainy monochrome tableaux stapled into the sleeve? With titles like "The Real Me", "I Am The Sea", Love Reign O'er Me" and "I'm One"?

The mind boggles, and you get the sneaking feeling that Pete Townshend has tried to out-"Tommy" "Tommy" and gone sailing right over the top.

The impression even persists when you start playing side one. The first thing you hear is a "Desert Island Discs" surf-crashing-on-the-shore sound-effect in sumptuous stereo while distant echoed voices intone the four principal themes from the piece.

Then it suddenly cuts into "The Real Me", and you hear that sound, as uncompromisingly violent as a boot disintegrating a plate glass window at 4 a.m., and simultaneously as smooth as a night-flight by 747.

Prime-cut Who, and suddenly you realise that Pete hasn't blown it after all. Face it, he very rarely does.

"Quadrophenia" is both less and more ambitious than its notorious predecessor.

"Tommy" tripped over its mysticism rather too often for comfort, and after being the indirect godfather to everything from "Jesus Christ Superstar" to "Ziggy Stardust", it didn't seem likely that Townshend himself would return to the scene of his former semi-triumph.

However, he has avoided most of the expected pitfalls with his customary agility.

The hero of this little extravaganza is Jimmy, the archetype mod. Frustrated, inarticulate, violent, thoroughly confused and prone to all the ills that teenage flesh is heir to.

Each member of the Who represents a different side of his character, and a recurring musical theme. Keith Moon represents the "bloody lunatic", John Entwistle is "the romantic", Roger Daltrey appears as the "tough guy", while Townshend casts himself as "a beggar, a hypocrite."

His odyssey leads him away from the constriction of his parents home to a dead-end job as a dustman, and by way of various other adventures to Brighton via a pill-crazed ride on the (you guessed) 5.15 train. Finally, he, ends up dexed-up and pissed out of his brain on a rock off Brighton Beach where he achieves some kind of satori and reconciliation with himself.

ON THE FACE of it, there's nothing very heavy going on there, especially when synopsised as ruthlessly as I've had to do.

Whereas "Tommy" took a headlong dive into esoteric symbolism, "Quadrophenia" is superficially mundane, as far as subject matter is concerned—but the implications of this autobiography of a generation go far deeper than those of the previous work.

As the prose on the sleeve puts it, Jimmy feels "me folks had let me down, rock had let me down, women had let me down, work wasn't even worth the effort, school isn't even worth mentioning. But I never felt that I'd be let down by being a mod."

That particular piece of disillusionment occurs when he discovers the King Mod from the seaside battles, the ultimate cool guy who everybody followed and mimicked, working in a menial humiliating job as bell-boy in a hotel.

When Jimmy eventually discovers himself on the rock, he finds his own peace by realising what he truly was even when stripped of his music, his friends, his clique, his beliefs. All that is left is himself, and that is more than sufficient.

To say that "Quadrophenia" is an affirmation of the strength of the human spirit is an invitation to accusations of pretension and screaming wimpism, but I'm afraid that that's the way it breaks down.

Beating a hasty retreat from the Philisophical Implications, Cosmic Messages and Assorted Heaviness Department, we can start looking at "Quadrophenia" simply as the latest album by The 'Oo. It would be an interesting critical exercise to demolish it, and I've no doubt that there's more than one typewriter jockey who'll try.

In some ways, it's extremely vulnerable to adverse criticism. Some of the more extravagant production touches, for example, even after a half-dozen listens, sound about as comfortable as marzipan icing on a half-ounce cheeseburger.

Also, the band have dubbed on so much synthesizer, keyboard and brass parts that, at times, one aches just to hear some unalloyed guitar-bass-drums-and-vocals Who.

In any case, does rock and roll need masterpieces, magnum opuses (apologies to my school Latin teachers; I know you tried hard) or works of genius? Isn't intensive listening to two-years-in-the-making double-albums antithetical to the spirit of true rock and roll?

Personally, I couldn't care less. If you're not prepared to listen to "Quadrophenia" in the spirit that it was made, then simply don't bother. If you're going to sling it on at a party or walk in and out of the room when it's playing, then you're not going to get a damn thing out of it and you might as well save your £4.30 for other purposes.

On the other hand, if you're genuinely prepared to work at getting into it and let it work at getting into you, then you might just find it the most rewarding musical experience of the year.

AS YOU JOURNEY through it, you'll find some real classic Who crunchers carefully placed to waylay you *en route*.

The second track "The Real Me" is almost as strong as "5.15" with its ferocious splintered chord work and vicious vocal, while Entwistle's bass seems to be plugged straight into this planet's central power source.

"Dr. Jimmy And Mr. Jim" which opens the fourth side, is as good an exposition of the raucous mod stance as anything Townshend's written since the "My Generation" days:

"What is it? I'll take it
Who is she? I'll rape it
Gotta bet there? I'll meet it
Gettimg high? You can't beat it . . ."

Basically, the early Who classics were straightforward expositions of an attitude, while "Quadrophenia" is an investigation of what went into constructing that attitude, and of its results.

It could be described as an obituary for the Mods by the band who did most to define that attitude.

I mean, we've all heard about how the Who were more a band who played to and sang about Mods than they were actually Mods themselves, but for those of us who were out in the provinces during the Mod era, Mod *was* the Who. And it is only fitting that the Who should be the ones to conduct this lengthy exorcism of the Ghost Of Mod.

After all, the spectre of those days has hung over the Who for the best part of a decade, and now Pete Townshend has summed up every stage of the Who's chequered past in one work.

There's even a flash of "The Kids Are Alright" between "Helpless Dancer" and "Is It In My Head."

"Quadrophenia" wipes the slate clean, leaving the Who free, hopefully, to follow it up with their freshest collection of new material since their very first album.

The Americans are gonna love it. What today's fourteen-year-old, who was six years old in the heyday of the Pill and the Parka, is going to make of it, Yog-Sothoth only knows. Ethan Russell's photo-booklet is gloriously replete with period detail, a perfect blend of documentary realism and the curiously dreamlike quality of events long gone imperfectly remembered.

"Quadrophenia" is a triumph, certainly. It's by no means unflawed, but a triumph it is. I'm glad that Pete decided to write it and that the band decided to do it, and I don't grudge a single day of the waiting time.

FADE TO BLACK and cut to Twickenham.

Pete Townshend opens up the door, immediately preceded by a large and presumably amiable dog named Towser (the facts, Ma'am, we just want the facts). Townshend is clad in bovver boots, extravagantly patched jeans and an Indian cotton shirt. He whips up a couple of coffees in large brown mugs and settles down on a sofa to get quadrophenic.

Now, talking to Pete Townshend is always a treat. He's intelligent, aware and articulate, qualities that aren't as prevalent among rock musicians as one might wish. Furthermore, he's capable of discussing the more esoteric aspects of his work with a remarkable detachment that's totally removed from the self indulgent, egocentric ramblings of many other acts.

First off, if the word "quadrophenia" is an expansion of "schizophrenia" as is indicated on the sleeve, why the missing "r"?

"It's a sort of jokey expansion of it, but it's a bit of a mouthful with the 'r'. It's something of a pun on 'quadraphonic' as well. The whole album has been put together as a quadraphonic composition. I suppose stereo is a bit of a compromise.

"We're fairly happy with the quadraphonic mixes we've done, but you know the problem with the transcription down to disc. It's all very well on tape, but when you try and get it down onto a record everything goes completely bersek.

"We were talking about a January 1st release date for the quadra-phonic version, but at the moment it's a bit of a myth. I heard the Doobie Brothers' quad album of "The Captain And Me" and it just doesn't come anywhere near the stereo version."

Okay, onto the album itself. Is it in any real sense an epitaph to Mod?

"It's probably a lot more than that. That's right in a way, but then songs like "My Generation" were that kind of epitaph in a more realistic sense. This album is more of a winding up of all our individual axes-to-grind, and of the group's ten-year-old image and also of the complete absurdity of a group like The Who pretending that they have their finger on the pulse of any generation.

"The reason that the album has come out emotionally as it has is that I felt that The Who ought to make, if you like, a last album.

"Also, in a way, I wanted to embrace the Who's early audiences—but also to give a feeling of what has happened to rock and to the generation that's come up with us. It's very peculiar that this album has come out at the same time as something like "Pin-Ups" because, although that's a more direct thing, the ideas are fairly similar.

"What I've really tried to do with the story is to try and illustrate that, as a study of childhood frustrations, the reason that rock is still around is that it's not youth's music, it's the music of the frustrated and the dissatisfied looking for some sort of musical panacea.

"Then we have difficulty relating to the business. We're not pure innovators, and we never rally have been. We've always been people who have latched onto things which were good and reflected them, and I don't feel anything at the moment.

"I mean, if someone like Bowie, who's only been a big star for eighteen months or two years, feels the need to start talking about his past influences, then obviously the roots are getting lost. The meat and potatoes, the reasons why people first pick up guitars, are getting forgotten."

HARKING BACK to what Townshend had said earlier about rock responsibility, there's a considerable case for the view that when rock starts thinking about what it's doing instead of simply reacting, then it's losing something of its essence.

"The most hilarious thing about arguments like that is the fact that people put forward the arguments in the first place.

"It shows that they're viewing the whole thing intellectually, that they're arguing intellectually and that what they're actually doing is putting forward an intellectual argument to denounce their particular rock star for becoming an intellectual—which is what they are. And they're blaming him for the fact that they've grown old.

"In actual fact, most of the American rock journalists that use these arguments are suffering from maturity, and it's unpleasant for them because they're in the rock business. A pop star somehow seems able to get away with it. I don't know why. Jagger and people like that are still able to get up on the stage and prance about like idiots.

"It's very difficult to write like an enthused child, which is really how rock should be written about all the time. It's very difficult to do that if you don't feel like an enthused child all the time, or if you're not a showman and can't switch it on and off like a light bulb."

A lot of people in my profession, I pointed out, prefer their stars to be noble savages.

"A lot of them **are** like that. I've never been like that, there's always been something missing. At times when I was heavily doped I never got any chicks. At times when I was playing good I never got any chicks—or any dope. You really can't have all three at once unless you're a physical dynamo.

"In the case of Iggy, I think the music suffers. Look at a band like Sweet, for example. They're probably a very straight bunch, dope-wise and wife-wise and god knows what, but I think their music does contain a lot of the tight, integrated, directed, pointed frustration of a fifteen or sixteen year old, although it doesn't quite get there and they're a bit out of place time-wise. They should have been around ten years ago.

"But someone like Iggy and the Stooges couldn't grasp that if they stood on their heads, because inside they're old men. I think that applies to many people. I think in a way that is why the freshest music that you can find at the moment is very, very middle of the road stuff.

"I think that there's a strong argument about whether a journalist's idea of what a pop-star should be really means anything. I think that our album clarifies who the real hero is in this thing.

"It's this kid on the front. He's the hero. That's why he's on the front cover. That's why he's sung about. It's his fuckin' album. Rock and roll's his music.

"It's got nothing to do with journalists, and it hasn't really even got anything to do with musicians."

[PART TWO] WHO'S JIMMY

AND NOW your starter for ten, viewers. See if you can recognise this rap. Are you ready? "Really what I've tried to do in the album is put the band in perspective. Each member of the band obviously thinks that he's God's gift to the music business and to The Who and that the world won't revolve without him. In actual fact, each member of the band is a very small piece of the band, and each member of the band is a very small piece of the boy."

Did you get it? Did you catch the use of the phrase "in actual fact"? Did you notice the mention of The Who? In that case, you have obviously sussed that what you've just read is Pete Townshend discussing "Quadrophenia", the Who's new double album, which, despite any qualms that anybody might have about four-sided rock song-cycles, is actually pretty damn good.

The scene is Pete's gaff in Twickenham, the subject "Quadrophenia", the scope grandeur. We continue.

"I've really had more control over this album than any other Who album we've ever done, from the beginning right through to the very end. I've directed it, if you like, and certainly people in the band have contributed fantastic amounts in roles that they normally wouldn't play.

"John Entwistle's role has been that of a constructive arranging musician, which is something he's never, ever done. On other albums he's worked off his frustrations by writing a couple of songs. Well, on this he's done a fantastic piece of arranging work, sitting in the studio writing out and then dubbing on fifty horn parts.

"So really what has happened is that the music on here is the first album where The Who have used each other's capabilities as musicians to the full. I've used my capabilities as a constructor and composer just to get the thing in shape, and then suddenly you realise when you play it that it's been written with a reason, that there was a driving force behind it."

So what was the first flash that ignited "Quadrophenia"?

"I think the first seed was that I thought that if we couldn't make a film, then, in Frank Zappa terms, I'd like do it myself. I'd like to either buy a camera and direct it myself, or alternatively, do a Frank Zappa thing with a kind of movie without pictures.

"That's where the idea came from, the idea of casting the four guys in the band as four facets of an archetypal mod kid's personality. It's obviously a kind of schizophrenic thing that I can relate to, because I know everybody in the band.

"I was probably more involved in the mod thing than anybody else in the band, and so it started off as a loose script and gradually grew into something where I felt that the characters could be represented musically by themes. Then it became quite a complicated musical task.

"Musically and impressionistically I'm not so hot. I've had to work fantastically hard on this. Lyrics come very easily me, but music is always very tough, and so stuff like "Quadrophenia" and "The Rock" were fuckin' incredibly difficult for me to get together without feeling that I was on a Keith Emerson trip.

"I wanted the music to be solid and really relate, and be emotive without creating a sort of "Big Country" drama. It was very tricky. It hasn't really come off but it's really great to hear it. It's amazing to hear a song like "Can You See The Real Me" followed by "Quadrophenia"."

A SCANNING of the storyline of "Quadrophenia" reveals a suspiciously strong resemblance to that of the "That'll Be The Day" movie, in which Mr Moon distinguished himself. What's the story, Pete?

Faint grimaces. "When I went to see "That'll Be The Day" I got about halfway through to the bit where he was on the beach and then I walked out in complete digust.

"I said to Keith 'You've been making this film all this time. Why couldn't you tell me that the story was very similar?'

"I wasn't irritated by the fact that it was a similar idea. I was irritated because it seems that the British rock public thinks that Brighton Pier, a fairground and Butlins Holiday Camp is all there really is to life.

"I'm a culprit in this respect, since 'Tommy' ends in a holiday camp, but this is how the bloody British mind thinks. Ray Connolly is a few years older than me, and his nostalgia is a different trip. This isn't a direct nostalgic thing, it's more a search for the essence of what makes everything tick. I'm trying to approach the thing and find an answer.

"Brighton Pier features very heavily in this, because of the two big events that I remember really being moved by. One was when we were playing at Brighton Aquarium and I saw about two thousand mod kids, and there were three rockers up against a wall. They'd obviously just come into it thinking that they were going to a party and they really were scared as hell, and the mods were just throwing bottles at them.

"I mean, there's no sort of hero in my eyes in something like that. There's no nostalgia. It just moved me to do something to perhaps make the music elevate people a bit.

"I know it sounds like idealism, but those people who were kicking rockers in on the front would then come in and listen to our music. So I knew then that I had what felt like a certain kind of power. There were all the tough guys looking at me, waiting to hear what I was about to say.

"In this album, the tough kid ends up as the bellboy. Jimmy ends up gaining a fantastic amount from the experience, but also losing a fantastic amount because of loose ends being drawn everywhere.

"The problem with The Who is that if I try to draw more out of their image and their history and out of rock than rock can sustain, you end up with a situation where there's nothing left that hasn't been milked or soiled, any emotion that hasn't been buggered about with, any mountain that hasn't been climbed by some plastic, made-up geezer who climbs to the top and says, 'I've seen God and He's a pig'.

"In the end, the loser is rock because people just look at it and say, 'I'm not interested in this shit any more,' and it becomes empty and it becomes Hollywood and it becomes plastic again.

"Because if the actual people involved can't act out a fierce enough role, then the business, seeing that it's starting to lose money, will invent people. People like Alice Cooper, good as they are, are inventions of a hungry industry. They might think they're real. I know better."

ONCE AGAIN, BACK to specifics. "Quadrophenia" was a long time in the making and a lot of assembly work must have gone into it. Hah?

"The reason why you end up with particularly strong material is that you have learned by past mistakes. I wrote about fifty songs for this and really creamed off the best.

"I had a much, much longer story. We could have made it a quadruple album. There's still a fantastic amount of material which is potentially quite good stuff, but what I really wanted to do was to make the album something that invited you to forget The Who a little bit and make you think about other things.

"So we started off with the sea. It was a big decision to do that, because I knew that people would say, 'Christ almighty, 'ere we are, an epic work.' But I really wanted that because the actual story begins with the kid sitting on a rock. He's gone out to this rock in a boat and he's completely out of his brain.

"You see, it's not really a story as such. There's a big difference between this and something like "Jesus Christ Superstar" or "Tommy". It's not a story, more a series of impressions of memories. The real action in this is that you see a kid on a rock in the middle of the sea and this whole thing explains how he got there.

"This is why I used sound effects: to establish atmosphere. Some of the sound effects I've tried to manipulate impressionistically. It's something that's new to me and I'm not particularly good at it, but I'm glad I did it."

A LARGE AMOUNT of the time that went into "Quadrophenia" was in post-production work.

"It took much, much longer to mix and blend than it did to record the backing tracks. It took about six months to mix. Stuff like "The Rock" and "Quadrophenia" were all recorded here at the house, all John Entwistle's horn parts. Extra synthesiser stuff, guitars, voices, drums and so on were added at the studio."

The Who have never been noted for their ability to make records with any rapidity. Apart from that Stones thing ("The Last Time"/"Under My Thumb"), which took about two days from idea to over-the-counter-sales and is thus the greatest piece of journalistic rock in the history of Western culture, they generally take an awful long time to figure out what they're gonna do and how they're gonna do it. Elucidate, Pete.

"Doing anything with The Who recording-wise always takes a billion years. Always. Dunno why. I mean, we can rehearse a stage-act and do a gig without any effort at all. Eighteen months after last playing together we can still walk on stage and play, but recording is something that we have to re-learn every time we go in.

"I think it's because basically I want the music to embrace more ambitious sounds, and the band is a pretty simple affair. It's bass, guitar, drums and the vocalist, and what happens a lot of the time is that ideas that happen in the studio have to be continually revised before they come to anything.

"Let me put it another way. I think we've been far too tight on ourselves. By that I mean that we've imposed so many rules and regulations on ourselves about what The Who are, what The Who can do, and what The Who can't do, what rock and roll is and what rock and roll isn't, what falls into our category and what doesn't."

A CURIOUS SITUATION thus seems to be emerging. One could put it unkindly and say that The Who were strangling on their own self-consciousness—or rather one could if they hadn't been vindicated by the excellence of "Quadrophenia".

But the problem is very real. What do you do if you're in the semi-fortunate position of being one of the world's premier rock bands, with each album that you issue a major event in its year? Pete Townshend can, one supposes, be forgiven for occasionally getting so wound up his own worries that temporary artistic paralysis sets in.

"I think it's more down to earth. That's why I felt, rightly or wrongly, that I could afford to take more chances with a fairly ambitious package, putting in a synopsis story and the photographs. I feel that I can talk about this thing in a far less guarded way.

"I eventually ended up with a set speech on 'Tommy'. People always used to ask me the same questions. They used to say, for example, 'If Tommy is deaf, dumb and blind, I assume that as a result of the miracle cure he became the Messiah'.

"I really don't think that it's going to happen with this because of a conversation I had with a lawyer from the States. She had to work out the dramatic copyright, which means that you have to present the thing and show that it has dramatic structure so that, although individual songs can be recorded, people can't put out an album called "Quadrophenia" or film it.

"She was trying to pin me down as to what character was saying what at different times. So I said, 'Well, I don't fucking know, the whole point of it is that the geezer's completely mixed up. He doesn't know and I don't know. I've just adopted this frame of mind in written songs'.

"Dr Jimmy and Mr Jim" is more about Mad Moon than anything else. "What is it? I'll take it/Who is she? I'll rape it" . . . that's probably Keith Moon. "I'll take on anyone/ Ain't scared of a bloody nose" . . . that could be me or Roger or anybody.

How about the problem of selling it to people who might not have the chance to hear it first?

"I think we're gonna lose a lot of sales because if people go into a record shop and hear the first track, all they're gonna hear is sea.

"It'll be a tough one, but I'm not really bothered whether mods of that era approve of it. The whole mod detail is really because it's an archetype, and that's what helps to build a character.

"The incredible thing about 'Tommy' is that you could listen to it thousands of times if you're stupid enough, and you still don't know what his clothes are like or what colour his hair is. It could be anybody.

"No, I can understand that consciousness because I'm guilty of it myself. I played the music from this album far, far more when I just had test pressings. When you get the whole package you tend to get into packaging consciousness.

"The reason that it's all grey and black and scruffy is so that it doesn't come on looking all tinsel and glitter. I'd call something like "Who's Next", a fairly straightforward album. I'm certainly not against albums like that. We've got a new "Meaty Beaty" album coming out soon, which is unreleased material drawn from over the years. It'll make fantastic background music."

That seemed to be that for the time being. Back out along the embankment looking forward to the tour.

What you think of "Quadrophenia" is your problem, and whether you buy it or not is Pete's. Anyway, having The Who back and functioning is something of a small blessing.

Now—let's see action.

PETE TOWNSHEND

Roy Carr | May 24, 1975 | *New Musical Express* **(UK)**

This interview given by Townshend to the *NME*'s Roy Carr in May 1975 doesn't seem moti-vated by the necessity to promote anything: Who rarities ragbag *Odds & Sods* had been released a year back, the *Tommy* movie—whose title role was taken by Daltrey and whose soundtrack was supervised by Townshend—had premiered two months previously, and the next Who studio album wouldn't hit the shops for another four months.

    Rather it seems Townshend entertained Carr simply to get off his chest his anguished feelings about the increasing irrelevance of the Who and rock in general. The following year, a group of people who came to be known as punks would start coming out with similar assertions, making very prescient both Townshend's broodings and his repeated references to his song "The Punk and the Godfather." —Ed.

PETE TOWNSHEND didn't die before he got old. Yet death isn't his problem, it's the passing of the years and his current position in what he feels is a younger man's occupation.

"If you're in a group," he begins, "you can behave like a kid—and not only get away with it, but be encouraged."

The name Keith Moon somehow springs to mind.

"If you're a rock musician," Townshend continues, "you don't have to put on any airs and pretend to be all grown up . . . pretend to be—in inverted commas—'normal' or even be asked to behave like you're a mature and a highly responsible person. These are just the trappings that society puts on most people—with the result that most kids are burdened down with responsibilities far too early in their life.

"You know the deal: as soon as you leave school you've got to find a secure job and hang onto it. I wrote 'My Generation' when I was 22 or 23, yet that song breathes of 17-year-old adolescence.

"But then I did have a somewhat late adolescence."

So what are you trying to tell us?

"Personally, I feel that the funniest thing—and also the saddest thing—about the current state of rock 'n' roll is that it's the pretenders that are suffering the most. Those people who, for a number of years, have been pretending to be rock stars and have adopted false poses.

"It's the difference between someone who has made rock an integral part of their lifestyle and therefore doesn't feel like they're growing old.

"You want to know something?

"I really hate feeling too old to be doing what I'm doing.

"I recently went to do a BBC TV interview and when I arrived at the studios there were all these young kids waiting outside for The Bay City Rollers. As I passed them by, one of the kids recognised me and said, 'Ooo look, it's Pete Townshend' and a couple of them chirped 'Ello Pete'. And that was it.

"Yet the first time The Who appeared at those same studios on *Top Of The Pops*, a gang of little girls smashed in the plate glass front door on the building.

"Anyway, as I entered the building, the doorman turned to me and smirked. ''Ere, what's it feel like to walk past 'em now and have nothin' happen, eh?'

"I told him that, to be quite honest, it brings a tear to my eye. Look, I don't want them to mob me because The Who have never been a Rollers-type band, what I'm scared of is hypocrisy."

Hypocrisy? In what way?

"Well, nowadays it's considered very passe to admit that you've got a burning ambition to stand on stage and be screamed at by 15-year-old girls. But when we started out that was something to be very proud of. If it didn't happen, there was something wrong with you.

"Though I haven't all that much experience as to what is happening contemporarily in music, I do feel that 'the-world-owes-me-a-living' attitude still prevails, not only in rock, but in every walk of life. So now everyone's gotta look like they really mean business and every bloody singer I see on *The Old Grey Whistle Test* looks a-n-g-r-y." He breaks off the conversation to pull relevant grimaces. "When I see this I go into hysterical fits of laughter.

"Sure. I know that I look angry when I play but usually there's no reason for it. I suppose it's an adopted aggressive thing, which is in turn a subconscious layover from those days when I *was* angry. I don't quite know what I was angry at, but I *was* angry, frustrated, bitter, cynical—and it came through in the music I wrote."

C'mon Pete, you're either evading the moment of truth or approaching it in a very roundabout manner. What's brought on this manic obsession about being too pooped to pop, too old to stroll?

"It's just that when I'm standing up there on stage playing rock 'n' roll, I often feel that I'm too old for it."

No kidding.

"When Roger speaks out about 'we'll all be rockin' in our wheelchairs' he might be but you won't catch me rockin' in no wheelchair. I don't think it's possible. I might be making music in a wheelchair—maybe even with The Who, but I feel that The Who have got to realise that the things we're gonna be writing and singing about are rapidly changing.

"There's one very important thing that's got to be settled." He pauses again. "The group as whole have got to realise that The Who are *not* the same group as they used to be. They never ever will be and as such . . . it's very easy to knock somebody by saying someone used to be a great runner and can still run but he's Not What He Used To Be." Townshend pauses yet again. "Everybody has a hump and you have to admit that you've got to go over that hump."

Yes we have . . . no we haven't—Townshend won't commit himself either way as to whether The Who are over the hill, but he intimates in no uncertain manner that the group are beset with acute problems.

"You've got to remember that there was a time when suddenly Chuck Berry couldn't write any more. He just went out and performed his greatest hits and I've always wondered what *that* was all down to?

"Jagger told me at his birthday party that he was having difficulty in writing new material for The Stones, which is unfortunate because nowadays so much importance is placed upon writing songs.

"To a degree, you could call it front-man paranoia—and even Roger gets it from time to time. Let's face it, Jagger carries a tremendous amount of responsibility apart from being The Stones front-man.

"Forget about that tired old myth that rock 'n' roll is just making records, pullin' birds, gettin' pissed and having a good time. That's not what it's all about. And I don't think Roger really believes it either. I think that's what he'd really like to believe rock 'n' roll was all about.

"Steve Marriott has chosen to live it like that and, as far as I can see, he's having a good time. Fair enough—but in my opinion Marriott's music falls short of his potential, which is a bloody shame because everyone knows what he's really capable of . . . there's all those old incredible Small Faces records piled up.

"For me, 'Ogden's Nut Gone Flake' is one of the classic albums of the sixties and, if it's the difference between that music and having a good time, I prefer that Steve Marriott suffer, because *I want the music.*

"Believe me, I don't want to sound too cruel and vitriolic, but I do think that you have to face up to the undeniable fact that there's no point in your life when you can stop working.

"You can't suddenly turn round and say, we're on the crest of a wave so now it's time to sit back and boogie. Deep down inside, everyone wants to do this but it's tantamount to retiring altogether. And personally, I can't do it.

"It's not necessarily to do with standards," Townshend continues, before I have time fire another question. "The Who's 'Odds & Sods' collection would have been released even if it hadn't been all that interesting, but it's all been put down in the past for being sub-standard."

Apparently the reason for its release was to make null and void the increasing amount of Who bootlegs currently being circulated, and once a second volume has been prepared and issued, there will be no need to backtrack. "If," says Townshend, "The Who were gonna wave their banner for standards, 'Odds & Sods' would still have remained unreleased. Standards have got absolutely nothing to do with it. I feel that it's the pressure at the front of your mind that . . . not necessarily your fans . . . but then, maybe your fans really are the most important people . . . are actually sitting twiddling their thumbs waiting for your next album.

"Every time they wait, they become more and more impatient. What Jagger said in that interview that he did with NME is that between the albums they are eagerly waiting for, he'd like to chuck out an R&B set to keep 'em happy. Fair enough if he thinks it'll make any difference—but of course it won't.

"It's just like making a 'live' album. The fans will say 'Thank you very much', but what we're really waiting for is the next studio album, so get on with it."

PHEWHATASCORCHA!

New subject: Townshend was once quoted as stating that the eventual outcome of any Who recording depended entirely upon whether or not he could keep Moon away from the brandy and himself from imbibing whatever it took him to get through a session.

"At the moment, what governs the speed of The Who is the diversification of individual interests. We would have been recording the new album much earlier were it not for the fact that Roger is making another film with Ken Russell.

"Roger chose to make the film and John wanted to tour with his own band The Ox, so I've been working on tracks for my next solo album. Invariably what will happen is that once we all get into the studio, I'll think 'Oh fuck it', and I'll play Roger, John and Keith the tracks I've been keeping for my own album and they'll pick the best. So as long as The Who exists, I'll never get the pick of my own material . . . and that's what I dream of.

"But if The Who ever broke up because the material was sub-standard then I'd really kick myself."

But the way you're going on, Peter, old Meter, it sounds like The Who is on it's last legs?

"However much of a bastard it is to get everyone together in a recording studio, things eventually turn out right. You see, though it has never been important in the past, we do have this problem that everyone has been engaged on their own project, so that the separate social existence that we lead has become even more acute.

"I mean, if I just couldn't live without Moonie and if I could go over to the States and spend a couple of months with him we'd probably be a lot closer. But as it happens, I haven't seen Keith since last August. I may have seen a lot more of John but as yet I haven't seen his new group *or* listened properly to his album because, apart from working on 'Tommy', I've been putting together new material.

"And the same thing applies Roger: as soon as someone decides to do something outside of the area of The Who the pressure suddenly ceases, because they are the people who put the pressures on me.

"Let me make this clear. I don't put pressures on them. I don't say 'we've got to get into the studio this very minute because I've got these songs that I've just gotta get off my chest.' It's always the other way around. They always rush up to me and insist that we've got to cut a new album and get back on the road."

So it's quite obvious that the pressures are back on and Townshend is feeling the strain.

"In a sense, rock is an athletic process. I don't mean running about on stage, but as a communicative process it's completely exhausting. It's not necessarily being a part of things," insists Townshend.

"Like I said, when I wrote "My Generation' I was already in my early twenties, so I was by no means a frustrated teenager. And that's what a lot of people often tend to forget."

But you were an integral part of that generation?

"Right," he retorts, "but we're also part of the Generation that we play to on stage today.

"Let me clarify that statement."

Yes!

"What I *don't* feel part of is not the Generation of age, but the Generation of type. I mean, who the hell were all those people at the 'Tommy' premier? Whoever they were, I'm certainly not in *their* gang!

"Yet funnily enough, whatever the age group, I feel much more at ease before a rock audience."

So why this current fixation about being too old to cut le Moutard?

"Because to some extent The Who have become a golden old-ies band and that's the bloody problem. And it's the problem that faces all successful rock groups at one time or another—the process of growing old.

"A group like The Kinks don't have that problem because, theo-retically, Ray Davies has always been an old man. He writes like an old man who is forever looking back on his life and, thank heavens, old Ray won't have to contend with such problems. But with group like The Roll-ing Stones, there's this terrible danger . . . now I could be wrong . . . but there's no question in my mind that it's bound to happen . . . Mick Jagger will eventually become the Chuck Berry of the sixties, constantly parody-ing himself on stage. And, this is the inherent danger that The Who are so desperately trying avoid.

"I can tell you that when we were gigging in this country at the early part of last year I was thoroughly depressed. I honestly felt that The Who were going on stage every night and, for the sake of the die-hard fans, copying what The Who used to be.

"Believe me, there have been times in The Who's career when I would have gladly relinquished the responsibilities of coming up with our next single or album to another writer. There've been a lot of people who said they would have a go but somehow it never quite worked out."

Why?

"Like a lot of things connected with The Who, I really dunno. Maybe it's because we've got such an archetypal style that's geared to the way that I write."

BUT BY HIS own admission, Pete Townshend has always considered his forte to be writing. The fact that he also happens to be a guitarist is, in his opinion, quite irrelevant. Yet even now, Townshend is astounded when other guitarists compliment him upon his instrumental prowess. He isn't bowing to false modesty when he insists that, after all these years, he still can't play guitar as he would really like to.

In his formative years with The Who, he compensated for his acute frustrations by concentrating his energies on the visual aspects of attacking the instrument. Every time he went on stage, Townshend insists he bluffed his way through a set by utilising noise and sound effects which eventually led to the destruction of many a valuable weapon.

"It's still true even today," he confesses without embarrassment. "I may be a better guitarist now than I was when The Who first started but I'm far from being as technically proficient as I would really like to be.

"What I like about the way that I play," he explains, "is what I think everyone else likes. I get a particular sound that nobody else quite gets and I play rhythm like nobody else plays—it's a very cutting rhythm style. Sorta Captain Powerchords!

"I do like to have a bash every now and then at a wailing guitar solo but halfway through I usually fall off the end of the fretboard. I might have a go, but I've resigned myself to the fact that I haven't got what it takes to be a guitar hero.

"Yet funnily enough I don't really respect that kind of guitar playing. I've got no great shakes for Jeff Beck or Jimmy Page. Sure, I love what they do, but it always seems to me that they're like the Yehudi Menuhins of the rock business. They're extremely good at what they do, but I'm sure they'd give their right arm to be writers—though not necessarily in my shoes.

"I don't really feel the showmanship side of my contribution to The Who's stage show is fundamentally a part of my personality. It's something that automatically happens.

"Basically, it stems from the very early days when we had to learn to sell ourselves to the public—otherwise nobody would have taken a blind bit of notice of us; and, like many things, it's been carried on through up until today. Yet I have no doubt that, if we wanted to, we could walk on any stage and stand there without doing all those visual things and still go down well with an audience."

So why this depressing down-in-the-mouth attitude. Could it stem, I ask Townshend, from the fact that a critic once bemoaned that, in his opinion, The Who, once the true essence of rock 'n' roll, now just go through the motions.

"Well, that statement was true—but on the other hand if it's unqualified then it might as well be ditched. But you've put the question to me and now I've got to try and qualify that other journalist's statement.

"To me, the success of any truly great rock song is related to the fact that people who couldn't really communicate in normal ways can quite easily communicate through the mutual enjoyment of rock music. And that was simply because, for them, it was infinitely more charismatic than anything else around at that time.

"For example, you're aware that there's this great wall around adolescence and that they can't talk freely about their problems because it's far too embarrassing. Personally, I feel that adolescence lasts much longer than most people realise. What happens is, that people find ways of getting round it and putting on a better show in public. And as they get older they become more confident and find their niche.

"Now why I think that journalist said The Who now only play rock 'n' roll is because on most levels rock has become a spectator sport. It's not so important as a method of expression as it once was. Today something else could quite easily replace it."

Townshend goes on to concede that rock doesn't hold as much genuine mystique as it did with previous generations to the extent that the stigma of the social outlaw has almost been eradicated. Those who have tried to become outlaws have failed miserably, hence the last-ditch shock tactics of Alice Cooper and David Bowie.

"For many kids, rock 'n' roll means absolutely nothing." He compares it to switching on a television set, going to the movies or a football match. It's just another form of entertainment.

"If what the kids do listen to consists entirely of The Bay City Rollers and the Top 10 then it must mean even less than most other similar forms of mass media entertainment because they're not really listening.

"The real truth as I see it is that rock music as it was is not really contemporary to these times. It's really the music of yesteryear. The only things that continue to keep abreast of the times are those songs that stand out due to their simplicity".

An example?

" 'My Generation'. A lot of people don't understand that there's a big difference between what kids want on stage in relationship to what they actually go out and buy on record.

"Perhaps the reason why so many young kids can still get into The Who in concert is simply because it's a very zesty, athletic performance. However, if we just restricted our gigs to performing songs we'd just written yesterday and ignored all the old material then I'm positive that we'd really narrow down our audience tremendously.

"I dunno what's happening sometimes," he bemoans. "All I know is that when we last played Madison Square Garden I felt acute shades of nostalgia. All The Who freaks had crowded around the front of the stage and when I gazed out into the audience all I could see were those very same sad faces that I'd seen at every New York Who gig. There was about a thousand of 'em and they turned up for every bloody show at the Garden, as if it were some Big Event—The Who triumph over New York. It was like some bi-centennial celebration and *they* were there to share in the glory of it all.

"*They* hadn't come to watch The Who, but to let everyone know that *they* were the original Who fans. *They* had followed us from the very beginning of 'cause it was *their* night.

"It was dreadful," Townshend recollects in disgust. "They were telling us what to play. Every time I tried to make an announcement they all yelled out 'Shhhrrruppp Townshend and let Entwistle play 'Boris The Spider", and, if that wasn't bad enough, during the other songs they'd all start chanting jump . . . jump . . . jump . . . jump . . . jump'.

"I was so brought down by it all! I mean, is this what it had all degenerated into?

"To be honest, the highest I've been on stage last year was when we used to play 'Drowned'. That was only because there was some nice guitar work in it . . . Roger liked singing it and both John and Keith played together so superbly. Really, that was the only time I felt that I could take off and fly."

PETE TOWNSHEND may well have some cause to feel sorry for himself; when the final reckoning comes he's got a lot to answer for—in particular, the Curse Of The Concept Album.

Though concept albums are by no means new to popular music—Gordon Jenkins and Mel Torme were churning 'em out almost a quarter of a century ago—it was "Tommy" (as opposed to "Sgt. Pepper") which unleashed a deluge of albums built around one specific theme. These ranged from The Fudge's horrendous "The Beat Goes On" through to J. Tull's obscure "Passion Play" up to and including Rick Wakeman's Disneyesque "King Arthur".

"None of which," says Townshend, as he bursts into laughter, "work."

Yet as we all know, Townshend himself has had no less than three stabs at the same subject. So how does he view the trilogy in retrospect?

"I don't. And if you're going to ask me which one I prefer, I don't really like any of them very much. I suppose I still like bits of The Who's original version but, the definitive 'Tommy' album is still in my head."

Perhaps it would be wise to quit this line of questioning and leave Tommy where he is. But Townshend wants the last word.

"I think that everyone in rock shares the same basic urges, and therefore, that it would be very unfair to me to say it's alright for The 'Oo 'cause we invented it. I have great doubts about that.

"For instance, when the Big Feedback Controversy was going on in the mid-sixties, Dave Davies and I used to have hilarious arguments about who was the first to invent feedback.

"I used to pull Dave's leg by saying 'we both supported The Beatles in Blackpool and you weren't doing it then . . . I bet you nicked it off me when you saw me doing it'. And Dave would scream that he was doing it long before that. Then one day I read this incredible story about Jeff Beck in which he said"—at this juncture, he adopts a retarded Python-esque android accent—"'Yeah, Townshend came down t'see d'Tridents rehearsing and he saw me using the feedback'. . . pause . . . 'and copied it'." Returning to his natural voice, Townshend scowls, "I never ever saw the Tridents and the man is pathetic.

"Obviously, Beck may feel deeply enough that he invented feedback—but for Chrissakes who gives a shit? Why even comment on it? It doesn't really matter, it's just a funny noise made by a guitar."

Townshend goes on to explain that the innovatory part of rock is not necessarily the part that he's proud of, even though he's regarded as The Who's ideas man. "I was trained in graphic design . . . to be an ideas man . . . to think up something new and different . . . like, let's give a lemon away with the next album!"

Thank you.

"In the early days of The Who we were tagged with gimmicks and subsequently it made me very gimmick-conscious.

"Now if I might return to 'Tommy' for a moment . . ."

But only for a moment.

". . . What I think is good about 'Tommy' is *not* that it's a rock opera or that it's the first or the last . . . that's of course, if you assume that there's gonna be any more!!"

Don't worry, there will be: Have a copy of Camel's "Snow Goose".

"What I feel is very important about 'Tommy' that as a band it was our first conscious departure out of the adolescent area. It was our first attempt at something that wasn't the same old pilled-up adolescent brand music. We'd finished with that and we didn't know which way to go. That's when we went through that very funny period of 'Happy Jack' and 'Dogs'.

"It was also a very terrifying period for me as The Who's only ideas man. For instance, though 'I Can See For Miles' was released after 'Happy Jack', I'd written it in 1966 but had kept it in the can for ages because it was going to be The Who's ace-in-the-hole.

"If you want the truth . . ."

And nothin' but . . .

"I really got lost after 'Happy Jack' and then when 'I Can See For Miles' bombed-out in Britain, I thought 'What the hell am I gonna do now?' The pressures were really on me and I had to come up with something very quick and that's how 'Tommy' emerged from a few rough ideas I'd been messing about with."

AND whereas The Beatles had cried that it was impossible to perform "Pepper" in public, the fact that The Who demonstrated that "Tommy" was an ideal stage presentation quickly motivated other bands to mobilise their might for the New Aquarian Age.

With more sophisticated electronic weaponry than they knew how to utilise, the likes of Floyd, Yes, and ELP adopted a more "profound" stance as, in a blaze of strobes, they began to bombard audiences with techno-flash wizardry, pseudo-mystical jargon and interchangeable concepts.

Townshend may have had a helping hand in starting the whole schmear rolling (it sure didn't rock), but he is adamant in his belief that many alleged "profound" music machines are working a clever con-trick on the public.

"All that they're really doing is getting together and working out the most complex ideas they can handle, packaging it with pretentious marketing appeal and unloading it on their fans.

"But"—and here comes the get-out clause—"does everything *have* to hold water? Obviously, it must mean something to the integrity of the band that's putting it together, but it's results that count."

Well the result, as Townshend puts it, has turned many a rock theatre into a dormitory.

"It might be difficult to fall asleep at a Who gig but, I can understand why some bands send their audiences into a coma.

"I don't like Yes at all.

"I used to like them when Peter Banks was in the line-up, because, apart from being extremely visual, he also played excellent guitar. With so many changes in the line-up, Yes is Jon Anderson's band and he might be guilty of much of that wishy-washy stuff they churn out—because Jon really is a tremendous romantic. Maybe he believes in the old mystical work, and maybe poetry moves him along—but I'm not concerned either way."

Just wait until the letters come pouring in.

"It's like that line in 'Punk and The Godfather' . . . 'you paid me to do the dancing.' The kids pay us for a good time, yet nowadays people don't really want to get involved. Audiences are very much like the kids in Tommy's Holiday Camp, they want something without working for it.

"That wasn't the way it used to be.

"The enthusiasm that evolved around The Beatles was *enthusiasm* as opposed to energy generated by The Beatles.

"You talk to them now about it and they don't know what happened! It was the kids' enthusiasm for *them*. Now when you see it happening again you can see how utterly strange it must have seemed the first time around.

"For instance, take the amount of energy and enthusiasm that's currently expended on, say, Gary Glitter . . . and Gary's just as confused as everyone else. All he knows is which curler to put on which side of his head—Gary readily admits this, and is all the better for it.

"Get in the middle of a crowd of screamin' kids—it doesn't matter who they're screamin' at—and there's a certain amount of charisma transferred to these people. But then, that's what fan-mania is really all about.

"When the real charismatic figures like Mick Jagger came along, then I think that rock started to change and *then the* kids began to create their own trends in fashion. The Mods not only used to design their own clothes but sometimes actually to make them; and the fact that they did hum-drum jobs to get money to buy clothes, scooters, records and go to clubs built this elite. Therefore it wasn't too long before the artists let that rub off onto them and in that sense, I think The Who were as guilty as anybody else.

"And I'll tell you why.

"Because in the end we wanted the audiences to turn up to see only us as opposed to the audience being the show and struttin' about like peacocks. We had to be the only reason for them turning up at a Who gig".

With rock and its peripheral interests having been systematically turned into a multi-million pound consumer industry, Townshend has observed that the customer no longer dictates youth fashion. That's all down to some designer employed by a multiple chain store.

"Everything nowadays is premeditated. Within days the whole country is flooded with what someone thinks the kids want."

He believes that the only invigorating youth movement in this country appears to be centred around Wigan's Northern Soul Scene.

"I wish that would spread more than it has, because I see it as a direct link with the Mod thing. But what is more important is that it's more philosophical in its attitude about not fighting and not boozing and not smoking. Even though they're ephemeral things they are nevertheless states of mind which are Very Good Things.

"Like the early Mod thing, this Northern Soul Scene has a fashionable aspect connected with it, but basically it's concerned with the exact opposite to the Mod preoccupation with getting pilled-up and fighting.

"Funnily enough, I'm still not certain why the original Mod movement was so obsessed with aggro. All I know is that at that time I felt an incredible amount of frustration and bitterness towards society and maybe everyone else felt the same."

BUT even as far back as 1968, The Who were somewhat trapped by their own image, when Townshend stated that the thing that had impressed him most was the Mod movement. He had been fired by the excitement of witnessing and subsequently taking an active part in what he felt was the first time in history that youth had made a concerted move towards unity of thought and drive and motive. "It was almost surreal" was how he was quoted at the time.

Somewhere at the turn of the sixties, the youth movement was derailed. Talk of a promised land and the eventual greening of America became suffocated as the consumer industry once again took command. and the Business in showbusiness grabbed the spoils.

When Townshend looks back in time, he can't help but laugh. "I don't think they were promises, I think it was just young people promising themselves something . . . having ambitions to do something . . . and, if you like, certain rock people were acting as spokesmen. So they are the convenient people to blame. That's if you want to lay the blame at anyone's feet.

"Basically, everyone had this mood that something was happening . . . something was changing. In essence it did, but unfortunately a lot of its impetus was carried off by the drug obsession. Everybody credited everything innovative and exciting to drugs . . . 'yeah man, it's pot and leapers and LSD, that's what makes the world great'.

"Then when things turned out to be meaningless and people had missed the bus, they quickly realised that they'd gambled everything on something that had run away. The same thing happened to rock. Rock got very excited and flew ahead leaving most of its audience behind. The Who went on to do what I feel to be some very brave and courageous things, but in the end the audience was a bit apathetic.

"It was back to what I wrote in 'Punk And The Godfather'—you paid me to do the dancing. That's why when I'm on stage I sometimes feel that I'm old to be what I'm doing."

Then, by way of contrast . . .

"Track by track, the new album that The Who are making is going to be the best thing we've ever done. But if people expect another grandiose epic then they ain't gonna get it. 'Cause this time we're going for a superb single album". Townshend, make your mind up, squire. If the last couple of hours are anything to go by, you're either—by your own admission—past it, or you're just after a bit of public feedback.

Ouch. Better not mention that word.

WHO'S LAST?

Tony Stewart | August 9, 1975 | *New Musical Express* (UK)

One of the more surprising things about Roger Daltrey is that such an assertive individual should have taken such a limited role within the Who. The former lead guitarist of Who-precursor the Detours voluntarily became merely the vocalist of the Who, removing the possibility of being part of the musical dialogue engaged in by his three colleagues and—whatever his considerable front man abilities—making himself seem creatively lesser, even dispensable, in the process.

This 1975 *NME* interview was granted to publicize his second solo album, *Ride a Rock Horse*, but is also used by Daltrey—with no little prompting from his interlocutor—as a riposte to Townshend's eyebrow-raising comments on the band in the same paper a few months previously. Daltrey states that he doesn't mind being "just" a singer, but his comments about being laughed at and marginalized by his colleagues suggest a more complicated reality. —Ed.

JUST HOW DO YOU conduct yourself when interviewing a man who's destined to become A Living Legend?

Do you ensure your shoe laces are tied, your hair's neatly brushed and that your breath smells sweetly? And then humbly sit opposite your subject, dutifully silent as you wait to hear his proclamations?

Or perhaps you just take along a bucket and spade in case the Centaur—as his latest album sleeve depicts him—craps on the rug.

After all, this is how Polydor are promoting Roger Daltrey.

The Centaur photograph exploits all the romanticism of Greek Mythology to intimate Daltrey *is* A Living Legend, as well as incorporating the sexual blatancy of the classic Satyr—the lustful beast which is reputed to be part man, part goat. But moulding the hindquarters of a goat onto Daltrey's fine torso would project a considerably less virile image than those of a stallion.

Look at the shot closely, and you'll see my (or his) point.

"It's nothing to do with me mate," Daltry asserts. "I can never consider that. I wish I could become Charlie Bloggs. I'm pissed off with it, because I feel it's not me. I'm not A Living Legend. A lot of old bollocks. It's all half-truths and I don't really want to be associated with that kind of thing.

"I don't really want to be A Pop Star, believe it or not. I'd like to have successful records, but that's it. And I'd very much like never to do any more interviews or anything."

Gee thanks, Roger.

"Well, you know, the *occasional* one. I suppose it's the price you have to pay."

Yes. But Roger also has an ulterior motive in talking to us, and that's to answer Pete Townshend's attack on The Who, carried in a recent NME article.

Stick around because the dirt flies like a sand storm.

SOMEHOW THOUGH, you just can't come to terms with Daltrey's new image. Here he is, in the Goldhawk Record company offices in London, sandwiched into a comfy chair between a filing cabinet and a stack of audio equipment, taking large hungry bites out of a pear, causing juice to trickle down his chin, the flow of which increases as he tries to talk with his mouth full.

His moods change faster than a streetful of Belisha beacons, going from Sullen to Friendly, and from Aggressive to Rationally Polite. And invariably he'll laugh at his own moods, throwing his head back and roaring like a triumphant bar-room brawler.

You could describe him as an earthy streetboy.

The interview, though, comes at an appropriate juncture. Sessions for the new Who album, "The Who By Numbers", have just finished, and after our rap Daltrey will go off to hear the final mixes.

"I'm really pleased with it," he says, chewing on the pear. "One song particularly, called 'Imaginary Man' I think is the best song Pete's ever written. There's a few mysteries in there, but it'll be a good album.

"The shape and form of it is similar to 'Who's Next' with a lot of varied material unlike 'Quadrophenia' which was really one vein. But I don't know what it's going to do, because I don't know what people are expecting.

"I think it's going to be *surprising*.

"There's not been a lot of style change at all. How can we? Moon still plays like Moon, John still plays like John, Pete still plays like Pete, and I still sing like me.

"The only time that we really change is after extensive touring, never when we're in the studio."

Yet the conversation doesn't dwell on the album for long, as it's quite apparent Daltrey wishes to discuss another topic. Like the Townshend feature.

"I never read such a load of bullshit in all my life," he comments, angrily. "To be perfectly honest, it really took a lot of my Who energy out reading that. Because I don't feel that way about The Who, about our audiences or anything in that way.

"It was an unbelievably down interview. And I still haven't come out of it properly yet.

"I've talked to fans," he continues, "and I think Townshend lost a lot of respect from that article. He's talked himself up his own ass. And there are quite a lot of disillusioned and disenchanted kids about now."

(In fact the tone of Townshend's rap was itself disillusioned. He was highly critical of the band as a working unit, their audience and even of their future. In his introduction to the piece Roy Carr admirably precised the prevalent attitude the Axe man expressed.

"Pete Townshend didn't die before he got old. Yet death isn't his problem, it's the passing of the years and his current position in what he feels is a younger man's occupation".

But that's not 32-year-old Daltrey's chief beef about the article. "My main criticism," he elaborates, "was the generalisation of saying the Who were bad. The Who *weren't* bad. I think we've had a few gigs where Townshend was bad . . . and I'll go on record as saying that.

"I think we had a few gigs where under normal circumstances we could have waltzed it. We could have done Madison Square Gardens with our eyes closed, only the group was running on three cylinders. Especially the last night.

"You *don't* generalise and say the Who was bad," he stresses, his rage stronger now. "Because The Who wasn't bad. Wasn't quite as good as we could have been, but it was because Townshend was in a bad frame of mind about what he wanted to do. And *he* didn't play well.

"Sure, we all have our off nights. But *don't* go round saying the Who was bad."

Did Pete sound like a Rock And Roll Martyr to you?

"Yes. Very much.

"You're putting words in me mouth, ain't ya?" He laughs.

Well sure. But only if there's room with the pear.

"Right. That's the impression I got. And it riles me when he generalises it to say the Who weren't playing well. The Who can play as well as they ever did, if we can get down to it and take it for what it is. He's just trying to make the Who something it isn't.

"I can understand his musical frustration," he continues. "He must be so far ahead now with just writing songs for The Who. But surely if The Who isn't a vehicle to get those frustrations out he should find another vehicle.

"But use the Who for what it is. A good rock 'n' roll band, that's all. And one that *was* progressing."

Was?

"I say *was* because we haven't done anything for such a long time. Hopefully when we get back on the road we'll still progress. But if we have any more statements like that I don't see how we can. Cos I know it's taken a lot of steam out of me and I'm sure it did with the others."

But Roger you said *was progressing*, which strikes me as a rather strange comment to make just as you complete a new album.

"I'm just talking about the road side of it," he clarifies.

"I mean, we are still progressing. We're never really The Who in the studio. That's one of the difficulties getting records made with the band. There was a lot wrong, but we rectified it on this album. We all got stuck in and made a record.

"But there's not a lot of room for a group because it's becoming more and more dominated by Pete. It's very hard to make a group contribution outside of what you actually do in the band. Outside of me just singing, for instance.

"John seems to do alright at it—but every suggestion I make I just get laughed at.

"But I can live with that. I don't care if I'm just the singer anyway."

ON THIS POINT, though, it was Townshend who complained he had to bear too much responsibility for The Who. There was, he bemoaned, too much pressure on him.

"There's all sorts of problems going down at the moment that have got bugger all to do with the music side of it," counters Daltrey, "which is usually lumped on my bloody shoulders. But I don't ever complain about it.

"I agree that because he's been the mainstay songwriter of the band he's obviously going to be under that pressure. But I think he enjoys that. As far as going on the road goes I don't think he's under any more pressure than any of us, really."

Townshend's argument—just to refresh your memories—was also that because the other three guys heavied him into the studio any songs he'd written for a solo album would be snapped up by them. And inadvertently he seemed to be moaning about the fact that Daltrey, Entwistle and Moon could work solo—but that he never saw his own efforts come to fruition—because of The Who.

Daltrey does feel it would be a good thing for Townshend if he did record a solo album, but denies it was impossible because of The Who situation. "You see, I think if he made a solo album he would get some of the musical frustrations out which he can't accomplish with The Who. Because he can do fucking incredible stuff that The Who'll *never* do. They just haven't got that sort of scope.

"That's why solo LPs are nice to do. They let your head run riot for a while.

"And I don't see why he couldn't have done his own album before this Who set, because I can't see this one getting released for ages because we've got so many problems, outside of just the music. Then The Who would have had second choice.

"And I don't see it would have hurt The Who."

"I think we needed this year break. We need to sort certain things out. Like, two months ago it looked as though we weren't ever going to record again—and now at least we've made another record. And I really want to get back on the road.

"I just don't feel I'm in group unless we're playing on the road. It feels like you're just another session man."

He pauses, having said his piece.

"Want a cup of tea?" he inquires politely.

SNIPPETS OF Daltrey's rap keep flashing up on the brain's screen like trailers at the cinema. And it could just be possible that's yet to come.

At intervals he's made oblique, but apparent, references to some kind of internal problems other than musical that are having a detrimental effect on The Who's well-being.

Something seems greatly amiss.

But as the mugs of tea are handed round—and you'll be glad to know Centaurs *do* have sweet teeth, because Daltrey started to crunch sugar cubes.—Roger seems reticent to divulge the relevant information.

"There's just certain things going down at the moment," he does proffer, not particularly helpfully. "You'll probably hear the whole story in about two month's time."

Can't we hear it now?

"I can't. There's a lot of litigation going on between our record company and our management and everything else."

A clue. But not exactly a scoop.

With a little gently prodding he does, however, begin to open up, revealing in unguarded terms there is, er, disagreement between the Who and their management.

"If we were free now to do what we wanted to do we'd have our record out in the first week of October and we would be touring England in the third week of October and the first week of November. And we'd be off to the States in the second week of November, then back here for some Christmas shows." He comes out with series of anecdotes which, due to the laws of libel, I can't repeat. Worse luck.

"If the record doesn't come out I don't know what's going to happen.

"We could still tour—but we wouldn't tour with a new act because it's hopeless trying to play people unfamiliar material. It's like, the *worst* thing any band can do. Even if it's vaguely familiar. Like Elton John at Wembley playing 'Captain Fantastic'.

"It didn't work.

"I wouldn't mind touring with the old stuff. But that's what it'll have to be."

Any dates pencilled in?

"There are, but I can't even talk about them because it's so vague at the moment.

"Maybe it will sort itself out and it'll go ahead, but I can't really see it somehow. It's probably gonna be December before we actually get on the road. The way things are going, and the lack of decisions and various things."

Christ. Some Main Feature, huh?

GOING BACK to That Townshend Feature—and considering all Daltrey has just said—it does seem somewhat unfair Peter Meter should blame Daltrey's involvement in "Lisztomania" for holding up the recording of the new album. Which he did.

"Obviously he doesn't want to talk about these other problems in the Press," suggested Roger quite rationally. "I do it reluctantly, but I suppose it's got to come out at one time.

"I can see if it does happen then I'm gonna come out as The McCartney Of The Piece. But there again, what do you do? You can't live on lies forever. But the last thing in the world I want to do is break The Who up. Anything I can do stop that happening . . . I'll do.

"Now The Who have acted." (Daltrey's referring to the legals). "But I don't know how long I could have gone on without them acting. I really don't.

"If the legal hassles hadn't been going on, yeah, then Liszt would have held up The Who recording for three months. Which isn't a long time.

"I know it was a drag for The Who, and I don't ever really want it to happen again. But there was nothing I could have done about it.

"As it's worked out, it didn't really matter anyway."

Perhaps at this stage it'd useful to clarify one or two other matters with so many insinuations whizzing around. Roger, how important is The Who to you then?

"Obviously very important," he responds immediately. "I mean it's part of me life, and it's the last ten years of me life.

"I can accept the fact now it's not going to go on forever. That's for sure. You do start to see the boundaries. But I just don't ever want to give up.

"The Who comes before anything really. It didn't come before Liszt but it was a group thing. I said, 'What do I do?'

"I think Liszt will do The Who good as well. That's one of the main things in my mind about it, because people—especially in the States—are gonna start thinking I'm Tommy. And I'm *not* Tommy. I don't think 'Tommy' is—The Who's best piece of work.

"Liszt is a quick way of showing people that I ain't Tommy. Which is, at least, a start in destroying that whole 'Tommy' stigma."

But again, when discussing his career in the movies, Daltrey is prone to relate it to his musical pursuits and his role with The Who. For instance, working with Russell, he says, has given him a better understanding of PT's song writing. "Ken is very similar to Pete," he explains. "He's very visual and thinks all the time. But unlike Pete I can talk to Ken. And he'll explain how he sees a situation to me, and I've got a terrific rapport with him.

"Unfortunately me and Pete have never actually got on, on that level. But I find now it's not important, because just working with Ken so much has taught me a lot about getting into things in the way I think you should.

"It's given me a lot more confidence.

"If you can't communicate on a talking level with someone, and you just go on feelings, and he's given you a sheet of lyrics and you've got a demo to work with, then you need quite a lot of confidence."

AT THIS POINT, however, Daltrey is understating his turbulent relationship with Townshend because, as our conversation unfolds—covering The Who's music and the sheer aggression and frustration it incorporates—it's necessary for Roger to explain why this should be such an overt facet. And in doing so he reveals considerably more about the personality structure of the band.

"It's probably because we're so different," he says, "and don't particularly get on that well outside the band. I don't want to be in a group with anybody else, although if I could choose three friends to go about with it wouldn't be those three.

"It's a very weird situation, but it does lead to frustration. But it's always worked because it's led to creating something."

And also led, it should be noted, to fights. On occasion.

"Yes. On occasion." Agrees Daltrey.

Well, your knuckles aren't bruised so the recording sessions must have gone well.

"Look!" He cries, laughing, and holding up his right fist. "Look at that!"

He displays one severely swollen and purple set of knuckles.

"No, no, no. We didn't have any fights at all," he points out. "That's a mosquito bite. Believe it or not."

A likely story.

"No. We didn't have any fights this time. We had fights in 'Quadrophenia'."

Tell us more.

"I've only ever had one fight with Pete and that was during 'Quadrophenia'. It was a bit of a shame because it was a non-argument, and the last thing I wanted to do in the world was to have a fist fight with Pete Townshend.

"Unfortunately", he adds petulantly, "he hit me first with a guitar. I really felt terrible about it afterwards. What can you say? Pete should never try and be a fighter.

"But when he was being held back by two roadies and he's spitting at me, calling me a dirty little cunt and hitting me with his guitar I become quite angry. And I was forced to lay one on him. But it was only one."

That was sufficient?

"Well," he roars with laughter, "when he came out of hospital . . ."

But according to Daltrey there has always been a clash between him and Townshend—with Entwistle and Moon as mediators. And perhaps for this reason Daltrey is able to contend with being laughed at in the studio when he makes suggestions.

"Like I say," he explains, "I can put up with being *just* the singer. It doesn't really bother me that much. It's just one of those things that make you feel—what's the word?—makes you feel a bit of a misfit.

"But I've always felt a bit of a misfit in the Who. That's another reason why solo things are good for me."

Cue. Change of reel, and subject.

Everything seemed to be going well for Roger Daltrey, solo artiste.

He's now grabbed himself a prestigious slice of the Movie Biz by doing the films "Tommy" and "Lisztomania"—with another, of which he'll reveal nothing except he has to have his hair cropped, on the starting blocks.

Even his solo-singing career had an auspicious debut, with the excellent "Daltrey" album, "Ride A Rock Horse", however, isn't too good.

The vocal performance is good, the musicianship is good, OK, but the material just doesn't have that stamp of quality.

And to date, business has not been brisk with the set, which is certainly not the kind of sequel one would expect (either artistically or sales-wise) following his first album.

"I'm pleased with it," comments Roger. "I like it. But then I'm bound to, ain't I?

"It is a very American kind of album and it's not particularly the English people's taste. But that was intentional. I aimed it at America.

"Maybe I aimed it too much at America."

Perhaps, though, Daltrey, who as a prominent British vocalist would have the world's established writers scrambling over each others' backs to get him to use their songs, has taken even more of a chance with the material than he did with the first set. Once again, he's used unestablished writers (like Leo Sayer was).

"I know it's a gamble and maybe this time it hasn't paid off, but I'm gonna carry on doing it.

"It's just that I get so many kids coming to with songs—and they're not all good—but occasionally you get the good ones, and I think it's worth taking a gamble. Maybe I've picked the wrong numbers this time . . . I don't know. Obviously I haven't in America. It's in at 60 this week.

"With a bullet.

"So my judgement's right somewhere.

"I just remember the days when I would have done anything for a helping hand. If I can help somebody who can't get a look in else-where . . . then it's a valid thing to do."

Not, I wouldn't have thought, if the album bombed, along with Dal-trey's sole reputation.

Polydor (who can improve your image as Charles Atlas helped build your body) do seem to be putting the big promo wheels in motion. This when discussed, moves onto Roger's own reluctance to be drawn into the area which he describes as "poshlust".

"But that's the business, I suppose," he remarks mildly. "I don't sup-pose kids want to buy records wrapped up in paper bags. They want a bit of glamour.

"You do need your Jaggers and Rod Stewarts, but they're trying to make me into one, and I'm not. And I never will be."

Just why is he in the business in the first place then?

You guessed it. "Cos I sings in a band called the 'Oo and I likes it. And That Is It."

But according to Townshend (in That Feature), Daltrey would like to believe rock and roll was "making records, pullin' birds, getting pissed and having a good time."

"That" retorts Daltrey disgustedly, "just shows he doesn't understand me at all. Because that proportion of my life which is devoted to that kind of living is such a minimal proportion. If he thinks that's what rock and roll is to me he must be kidding.

"Just coz I don't live in a studio like he does doesn't mean to say I don't like rock and roll much."

He pauses.

"There's a terrible battle going on between me and him, ain't there?"

In fact you could say this last quote of Townshend's proves to weigh heavily on Daltrey's mind. It isn't until near the end of the interview when he decides to elaborate on [t]he point.

"I'm just thinking about what he said," he said. "That I'd like to believe that rock and roll was birds, booze and fun. The naivete of that is that [t]he last few bad gigs the Who did were, in my opinion—apart from his head trip—bad because they were physically out boozing and balling all night. And by the time it got to the show at night they were *physically incapable of doing a good show.*

"So . . . put that in your pipe and smoke it.

Was that all of you?

"No. That was Townshend. Moon does it, but he can control it. On a few of the last gigs Townshend was pissed and incapable."

Now Daltrey's anger is rising.

"So don't talk to me about booze, because I've never been onstage drunk in the last seven years, Mr. Townshend! I don't know if you've ever noticed, maybe he hasn't but I have. I remember every show we've ever done!

"I'm just getting a bit fed up with these left-handed attacks."

And now he's retaliating.

"One of the sad things is that Pete and I are probably never gonna be able to communicate," he explains coolly. "I think I'll have to sit down and write a letter to the band, because there's no way of ever speaking to them about it."

JESUS. What's the future going to bring then?

Maybe Daltrey is outspoken, vitriolic and often enraged by the circumstances surrounding The Who, and yet underneath it all runs a deep devotion for the band. He may criticise Townshend for what he describes as "pathetic" guitar playing on one gig, and yet he'll get back up on stage and work with him again.

"The only other way is to give up, init?

"From my point of view . . . I think I've got better on stage in the last six years . . . and it really frustrates me that the people who were heads, hands and feet above me before are starting to fall by the wayside. I think it's unnecessary.

"That's why I want to get back on the road and do it. Because I know they can do it.

"And if they don't, then the Who breaks up. We're not a government. It's only a rock and roll band, after all.

"It'll be a terrible shame and a lot of people will be disgusted with us for letting it break up. But what can you do?

"In a way," he continues, "I don't mind if the Who do finish, because I think we've done a helluva lot and I'd hate to see i[t] fizzle. I'd hate to see anything mediocre come out by The Who."

And in a more dis-spirited moment he comments: "If I feel I've come to the stage where I can't give anymore into rock, and I can't do the things I like, then I might as well take up acting.

"I might as well."

JOHN ENTWISTLE:
THE WHO'S GREAT BASS GUITARIST

Steve Rosen | November 1975 | *Guitar Player* (US)

John Entwistle has considerable accolades to his name. His bruising instrumental section in "My Generation" was the first-ever bass solo on a rock record. Moreover, his was one of the most melodic, prominent, and innovative bass styles of all time.

Not that Entwistle was inclined to shout these achievements from the rooftops. The man known to Who fans as the Quiet One was as undemonstrative a celebrity and stage performer as they come. Almost certainly as a by-product of that, his surname was consistently spelled wrong by journalists long after they'd got their heads around the fact of how to render the no-less-tricky "Townshend."

However, this interview with a specialist musician's magazine enabled Entwistle to explain at length his philosophy about his instrument and his contribution to the Who. —Ed.

As bass player with the Who, England's John Entwistle is often passed over for the gyro-gymnastics of Peter Townshend and the out-front frenzy of Roger Daltrey. And though his 4-string playing creates the foundation of the band, John's toppy sound is often confused with Pete's lead lines.

The first meeting between Entwistle and Townshend took place when John was twelve (he's now thirty), and they began working in bands together two years later. Sometime after this fortuitous pairing, while carrying a homemade bass under his arm, John was stopped in the street by Roger Daltrey, who then and there asked him to join his group performing in a pub at thirty shillings a night. Eventually, Townshend (then in art school) was brought in as rhythm guitarist, and later still Keith Moon worked his way onto the drummer's platform. The Detours (which became famous as the Who) was formed. It was a versatile amalgamation, reflecting influences of such groups as Johnny and the Hurricanes, the Crewcats, Nero and the Gladiators, Johnny Kid and the Pirates, and the Beatles before it evolved its own, now familiar sound. Entwistle, as artist and songwriter, has tried to avoid the ruts that inevitably form under the wheels of a long-lived rock and roll band by recording LP's all his own, as well as by playing with musicians not included in the Who personnel. Solo albums include *Smash Your Head Against The Wall,* [MCA, 2024], *Rigor Mortis Sets In* [MCA, 321], *Whistle Rymes* [MCA, 2027], and *Mad Dog* [MCA, 2129]. Dressed in his perennial black outfit, Entwistle talked about his early work with the Who, as well as his current playing with his own new band, Ox.

What was the scene like when you first started playing?

I sang before I was seven; my grandfather used to stand me on a chair in the local workingman's club, and while I sang, he went around with the hat. My mother forced me to play the piano when I was seven, but I convinced her that I could carry on teaching myself the piano and learn trumpet at school. But there were too many trumpet players, so they made me play French horn instead. Then, when I was about fourteen, I made my own bass. I never played guitar.

Why did you fashion a bass and not a guitar?

Everybody I knew played guitar, and everybody needed bass players, and they just weren't about. When I first started playing in England there were only about four bass guitars on the market, and they were all very cheap. You couldn't buy a Fender bass or a Gibson. They were all like these very cheap tuxedo basses; I think the most expensive one you could get was a Framus-style bass—a big sort of acoustic thing—and a few Hofners. I had some photographs of Fender basses, and I just looked very closely at the pictures and tried to make one. I wanted a nice long bass, and so I made the neck really long—it ended up about 5'6" long. When I took it in to be fretted they took the fret measurements off a Hofner violin bass, and it ended up with about 9" of fingerboard with absolutely no frets on it. It had drum material for the scratch plate, the control knobs were stuck on with glue, the wire came straight out of the pickup, and it had a square neck as well. It was terrible.

What type of amplifier and guitar were you using when the Who first formed?

When we first started calling ourselves the Who I used a Marshall 50-watt amp with a 4-12 cabinet. I had the first 4-12 cabinet that Marshall made. We more or less forced them to make 100-watt amps by changing to Vox, who had already made one. Marshall decided that if they were going to keep us, they'd have to make a 100-watt amp. They used to make their amps with speaker material on the front, and they looked completely different. I said, "I don't like that; I want it all black," so they changed them. I bought another 4-12 cabinet, and then Pete bought another 4-12 cabinet, and it went on and on and on. We had more equipment than any other band in the country—it was ridiculous. I was using a Fender Precision on the first albums, and then I had an Epiphone and a Rickenbacker. Then I got rid of the Precision and got a Gretsch bass, which I could hardly play. I played it for ten minutes, and my hand got worn out. Then I had three Dan Electros in a row because you couldn't buy the strings small enough to vibrate properly. I only used the guitar until one of the original strings busted, and then I bought another one.

Why were you going through all those different bases?

I was trying to find something I could play. I felt comfortable with the Rickenbacker, but the neck warped, and it started sounding very strange, so I changed to a [Fender] Jazz Bass. The first *proper* bass setup I ever used, I had a big cabinet with curtain material on the front, and we used to carry our own equipment then, hire a van to take us to the concert. Because we thought it was too heavy, we used to hang the 18" speaker on a nail every time we'd go to a concert, and when I played a bottom *E,* it would fall off the nail. So we'd have to stop halfway through the number and hang it back on the nail. The first time I could ever play my E string properly was after I'd been playing bass for about three years. I'd never actually touched the *E* string; I was just playing on the first three strings.

And the first time I actually touched the *E* string was when I got my first 4-12 cabinet, and I was using an Epiphone semi-acoustic bass.

You're now using a Thunderbird bass?

Yes, I started getting into a bit of a rut using a Fender, and I found that we were playing bigger places, and it just didn't have enough bottom. I was using Hi-Watt amps with that Fender bass, and I was getting a nice trebly sound out of it, but there didn't seem to be any bottom in the band. The bass is very important, so I changed to Sunn Coliseums just before *Who's Next* (released in 1971, MCA, 2023). I had this Thunderbird bass for quite some time. In fact, at the time it was in a shop being sold for me because I just couldn't be bothered to use it. But they couldn't sell it; nobody wanted it, not even for a hundred pounds, which is like $250.00. So I said, "Oh, blast, I'll take it back." I thought I might as well try it out on stage, and it was perfect, though it didn't have enough treble, and it still doesn't. It's very difficult getting enough treble; you have to turn the treble pickup right up. All the Thunderbirds are the same, they're not exactly boomy, but there's no *presence* there unless you use a very "presencey" amp like a Hi-Watt. Sunn hasn't got that much treble either. The Thunderbird I'm using now is a '64. It's in pretty good condition, but I'm going to start using my "Fenderbirds" on stage. Once I realized Thunderbird was the bass I was going to be playing for a few years, I panicked because they stopped making them. I went to Manny's [156 West 48th St., New York, NY 10036], and told them to buy up the whole stock, so consequently I got ten two-pickup Thunderbirds. Some of them had harmonic, microphonic pickups, so I couldn't use them, and with the rest, I just couldn't get the action as low as I wanted. So I used the pickups and hardware and bought some blonde Fender Precision necks and had some old style Thunderbird bodies built for the Fender necks to fit, and I've been using them on stage more than the Thunderbirds. I use them for recording as well. Blonde Precision necks are my favorites; those and Rickenbackers. Thunderbird necks tend to be too thin down at the bottom. I get my fingers all tangled up when I go to the first fret.

You play with both your fingers and a pick?

I play with my fingers most of the time. I don't like playing with a plectrum. I use it for stuff like "Boris The Spider" [*Happy Jack*, MCA,

2045] and "My Wife" [*Who's Next*], but I'd much rather play with my fingers. I can play faster with my fingers anyway; I use all four. When I first started playing I was using my thumb, and I thought this was a bit stupid, because I'd learned the piano, and the trumpet, and the French horn, and learned to use all my other fingers, so I might as well use those. I started using my first finger, then my first and second, and then sort of brought all the others in. Only about two English bass players played with their fingers at that time. Everybody was using felt picks and thumbs. When I use a pick it's a Herco heavy tortoiseshell.

What type of strings do you use?

Rotosound. I *have* to use them—I designed the flaming things! Poor Greg Lake, Chris Squire [laughs]. I was looking for bass strings which vibrated properly, and I couldn't find a good *E* and *A* string on any set at all, except maybe for LaBella—they weren't too bad. But I wanted a round-wound string. I was approached by Rotosound, and they said they'd make some strings for me, exactly what I wanted. So I went to the factory, and they brought out a set of their round-wound and asked what I thought of them. The *E* and the *A* didn't vibrate properly, and the *D* and the *G* weren't heavy enough. So I sat there all afternoon while they made me strings with different cores, and different gauges, and different types of wire, and finally got through the *E, A, D, G,* and got a balanced set. And I said, "They're fine, make me as many sets as you can." They started making them and said, "Look, we'll put your picture in the string sets, and we'll put these strings on the market." So they issued them as "Swing Bass," and they've been out ever since. A lot of people use them and get the same sound as me. I wanted to get a sound like a piano, which is why I wanted round-wound strings; I found that I could play chords and get a lot more sustain out of wire wound, so that's really why I set out to get the strings done. We did the same thing with strings for medium and short scale basses, though shorter scale basses don't seem to sound as good as medium or long; they don't have the same kind of harmonics happening. The Thunderbird is a long scale.

What type of equipment do you use in the studio?

If I need a very trebly sound I use a Sunn Coliseum with a 4-12 cabinet, but most of the time I find that we need a sort of bassy sound, so

I use an 18" speaker with a Sunn Coliseum. On stage, I use two Sunn Coliseum stacks with Ox, and four with the Who. I use the straight Coliseum amp with a slave going through four 18's, two in a big reflex cabinet, almost like a PA cabinet, and two in just straight compressed cabinets. Then I use two other amps, one for midrange, going through two 4-12's and then an amp coming from the preamp out into the front of the next amp, with a lead cord which goes through two 3-12's, which are like PA cabinets as well. This is so I can project the sound but still have some sound on stage. The 18's are Vegas and the 12's are all the normal Sunn speakers.

What setting do you use on the amps?

I more or less have to use the equipment flat out with the stuff I'm using with Ox. I'd much rather use a lot more equipment, but it means I'd probably drown the band completely out. To get more treble I use an MXR, the little red box. It has a reverse limiting effect; it spreads the sound out and sustains it. It also doubles the volume. The only other pedal I use is a phaser, though I have quite a few other pedals at home—Morley echo pedals, power-wahs—but I really haven't had time to incorporate them. I don't want big rows of switches all over the place; I trip over the phaser as it is.

Was it difficult to coordinate your playing with the singing?

When I'm singing, I don't play bass as well—obviously, I'm thinking about the words. But I had a lot of experience with it in the early days, because I was doing a lot of vocal backing at the local dances we played.

Because Townshend tends to be more a rhythm than a lead guitarist, do you have to fill in more with a second lead line as well?

Oh, yes. Pete plays rhythm and lead, and I play bass, rhythm, and lead. We just play as much as we can. Once the Who gets on stage, everybody starts playing a solo straight away. With Ox, I've taken over a lot more lead work. Maybe if I'd been with another band I might be one of those very tasteful bassy players, a proper bass player, really. I've never truly considered myself a bass player. I think I'm a lead/ rhythm bass player. Because the Who was a three-piece, and we tried to reconstruct the same sound as on record, I used to play most of the time with a plectrum and played rhythm figures on the bass. Then, when we started doing more complicated stuff with *Tommy* [MCA, 10005], I started playing lead figures. Occasionally before that, when the guitar went off, I'd have to take over a solo and turn everything full up and go into a solo.

Do you change your instruments in any way?

Not really. When I get hold of an instrument I put a set of Rotosound strings on it and set the action as low as possible. I prefer playing with a very low action, but that's about all I do to it. I immediately take off the hand rest and the tailpiece cover, a thing of the distant past.

On large project pieces like Tommy *and* Quadrophenia *[MCA-100041], do you try to get a particular sound for each track?*

Yes. I think if you listen to my bass parts on their own they sound unbelievably disjointed, but when you play them with the other instruments on the track, they fit. That's what comes with playing with Keith Moon. I mean, if you play Keith's drums alone, it sounds like an avalanche. But once you put it in with the track it's okay. Keith must be the hardest drummer in the world to play with, mainly because he tries to hit nearly every drum at once. And if you try and fit in with one of his beats, you have to play like him, *bippity-bippity,* all over the place. It's really difficult; he doesn't play a hi-hat either, so you've got no sort of backbeat going. I just try and fit in the bass runs with what the drummers are doing on the tom toms and bass drum. I have to look at them all the time, so the audience sometimes gets forgotten. There are some shows I've done with the Who where I haven't even looked at the audience once.

Is this why you don't move, so you can concentrate on playing, or is it just part of the image?

Half-and-half, really. I've tried moving a couple times and really haven't gotten on with it at all. I don't think it helps with bass playing at all to move about. I think it may do with guitars, because guitarists can play a chord and let it sustain and then move or jump up in the air and play a chord while they're up there and then come down again. But a bass player has single notes and things to play, and moving about means you have to play a simpler part.

Do you compose on the bass?

I used to; then I changed to composing on the piano. Now I've gone back to bass again. I do a bit of composing now on synthesizer as well.

Have you found that playing piano, French horn, and trumpet has influenced your bass work?

Only insofar as it's enabled me to play with my fingers on the right hand. With piano I use both hands, with trumpet you loosen up your right hand, with French horn you loosen up the left hand, and it's enabled my hands to move faster. But that's as far as it goes.

What is a synthesized bass [played on Whistle Rymes*] and an 8-string bass on [*Mad Dog*]?*

A "synthesized bass" was just something I did on an ARP Soloist. It was just like a *doiiing, doiiing*. The bass part was so simple I just couldn't be bothered to play it on bass, so I played it on synthesizer. The 8-string bass is a Rickenbacker I have, which goes up to an *E* octave, *A* octave, *D* octave, and *G* octave. It sounds like a bass and a guitar playing in unison, which is nice.

Have you ever tried playing a fretless bass?

Yes, I can play one when someone else is playing, but it doesn't suit my style. You can play half- and quartertones, but I just wouldn't use one on stage. I might use it for recording. I like the safety of the frets about me. I do have a big guitar collection though, 57 of them. I have a couple of 1953 and 1954 Gibson violin basses, a couple of Les Paul basses, two Explorer basses, a Gibson Discoverer, a couple of old Thunderbirds, and about five old Gretsches.

Do you play acoustic bass?

I can, but it doesn't interest me because I can't play what I want to play on it, I can't play fast or anything. I use an Earthwood acoustic guitar bass instead, because you get roughly the same sound.

Do you ever rely solely on volume and make the playing secondary?

No, in fact I can play far more intricate stuff when I'm playing quietly. Once you turn up the volume you tend to lose a lot of note separation. The ideal volume is with the amp on number 1. I'm really looking forward to the time when I can join a dance band or something and play through a nice little Ampeg.

Are there any contemporary bass players you listen to?

Not that many, actually. [Paul] McCartney I like, because his bass playing is very tasteful. Larry Graham, I suppose; he's doing the same thing in a soul format that I'm trying to do in rock—turning the bass into a lead instrument. I really believe in the bass as a lead instrument. I think a bass solo, played with a trebly sound, can be as exciting as a lead guitar solo—if not more. I like Jack Bruce's technical ability, but I don't really like his sound. It's too burpy. People are playing the bass better now; gone are the days when they used to plod through four-to-a-bar. The transition from double [upright] bass to electric bass has taken since 1953, but I think a lot of people are realizing that bass has many possibilities. You stick it through effects pedals, and it sounds pretty good. A lot of the stuff with the Shadows had bass solos because the bass player was the leader of the band. I was raised on Duane Eddy and Eddie Cochran, so when I was playing at home I used to stick tremolo on the amp and play Duane Eddy numbers on the bass. He was about the greatest influence on me; that's part of the reason why I use a trebly sound as well. And also, after you've played an Epiphone Revoli for a year, and you sound like a landslide or something—a big sort of blurred boom—you really go to the opposite extreme when you change guitars. I changed to a Rickenbacker and used full treble all the time. We found that it cut to the back of the audience as well, so you could hear what the bass was playing, instead of a blur.

Do you practice?

No, but I'm in the studio so much I don't really have to. There's something very boring about practicing bass. You can sit down in a tune-up room before a show and get more achieved than you would sitting down for three hours practicing at home. There's something very strange about standing on your own in a room and trying to play. You can practice scales and stuff like that, but I prefer not to know where I'm going on bass. I'd hate to know that I was going to slide up to an *F#*, and then play a *G#*, and then an *A,* and know exactly what notes I was going to play. I think it would hinder me. It hindered me in the beginning; I didn't know what notes I was going to. I used to get very confused. I also had perfect pitch when I started playing the bass, but the Who used to tune a semitone above concert because the equipment sounded better, and my ears just used to go berserk. We tuned sharper because it made the strings tighter and made the speakers work better. It played havoc with my hearing; I could never get *in* tune because I knew it was *out* of tune.

Have you ever had any training on bass?

No, I sort of picked it up myself. Up until six years ago I couldn't read bass lines—I never bothered. I used to guess more or less where octaves and notes were; I got along okay. I used to work it out at rehearsals and in the studio. I'd sort of block off my mind and play. But now I know where I'm going, roughly. I can read, but I wouldn't dream of doing it unless we're in the studio, and we've got a very difficult number to remember. For some of the stuff on *Quadrophenia* [MCA, 10004], I wrote down chord sheets, and I found it helped. You get halfway through a six-minute number, and you don't know where it's going. Suddenly you get a brain block, panic, and go "Ehh," and you've made a mistake—then the whole band has to start again. So I just use chord sheets.

Do you think people mistake your bass for Pete's guitar because the sounds are so similar?

Yes, it does tend to happen. A lot of people in England, when "My Generation" [*My Generation,* MCA, 2044] first came out, thought that Pete was playing the solo, the bass solo. And for months, when we were playing it on stage, that solo would come up, and they always used to look at Pete. And after the bass solo was over they used to clap for Pete. I use a very guitar-like sound, so if the audience don't know about the instruments they're obviously going to get confused. The offensive thing is they automatically think it's Pete. Yet they can't understand why Pete just has his hands on a chord he's just strummed, and there's a lead figure coming out, and they're still looking at him and saying, "How's he doing that?" I did that solo with a plectrum, because in those days our manager, who was also our producer, didn't think that fingers recorded very well. But all the stuff I did on *Quadrophenia* and *Who's Next* [MCA, 2023] was fingers, and all the stuff I do on my own albums is fingers.

Where does the substance of your phrases and riffs come from if you don't really listen to that many other players?

A lot of it stems from classical music; I play a lot of octaves with thumb and first finger. I tend to always keep my hand in the shape of a chord in case I want to hit an octave or a fifth. I find it very hard to play simple rock and roll bass parts. I don't really like them; they're boring. They achieve what they're expected to achieve. You can get a rock and roll beat going, but they're not particularly exciting to play—no more than playing one and three in a waltz is. I'm trying to create things to do with the bass; I just had a 6-string bass designed for me, a long scale one. The top two strings are tunable to C and F in fourths, and it has a C string and a bottom B, just to widen the scale. This is made by the same people in England who made my Fenderbirds. They also made a hook bass for me, shaped like an executioner's axe. I just try to do new things.

WHO SAID THAT! THE 1978 PETE TOWNSHEND INTERVIEW

Tony Stewart | August 12, 1978 | *New Musical Express* (UK)

Who By Numbers (October 1975) had been an album likeable for its pitiless self-examination, but its somnambulant texture had done little to assuage a young generation disillusioned with the lethargy of the rock aristocracy. By the time of the next Who album, *Who Are You* (August 1978), that rock aristocracy had been shaken to its foundations by the arrival of the punk movement.

Townshend, though he took punk a lot more seriously than most of his peers, emerged from its impact with a surprising amount of positivity, as can be seen from this extensive *NME* feature. —Ed.

THE POLICE found Pete Townshend unconscious in a Soho doorway the day after he'd been to hell and back.

In the grey light of a cold dawn, the copper recognised the soiled and dishevelled figure that stank of stale booze, and gruffly shook him awake.

"'Ello, Pete," he said, smiling benignly. "If you can get up and just walk away as a special treat you can sleep in your *own* bed today."

Eyes screwed up against the harsh daylight, cold and confused, Townshend staggered to his feet. As he slowly made his way along bleak and deserted streets to the tube station, the painful memories of the previous day started to come back . . .

He'd been at a business meeting with his former manager Chris Stamp, his accountant and the infamous rockbiz troubleshooter Allen

214

Klein. For six months he'd been trying to get back payment of his American songwriting royalties, and it was the final meeting in a series of many.

Klein apparently produced sheets of figures, totally confused everybody, haggled over his cut for collecting the monies, and after 12 hours presented Townshend with a cheque. Townshend was emotionally drained, exasperated and infuriated by the whole ordeal.

"I said to Chris Stamp," he recalls, "'I don't fuckin' believe all that! I don't believe that after all these years in the rock business that I've sat through all that shit, and gone through all that for six months *just* to get a cheque.'

"I felt like a piece of shit!"

But his tortuous journey into self-abuse to visit the hell of his own personality had only just begun. And after drinking his "compulsory bottle of brandy", he and Stamp went to the Speakeasy to see John Otway and Wild Willie Barrett perform.

"I burst in, ignored John and Willie who were on their last number, smashed a few glasses, trod on a few toes and hit a few people, all friends of mine, I dunno why I went. I should have just gone and banged me 'ead against a wall.

"Then I thought I saw Johnny Rotten.

"Then I said to Chris, *'Oo's that there?'* An' he said, 'It's one of The Sex Pistols. It's . . .'

"And I'd already gone, and I'd got him and cornered him against the bar. I said something like, 'What the fuck are *you* doing here?' And he said, 'Well, what the fuck are *you* doing here?'

"I thought he was Johnny Rotten for about the first five minutes I was talking to him. Then I suddenly realised it was somebody else. It turned out to be Paul, the Pistols' drummer.

"And I sat him down and I was really preaching at the poor little sod. Then Steve Jones, the guitar player, came and sat down and I went, *'Rock and Roll's gone down the fuckin' pan!'* and I tore up the royalty cheque.

"About half way through the tirade Paul looked at me really confused. He didn't really know what I was talking about. And he said, 'The Who aren't going to break up are they?'

"'*Break up!*' I said. '*We're fuckin'finished! It's a disaster!'*

"And he said, '*Ahhh, but we like The Who*'.

"I went, '*YOU LIKE THE 'OO? AHHHHHHHHHH!*' And I stormed out of the place, and the next thing I knew I was being woken up in a doorway in Soho . . .

"And I got in and me old lady was waiting for me . . . sitting there with the rolling pin, but too tired to use it. She said, 'Where have you been?'

"I said, 'I've been to hell'. And I really did feel that I'd actually been to hell, and that's what the song 'Who Are You' is about."

Paul Cook later said that you thought you were past it—which may well have been the impression you gave.

"That's a polite way of putting it.

"I felt like a raging bull. I obviously collapsed just as soon as I walked out the door, but I didn't feel so bad just because I'd been drunk in the Speakeasy; it was because I'd been stone cold sober at a business meeting in Tin Pan Alley.

"That sort of thing had nothing to do with why I picked up a guitar in the first place.

"I think," he adds, "the whole new album will serve as an encyclopedia of rock and roll for the up and coming group—where *not* to get caught."

IN THE THREE years since he last allowed the rock press to interview him at length, Pete Townshend has changed very little in appearance.

Conscientiously the '70s Mod, he still gives the impression of being haunted. Not even the smart white shirt with a buttondown collar, the crisply tailored khaki trousers and the cumbersome Dr Martens he wears hide the nervous tension stiffening his thin, angular body.

Suspicious and uneasy, his eyes dart around their sockets; but it's understandable that he should be wary at first.

His last major interview with *NME* in May 75 told of his own disillusionment with Rock and The Who and led to a public feud. Three months later Roger Daltrey retaliated; he accused Townshend of going onstage drunk, betraying the group and their fans, and generally continued a vendetta that many expected would finally finish The Who.

"When Roger said I was drunk," Townshend says, "he was right. Drunk? Was I drunk!!

"I felt part of rock and roll was going on the road, getting drunk, having a good time and screwing birds.

"But on that particular occasion I couldn't handle it . . . and I was falling to bits.

"At the same time I was going slightly barmy. I was hallucinating; I was forgetting big chunks of time: I think only because I was drinking so much.

"Like I was waking up in bed with somebody and not knowing what had led up to that particular point. Then I was going home and trying to face me old lady.

"So it was a really peculiar period."

The Who survived, but Townshend declined to be interviewed.

"There's only one direct line between me and the public and that's through the songs. And that's obviously where I want to be judged, not on the strength of what I say in interviews.

"Because interviews are opinions. Songs are actions."

Yet he did once break his silence, even if he remained unquestioned, to write *Pete Townshend's Back Pages,* published in *NME* last November. It was a courageous attempt to exorcise the ghosts of disenchantment and the frustration of 'old-age' that haunted Townshend's career during the mid-'70s.

Undoubtedly cathartic, the piece ended optimistically; and it's this spirit that's been captured on the new album, "Who Are You".

While it may be idealistic to believe that Townshend has agreed to be interviewed again because the psychological scars have disappeared, you can't help but suspect that it's also a timely way of promoting the LP as The Who aren't playing concerts. But that suspicion undermines Townshend's dignity.

Now regarded as the spiritual Godfather of Punk, and arguably the single most important precursor of Rock's New Age, he's abrasive, animated and candid. Once he overcomes his initial reserve, he relaxes into a comprehensive interview lasting three hours.

Obviously the traumatic years have changed his attitudes, but more significantly he has regained his artistic confidence.

"I'm really quite relieved that we managed to get the new album done," he says.

"But I'm pleased with the writing. I particularly like 'Trick Of The Light', a song John wrote. And I'm glad I managed to get 'Guitar And Pen' and 'Music Must Change' to be as optimistic *and* razor-edged.

"They're not screaming vitriol, but they're still quite hard . . . Not in the aggressive way that 'Who Are You' is hard; that's probably the most archetypal, old-fashioned Who-sounding track on the album . . . very much in the tradition of 'Won't Get Fooled'.

"But I know we're evolving," he adds confidently, "no question about it."

Were you in a better frame of mind when you wrote the songs for "Who Are You" than you were in 74/75?

"Oh yeah," he answers without hesitation. "In a much better frame of mind than after and during 'Who By Numbers'. At that particular period I felt the band was finished and I was finished and the music was *dying*. There was very little sign that the New Wave was gonna emerge.

"I started to get disenchanted not only with what we were doing and everything around the band, but because nobody else seemed to be pushing either.

"The band came through that very down period. I came out the other side giving up on the rock business *and* giving up on the band, but discovered three other blokes that I really liked. I stopped treating them as a group of partners and started to think about them as people to drink with.

"Suddenly I realised I liked them and liked working with them. It was a bit of a discovery.

"When the New Wave came along it was, for me, a great affirmation. I thought, 'Aye, aye, we're not dead yet'.

"I felt it was the closing of a circle. It was part of what had been nagging at me: it didn't seem the music business was *ever* gonna get back to rock again, and that we were incapable of going back. We were getting older, getting more mature and we were settling down.

"Like there's a big difference between me playing the guitar today and me playing even six years ago. It's not just that I don't wanna play in the same aggresive way, but I haven't got the ability to do that. I've knocked down that wall of screaming and shouting so often that it's no fun to knock it down anymore. So I'm going over and knocking at another wall.

"It's not necessarily one that's so romantic or *macho* or young and proud, but it's nevertheless a wall; and I like smashing at it.

"Nowadays when I write I push myself in another direction. I try and work out chord changes that turn your head inside out; I might spend a month messin' around with a particular synthesiser sound just to try and get something that's gonna last for ten years and not sound jaded in a week.

"I'm trying to discover something else that's as good as a wound-up electric guitar."

UNLIKE YOU, a lot of musicians in your class-group felt threatened and intimidated by the New Wave. They thought they were finished.

"Well, I can understand that. A lot of bands that felt finished I hope are finished.

"I think The Who are standing on a different bit of ground. If you feel intimidated you have to get territorial. Say, 'I'm on this patch of ground; if you want it come and get it'.

"The strongest survive, and if a new band wants that patch badly enough, it'll get it.

"I don't think enough people did that. If anybody should have felt completely superfluous, it should have been The Who. The roots of practically every New Wave act I saw seemed to be The Who. Then I realised that made *more* of us.

"There was a line between us and the kids on the street; people The Who are finding increasingly difficult to reach.

"At least it makes us feel we've achieved something over a longer period of time.

"I'm a rock idealist," he laughs. "I'm not interested whether I make money out of it. I'm interested that when I picked up a guitar to write *I'd* been listening to people like Dylan.

"You can use music to communicate with people and to affirm that you share certain feelings about the world and about the music that we enjoy. And I think that lasts to today.

"So now I spend my time communicating through my music to people that are about 33 years old, used to live in Shepherd's Bush, sometimes wear Dr Martens . . .

"When I was a kid, and when I was in me middle-20s, I had something that they don't seem to have today. And I felt very glad I could reach younger people. It's just an amazing kick that rock and roll has managed to sustain.

"Admittedly I was wearing dark glasses at the time, and looking at everything in a grey way, but after 'By Numbers' I saw people like Electric Light Orchestra and ELP. I thought about what *we* were up to, and the Stones and Mick Jagger's silk pyjamas and Elton John and Rod Stewart.

"I thought, 'ell, it really is dead.'

"Luckily the New Wave came when I was already down. They say if you're down far enough the gutter looks like up. Well, the gutter is where modern rock bands, all rock music comes from. It's where it starts and you've got to be in the gutter to see it.

"And the New Wave began when I was feeling really wretched. So I took most of the insults as grand compliments.

THE JAM WERE probably influenced more by The Who than any other New Wave band. When they released their first album "In The City" they were regarded as the surrogate-Who to the extent that one critic claimed they were more entitled to Who licks than The Who were themselves.

"Entitlement to a lick is a complete waste of words anyway; cos all rock comes from somewhere. It all evolves, is handed on, taken, snatched, ripped off. You're entitled to it if you've got it. Possession is nine points of the law.

"He's probably right," Pete adds with a chuckle.

But why are you so benevolent towards them? Don't you want to retain the music yourself? For one thing blatant mimickry (which it was at first) is unhealthy in rock and roll.

"I don't think it's a good thing for The Jam, because they've got a helluva lot of potential. Seems a waste of time.

"But I don't think Paul Weller writes because he wants to emulate what The Who did. He just sees what The Who did as being a particular way of reaching a public which would work again.

"It's not so much blatant mimicry as outrageous commercial *Stigwoodism*. He's doing it with *Saturday Night Fever*, turning Travolta into another Elvis Presley, and the old man hasn't turned in his grave yet.

"So why not do it on other levels? It's smaller, but it's the same thing.

"I'm not trying to justify it and nor do I want to appear Mary Poppins-benevolent either."

But surely it's got something to do with the rock audience now being too big for any one band to meet?

"We can't even play for the 30 year old B-O-Fs who want to come and see us at Wembley Pool. We could probably play six weeks at Wembley, and only towards the end the audiences would start to trail off.

"We could travel in America all year round playing to full-houses. So it just goes to show there's not enough bands to go round.

"I've always said to Roger (Daltrey), who wanted badly to go to Japan, 'What's the point? We'll go and they'll probably love the band, and then there'll be an amazing demand and we won't be able to meet it'. We might as well not go and prick-tease.

"It's a strange situation. And yet a lot of younger bands that I'd quite happily spend time listening to don't make it."

Well, seeing a band in a club is genuinely exciting, but once they get into a vast stadium the vitality is dissipated and very often the essence of rock and roll is lost. Unless, of course, it's somebody like Dylan, when just to actually see him contributes to the excitement of the event.

"It did happen with Dylan, didn't it? I couldn't believe it. My old lady took the tickets, but after the last couple of shitty albums he's put out, I couldn't be bothered to go.

"And she said he was *AMAZING!*

"I said, 'You're kidding. 'Ow could Dylan possibly be amazing at this point in his life?'

"I was just incredibly surprised he could actually do it. Perhaps it's because he's conscious of his writing today, in the same way that The Who are of 13 years of history. But in a different way.

"He doesn't treat his history in the way The Who treat theirs.

"We treat our history like Who fans. We look back on it as something almost sacred, not to be tampered with. You don't take a song like 'My Generation' and rearrange the fuckin' thing. You don't have black women singing on it.

"But I suppose we're denying ourselves a true evolution, which is one whereby the music continues to live rather than being ice-box material which is constantly de-thawed and then shoved back in the ice-box again.

"The Who *are* doing something wrong, and I don't really know what it is; I feel that passionately at the moment."

Perhaps it's because you're denying yourself the feeling of being involved in rock, because you don't tour and "Who Are You" is the first new album in three years?

"The only time I feel the joy of rock and roll is when I'm actually on stage. But getting to the stage is another story: getting on a plane with Moon, going to an hotel, getting stuck in some dive in the States.

"Then you come back from a six-week stint feeling like a superhuman, but nobody around you recognises it, and you don't relate to your own family.

"What's *that* all about?

"It's just disorientation; unless you're gonna spend your life on the road until you get killed in an aircrash. Yeah, Lynyrd Skynyrd!

"I don't wanna die in an aircrash. And I also don't wanna drink a bottle of brandy every day, cos that'll kill me too.

"Different people want different things. I heard that Jagger said the Stones would be on stage until they're 50, and look at the human wreckage they've already left behind them.

"I don't want to be responsible for that for the rest of my life. I can excuse a lot of wreckage The Who have created, put it down to experience maybe. But now I can't do it.

"I could handle a nightly engagement at the Hammersmith Odeon. I said to Bill Curbishley (The Who's manager) I'd play every night of the week at the Odeon, but not to ask me to go round the world again because *I'm not gonna do it!* They're trying to persuade me to agree to three three-week tours of America.

"But I haven't got that kind of need anymore. I don't *need* to get up and play.

"I enjoy it when I'm there . . . and I might need it more than I think I do.

"But when I say there's something wrong with The Who I'm really talking about the stage. We still go on and do that same old act again and again. It's so backward looking.

"The Who must never be a parody of ourselves. It started to happen in '76 and I don't think we realised it. I was really fucked up after that."

After you played that Kilburn gig for *The Kids Are Alright* movie last Christmas, the producer said he thought it'd given you the bug to play concerts again.

"Roger, Keith and John all came off bubbling. Roger said, 'Right Townshend, now you must feel like going back on the road'.

"That performance made me feel more than ever that we shouldn't go back on the road. And everybody kinda went, *'Eurghhhhh!'* Then Roger said, 'You're barmy. I'm not gonna let your feelings of depression affect me'.

"Of course there's always a chance that the band affect the way I feel about it. But until I can actually feel they share my neurosis then it's hard to begin to even talk about the problems I feel are there.

"The group has gone past the point of no return, and I haven't now got the machinery to find me way back. But I do accept that somebody like Roger could, if he wanted to, probably bring me back.

"But he'd have to work on it, because I feel such a long way from that desire to get up and play the guitar.

"Like I said about the album, I'm relieved we got it out. I think it's a miracle, and not because it took too long or any of the hardships."

On just one hearing, it still seems a positive album.

"Yeah. There's nothing that gets you at it like a few problems. We've been through some amazing ups and downs. A little thing like a tape-recorder breaking down is not known to stop us. It's just that it did happen a helluva lot."

Did you ever think The Who were fated?

"No. Glyn (Johns) used to. In fact he actually ran out of time completely. He'd worked a year longer on the album than he planned."

He digresses. . . . "See, I like to keep a space open as far as the band live performances go. We have to find another way to do shows if it's gonna fit in with being a young married with a couple of kids who're nine and seven and need to see me every day.

"That's something I could never account for when I was 19 and wrote *'Why don't they all fade away?'* I never fuckin' knew one day I'd have two kids I missed with a physical pain when I was away from home.

"'Ow do you deal with *that*? Big fuckin' rock star!"

WE WERE TALKING about communication, and you seemed to suggest you only appeal to 30-year-olds in suburbia. Does that mean you feel bands like The Clash, Bethnal and The Jam now communicate with the teen-generation?

"Not entirely to the younger generation. As you probably know as well I do, a lot of the so-called young punks that you used to see down the Roxy were all about 50.

"But a lot of them were also very young people who were isolated. They couldn't find anything in The Who's music that appealed to them.

"It was weird. Just as somebody started to speak up, thousands of people said 'Right, I want to hear that!' They didn't care whether it was music, or whether it sound any good. It mattered more that somebody was saying it.

"I think The Clash are an amazing band. I hope they don't break up, but unless they go to America they will.

"They're probably now regretting having said, 'We never want to go to America; we're never gonna leave England; fuck America and the materialistic Cadillacs an' all that crap!'

"But it's *not* like that.

"The Clash have not received the kind of recognition they, yes, *deserve* in this country, apart from a certain inspired minority, like myself. It would be balanced and more powerful in the American environment.

"They'd be acceptable in street terms because they've got their own cultural ground. They would feel a kinship in the States rather than feel intimidated. Whereas it's difficult to feel you've achieved anything in England if you think that achievement is measured by results.

"America's big enough to make a small result look bigger.

"The Who fans there don't number anything like Elton John's, but it's still a significant enough group to pay the bills and allow you to go on and make you feel you're achieving something.

"But you could put Elton's 15 million fans against our million, and you'd have a different substance of people. They'd buy his records for *entertainment*. They wouldn't listen to the lyrics . . . they'd listen to the clever production and the musicians' session ability."

But nowadays don't people just buy Who albums because they want to know what you're going to reveal about *yourself* next? Certainly this was true with "By Numbers", which contained songs like "However Much I Booze".

"If all you had to do to sell records is be honest . . . it'd be really easy.

"'Who By Numbers' was revealing, I suppose, because it was all that I had left at the time. I just thought, 'What am I gonna do because I'm fucked up, not writing anything?'

"Not all the songs I submitted for that album—about 30—were like that. There's one little chink in the armour, and that's the ukelele track, *'I like every minute of the day'* ("Blue Red And Grey"). I put in five other things like that."

Do you think it was an album of despair?

"Not entirely. It's just a statement of fact.

"You don't despair about something that you feel has already gone down the pan, and I just felt the band was down the pan. I felt the situation between Roger and me was irredeemable.

"The things I said I genuinely meant at the time. The reason they got up his nose, and why what he said in reply got up my nose, was because we were both speaking the truth about one another. We both made it clear we hated one another's guts. And you only hate somebody if you don't know 'em.

"I really feel the reverse now. Now if I was gonna pick three friends, I'd *start* with those three.

"Everybody's changed in the band in the last three years. I think 'Who By Numbers' was partly responsible for that.

"But the other thing that's been played down like mad—because it's very painful for the band to talk about—is that we were going through litigation with our management, Kit Lambert and Chris Stamp; people we loved.

"I felt myself being pulled in two directions, and in the end I had to let go my friendship with Kit and Chris, and run with the band.

"And I *don't* like that, but I knew what I had to do.

"It's like if your two kids are drowning; which one do you save? You don't necessarily save the nearest. Somewhere along the line you make a choice, and the choice may be selfish. In retrospect I made the right choice.

"It was when 'Who By Numbers' was finished that I said to Roger, 'Alright, let's get together and blow 'em out'.

"Then he dropped his armour, and we immediately became very close. He'd seen me very much as an enemy, and it explained a helluva lot. Like when we were doing 'Quadrophenia' I couldn't understand why he was so aggressive toward me and about the album."

Ripped apart by mixed loyalties and your own feelings of gloom, there were those lines on "They Are All In Love" on "By Numbers":

"Goodbye all you punks stay young and stay high/Hand me my cheque-book and I'll crawl off to die."

Why didn't you?

"I think I did.

"What the lines are about is that we went on to sue Kit Lambert. It's not really what it seems to be about.

"Punks didn't mean what it does today. Punks is what I used to call the New York fans who used to try and get you by the ears and pin you down and take you home in a cardboard box.

"The song was about what the band had become. It was about money, about law courts, about lawyers, and about accountants. Those things had never mattered and the band had a backlog of tax problems and unpaid royalties. We had to deal with it.

"I really felt like crawling off and dying."

So it wasn't abdication from rock and roll?

"Only in as much as I didn't think we were gonna be able to go on. I couldn't see how we could if we were gonna worry about these kind of things."

It must have been hard for somebody who's a rock and roll idealist.

"I blame The Who fans for this!" Townshend goons. "If they hadn't bought the records, if they hadn't come to the concerts, we wouldn't have had all that money, we wouldn't have had to buy Shepperton Studios, and I wouldn't be here.

"So it's their fuckin' fault!"

"It certainly hasn't changed my idealistic stance. I can't be hypocritical about it. But I'm not in the place I thought I'd end up.

"When the band started off in 64/65 I really thought we were just gonna explode. I thought I was gonna die. Looking at the footage of *The Kids Are Alright* it's a bloody wonder we are still here today.

"I never ate; it was all dope-dope-dope, and *'orrible* vibes of aggression and bitterness.

"Out of that we were saying, 'We are the mirror for the desperation and bitterness and frustration and misery of the misunderstood adolescents; the people in the vacuum'.

"I never expected to be able to afford a reliable car or go somewhere wonderful for me holidays, or buy a big house, or run a business. And I don't know if I *want* to.

"How many people do *exactly* what they want to?

"I've done what I want to for ten years, so I don't mind the odd things that I don't want to do now.

"Meher Baba says, 'Don't worry, be happy'. I think that's what rock and roll's about.

"But it doesn't walk away from the things that aren't right. It lays everything out on the table, all the problems that you've got, and all the problems society has. It doesn't squash that or screw 'em up and throw 'em away. It fuckin' lives with them!"

YOUR DEFINITION of rock and roll in *Back Pages* was: If it screams for truth rather than help, if it commits itself with a courage it can't be sure it really has, if it stands up and admits something is wrong, but doesn't insist on blood, then it's rock and roll. We shed our own blood, we don't need to shed anyone else's.

"*YEA THE TEAM!*" calls Townshend, punching the air and laughing.

"It shouldn't be said as poetically as that, but that's really what it's about.

"People talk about not taking rock too seriously. But to me it's everything; so I can't take it seriously enough. If it is your release, the key to happiness, then you should take it seriously."

For somebody who follows Meher Baba's philosophies (and rock's), you've had more than your share of torment and despair.

"That's cos I'm silly.

"I remember Patti Smith said, 'How can somebody like Townshend follow Meher Baba and be such a miserable bastard?'

"Could it be I'm happy when I'm depressed?

"I dunno. I definitely like a bit of drama. Like I said, I'm happy when I'm taking things seriously.

"It's also difficult to practice what you believe, what you aspire to. It's one thing to say '*I hope I die before I get old*' and it's another matter to do it. And it's easier to please other people than it is yourself.

"So I'm not worried about making my life cosily happy.

"But I know now my need for security and stability is greater than it ever was. People used to say to me, 'Townshend why don't you learn how to relax? Go away for a week and have a holiday'.

"I'd say, 'I don't want a holiday; work's a holiday, music's a holiday to me'. Utter crap like that.

"Now I do need to get the business and music out of me 'ead. If you think about one thing obsessively for 15 years you eventually go barmy; and I went barmy with rock and roll and The Who.

"Though keeping it at a distance and being objective about it for a couple of years, I feel fresher and happier."

Do you think that shows on the new album?

"I hope so. The lyrics I wrote are hard-edged and cut in the way I want them to, but not in a bitter or aggressive way. They've got venom. But there's also a bit of joy in the music.

"I don't mean it's doom-laden music with pretty lyrics in the back-ground; the balance is right.

"A lot of the material on this album was inspired again by the *Life-house* film. I revived it in the middle of last year to try and persuade The Who not to release an album this year. For the band to do a big film instead of an album—and reach fantastic amounts of people would mean we wouldn't have to play so many concerts.

"The band went along with it, so I've developed the *Lifehouse* script. It's what first inspired a lot of music on 'Who's Next'.

"Basically it's a story about music, the rediscovering of music and what music is. It's not just about rock and roll, it's got a mystical quality.

"Seven years later a lot of what I wrote about has since become accepted, particularly in America where they're into metaphysics, the connection between your mood and the way you live your life, and the vibrations in the air.

"It was all spacey talk when I first started. The rest of the band thought I was insane . . ."

Or ready to join the Moody Blues.

"Right.

"But the story has inspired me to write songs like 'Guitar And Pen', which are not just about music but also about writing a song.

"If you've got the ability to write a song that reaches people, if you've got the ability to play guitar in such a way that it makes people jump up and down, then it's a God-given thing."

Isn't "New Song" on "Who Are You" part of that too?

"It's really about rock needing to do the same things, say the same things again and again.

"It's like I said before: it never lets go; it always admits to the same thing; it carries its own crap along with it. It never throws it on to someone else. It can't, because when it does it's then guilty of what the rest of the world does.

"In that sense a good bit of rock is still fairly pure.

"How long it can stay that way I don't know."

You said earlier The Who mirrored the frustrations of the people in a void who otherwise weren't represented. Do you still do that with your music?

"Only partly, because I'm not trying to do the same thing anymore.

"Things have apparently changed around me. Every man is a pivot for his own private universe, and that's the way I still feel.

"I'm still Townshend and I'm writing every now and again, but not necessarily to change things. Perhaps now certain things could be left as they are. Certain things you can't change. Certain things aren't worth worrying about. Rather than getting so desperately unhappy I come out with something 'Who By Numbers'."

But you haven't any teen-anthems like "My Generation" and "Won't Get Fooled", and perhaps that's part of The Who's problem: you've alienated yourself from the audience. Paul Weller claimed the songs you write now are self-indulgent, that you come on with "all this martyr shit" and that you can't rest on your laurels for the rest of your life.

"There's an element of truth in what Paul said.

"There have been periods, and I'm sure there'll be more, when I felt like an amazing martyr. If you think you're doing something that you don't wanna do, then automatically you feel like a martyr. Particularly if you feel you're doing it for a cause.

"To me rock's a cause. So I often end up going on stage or into the studio when I don't really want to.

"As for resting on me laurels, that's the last thing anybody should want to do.

"He's really saying anybody over a certain age who's achieved anything should just go off and DIE! It's exactly the same thing I once said. Life isn't like that. You think it is when you're 17—sometimes even if you're older.

"If somebody wants to judge me in terms of what I've produced in the band, and then write me off, fine."

You've said before, in Back Pages, that you find it hard to accept you're regarded as "well-nigh a saint". But that's because you're articulate and above all appreciate the social and political power of rock. When the New Wave emerged, rock did turn full-circle. It was again about the rot in society and government: some of the issues you wrote about for another generation; most of all about adolescent confusion, with songs like "I'm A Boy".

As a Who fan there's frustration for me now, as I want to know what Townshend has to say about the National Front or about the way this country is. But you haven't said anything.

"No."

Is there a reason why not? Are you oblivious to it?

"No, no, no.

"It's actually because I'm now actively doing something about it, whereas when you're an adolescent you're not capable of doing anything.

"If I wanted to I could become really practical, and not just write a song which I know now doesn't change anything. It just lets you know that there are other people who feel the same way.

"I could actually be a right pain in the National Front's arse, if I wanted to be.

"But I don't really like Vanessa Redgrave and Jane Fonda and people involved in petty power politics in unions. But if The Who wanted to, they could. We know Lords here and MPs there.

"We not only meet people with problems, we do something about them. And that's important because you feel what's happening on the streets and you're a part of it.

"If you haven't been in a black squat in Brixton, grit your teeth and try it. It's nothing like those squats in Westbourne Grove where they spend their money not on their rent but on their *pot* and heroin.

"It's people with families, people who go out in the day labouring; and mothers who try to keep their families together, sometimes large ones. And they've got *dignity!*

"But what kind of fuckin' music does that make? And how long can you go on doing it?

"I've got to the point in my life where you can't do it all, and rock is not capable of changing society. The only thing that's capable of doing that is power.

"So I'm more concerned now with trying to make music that makes people feel better, rather than worse.

"I don't suppose I ever really wanted to make people feel bad. But I definitely wrote songs like 'My Generation' to intimidate anybody who was driving round in a Rolls Royce.

"The stupidity of writing it was that nobody in a Rolls ever listened to 'My Generation'. Nobody in a Rolls was ever even *slightly* scared of people with safety pins in their ears."

But rock's an instrument to make people aware of things, even if it doesn't effect change. And some people who need it haven't got that voice. Whether it's minority groups like squatters, blacks and gays, or disturbed kids living in highrise blocks, they want *somebody* to speak for them.

That's why The Clash came from nowhere and were accepted almost immediately. It's why McLaren manipulated the whole Sex Pistols charade, which it often was. At least some truth was coming out.

"So many kids relate to me because . . . I'm in middle-class confused misery!" He laughs loudly.

"I don't know where The Clash are coming from, or even where Johnny Rotten's coming from. But I know that when I wrote 'My Generation' I was in a flat in Belgravia looking down at the Rolls Royces. It was only 12 quid a week, but it was still in Belgravia.

"There was an embassy over here, another over there and the Queen Mother went past every day.

"I've always thought that was a bit peculiar.

"I hope now people will understand what I feel about the important issues, just through the way I am as a person, and the way the band conduct their lives.

"If the band are gonna be worth anythin' they've got to stand up first as people. Their opinions don't matter. It's what they do that counts; not what you say.

"So I'm more concerned with doing; rather than pointing fingers saying 'That's wrong and that's wrong!'

"But there again, it's less important to say it when other people are saying it, and when they're being heard."

Didn't you ever want to be all-powerful and shout: listen to me! This is RIGHT!

"No. Unfortunately the only time I'd get like that was when I was pissed, and then I'm extremely uninterested in intelligent matters. I'm much more interested in getting in fights.

"I feel something incredible has happened in my life, with Meher Baba. That's what I'd be most happy to pass on to other people. But it's something you can hardly ever mention."

Time passes.

But to suggest Townshend is uncommitted would misjudge an awareness and sense of outrage that he simply chooses not to project in his music now.

He condemns the National Front, abhors pornography and, to precis, is genuinely concerned that the quality of life is eroding for many kids. He talks about it all with conviction.

Three years ago he couldn't even accept that his own role in rock had evolved into something different. Over a decade in the unreality of the music business inevitably put a distance between him and the audience of which he was once a part.

Now he has come to terms with it, and has made an album he says is "an encyclopedia of rock and roll for the up and coming group": the reality of his environment.

And he's no longer thrashing round in a malaise of bewildered despair.

"It is very difficult to see the problems people have in society. And to that extent The Who have lost their roots and lost that reality.

"Roger was really upset about a *Daily Mail* article where they talked about him being in his big 'ouse. Bill Curbishley said, " 'Ell man, admit it! It's true. You ride around in a helicopter . . . you're not a Shepherd's Bush geezer'.

"And Roger was saying, 'Fuck it! I *am* still a Shepherd's Bush geezer'.

"Without starting another journalistic interchange with 'im . . . I certainly don't feel I'm in the same piece of space. But it's hard to see how you change. Things change around you."

Three years ago you talked about being too old for this kind of life and activity. Do you still feel that with The Who and rock? Does it depress you as much?

"No. I don't feel the same as I did.

"But a lot of crap, well-meant crap, well-meant, supportive, encouraging crap, has been written to me lately: You're only as old as you feel.

"*I know that!*

"I know some 60, 70 year old people are like adolescents. But they don't prance around on a rock and roll stage.

"It's not age; it's being realistic about the practicalities, particularly of the road. You have to be fit to do a year touring the States, because you don't lead a regular life and you don't have a stable existence.

"You travel a lot, which is exhausting. You're under immense pressure. Your ego is fed left, right and centre. You tend to look for escapes by going to parties, boozing and God-knows what.

"I can get in good physical shape quickly to do a certain amount of work with The Who, by running or some kind of excercise. But I never used to have to do that.

"And Moony goes to a health farm to get in shape, just to bang the snare drum.

"It's absurd. Life wasn't always like that.

"Most of all, you've got to be in psychological shape so you don't fuck up. It's not just youngness in heart.

"I don't feel young in heart. I didn't feel young in heart when I was 19. I believe I am over a million years old, if you want to know the truth. It's like; hand me my straitjacket.

"'Oo wants to feel young in heart?

"Leave it to the butterflies."

THE KEITH MOON EXCLUSIVE

Eamonn Percival | September 1978 | *International Musician and Recording World* (UK)

This interview with Keith Moon was his last: while the relevant issue of *International Musician* was still on the newsstands, the drummer fatally overdosed on medicine prescribed to curb his alcohol use. His death, aged thirty-two, automatically transformed Eamonn Percival's routine feature into a poignant valedictory.

It proved a fitting epitaph. Although one could make the point that it was notable how unimpressive was the increasingly "wasted" Moon's work on *Who Are You*, there's no disputing the assertion he makes here that he revolutionized the role of the rock drummer. Moreover, for all his madcap legend, Moon throughout comes across as very thoughtful about his craft. —Ed.

Since International Musician last spoke to Keith Moon two years ago, a lot has happened to him and The Who. This year the band celebrate 15 years together and have just released a new album, "Who Are You". With the purchase of a large part of Shepperton Studios, The Who are finding new creative directions while remaining very active. Their reported decision not to tour again has caused a great deal of controversy. I.M. recently spoke to Moon about drumming and the future of The Who.

Is there anything new in drums which interests you?

Yeah, the new synthesized drums. There's a company called Syndrum who make a set which comes with a sort of small computer. You can get bird calls and all different sorts of sounds. It's very good. Obviously, it's not like the real thing but the effects are quite startling if you use it set up next to a straight drum kit. It's great to go from one to the other, playing the same pattern, because the way it's reproduced through the Syndrum gives it a really different dimension.

Have you used them on record?

Yes, only experimentally, really. On the new album, they're in there somewhere. They're quite easy to control. When you set them up, you've got a chart which you work from. You set the decay and the rest and it's basically like a small Moog but connected to the drums instead of a keyboard. It can be a bit of a hassle if you're playing as it can be difficult to turn round and readjust the controls. They're still experimental, for onstage use at least.

I don't really see a full synthesized kit. But they're great to add colour and that's important. I've got 16 drums in my kit and on every song I use a different set of four or five so eventually I've used all 16 drums. Sometimes I use the timpani, sometimes the timbale, sometimes I do runs that'll go right around eight drums and sometimes I'll just use bass drum, snare drum and hi-hat. I've got everything I need there. I can cover from a roar with the timpani right up to the smallest timbale which is about 6". That's why I have so many drums onstage because, with The Who, there's Pete who plays a lot of chords and John who plays very intricate bass figures that I work with and we have this empathy between us.

How much of the interplay between yourself and John Entwistle is worked out and how much is spontaneous?

Well, we rehearse the length of the song, whether it's verse, solo, middle-eight, verse, solo and then ad lib ending or whatever. We don't sit down and work out fills. Each of us works out our own part and then, when we put it all together and start to play, it comes out extremely powerful. You can't really work things out too much. We do certain things, certain build-ups and things but you can run into a danger of becoming an automaton if you do everything exactly the same each night. You just stop thinking and it ends up the same every bloody night but, with us, it's different. Sometimes I'll build up with timpani, sometimes I'll build up on cymbal or with a roll around the kit. There are so many variations on each effect.

Your use of cymbals has always interested me. Quite often you will start a break on cymbals alone without the bass drum behind it, which is something alien to most drummers.

That gives me absolute top. If you hit the bass drum as well, you bring in some bottom; the cymbal gives you top and with both, you get something in between which is neither fully cymbal nor fully bass drum. Sometimes I do a single-stroke roll on cymbals for a "whoosh" effect. Again, we get back to colour. I believe very positively in colour in drumming. You know, there's so many drummers that can go through the routine but they don't add colour anywhere. They don't paint with the kit. That's what I like doing. I like painting, adding colour and effects and shocking people. Constantly, while I'm playing, I'm thinking two bars ahead. That gives me a chance to, if I'm in the middle of a roll, to do something I've already thought out so I can get out of the roll and into whatever I was already thinking about. Then when I'm there, I'm thinking another two bars ahead.

Having played certain songs for 14 years, do you find it difficult to actually think of new fills and breaks?

No, if I thought about it, I'd be in trouble. There are some parts that just naturally happen and I'll think of a figure that I'll put in at a particular point. A lot of them are very unconscious. Sometimes I'll think of a pattern and immediately forget it and store it subconsciously and then two bars later, I find myself playing it. Sometimes when we go on tour, there might be a number where there is just a guitar and drum pattern or fill and it would be very easy to do the same thing every night but it doesn't work that way because the atmosphere is different at every place you play and the atmosphere on stage is different so you get different fills happening. I'm very adventurous with things like that, I don't like to remain static. I know when I've played a certain figure before so I try something else.

How much do you rehearse?

Well, as you know, I don't practice on my own. When we're going out on tour, we usually rehearse for three or four weeks and that's about three days a week, so we probably have about eight or nine rehearsals spread over a period. If you rehearse every day, you start getting cliched and you end up like an automaton, you can rehearse it to death. As far as we go, as long as we have the bare bones of a song, that's the way we rehearse. It's just to get the bones the verses, solos and the general framework of the song. Then, within that framework, we're free to experiment and we all experiment. It's rather like plasticine, you've got the thing there but it's malleable. You can actually shape it and stretch it but you're still left with what you started out with.

Do you tune your drums yourself?

Yeah, I do. I work very closely with Bill, my roadie. I'll go round and tune the drums and then go out front while Bill plays them. I just tell him, "use the blunt end and whack it as hard as you can". I get the tuning right and if we have three or four dates and we can't get to the hall in time for a soundcheck—I can't really walk on stage in front of the audience and start tuning the bloody things up—Bill knows how it should be tuned and he tunes it for me. After a show sometimes when the crew are breaking everything down, I occasionally go up and have a look around the kit and see if any heads need changing or anything. That happens quite a lot. We change the heads on every second show because I play very hard. What happens is the skin itself tends to lose its resonance after a couple of shows. You've thrashed the life out of it and it just gives up, really. We don't change all 16 drums, only the tom toms, snare drum, bass drum and one of the floor toms that I use a lot. The timbale are usually OK, but I suppose no skin stays on for longer than a week. They do lose their tone after a while and I do tend to hit them hard.

Do you have to work hard to keep fit?

Yes. I've just joined a health club because basically it's a question of keeping your stamina. You have to psych yourself up to it. I used to belong to a health club when I lived in Beverley Hills and I'd go there for a sauna and ride bikes and do press-ups and things. It is important to keep the muscles going. You need a lot of stamina to keep up a two-hour show. A drummer has to use more parts of his body than anyone else. I mean, it's not so important for John Entwistle to keep in top physical form because he just sort of stands there and basically just uses his hands. *(laughs)* He does a lot of hand exercises—a lot of wristwork!

Your kit has grown since last time I spoke to you. How and why has it got bigger?

Well, I added some timbale. The kit changes really as the act changes. When we're doing some stuff from Tommy, there are some really big heavy drum breaks where I bring in timpani and the big floor toms and some timbale for light and shade, so you're not confronted by a big rumble. That can sound very dull, so I use the timbale mainly for accents. You have to hit them hard but then I hit all the drums pretty hard anyway. They're miked up through the PA anyway and, as long as I've got the kit sounding good, it's OK. I have my own PA system virtually so I have to check the sound that comes out of the drum PA. Bill will go round the kit and I'll listen and see what has to go up or down. So, it's not that important to whack 'em hard although I do whack 'em hard. I'm a very physical drummer. In fact, we have to use special mikes for the drums because the amount of air, from hitting it so hard, would produce this "popping" sound—like someone blowing into a mike. So they put windshields on and that helps the tonal reproduction.

Is there a nucleus of the whole kit that you tend to work from?

Yeah. It's obviously the bass drum, tom toms, snare and hi-hat. You see, with double bass drums, I have the hi-hat locked in a half-open position so you get a "swoosh". I don't actually use it as a hi-hat. Both my feet are on the bass drums. So, basically I get a good ride, hi-hat sound. They just bring in the crowbars! Everything is tightened down and nailed and strengthened with extra screws drilled in. Everything is double braced so I can get up, as we do at the end of the act, and actually stand on the kit without breaking the fittings or ripping them away from the wood. Inside each drum I have a metal plate to support them so I can actually stand on top of the kit. The whole thing is solid as a rock.

What other drummers have you been listening to recently, or do you listen to other drummers?

Not really, I've been down to a couple of places like the Vortex and the Marquee and it's very odd because I see a lot of myself reflected in their styles. A lot of the atmosphere and a lot of the things they play. It's a bit brash, which I love. I think it's great, just thrashing away, but a lot of the drummers have not developed a definite style. That's something that comes from years of playing, I've picked up bits of Elvin Jones, Krupa, Philly Joe Jones—they were the sort of people I listened to for drumming.

The whole big band scene?

Yeah, mostly big band drummers. They're very dynamic, really wild.

Do you listen to the super-technicians like Cobham, etc.?

No, I'm not really into technical drumming. I don't play a technical drum at all. That Billy Cobham kind of control and discipline is incredible, beautiful but it just isn't me. Then again, I'd be lousy at playing what he does and he'd be lousy at playing what I do. I don't really get off on being able to do so many paradiddles. It doesn't impress me too much. I feel much more at home being very brash and spontaneous.

A few years ago Chris Welch said you deserved an award for "revolutionising rock drumming"

Well, you see, the drummer was always at the back and was very rarely noticed. He was the least photographed, the least interviewed. When The Who started, I began playing a constant drum solo throughout the act and Chris Welch saw us and probably thought "I've noticed the drummer for the first time". In that era, nobody ever took any notice of the drummer. It was all guitars and singers. When I started twirling the sticks and standing up and those kind of things, nobody else did that kind of thing in rock. I'm a total extrovert, I love to be involved. I don't like this great big kit in front of me and the audience.

I envy the guitarist who can go over and get that much closer to the audience. I can't do that, I have to sit at the back, so I acted in a different way and started to draw attention to the drums in a different way by acrobatics and all the tricks. So, a lot of people used to say "God, look at the drummer!" so I suppose there was a certain amount of revolutionising the drummer's role. Actually bringing the drummer out as an integral part of the group. The group wasn't just made up of a singer and a lead guitarist. You used to watch pop shows on TV and they'd just show the singer, the rest of the band being just a backup group and nothing else.

When I started showing off a bit, the directors would notice. There were two great directors, Mike Lindsay-Hogg and Mike Mansfield and they started getting the camera on the drums. "Ready, Steady, Go" and "Top Of The Pops" really treated the band as a whole and, up until then, it was just Billy Fury and his group or Adam Faith and his group. Most of the TV in those days was only a couple of cameras, one trained on the front of the singer and the other getting a side shot of the singer and they never bothered with the rest of the group. They were always there as part of the furniture. It wasn't until Townshend started smashing guitars and I started smashing up the drums that the producers of the shows began to realise that there was more than the singer in a band. They'd actually line up a camera for the drums, which was a first. People started to actually notice the drummer.

What's in the future for you and The Who?

Well, films basically. We've just finished "The Kids Are Alright", thank God! We've been working on that for two years. We've already started pre-production of "Quadrophenia", the casting and that kind of thing and we've got the money for it at last. That's the biggest headache—getting the money to do the picture. Roger's doing the McVicar film which will be done down at Shepperton and Pete's been working on the Lifehouse project for quite a while. There will also be soundtrack albums from these plus the studio albums. I often get asked about when The Who will be going on the road and the simple answer is, I just don't know.

Do you miss going on the road?

Not really, because I'm still involved in so much Who. Everything I do is still all to do with The Who. I enjoy going out on the road. I still get up now and again, and sit in with bands and play but as to putting together another road show and going out on a big tour . . . we've been doing that for 15 years and you can get a bit bored, especially when there are so many new directions opening up for us. We've toured and we've done our bit as regards live tours. I mean, let's not count it out but let's not put it too high on the agenda. There are no plans at the moment for a live gig. You have to look at it very carefully. If we do one here, we get insulting letters from America saying "You do one in London but you won't come to New York. We're just as big fans here as they are there!" You've got to be fair and go to New York, you can't just do one-offs.

The Who, unfortunately or fortunately, attract a big audience and, unfortunately, once you decide to go on the road, you're committed to doing everywhere. If we were to do it, it would mean rehearsals, a new act, and we've got such a lot on our plate at the moment, it's impossible. For years, all we did was tour and now we've got the opportunity to turn Shepperton into a real working project with films, commercials, video theatres, rehearsal stages, our own production companies and all of that. That's as exciting for me as being on the road. I love playing drums but there is more that I can do. Playing drums got me in the position where I can now do other things but to go on the road again, I don't see it as being viable for quite a while.

Can The Who exist without live gigs?

Oh, yes. Very much so. The Who are still working but we're working in a different way. It's very difficult. You spend a lot of time on the road and people start screaming for a new record, you spend time in the studio on a record and people start screaming for a tour—you just can't win. You asked me last time about couldn't The Who do small clubs unannounced and the fact remains that it wouldn't work for us; if we went back on the road, we'd go back as THE WHO. It wouldn't be fair to the fans to do a small gig. I think you should do a gig in a venue where everyone can see you. You should give all the Who fans the same chance and not go to some out of the way place. You'd get people saying, "Bastards, what's special about that place?" I don't want that kind of criticism. You can see why it's so difficult. We've just got so much to do first.

THE *ROLLING STONE* INTERVIEW: PETE TOWNSHEND

Greil Marcus | June 26, 1980 | *Rolling Stone* (US)

The Who quickly replaced Keith Moon with ex–Small Faces and Faces drummer Kenney Jones and expressed a defiant determination to carry on, but one tragedy was quickly followed by another. A 1979 Who concert in Cincinnati saw eleven fans crushed to death.

Despite such horrendous setbacks, the Who entered the eighties as a more commercially successful entity than ever before, the disdain of punk proving no match for the burgeoning nostalgia market.

This interview sees Townshend grilled by veteran music journalist Greil Marcus. Where Townshend had in recent years been publicly agonizing about whether the Who had a legitimacy and a future, he now seems comfortable in his part of a moneymaking machine. That may be because he is getting his sense of validation from his now properly inaugurated solo career: well-received Townshend debut *Empty Glass* was released in April 1980. Marcus—long as devoted as Townshend to the cause of rock as social force—is mainly the one brooding over issues of wider concern. Nevertheless, Townshend remains as coruscatingly—even suicidally—honest as ever, at one point even proclaiming, "I don't think *I'd* go and watch the Who."

Notes: The GPO was the General Post Office

Keith Moon died aged thirty-two not thirty-one. —Ed.

The interview that follows took place on April 17th, just a few days into the Who's eighteen-date spring tour of the United States and Canada: their second new-world tour since drummer Keith Moon died at thirty-one on

September 7th, 1978, and their first since eleven people died in the crush of fans trying to force their way into the Who's concert at Cincinnati's Riverfront Coliseum on December 3rd, 1979.

That event made headlines all over the world, most often as a condemnation of rock & roll (as on CBS news), or simply of America. Sixteen years as a unique and seminal rock & roll band aside, what happened in Cincinnati has probably made the Who more famous than they have ever been. Millions who had never heard of Keith Moon now think they know who the Who are.

In the world of rock & roll, the Who's status has also changed. People have rallied around the band. Though the Who have never placed a Number One album or single on the 'Billboard' charts, they have represented the very spirit of rock & roll to a growing mass of fans; the Who's confrontation with disaster has made the group even more important as a standard-bearer, and raised the possibility that, having only just returned to live performances after two and a half years off the road, the band might be forced off the stage for good. The T-shirts fans are wearing tell the story: I SURVIVED THE WHO, on the backs of a few, THE WHO CARES, on the backs of a lot more.

In the San Francisco Bay Area, where Townshend and I talked, excitement, at least in the media, was pervasive. For days preceding the Who's three sold-out concerts at the 14,000-seat Oakland Coliseum Arena, the drums were beating with a message that could not be missed. Along with the usual ticket giveaways, radio stations programmed "all-Who" weekends, "the Who A-to-Z" weekends (and they have a Z, too: "Zoot Suit," the B side of their first record, cut in 1964 as the High Numbers), ran long, pretaped interviews with Pete Townshend, and fondly recalled the Who's "American debut" at Monterey in 1967 (it wasn't; it was in New York in 1966). Smaller cinemas put on double bills of the band's two 1979 films, the fictional 'Quadrophenia' and the career-documentary 'The Kids Are Alright,' both of which had died early at local first-run houses. The day the Who left town, the radio jumped on 'Empty Glass', Pete Townshend's new solo album—with vocals, guitar and synthesizer by Townshend, piano and organ by John "Rabbit" Bundrick and bass by Tony Butler of On the Air, a band led by Simon Townshend, Pete's brother.

Such a buildup (and follow-through—two weeks after the Who left town, the airwaves were still full of their music) was common in the late Sixties, but nothing like it had been heard since: not for the Stones, not for Dylan, not for anyone.

The Who are, in some ways, a new band: along with Kenney Jones (who replaced Moon on drums), they have added Rabbit on piano, organ and synthesizer. After the end of the spring tour the Who returned to England to complete an album, tentatively set for release in the fall. They hit the U.S. in June for another tour, this time touching down in Los Angeles and heading for the South.

At the same time, the band is caught in its past. It's not the immediate past, of Keith Moon's death and the disaster in Cincinnati. ("We can do fourteen dead here," said a woman outside the Oakland coliseum, handing out fliers for the forthcoming concert by John Lydon's PiL. "We can beat Cincinnati." The Bay Area has always had the world's stupidest punks.) When we talked—before the show I saw—Pete Townshend spoke of the Who's history as, among other things, a burden: "A great knapsack—you carry it around, and nobody ever empties it. You've got the old stale sandwiches in it, as well as the new ones." But that history—and the Who's history may be more vivid, more coherent, than that of any other band with a tenure even approaching theirs—can also be a crutch.

As their show opened—with "Substitute" (1966), "I Can't Explain" (the band's first record as the Who, 1965) and "Baba O'Riley" (1971)—it was impossible to think of the songs as oldies, or even as classics. With the volume loud enough to be totally satisfying—and loud enough to leave me with a partially paralyzed lower lip and a sore wrist for three days—the songs were undeniable: rock & roll facts, preexistent entities waiting for the Who to discover them. The Who didn't sound like they were referring to what had gone before: they sounded as if they were starting all over again, from the necessary beginning.

But as the show moved on—and into the more abstract and less social material from 'Tommy,' or 1978's 'Who Are You'—the performance, at least for me, settled down. Other fans—the teenage junkie behind me, the college students in front—grew ever more excited, but in a way they also settled down: they were waiting for their favorites, and the shape of the concert insured that they would get them. If the show was not quite the Who's Greatest Hits, it was the History of the Who. Aside from a couple of numbers from `Quadrophenia' and "Dancing in the Street" as part of a three-song encore, there were no surprises: no unrecorded material, nothing from the unfinished album, no obscurities, be they "I Don't Even Know Myself" or "Pictures of Lily" or "The Seeker." The band gave the audience what it wanted, but they didn't entice the audience to want more than it had thought of wanting—which is what the Who, like all great rock & roll bands in their great days, have been all about.

Technically the show was superb: shot through with fun and movement. Roger Daltrey seemed to run in place for two solid hours. Townshend's crouched leaps were thrilling—spectacular but not gaudy, aggressive but not cruel. No one in the Who ever seemed bored by the material. The band changed the show over the next two nights. They cut it down, stretched it out, shuffled the songs, varied the encores—and, according to one fan who saw all three concerts, Townshend never played the same solo twice. The band sounded as compact and uncompromised as it ever has. Rabbit and a horn section added a kind of subliminal fullness. But it was a show based on the "stature" Pete Townshend talks about below, not a show intended to subvert it.

To a man, the Who looked terrific. Roger Daltrey and Kenney Jones were dressed in T-shirts and denims, and worked like athletes. John Entwistle, as always, stood stock still, and this time, wore a neat white suit, which set him off perfectly. As for Townshend, he appeared onstage in an impressive navy blue jacket: he looked like a world-beater. When, after a few numbers, he took it off, revealing a Clash T-shirt with the sleeves rolled up, his pants suddenly seemed baggy—and he struck me as just another rock & roll anomaly. Just another Buddy Holly: the kid you laugh at, if you bother to do that, the kid who one day comes out of his shell and changes your life.

As that Clash T-shirt was no doubt meant to show, Townshend remains a fan. Since "I Can't Explain" he has been one of rock & roll's first-rank creators, definers; but since a memorable interview appeared in these pages in 1968, he has also been its premier participant-philosopher—or if you *like, player-coach. What follows below is merely the latest installment of that career. —G.M.*

It seems to me that the love songs on 'Empty Glass' are much more personal than they've been for the past few years—not confessional, but clearly directed to a person. There's a passion in "A Little Is Enough" that seems very new.

I think probably because I've had a harder time, lately. Before Keith died, I decided that practically all the personal problems I had—whatever they were, whether it was boozing, or difficulty at home with my family—was because of the Who on the road. When we came off the road, I spent two and a half years not touring—under great pressure from the band to tour, but I resisted, and said, "No, I want to try it, and see what happens." I got to the end of that period, and all my problems were still there. Some of them were worse. But what was strange about that time was that it somehow opened me up: I was able to put a slightly different slant on the qualities that I look for, or that other people look for, in life.

With a song like "A Little Is Enough," what was interesting to me was that I was able to very easily put into words something that had actually happened to me when I was a thirty-four-year-old. It wasn't self-conscious; it wasn't a song written from a *stance*. It wasn't objective. It was *purely* personal: instant, and purely transparent. It's very emotional, but it's also very straightforward and clear. Just the fact that you can't *fucking have the world*. If you're lucky enough to get a tiny piece of it, then—fine. When that's applied to something as *immense* and *intangible* as love—whether it's spiritual love or human love . . .

I suppose I wrote the song about a mixture of things: I wrote it a little bit about God's love. But mainly about the feeling that I had for *my wife*—and the fact that I don't see enough of her, and that when we are together there're lots of times when things aren't good, because of the period of adjustment you require after a long tour: stuff like that. She would always want a deeper, more sustained relationship than I would—but in the end I suppose we're lucky that we do love one another *at all.* Because love, by its very nature, is an infinite quality, an infinite emotion—just to experience it *once* in a lifetime is enough. Because a lot of people don't—don't *ever* experience it.

A lot of the songs on the album—well, "Let My Love Open the Door" is just a *ditty*—but particularly "A Little Is Enough" and a couple of the others—"I Am an Animal," I think—are getting *close* to what I feel I want to be writing: in terms of somebody who's thirty-five writing a rock song, but one which isn't in the George Jones-Willie Nelson tradition—"I'm a smashed-up fucker standing at the bar. . . ." "Empty Glass" is a direct jump from Persian Sufi poetry. Hafiz—he was a poet in the fourteenth century—used to talk about God's love being wine, and that we learn to be intoxicated, and that the heart is like an empty cup. You hold up the heart, and hope that God's grace will fill your cup with his wine. You stand in the tavern, a useless soul waiting for the barman to give you a drink—the barman being God. It's also Meher Baba talking about the fact that the heart is like a glass, and that God can't fill it up with his love—if it's already filled with love for yourself. I used those images deliberately. It was quite weird going to Germany and talking to people over there about it: "This 'Empty Glass'—is that about you becoming an alcoholic?"

That George Jones tradition—which is apparently where the person in Germany plugged in "Empty Glass"—can be just as stultifying as if you felt it always necessary to write in the voice of a seventeen-year-old: as if that were the only way a song you wrote could have any validity as rock & roll.

I think what's always been my problem, though, is that I've always been *fascinated* by the period of adolescence—and by the fact that rock's most *frenetic* attachments, most long-lasting attachments, the deepest connections, seem to happen during adolescence, or just postadolescence. Rock does evolve, and it does change, and it does go through various machinations, but to *you,* as a listener, someone who needs both the music *and* the exchange of ideas—you always tend to listen in the same way. You expect—and you feel happiest when you get—an album that does for you what your first few albums did. You're always looking for that: you're always looking for that *first fuck.* Of course, you can never have that first fuck, but you're always looking for it. Occasionally, you get very close. Always chasing the same feeling, the same magic.

I think the strangest thing for me—and I think perhaps the Who are unique in this respect—is that we *seem* to be able to continue, even though I think my writing is clumsier than it was in the early days. It's less easy for me to completely open up, because I'm not *alone* anymore. When I wrote the first five or six hit songs for the Who, I was *completely and totally alone.* I had no girlfriend, no friends, no nothing—it was me addressing the world. That's where the power of that early stuff comes from. But despite the fact that the later material is less transparent, less wholesome to some extent, we still appeal to a very young audience. Sometimes preadolescents. But always, *always,* there is a very, very strong *grab*—a deep, instant grab—which lasts . . . forever. It's not like a fad. People who get into the Who when they're thirteen, fourteen, fifteen, sixteen, never stop being fans. The Who don't necessarily captivate the whole teenage generation—as each batch comes up every year—but we certainly hit a percentage of them, and we *hold* them.

Just after Cincinnati, just after the news hit that eleven people had been killed trying to get into your show, there were statements on the radio from you and from Roger Daltrey and my wife was very disturbed by something Roger said: simply a reference to the people who had died as "the kids." She said, "But they weren't all kids—one of those people was a mother with two kids of her own." What that expression meant to her was that the audience was no longer real to the band: the audience had become faceless, physically present but also somehow invisible. Whoever was in the audience, they were "the kids." It was as if there were an enormous gulf separating the band from its audience—as if there were no way to feel the kind of identification she and I felt when we first saw the band in 1967, when it became obvious that the band and its audience were part of the same reality, a reality we were both creating, or a story we were both telling. Do you think there is that kind of gulf?

Yes. I think there is. When I think back to the days at the Marquee—we got a regular Tuesday night residency, which was a big coup for us, because we didn't even have a record out. The first night, there were maybe fifty people, the next night, two hundred, and after that we were packing it. We were a cult within a cult—our whole audience was nineteen years old, as we were—and there's a great feeling of affirmation when the audience knows they're sharing in the success; they're making the success happen as well. So you become *incredibly* close. The two or three thousand people who regularly attended the Marquee residency—I think I know them all by their first names.

One of the problems, today, is not an obvious one. Roger—who, dare I say it—tends occasionally to jump to conclusions about what's going on, and maybe sticks to them until someone can talk him out of them, jumps to a *wrong* conclusion when he feels that the gulf is created by a difference in age. I think it's more to do with a difference in *stature*. The Who are an enormous business machine, surrounded by all kinds of controversy—and I suppose a great amount of media power. A lot of that comes from the success of things that are happening *around* the band. The *Tommy* film is a case in point: an average, entertaining film, blown all out of proportion—the David Frost show, Allan Carr with his famous parties, Oscar presentations. It's really got very little to do with *front-line* rock & roll, but it does affect the way people see the band.

But there is also the fact that the band's history starts to accumulate. To be in existence for fifteen years, and still be working, still be appearing on a stage. . . . People can actually pay money and go and see this band who have got—not so much a wonderful backlog of material behind them, but who have actually got a history.

It's like discovering a new author. You run out of books to read, and suddenly you discover that you like F. Scott Fitzgerald. You start, and you read all his books, and you're really pissed off the day you come to the end of them. Then you go on to your next author—you might discover Salinger. And you go through that lot. And you get pissed off when you run out. This often happens to you when you're quite young—and what's a big kick for a lot of young kids who get into the Who is the discovery that there's so *much* to get into. We do exist now, we are putting out product, but there's a lot more they can find. So although there is a gulf, I think there is also a fascination in the fact that people might feel that gulf to start with, but also feel there's an opportunity, by a kind of investigative listening, and studying, and reading books about the band or going to see the films—there's a chance they can *get* closer.

All I can tell you is that I meet kids on the road—and they are kids, sixteen to twenty—and they treat me just like the guy next door. They've got *no* deep respect for me; there's no fanaticism. It's an absolute, one-to-one relationship. There's a familiarity, a sense of naturalness. I think that could only come about if they felt close to me. It doesn't happen with everybody—but it happens with quite a few people.

Of course, it's going to be different if you're fucking eighteen- or nineteen-year-olds—I don't think *I'd* go and watch the Who, even if I lived in America. I mean, I'd sit and wait until the Clash came: I'd go and see them. And hope I'd get one of their good nights!

Is there any point to the Who carrying on, as a touring band, any point beyond pandering to an audience that has become so conservative, so fearful of new experiences, that latching onto a rock legend—and whatever else the Who is, it is that—can become a reactionary defensive way of resisting new and challenging music? That isn't to say—or to deny—that your music today is unimaginative, old-fashioned, or whatever—that's irrelevant. I've been struck, over the last few years, by the fact that the great bulk of the American rock & roll audience will do almost anything to avoid having to deal with something that's radically new.

Me too—I think you're absolutely right. It's very, very strange: in Britain, at the moment, we've got 2-Tone, we've still got punk, we've got mod bands, we've got heavy-metal bands, we've got established supergroups, we've got all kinds of different *families* of music—*each* of which takes an enormous amount of adjustment. They're intense, and very socially . . . jagged. They don't fit neatly into existing society: they challenge it. And yet in America, kids seem to be quite happy. Rock, to them, is enough: establishment rock *is enough*. That seems very peculiar to me. There are obviously lots of subdivisions of music in America, but I think that's something record companies dream up. In reality, whether it's black music or white rock music, I think the truth of the matter is exactly as you've said. It's not necessarily something as big as fear—it's fucking *uncomfortableness,* listening to a Sex Pistols record. It worries you, because somebody is speaking the truth.

People in the States don't necessarily refuse to admit that problems exist, but it's a country that believes in *success*—that ultimate success lies in the hands of man. Whereas, *rock* doesn't. Newer rock, particularly, actually affirms the *futility* of man, in all respects but one. It says, in a word, in a sentence, what Meher Baba said: "Don't worry—you're not *big enough* to deal with it." It's just gone *too crazy.* Do your best and leave the results to God.

When you listen to the Sex Pistols, to "Anarchy in the U.K." and "Bodies" and tracks like that, what immediately strikes you is that *this is actually happening.* This is a bloke, with a brain on his shoulders, who is actually saying something he *sincerely* believes is happening in the world, saying it with real venom, and real passion.

It touches you, and it scares you—it makes you feel uncomfortable. It's like somebody saying, "The Germans are coming! And there's no way we're gonna stop 'em!" That's one of the reasons: a lot of new music is harder to listen to. So you get a band like the Clash, and they come out with a nifty little song like "Clampdown," and you can't hear the words, and they'll play it on the radio in L.A. You read the fucking words, they scare the shit out of you. Or the Pretenders—Chrissie Hynde's got a sweet voice, but she writes in double-speak: she's talking about getting laid by Hell's Angels on her latest record! And *raped.* The words are full of the most *brutal,* head-on feminism that has ever come out of any band, anywhere!

And yet it's only because it's disguised that it's getting played, and getting appreciated. To some extent, both the Clash and the Pretenders are getting played because their music is slightly more palatable, slightly closer to the old form. I saw so many new bands go *down* in England, so many great bands, because unless you were in exactly the right frame of mind, felt the same way, felt as abandoned, felt as anarchistic, and felt as I-don't-give-a-shit as they did, you just couldn't enjoy it. And in fact—to answer the question you asked at the beginning of all this—for the Who, at the moment, to go out as an established band, requires a lot of that don't-give-a-shit attitude. We *don't give a shit* whether the audience has a problem or not. All we know is that *for us*, to go on a stage, get instant communication, know that people have done their homework, have an instant connection with the audience, *go* backstage afterward into a dressing room full of the most beautiful women you can ever hope to lay your eyes on, never have *anybody* say anything nasty to you, everybody's friendly, everybody's *wonderful*, people don't throw us out of hotels anymore—

I mean, life revolves quite nicely—you know what I'm saying? I'm getting paid a lot of money for the privilege. The first ten years in the Who were fucking *awful*; miserable, violent, unhappy times. It's nice to now sit back and enjoy it. It might be brief; for the sake of rock music in some ways I hope it is brief. For me, maybe I don't hope it's brief.

We've very much dropped our idealistic stance in terms of *our* weight of responsibility to rock's evolution. We haven't stopped caring about where it's going to go; I think we've realized that we're not capable of doing *that much*, in terms of actually pushing it forward. If we have got a chance of pushing it forward, I think we've got a better chance of doing it on the road than we do on record, to be quite honest.

So can the band still make history? Obviously it has made rock & roll history, and it's certainly affected social history as such. You seem to be saying that can't continue.

Maybe only history in terms of *statistics*, now—how many years we've been together; how many disasters we can survive.

Which is not what I meant. I meant exactly what you meant: pushing the music forward.

Well, I don't know. Who's that down to? Is it down to me? As a writer? I don't know. I think if it's down to me as a writer there might be a chance, but I don't know how much stamina I've got left.

Let me put it another way. What strikes me most about what happened in Cincinnati is that it seems, now, not to have happened at all. It has not become part of the rock & roll frame of reference, as Altamont instantly and permanently did. It seems to me that it was an event that should have signified something new about the relationship between bands and their audiences, or about rock & roll as mass culture, was taking place. It ought to have forced people to reexamine a lot of assumptions, a lot of what they took for granted. That hasn't happened.

Will that event have an effect on the Who's music? I don't mean in terms of the Who putting out a nice little commentary about it, as the Grateful Dead did after Altamont with "New Speedway Boogie"; I mean over the years, in a more profound way.

I think what's not apparent to the outside world, in the Who, is our—bloody-minded brutality. Our—determination. Our stamina, and our *strength*. It's not apparent, because we seem to brood so incessantly on our weaknesses, we seem to have so many phobias; like everybody who really cares about rock, we spend so much time worrying how many more years. . . . But the amazing thing, for us, is the fact that—when we were *told*, told about what happened at that gig, that eleven kids had died—for *a second*, our guard dropped. Just for a second. Then it was back up again.

It was, fuck it! We're not gonna let *a little thing* like this stop us. That was the way we *had* to think. We had to reduce it. We had to reduce it, because if we'd actually *admitted* to ourselves the *true* significance of the event, the *true* tragedy of the event—not just in terms of "rock," but the fact that it happened at one of our concerts—the tragedy to us, in particular, if we'd admitted to that, we could not have gone on and worked. And we had a tour to do. We're a rock & roll band. You know, *we don't fuck around,* worrying about eleven people dying. We *care* about it, but there is a particular attitude I call the "tour armor": when you go on the road you throw up an armor around yourself, you almost go into a trance. I don't think you lose your humanity, but, think: for ten, maybe fifteen years, the Who smashed up hotel rooms—why? Where's the pleasure in it? We actually quite relished general violence. I don't understand why it happened. It doesn't happen now, but it did happen, for a long time. I think that, for me, tours were like a dream.

I was literally wearing armor. The only thing that would ever crack it, for me, at a show, would be if my wife and kids were there. Or my brother—he'd be, what? Eleven or twelve years old. Simon: he's got a band of his own now, On the Air. I used to really worry about him. He'd like to be right up front, and if I saw trouble happening—that would be my link. That would pierce my armor.

In a way, I think you're wrong about what you were saying about a gulf. When I say armor, I mean armor that actually *allows* you to be more abandoned, and freer, that allows you to be tougher, harder—*genuinely* tougher and harder. I'm not trying to glamorize it, and it's not something that I'm necessarily proud of. The Who's macho tendencies, in some ways, weaken our audience: our audience is about eighty percent male.

You say that if you had allowed yourself to really think about, to really face the true tragedy of what happened in Cincinnati, you would have had to stop—but you couldn't stop, you didn't want to stop, there was no point to stopping. But once the tour was over—or maybe a year after; or two years—isn't it important, if the band is going to continue to make sense of where it's been and where it's going, to somehow integrate that event, to absorb it: to allow it to affect you, in terms of the music you make and the way you perform it?

I don't know, because so far, we've had a series of quite unfortunate reactions.

How do you mean?

I think the way festival seating was blamed, wholesale, for practically all the problems, was quite a nasty, negative overreaction—because I *like* festival seating. When I go to a concert I don't want to have to fucking sit in a numbered seat, and get clobbered over the head every time I stand up. I like to be able to move about, I like to be able to *dance* if I want to, or go and buy a Coke if I want to, or push my way to the front if I want to or hide in the back if I want to! I also know, from the stage, that you get the best atmosphere with festival seating.

Yesterday was a case in point: the second date we did in Seattle. I saw five or six punch-outs, because of people just not wanting to stand up at the same time as the person in front of them. You see one guy punching some guy out 'cause he's standing up, and fifteen minutes later *he's* standing up and the guy behind *him* is punching him out. Everybody's got a different reaction time—a different moment when they feel they want to get up and jump. One person thinks that the time to get up and jump is the guitar solo in "My Wife," and somebody else thinks it's when Roger goes, "See-ee meeee, fee-eel me—" I mean, who knows? You don't get that kind of conflict at general-admission shows.

That's one reason. Another is that immediately after the Cincinnati gig, to protect ourselves partly from *legal* recriminations, we doubled, trebled and quadrupled external security at halls. The *problem* with Cincinnati was external security, external control: external people control. People in large numbers *need controlling.* They're—they're like cattle. But a lot of kids complained; everywhere they'd look there was a cop. It spoiled their evening for them. They felt, okay, it happened in Cincinnati, but *we don't need that.* There was an article in the paper in Seattle, complaining about the fact that there was *too much security.* It said, "This isn't Germany. The kids in Seattle *don't* rampage. There's never been even a slight *injury* at a concert . . ." et cetera, et cetera, et cetera.

All of which is quite meaningless: "It can't happen here." That's just what I meant about the event seeming not to have happened, to have been deflected.

Probably—but at the same time, it was interesting that the first serious problems they had at Seattle coliseum were at our two gigs [this tour]: the first two gigs they've done with reserved seating on the floor. It's the first time they've actually had audience-inflicted injuries.*

The other side of it is worth mentioning: the fact that the Who don't just get their strength from wearing armor. We did go home, and we did think about it, and we talked about it with our families and our friends. I went home to about ten letters, from the families of the kids who'd died: letters full of deep, deep affection and support and encouragement. It wasn't like these people were being recriminatory. The father of the girl who died who had two children was writing to say that it would hurt *him,* the family, the friends of the family and friends of the girl, if they

---

*The Who's April 16th show was *not* the first concert at the Seattle coliseum to use reserved seating on the floor (there are about half a dozen such shows each year) and—according to a Seattle coliseum guard—it's not the first incidence of audience-inflicted injury in Seattle.

knew that because of what happened, because of her death, we changed our feelings about rock. They understood her feelings about the band, and about the music—you know what I'm saying?

We actually left the States—I know Roger and I had a long conversation about it—with an *incredible* feeling of, without being mordant about it, of *love* for the American people. Everybody had been so positive, and so supportive and *understanding*—even to the point where people would come up to me and say, "We know it wasn't your fault." And to some extent it *was* our fault. It's not exactly the way the Cronkite report made it look, but there was a great share of responsibility there, and people were so willing to—not so much to *forgive,* but firstly to get us back into shape, so that perhaps it was possible for us to behave in a truly realistic, responsive way about the whole thing.

I think only time will tell. If I could dare say it, I'd say that Cincinnati was a very, very positive event for the Who. I think it changed the way we feel about people. It's changed the way we feel about our audience.

In terms of affection?

In terms of affection, and also remembering constantly that they are human beings—and not just people in rows. And I hope the reverse: that people who come to see the band will know that we're human beings too, and not this *myth* you were talking about earlier.

I mean, I watched Roger Daltrey cry his eyes out after that show. I didn't, but he did. But now, whenever a fucking journalist—sorry—asks you about Cincinnati, they expect you to come up with a fucking theatrical tear in your eye! You know: "Have you got anything to say about Cincinnati?" "Oh, we were *deeply* moved, terrible tragedy, the horror, loss of life, *arrrrghh*—" What do you do? We did all the things we thought were right to do at the time: sent flowers to the fucking funerals. All . . . *wasted.* I think when people are dead they're dead.

When I was in England a couple of months ago, there was constant talk of youth-culture violence, particularly from skinheads, and there seemed to be a general feeling that the violence was increasing. Geoff Travis of Rough Trade [a record shop and label in the Notting Hill area of London] spoke of the violence, in his store and on the street, as a day-to-day fact.

I asked him why he thought this was happening, and he gave me various explanations having to do with the economic and political situation in Britain—but he also said that he thought 'Quadrophenia,' the movie, had had an effect. He thought that the movie glamorized violence between youth movements, and also very much exaggerated the mod-rocker violence that did take place in the early- to mid-Sixties, when the movie is set—that the violence was nowhere near so intense as the movie shows it to be. What do you think about that?

Well—I'm sorry to say that I suppose in a way I think he's right. It's very difficult when you make a film—when you *produce* a film—because in the last analysis you have to hand it over to the director. I wrote the script, originally—the first draft screenplay I wrote with Chris Stamp—and there was no riot scene at all. Not at all. For me, *Quadrophenia* was about the fights, and the riots, happening in the kid's *head*. The *threat*: "I'll do anything, I'll go anywhere"—and what you're dealing with is a little wimp. Who's fucking *useless*. Who couldn't fight anybody. He had his few pills, and his bottle of gin, and he *felt* like he could.

It was a study in spiritual desperation: the fact that all that desperation and frustration leads somebody to the point where for the first time in their life they realize that the only important thing is to open their heart. It wasn't about blood and guts and thunder—in the way that the film turned out to be.

It wasn't about the clash of youth cultures.

No. I suppose the director, Franc Roddam, thought it would make good cinema. And I think to some extent it's possible [the film] has sharpened [the violence] up, but I think it runs a bit deeper. A lot of skins would naturally go and see *Quadrophenia,* but the thing that makes skinheads violent is that—well, fundamentally they're fascists. They despise *everybody*—who isn't like them. It's a kind of *toy* fascism, fed by organized fascism: fed by Martin Webster and the National Front.

You know, I'm not afraid to say that I think fascism *stinks,* and I think a lot of skins stink. But I suppose I think any violence stinks, and if you pin down any of these kids, you could actually get it across to them that neither their violence nor their outfits nor their stance is going to *change* anything in British society. But most of all, they're wrong anyway: there's nothing wrong with our society. It's perfectly all right as it is. The way all societies are is that some people get, and some people *don't*. And if you don't fucking *get*, you don't go around slashing people on the face because you've not got enough money to buy a car. You bear it with dignity. The problem to some extent—when you've got a film like *Quadrophenia*—is that it's *exploited* something that's already there: the violence was already there. I don't know quite where the responsibility lies—maybe you could use the same terms I used for Cincinnati: I suppose the responsibility lies in direct proportion to everybody who makes money out of it.

Earlier, we were talking about the different strains of music that exist in Britain now, and you said each was jagged, challenging, didn't fit easily into the social order—and that things didn't seem to be that way in America. In America, when a problem becomes evident, it's common to hear, "Oh, it's just a problem in communications"—as if there couldn't really be anything that truly divides people. Whereas in Britain, the class system is recognizably the basis of the way the country works—it's part of the way this country works, too, but not recognizably—and, in Britain, there is an understanding that real things can divide people: that, inevitably, they do. That, to me, is one of the reasons you can have intensely different audiences and musics, each "jagged," not because one form of music simplistically represents a given class, but because the idea of clashing, of being separated, is part of the society itself: it's not the slightly unreal concept it often is in America. Such conflict implies change, and yet you're saying society as it is right now is just fine—perfect. I'm quite taken aback to hear you say that. It seems to me you're saying a lot more than that it's pointless to try and change society.

I'm saying it's pointless to try and change it through violence. And it's pointless to try and change it through *complaint*. Probably anarchy . . . Anarchy in organized society means standing up and saying, "Listen, I don't fit in, and I refuse to fit in"—and, presumably, you end up in jail. But you don't necessarily have to hurt anyone by being an anarchist; the old image of the anarchist walking around with a bomb, about to blow up the British Museum, is *dated*.

No—I don't think society's perfect at all. What I'm saying is that a lot of the problems that lead to violence, that occur within separatist youth movements in Britain, come from resentment that somebody is better off than they are, and they can't understand the reason why. And they then feel that if this person is better off than they—if there's a Rolls Royce to be had, and it happens to be driven by a Pakistani, then he doesn't deserve it: it belongs to *me*. Charlie Wilkins from Camden Town. With his Dr. Marten boots with steel-toe caps, and his hair shaved off. He probably works for the GPO—and has probably got an IQ of four. And deserves a Rolls Royce as much as a kick in the head. I mean, he deserves *nothing*, is what I'm saying.

Why do British rock movements last so long? There are still Teds, or the Ted-rockabilly subculture; there are mods again; there are still skinheads, after more than a decade. London and towns outside it are full of very young kids in pure 1977 Sid Vicious regalia. Why do these movements last so long, and without developing?

I don't know. There is that deeply ingrained sense of class, and it shatters down now into separatism—but it goes a little bit deeper. There's a need for uniforms; and to some extent it doesn't matter which uniform you choose, just so long as you choose a uniform.

A lot of skins are just kids that like the look. They like football, they like to go and jostle at football matches, get involved in a few punch-outs, but not *kill* people. Not slash people. It's something like getting involved in a fight, and going down to the pub the next day as the hero, with a black eye.

What's important about the uniforms is that they're so *extreme*. You adopt the heavy-metal uniform: you wear a denim jacket, you cover it with badges of this band and that band—UFO—you take your cardboard guitar, and you go down to the Roundhouse, and you wave your long, greasy hair—

Cardboard guitars? To mime playing along?

Right. Then rockabilly: bright pink jackets, with velvet collars; drapes that go halfway down your legs, great big brothel creepers—

Brothel creepers?

Shoes with great, thick crepe soles. And drainpipe trousers, pink socks. Punk: people with beehive, pointed hair, their legs chained together, girls going to clubs with no skirts on. Mod: short, clean haircuts, military clothes—

They're all so fucking extreme: I think it *invites* a them-and-us situation, *wherever it occurs.* The way Franc Roddam tried to *justify* the sensationalist violence *in Quadrophenia* was by analyzing the relationship between the two friends: Kevin, who was the rocker, and Jimmy, who was the mod. Despite the fact that they were friends, and had a hell of a lot in common, and could have gone on to become closer, Jimmy ends up finding himself beating his own friend up, simply because he's wearing the wrong clothes.

It's so *clear* who are "they" and who are "us"—animosity comes quite naturally. Quite why there is the need for uniforms, I don't know. I'm still trying to work that out.

THE GUITAR GREATS:
PETE TOWNSHEND

John Tobler and Stuart Grundy | 1983 | *The Guitar Greats* (UK)

Pete Townshend has always been more than a great composer. A pioneer in combining lead and rhythm work, playing electric guitar in a quasi-flamenco style, harnessing feedback, and purveying volume, he is one of rock's most extraordinary guitarists. This chapter from the book based on the eighties BBC radio series *The Guitar Greats* gives an insight into how his remarkable techniques developed, as well as providing more general Who history. —Ed.

Notes: for "*Chinese Eyes*" read "*All the Best Cowboys Have Chinese Eyes*"

Pete Townshend needs little introduction—he is, although he would perhaps reject the term, a celebrity. Pete was born on 19 May 1945, in London, to a musical family—his father was a musician, of which Pete was very proud and he enjoyed going to see his father play.

'It was mainly what I'd call post-war dance music, highly arranged big band stuff, with over twenty pieces, with a bit of Dixieland jazz thrown in and mainstream jazz when he had the opportunity, plus a wide variety of session work, sometimes playing bass clarinet on symphonic works, and at other times, playing bass or baritone sax for a rock album. But we didn't have much music at home, apart from when he was practising or when he had a jam session with a few friends. We never had a piano in the house, and I don't think my parents have got a decent record player even now—I think there are quite a few musicians like that, who don't necessarily live in an atmosphere of music, because I suppose they don't always want to take their work home with them.'

No pressure was applied to Pete to make him learn an instrument, and his first musical attempts involved playing the mouth organ in the bath. 'I did think about playing clarinet at one point, but I couldn't get the embouchure right to make a note, so I waited until I was eleven or twelve and could get hold of a guitar and eventually my grandmother gave me one for Christmas which I think cost her three quid—she was robbed! It was a bit of a disappointment, because it was much harder than I thought, and because it was such a poor instrument, it was really difficult to play. I think a lot of learners suffer from being told that they'll be bought a better instrument when they've shown they have a bit of flair, but the irony is that if you pay a lot of money for a good instrument and the kid doesn't work out well on it, you can always sell it for more than you paid for it, because good instruments hold their value, whereas rubbish instruments don't. Obviously, a lot of people can't afford to pay £60 for a good learning instrument, but it's worth doing, because I think it's very hard to gauge your potential on a bad instrument. So I mucked about for two years, not achieving very much and sitting in my bedroom playing a few chords, and it took me two years before I got a plectrum and a chord book. The first decent instrument I had was a banjo, so my guitar playing style developed for about 18 months around almost a Dixieland banjo style, and there are still traces of it in my playing today, that rhythmic, chordal approach.'

During the late 1950s, Townshend was in fact a member of a traditional jazz band. 'John Entwistle and I had a band with a couple of schoolfriends, but we were more interested in the glamour of rock, and trad. was about to die—a lot of the musicians were getting old and losing their energy, and the Acker Bilks, Kenny Balls and Ken Colyers were obviously just about to move into cabaret. There was still a small cult following for jazz as a result of the Aldermaston marches and so on, but it was in its dying years, and we could sense the rock revolution coming up on the horizon, through Elvis and Bill Haley, and to a lesser extent, through bands like the Shadows. Once the Shadows were established, that was all we wanted to do, so John chucked away his trumpet and built a bass guitar, and although I still play the banjo to this day, I concentrated much harder on guitar—I literally shut myself away for three or four years and learnt properly.'

Historically, soon after rock music supplanted traditional jazz, rock itself became somewhat uninspiring, only being rescued by the Beatles and their ilk, although Pete, it seems, was unconcerned. 'I didn't care, because I had none of the aspirations then to do what I have done, and I wasn't interested in songwriting. Remember, my dad was a member of a band, and guitar players then had few courses of action. They could play in a small combo doing clubs and hope that one day they might get into a rock band, but then I always thought of myself as a rhythm player, and had no aspirations to be like Hank Marvin. I never wanted to front a band or sing, I just wanted to play rhythm, which fitted in very much with my status within the group of friends I had at the time, because I wasn't in any way a charismatic part of the team of geezers I hung around with then. I was the shortest and probably the least significant, and that was the way I was thinking—it was only later on, under great pressure from record companies, that I started to write and take a slightly more aggressive role.'

Aggression certainly appeared to be a major Townshend character-istic at one point during the Who's early career—was it due to pressure, or simply the discovery of a burning ambition? 'I don't know, but I think a lot of it came from the way Roger (Daltrey) led his life during the early days of the Who, when we were called the Detours. He was a very challenging guy—not freely aggressive, but he knew what he wanted and how to get it, and in a sense, he taught me how to fight for what I wanted, and as I started to improve and become more positive and forceful about what I was doing, he readily allowed me to take over from him as lead guitarist in the group, and at that time, of course, we didn't have a rhythm player, and I just played lead. We were one of the first bands to use that trio line up, loosely modelled on Johnny Kidd & the Pirates, whose guitarist, Mick Green, forged that particular guitar style later used by me and Hendrix and Eric Clapton and Wilko Johnson.

'I got an early introduction to rhythm & blues music through an American friend who went to the same college as I did—that was when I was sixteen, so I got into stuff like (John Lee) Hooker, Jimmy Reed and B. B. King before anyone else, and the only other people who were as clued up with records were the Stones, and in fact, we had virtually identical record collections, although it later emerged that quite a few other people were fairly well educated in the blues, but at the time, it was a bit of a plus.'

Like so many notable British musicians from the '60s, Townshend attended art college. 'It's because rock is art, and I don't think you can argue with that anymore. I think a lot of art college people were trying to do the kind of art which they had a preconception about, and they suddenly realised, and were actually told by people like Peter Blake, one of the great pop artists of that period and still a good friend of mine, that rock or pop music was a new art form, although not necessarily one that had to be taken incredibly seriously.'

Townshend's guitar technique was not the result of lessons. 'My father got me started, but tended to leave me to my own devices, although he was very encouraging, and told me to learn some basic musical principles, which I did, concentrating mainly on chords and harmony rather than sight reading.' It's often suggested that too much formal training detracts from a player's individuality . . . 'I'm not sure about that—it's potentially a problem because you learn using exactly the same procedure, sitting the same way and practising exactly the same scales as the other people you're competing against, and virtuosity becomes the premier attraction, but let's also remember that in classical music, it's interpretation that's important. Like Rodrigo's Guitar Concerto, which has been recorded now by about eight players, who play exactly the same part, but interpret it all very differently.'

His own group, the Detours, who started around 1961/2, were together for about four years. 'That band went through a few changes, so many, in fact, that it would be boring to note them all, because Peter Vernon Kell, who now runs a record label and a production company, was the only one who ever did anything else musically, and he played guitar with us for about two months. There was a drummer, a couple of singers, a couple of keyboard players and a couple of other guitarists, but they were just people who passed through the band. We got a hell of a lot of work, and we were good at copying other people's music, but the aims of a small band playing at the White Hart, Acton, are quite modest, and our idea was really to have a good time. The atmosphere then was very similar to how it is today, with a lot of young people walking around saying that the end of the world is nigh, and they might as well get it while they can, so we weren't willing to wait for success. So for us, a good time was maybe a season at Butlin's, where we could spend six months in the summer knocking off birds, getting drunk and being paid for the privilege, sunbathing during the day, and doing Cliff Richard impersonations every night—but we failed the audition.'

However, despite this somewhat unambitious approach to a career, the Detours were making experimental moves musically. 'The R&B records I mentioned included a lot of music I had never come across before, like I'd never heard Ray Charles doing R&B, only his smoochy stuff, and Howlin' Wolf, and Jimmy Smith's organ playing . . . Roger started to get very interested in R&B, and we started to introduce it more and more—I found this music much more a vehicle for the expression I felt akin to. Once I wrote a song, it really freed the band and me a lot to start developing our own image, our own stance, and to talk about our own lifestyle and environment and who we were. The fact that blues singers sang about real life was quite important, and affected Roger and I and eventually the whole band.

'Then we got Keith Moon, who was an enormous catalyst for the sound of the band, because his style never changed—right through his life, it was always that incredibly fluid, rumbustious, extravagant style, but still very musical. He had an incredible intuitive response, so you could sound like you were going bananas, but in actual fact be playing quite disciplined stuff. He was like the missing link, and we only worked with him for six months before we were "discovered". Then came the scenes with our first manager, a local Jewish entrepreneur, who introduced us to Pete Meaden, and then Kit Lambert arriving and finally taking over the management, which all happened within about two months.'

During the first half of 1964, the group briefly changed their name to the High Numbers and released a single, the only one they made under that name, 'I'm The Face', which was not a success, despite the climate apparently being perfect.

'I think only 300 records were pressed, and the rumour is that Pete Meaden's mum bought them all! Pete was a very deep influence on the band—apart from some of his image-grooming maybe appearing to be trite, he actually made us very conscious of the audience, and aware of the idea of reflecting their feelings rather than just ramming music down their throat.'

It has been said that the Townshend visual style was partially to compensate for his lack of musical ability on guitar and Pete himself agrees. 'I was tremendously frustrated because I wasn't moving ahead fast enough, and I was in an arena of incredible guitar players, like Eric (Clapton), who didn't start until he was seventeen or eighteen, and a year later was blowing people's minds in the Yardbirds, whereas I'd been struggling along since I was eleven, so there was some frustration there, things I felt I should be able to do which I couldn't do, and I compensated with visual things. I found it was easier to get more effect from the things I could do, and that's still the case today, where I can get the audience screaming and cheering as though Bruce Springsteen had just walked on by simply smashing a guitar. Not everybody could do that, but I can do it and get an audience on their feet, and I could spend two hours trying to play clever guitar solos and have to work bloody hard to get anything like that kind of theatrical effect, because rock, to me, in live performances is still a theatrical event, and its pointless to ignore that.

'And that's what's so unique about the guitar, as a new instrument—it has new qualities which are still fairly fresh, and can do so many different things, like on Jeff Beck's last album, where it sounds like a violin, with that expressive quality, or it can sound incredibly angry and incredibly sweet, and it's still available in its original form, a classical guitar with nylon strings, or in country & western hybrids or folk hybrids. All these styles and types of sound are still available, but the main thing is that it's an instrument you can stand up with on stage, wear round your neck, hold like a machine gun and turn up bloody loud! It's a perfect theatrical tool.'

So what about the idea that the guitar was on the point of being made extinct by the synthesiser? 'I think that people in the music business always believe, in a visionary sense, in technology always advancing at exactly the same rate, but I tend to disagree, because I think we're already in a situation where synthesiser development is running too fast for musicians to keep up—only now, for example, is the mini-Moog being used properly and expressively.'

We returned to talking about the Who's ability to reflect the feelings of their audience, many of whom, in the early years, were 'mods'. 'I don't think we exactly performed that function—they could relate to us in several different ways, partly through the songs we wrote and archetypically through "My Generation", and the first three Who singles, "Can't Explain", "Anyway, Anyhow, Anywhere" and "My Generation", were the ones where I tried hardest, and were overtly aimed at trying to reflect street level frustration, because there was something happening at that time. The atmosphere was very doomy—there was Bertrand Russell standing on a podium with an audience of 20,000 in Trafalgar Square, everybody saying that he was a genius, a doctor of this and that with sixteen degrees, and he said that the world was going to end in two years. The old bugger was 82 years old, and we're still here, but he gave us all a bit of a fright, and I think one did walk around in a bolshie mood. Later, I think we tended to use more subtle devices, and it wasn't always by dressing the same as the audience or anything like that—really, the Who discovered a technique and we don't quite know how it works, and it's evident to me that Springsteen has discovered the same technique. It's quite interesting that the first rock concert he saw had the Who performing, and he saw something we had that other bands didn't have. We weren't a band with a figurehead, like the Stones with Jagger in front, we didn't have a particularly powerful image, and we didn't make particularly wonderful records, but there was just something there, some trick. If you talk to early Who fans, they'll tell you it was more than the music, it was a magic, and I think that was something we learned to get back from the audience, something to do with audience/performer awareness.'

Once Pete had discovered the ability to write, he seemed to become very prolific very quickly, with which he agreed. Was, for example, 'Anyway, Anyhow, Anywhere' written quickly?

'Yeah. I actually wrote that song about Charlie Parker, when I was listening to one of his solos, and I just scribbled those three words on a piece of paper because I thought that was how he sounded, so free and liberated. Roger helped to write the final lyric—he wanted it to be more about the street, and we finished the lyrics off together.'

One aspect of the Who's early recordings which many found appealing (perhaps a very early foretaste of the punk rock movement of ten or more years later?) was the roughness of their quality. Was this intentional, either on the part of the group, or of their producer, Shel Talmy? 'Shel was sort of a factory producer, a good hard worker who wanted to make records as efficiently and economically as possible, and wanted hits but didn't want to spend too much time messing about with what the artist wanted, so often we were very unsatisfied. Later on, when we really tried hard and spent a long time in the studio with Kit (Lambert), we ended up with results that weren't always better anyway, and I think Shel's skill was in using studio set ups and mikes and things to their best advantage, like the use of the early limiter/compressors and stuff like that, which nowadays everybody raves about—can they get hold of an old valve limiter/compressor so that they can get that old horrible sound? (Laughs). Even that was in its infancy then—a limiter/compressor wasn't something you used for effect, you used it for control. We made our first album, *My Generation,* in two days, two four hour sessions, all the tracks and all the vocals and everything.'

As a songwriter who was also a guitarist, was there a tendency for Pete to write in a way which catered for his own style of playing? 'I did start to get a little bit in a rut—there was always a feedback passage where I could go "Yaggadang!", and I still tend to do that to some extent. Yes, of course I write for the style I play in—even if I write on acoustic guitar, I tend to leave myself room, and I hope on my next solo album to include more straight up guitar solos, but then again, you have to concentrate on what you're best at, because everybody's evolving in such acutely different directions.'

Was Pete prone to experimentation in those early days, for example, with feedback? 'I started to get into really rough-sounding guitar through listening to John Lee Hooker records, and I suppose his sound was rough because he had a rough guitar, and probably a tiny amplifier, so it was very distorted. John Entwistle used the first 4 × 12 cabinet that Jim Marshall made, and the first Marshall amp, and I really liked the sound of that. It was developed for bass originally, and I asked him to build me a speaker cabinet for guitar, which I drove with a Fender amp, and used at ear level, so I'd literally get the whole force of the thing blowing my head off. Before that, people put their amps on the ground, or at most on a chair, but I decided I wanted it higher, and thus it was also blasting right into the guitar pick ups, and I got feedback immediately, which at first I dealt with as a problem, but I quickly began to realise that it could be controlled musically, and once I'd got my semi-acoustic Rickenbacker, I could actually play songs on one note on feedback, just picking out the harmonics by moving the angle of the guitar, and I got really good at it. I was never interested in outboard equipment, like echo effects or wah wahs—I used to leave those to other people to muck about with.'

We have already mentioned the fact that Pete was world famous for destroying his guitars, but how did it actually start? 'It happened initially by accident, and a few pretty girls in the audience laughed, so I decided to make it look deliberate, and I'd luckily just got myself a spare guitar— I broke a Rickenbacker 6-string, and I'd just bought a 12-string—so I finished it off, and they rapidly stopped laughing, and I think I emptied the hall, but it filled up again the next week. In the end, it reached the daily papers and stories were printed about it, and it just got out of control. Once Keith realised he was getting left out, he started smashing his stuff up, and it developed from there, and eventually became less of a spontaneously jumped on gimmick than a potential outlet for frustration and a great theatrical device we could use when things weren't going too well. And we also liked the fact that when we decided the show was over, it was over, and there was no way the promoter was going to tell us that we hadn't played long enough, or that we were going to get any of this encore rubbish, which occasionally used to happen.'

One of the Who's strongest aspects has been their often superb (and frequently lengthy) live performances, although Townshend, for one, has more recently disclosed that he enjoys playing on stage less and less as time goes on. 'I don't know whether I've ever really enjoyed it that much—I've always had reservations about it, but I think I both enjoy and abhor it to the same extent now as I did then. Roger and I both find it very difficult being rock musicians carrying a large past, apart from simply getting older and finding it physically difficult to sustain stamina over a long period of time, although that's one of the easy bits, and after a week of touring, you're usually in incredible shape . . . with the Who, anyway. But it's really the fact that a player like B. B. King has a certain dignity which I don't think I'll ever have. I'll probably still occasionally want to get up and play when I'm his age, but his material isn't really concerned with youth and youth subjects as so much of mine has been for such a long time—I wrote *Quadrophenia* when I was twenty-nine, so I was middle-aged by then, and I was still writing about Brighton beach and punch-ups and popping pills.'

Advancing age seems always to have been one of Pete Townshend's major concerns, and still seemingly worries him greatly. 'I think it does more than I let on, actually, even though I let on quite a lot, because I really enjoy the company of younger people more than I should, and although this may be heresy to a few of my mates, I'd almost prefer to see the Original Mirrors than Bruce Springsteen.'

During 1967/8, the Who were making hit records, yet, for a highly-successful band, they seemed to be suffering financial embarassment. 'Yeah, we were really broke, partly because of the guitar smashing, but also because having hit records in Britain didn't make you a lot of money. I used to do better than the rest of the band, because I wrote the stuff, and towards the end, John used to write the B-sides, so he had an income from that period, and then we started to share the B-sides out among the guys in the band, but even if you sell 100,000 singles, you don't make much money, and we were trying to run a very hard touring band who were over-equipped hardware-wise compared to other bands at the time, with a much larger PA, much larger amplification and lots of spare equipment, which was necessary. Eventually, everything we put out seemed to peak at eight or ten or twelve, then we'd get a brief period of successful touring in Britain and Europe, and then the record would slide out again, and we'd have to climb the same mountain again, and I got really sick of it. I'd kept "I Can See For Miles" back for about eighteen months or two years as a kind of ace in the hole, and we finally stuck it out and I thought it would be the Who's first real number one record, but it didn't do at all well, and was one of our least successful records, which wasn't through lack of play. I was bitterly disappointed and disillusioned, and I just decided to go for broke and do something completely mad, and started work at that point on "Tommy", which took easily a couple of years. It didn't start off as work on "Tommy"—I started on two other things, one of which was called "Rael", a full blown rock opera thing which didn't get completed, and turned up as a cameo track on one of our albums. We must have started "Tommy" in early '68, because it took ages and ages to finish—not because we spent a lot of time in the studio, although we did decide that we were going to spend a lot of money on it, but mainly because we kept having new ideas, so we'd go back and re-record tracks, because we wanted to include a theme from another song. That was a drawn out period of recording.'

'Tommy' is generally regarded as the Who's finest hour, or at least their most ambitious and successful project. How does Pete feel about it more than ten years later, as it certainly appeared from the outside to have become a millstone around his neck at one time?

'In my life, it probably still is, because I'm still involved with the publishing, the follow-ups, the amateur dramatics, the touring productions, the West End production and everything else, but from the band's point of view, I think we're well over it now. It really was a millstone during the Woodstock period—we played Woodstock, and after a long quiet period, the *Woodstock* film came out and the record went back up the charts, so we had to play "Tommy" for another nine months on the road in America, when our tours were just exploitative. But equally, it sold more than probably any Who record ever made, and helped us significantly financially, and gave us a lot of credibility with American audiences, more than some of the other bands who had benefited from Woodstock, like Ten Years After, because it was considered a very serious work, even though half of it was tongue in cheek, and it was the record that finally broke us once and for all in the States.'

Another facet of Pete Townshend's life has been his patronage of other promising musicians, and in 1969, Joe Walsh was the recipient of encouragement above and beyond the call of duty, his band of the time, the James Gang, being invited to support the Who on tour.

'Yeah, when the Who first played alongside the James Gang, I immediately recognised Joe as a very important player. His style was lyrical and flowing, but his chord work, both on keyboards and on acoustic guitar, was very much a derivation of my work, which made me feel flattered —I felt he was a great synthesis of the American lazy, Hendrix-y kind of guitar style and the more English sound, and I really liked him because of that, and I also really liked their first record at the time, so I gave them a plug wherever I could'.

This was the era of the huge open air festivals, and as well as Woodstock, the Who played the 1969 and 1970 Isle Of Wight extravaganzas—how did he feel the two compared? 'The Isle Of Wight was very different, and I enjoyed it much more than Woodstock, which I didn't enjoy at all. Both the Isle Of Wight festivals were wonderful—when Rikki Farr first came round to tell me that Dylan was going to play the 1969 festival, I didn't believe him, because the last time Dylan had played in England, he'd been booed off stage at the Albert Hall, but when it all came together, I was really pleased. I enjoyed both years, and they were great festivals.'

No profile of Pete Townshend would be complete without some reference to Meher Baba, his 'guru', an Indian mystic whose memory Pete has kept very much alive since Baba's 'bodily demise' in 1969, only a couple of years after Townshend had learnt of his teachings. 'I discovered Baba in 1967, or at least definitely before *Tommy*, because I was really conscious of trying to write that in the Sufi tradition, to have a multi-layered story which could be read either as a series of rock songs, or just a story, or a story with religious overtones, or a spiritual tale, or what you will. I wasn't exactly sure what he was about at the time, and its probably taken me to the present day to fathom what he really is all about and what he was really saying, and what he was doing when he was living in India, although I've obviously been very deeply and personally involved in the work of disseminating books and films and stuff to anybody that wants to know, as one of the only people with enough spare cash to do it really. Initially, Baba affected me deeply, and it was manifested most instantly on *Tommy*—there's a credit on *Tommy* which reads "Avatar, Meher Baba". My interest started when I stopped using drugs, which was a very sudden, immediate, impetuous decision. All my friends and the people in the music business were very druggy people—narcotics weren't common, but hallucinogenics, marijuana, LSD and stuff like that—and I just decided after the Monterey Pop Festival in 1967, which was the first big festival we played in America, that I'd had enough of it. I looked at all these hippies walking round in California, and thought, "This has got nothing to do with Shepherd's Bush; I've had enough of it". As soon as I stopped, I realised that I'd been replacing with drugs an important vacuum of experience and knowledge-gathering and feeling and emotion-gathering that needed filling, and I started to read and search, and looked fairly light-heartedly at certain sort of mystical things.'

The next subject we discussed was about the possibility of the Who ceasing to perform live, and just how they coped with the problem of playing lengthy sets, and what material they included from the vast catalogue of songs accumulated during a career taking in nearly two decades.

'There would be debates, but we tended to end up playing what was obvious. If we do any long shows again—although they may not necessarily be long tours—they'll inevitably include lots of the songs we're still doing, that we can't leave out, like "Won't Get Fooled Again", "Baba O'Riley", "Substitute", classic standout tracks which don't necessarily have any stigma attached to them and haven't been analysed as deeply as the "Tommy" things or "My Generation". They're just really great rock songs which get everybody at it, so we'd inevitably use them, and we don't change the way we play them much at all, because for twelve or thirteen years, we'd been using exactly the same line-up—the biggest change that ever happened in the career of the Who was when we brought in a keyboard player. We did attempt it once before, when we were working on *Who Are You?*, and Nicky Hopkins came over from the States to work with us, but he's a very frail guy, and he was really sick, so we decided not to drag him round the world on the road, although we did rehearse with him. Then we dropped the idea for a long time, but when Keith (Moon) died, I pushed very hard to get a keyboard player in, or another guitar player. We had routined a couple of tracks with Rabbit

(John Bundrick) when Keith was alive for recording, and I'd liked the way he played and we used him, but I suppose it was me wanting someone to play against—I felt I'd always been caught into providing the rhythm, the backbone, particularly on the earlier material, and I wanted to be free to play solos and one note lines, and sometimes just not play at all. The other element was that songs like "I Can See For Miles" and "Dr. Jimmy & Mr. Jim" from *Quadrophenia* are very complex harmonically and use juxtaposing chords on different instruments to get a particular effect, and sometimes even more complicated than that, like taking the left hand of the piano and playing it on the guitar, and there were things like that which we just couldn't do—we couldn't get the fullness of sound that we wanted in sections like "See Me, Feel Me" in *Tommy,* which needs a good sustained sound behind it, and I felt it would really help a lot, so I'm glad we've done it, and I think the keyboard is the right thing with which to augment the Who.'

How much does fatigue have to be taken into account by Townshend, as a rhythm player who has to drive the show along, acting almost like a dynamo—does he have to go into training for a tour, and how does it affect his hands and the way he plays? 'Since I've been slightly less brutal on my hands, my playing has improved a bit—funnily enough, it improved after an extremely childish, brutal event where I punched a wall and broke a finger, and had to do the last American tour with a cast. It changed the way that I held the pick, and turned out to be an advantage, because I used to hold it very loosely—it almost used to float in mid-air and I'd keep catching it, to get that fluid, percussive fast rhythm sound. I started holding it a lot harder, and a lot of modern players are discovering that the harder the pick you can afford to play with, the more fluid your solo style becomes. But yes, I used to not only psych myself up physically but mentally as well, and almost start to withdraw two weeks before a tour or an important show. Sometimes I ran a bit, but never a hell of a lot, because it was just nervous energy. I've always been naturally fit, although I've never looked it, which I think has been one of the great things about being on stage with the Who—I always looked like a corpse, but to act like an athlete is kind of an anathema—dichotomy, rather.'

The familiar image of Pete Townshend on stage is of him swinging his arm in a huge circle as he strikes a chord, something which he adopted after seeing Keith Richard play. 'Yeah, it was in '63, when we were called the Detours, and we played with the Stones when they'd just started at St Mary's Ballroom, Putney, and he was literally limbering up as the curtains opened, and I just copied what he was doing. He did it once, and I did it forever . . . He's always been my favourite player, and the Stones have always been my favourite band.'

The guitars on which Townshend performs, unlike his style, have gone through several changes . . . 'The first decent one I had was an Epiphone which Roger gave to me, a solid guitar with quite a small body and little black pick-ups on it—Epiphone was about to merge with Gibson at that time, I think. Later on, I flogged that and got my first Rickenbacker, and I used Rickenbackers up to about '66, I suppose, and then I got fed up with how weak they were strengthwise, and they were also very hard to get and very overpriced—I hadn't helped because I'd been using them, and the Beatles hadn't helped because they had too, and they were very striking-looking guitars.'

But don't guitar makers form a queue to make instruments for someone like Townshend? 'To some extent, I suppose—the custom-makers line up because they want the money, as there are very few people that can afford to pay £2,000 for a guitar, which is what a really excellent instrument costs, and that's because the wood is so expensive, because the pick-ups are so carefully wound, because so much craftsmanship goes into it, and because there aren't factories doing it, but just small companies, hundreds of people. The large companies pursue you for endorsements, which I've never given, so I've almost always had to pay for my guitars—I turn them down because I don't want kids to think I can get something for nothing and they can't. . . . After Rickenbackers, I went on to Gibson SGs, with a small solid body, which I used for about another three years, then I started using Fender Strats and Telecasters during Hendrix's reign. Then I went back to Gibsons, Les Pauls, and after that, I tried all kinds of things—I used a guitar called a Coral once, but not their sitar/guitar, and all kinds of cheap guitars which I liked the sound of—the Coral had a Danelectro pick-up—and then I went back to Fenders for a short period, and then I used a Les Paul De Luxe, which has very small pick-ups on it, but they're too heavy, and as I got older, I found that I'd get this incredible pain across my collar bone just from the weight of the guitar across the strap, and I think it buggered up my collar bone. So I looked for guitars with lighter bodies, and in the end, I got them made, first by an American company called Scheckle, and finally by an English company, Giffin, who make all my guitars now, and they're not too expensive either.'

One of Pete's 'extra-curricular' activities during the late 1960s was working with a group he championed, Thunderclap Newman, and on several of whose records he played bass using a pseudonym of Bijou Drains. 'The name didn't really mean anything, but what was most interesting about that was that I played the bass while engineering the record, going from two track Revox to two track Revox.' But wasn't he disappointed that, after scoring a number one hit with 'Something In The Air', the band achieved little else?

'No, not really—I think it would have sustained had Kit Lambert taken over the production and management of the band properly, but also it was really a lack of follow-through in the band. Speedy Keen was the drummer and writer, and I was very much his mentor, in the same way that Kit Lambert was my mentor. Once we'd finished the album, which was meant to be a very light-hearted homespun affair, the Who went out on a massive American tour, and when we got back, it was all finished. They'd tried to put out three singles from the album, but the album really wasn't singles material. They would have done better to wait, and they also made the mistake of trying to do live appearances, which were a disaster.'

At this point, we turned the clock back to influences—'Syd Barrett was an influence because I used to love early Floyd, and I think Roger Waters was a bit of an influence as well, although to a lesser extent. Syd influenced Eric (Clapton) as well—we went to see the Floyd at the UFO Club a couple of times together, and I went to see them every time they played there. They were just unbelievable, one of the most literally frightening bands I'd ever seen, and it wasn't just because everybody was doing LSD. They were frightening when I saw them at Alexandra Palace and I was stone cold sober, which may have been the worst way to see them. They were spine-chilling—Syd was just manic, and everything went through dozens of echo units, and you couldn't tell the beginning from the middle from the end. I listened to John Fahey a lot and still do, and to another player called Robbie Basho, who incidentally shares my interest in Meher Baba, and was on John Fahey's label, Takoma. What I get from Fahey's playing is almost the same as I get from listening to a Terry Riley record, cyclic electronic music, and it has a similar kind of round quality.'

Which leads to the 1971 album, *Who's Next,* on which Townshend used synthesisers in the style of Terry Riley, even calling one track 'Baba O'Riley'. 'That was an interesting period for me—that John Fahey type guitar playing, the constant bashing away fingerpicking style was similar to the electronic music of someone like Terry Riley or (John) Cage, certain things they did. I was introduced to that whole kind of area of electronic music by Tim Souster, who also introduced me to the synthesiser. I got a great big ARP synthesiser and started to work on a film script, which is called *Lifehouse,* and which I'm still working on today. It examines the whole theory of music, where it comes from, how it affects you, and all that kind of thing, and I used that kind of mood as a backdrop for Who music.'

Surely making *Who's Next* must have somehow changed Pete's approach to guitar playing? 'Maybe it did a bit—remember, this was also the first album since the very early days that we'd done with Glyn Johns, and it was our first album that he'd produced. Kit Lambert had done an incredible amount of preparatory work on the album, taken us to New York, where we re-recorded all the tracks I'd done as demos, and routined and rehearsed them before we went in with Glyn. Joe Walsh had just given me a really great Gretsch guitar, the kind that Neil Young once used, and is currently used by the Stray Cats, and I really got into solo playing quite a lot. Nicky Hopkins did a lot of keyboard work on that album, and most of the tracks were done live, just with piano, guitar, drums and bass. What I was doing was overdubbing the rhythm guitar, and putting the solo guitar on while we were doing the tracks, which was a complete reversal, and was Glyn's idea, which I thought was brilliant at the time.'

Was the fact that the Who didn't like some of Townshend's songs part of the reason for him doing the *Who Came First* album, which many consider to be his first solo album? 'I don't really think of that as a solo album, because I used a song by Ronnie Lane and a song by Billy Nicholls on it, and I had very little to do with those apart from the fact that they were recorded in my studio. It was more of a devotional album, really, which we did together in reaction to the fact that the Meher Baba limited edition albums that we'd put together, of which there were only 2,000 copies printed, had sold so well, and there was tremendous demand for the material. I offered it to my record label in America, and they said they'd donate the funds to a Meher Baba charity, and I thought it was worth doing.' The authors have always considered one track on the album 'Sheraton Gibson' most attractive. 'I loved that track—"Sheraton Gibson"—I think it's sweet, and I like the fact that it was the first time I ever played the Chet Atkins guitar style, which I used to play when I was a kid. I studied his playing—he played with a thumb pick, and that was the first time I ever managed to pull it off on a record and have it sound like anything.'

Who Came First was a completed project, but having already mentioned the *Lifehouse* project, were there other items which were in the course of completion which related to Pete? 'Because I've always had a studio at home, and always had fairly free access to studios—at the moment, I'm lucky enough to have three studios operational, all at various levels of technical excellence—I tend to get a tremendous backlog of material, not only of my own stuff but of bands that I've worked with or people that I know. For example, before Roy Harper went over to the States he was going through a troublesome scene with his record label, and just didn't have the money to record, so I lent him a machine, and I presume he churned out a few songs . . . and I've always had that—if I ever feel like doing anything, I do it, so I've got a tremendous amount of stuff, some of it unfinished, some of it off on a tangent because I do it purely for pleasure, and some of it experimental, but a lot of it's complete and just not very good.'

Following the enormous success of *Tommy,* the world seemed to be waiting for a similar Townshend extravaganza, which eventually appeared, although perhaps with less striking results, as *Quadrophenia.* 'That was actually a very quick project—I started writing it on holiday in France in May or June, 1973, and it was out in November, and we were on the road with it immediately. It was very quick, and while we were recording it, the Who also built Ramport recording studio. *Quadrophenia* was a slightly weird project for me, because perhaps I was moving a bit too fast for the band, but I wrote the story and then the music, and I took in a batch of demos that fitted together like a jigsaw. Very unlike *Tommy,* where there were just five or six songs to start with, and we talked about it, and John and Keith would come in with ideas—for example, at the end of the story of *Tommy,* I wanted to have some kind of church affair, some kind of nutty cathedral at the end, and Keith suggested that it should be a holiday camp, so there was a lot of exchange there. *Quadrophenia* was completely intractable—if you changed any part of it, it wouldn't work, so there wasn't room for an exchange of ideas, and although the band were very pleased with what they did on it, they did feel a bit cornered, particularly as it was a double album.'

Shortly after the release of *Quadrophenia,* the Who's career seemed to enter a hiatus, the next four years providing little in the way of new material other than a rather strange collection of old tracks whose title, *Odds And Sods,* was all too appropriate, and an equally disappointing new LP, *The Who By Numbers.* 'Yes, but there were two factors involved in that. One was that our management had fallen apart—Kit Lambert had moved out of the picture because it was becoming impossible for him to work with the group, because the group was still really quite disciplined and he'd become very undisciplined. And the other factor, of course, was the bloody *Tommy* film, which occupied a massive chunk of time, and in fact went right through that whole period.'

Despite its taking up so much of Pete's time, the *Tommy* project, and particularly the film, had made him a good deal of money. Does being rich affect his creative output? 'I've found that if I've ever been lucky enough to have a lot of money in the bank, I've always been able to think about something to do with it very quickly, either to pour it back into some fairly massive creative project or some business scheme, or else there'll be something that I need, like some musical instrument I can't live without, or a new mixing desk. *Tommy* did make a lot of money for the band, which we spent almost exclusively on buying Shepperton Studios, or about a third or a quarter of it, and putting together a big PA company, so that our roadies had something to do with their lives. So it wasn't as though we were walking around with wads of money, not feeling as though we had to work, but then I don't think it's ever been money that's driven us.'

Pete had always seemed to be the member of the Who to take the major responsibilities on his shoulders . . . 'I don't know that that's entirely true—each individual in the band took as much responsibility as I would allow them to share, and with *Quadrophenia,* I took the whole project on my shoulders and wouldn't let anybody else in. It wasn't a question of them not wanting to. I still suffer from that to a great extent today, and I'm very closeted not only with creative things, but with any-thing involving emotion—I like to keep it private until I feel it's been sufficiently edited to unleash on the unwitting public. I think I'm an extrovert, but I do oscillate—sometimes I feel very extrovert, sometimes I don't, and I definitely get very maudlin and moody occasionally, but then if you can get really high naturally, then you can expect to get really low naturally too, and everybody goes through that, but not everybody lives their life under a microscope.'

In 1977, Townshend was involved in an album titled *Rough Mix,* on which he shared the billing with Ronnie Lane. 'That was really spontane-ous—Ronnie wasn't getting taken seriously by his record company, and he told me that he reckoned that they'd take him a bit more seriously if I agreed to produce the record that he was about to make. I told him I really couldn't do that, despite the fact that I'd recorded a lot with him at home, and we were very close at the time, because it would be awful if he ended up seeing me like Glyn Johns or something, walking away at the end of the sessions saying "I don't want to see him for another two months, because he's told me some horrible truths, like I was sing-ing flat and it was a crappy song". So I agreed to play on a record with Ronnie, if he could get Glyn to produce it, and Glyn agreed immediately, so we did it. It didn't turn out to be a creative collaboration as much as a three-week party, and it was great fun.'

1978 saw the untimely death of Keith Moon, whose last work for the Who was on the *Who Are You* LP, a record which to some gave the impression that it had been created largely for the American market. 'That's very true—the backdrop to that album was the punk movement in this country, which initially alienated all the established musicians because it was so incredibly aggressive towards them, despite the fact that a lot of people quietly welcomed it. I welcomed it loudly, but it didn't help, and they still called me rude names, and one tended to feel that Britain was going through an explosive situation, and we should look to where we could manage to survive for a bit longer, so we were more conscious of the American market than we had been up to that point. It's just starting to happen in America, but of course not with the same venom, and there's quite an interesting band called the Dead Kennedys, who've got the same kind of venom as the Sex Pistols, but none of the genius. As the Talking Heads said, "I'm still waiting for the music revolution to happen", and I think it hasn't happened there because a lot of America is so staid and middle class, and how spread out it is. It could possibly have succeeded in New York, but even New York's incredibly cosmopolitan, and the white teenage situation in New York is a minority, whereas in London, it's a landslide.'

During 1979, Pete Townshend played several public shows which were, to say the least, out of the ordinary. One was for Amnesty International, where he and John Williams, the noted classical guitarist, duetted on Pete's 'Won't Get Fooled Again'. 'The first day of that went on for ever, and seriously, I think I fell asleep on stage in the middle of the song and actually came round, but everybody in the audience was doing it too, because the show went on for nearly four hours, and everybody was sitting there after their big dinners and two bottles of wine. I enjoyed doing it, but most of all, I enjoyed meeting John, because he's not the kind of man I expected. I've been a great admirer of his classical playing, and although I don't much like Sky, his rock band, I admire him for that as well, that distilling of styles, which is an idea I like, and I'm sure I'd enjoy them live.'

The Who also appeared during a series of charity concerts for the benefit of the people of Kampuchea, which were held at London's Hammersmith Odeon, and Pete also played as part of Paul McCartney's huge 'Rockestra', although he claims not to have been too happy about it. Far more serious were his appearances at various 'Rock Against Racism' concerts—does Pete feel that, as a rock music personality, he should be involved in politics?

'When I started, I felt that it was beyond our scope to effect any changes whatsoever, because we weren't really respected as human beings—which I think goes for the rest of the band as well—and we only wanted to talk to our particular audience, although not necessarily just our generation. In later years, we realised that we were getting the respect of people outside the rock field, so then it means slightly more to say what you think and do things rather than just talking. I obviously did the Rock Against Racism things because I identify with the motives of the people involved, but I got very severe on the subject a long time before, after the altercation with Abbie Hoffman at Woodstock, where he tried to use the Who's performance—right in the middle of *Tommy*—as a platform for some diatribe about the Chicago Seven trials and John Sinclair being in jail. For a long time, I just stood back and whenever a political issue came up, I tried to keep out of it, because that really tainted it for me, and I don't think I became more open again until the Rock Against Racism thing—it seemed that fascism was getting a foothold against a backcloth of unease in this country, and I didn't like the look of that at all. We've learnt our lesson once in Europe, and it just seemed a waste of time to go through it all again, and I felt I couldn't sit in my shell for ever, and say it was nothing to do with me or that my money would get me out of it, like in the last war, when all the singers and artists and film directors got out of Germany the first day there was a sign of a jackboot, and were all over in Hollywood. That's all very well, but there were a lot of people left behind who couldn't move. So I've changed quite a bit, and the band's attitude to playing for charity has changed, because initially, we played charity shows, but didn't let anyone know we were doing it. It's our business whether or not we give our money away, so for a long time the Who ran a charity, the Double O Charity, which still gives a lot of its earnings away to charity. I think it was formed about the time of *The Who By Numbers,* and we were giving away quite phenomenal amounts of money, and nobody knew, which I suppose made us feel fairly smug, but when somebody says "Why don't you do a charity concert, you filthy rich pig?", you eventually have to tell them what you've been doing, and people realise that you're receptive to doing charity work, or concerts for no money, and they descend like hawks.'

In 1980, Pete Townshend finally released a solo LP, the excellent *Empty Glass.* One of the more popular tracks included was 'Let My Love Open The Door' . . . 'Yes, it's got three chords in it, hasn't it? When I was getting the songs together for a gig I did recently, I realised that all the songs I wanted to play had the same three chords in them, the old kind of "Pure And Easy" thing . . . but that song was very spontaneous, and I did it on a computerised organ machine, and then decided to put a vocal on it, just singing the first thing that came into my head, and that's what came out. I did the same thing with another song on *Empty Glass,* "Little Is Enough"—a computerised organ performance, doing it all in one go with the drums and the bass, and then made up the vocal as I went along, and I had to think fast for that one. "Little Is Enough" is a much better song, and about my favourite song at the moment, because I think it's the way I feel about life—a little has to be enough in this day and age, not just of money and food, but of love too, because there isn't enough to go round, it seems, and you grab the little bit you can get and try to make it last.'

1980 also saw what was termed by the press as a 'Mod revival', echoing the attitudes and especially the fashions of the first half of the 1960s, when the Who were the favourite 'Mod' band. Had Pete considered that a genuine revival might happen? 'No, but I think there was a revival of sorts, which was absolutely, directly, specifically tied up with a modest little English outfit called the Jam—I think they started it, and I think they'll finish it. When the Jam move on to something else and evolve, which they inevitably will, because Paul Weller's too clever to stand still for ever, and too agitated, and so are the other members of the band, I think they'll take their fans with them. A lot of the kids that you see riding around wearing parkas with The Who written on them don't even know who the Who are—they're Jam fans who've seen Paul wearing a Who badge, although some of them may have investigated Who records. When the first Who album was reissued by Virgin, it sold well, and probably not exclusively to Who collectors, but also to that bunch of kids who follow the Jam—when you think that the Jam's singles go directly to number one sometimes, and sell 400,000 copies in three weeks, they've got a pretty significant following in Britain among the twelve to eighteen age group. It made me feel good when Paul stuck one of my early songs, "Disguises", on the B-side of one of his singles.'

Apart from the Jam, who does Pete rate among the current crop of bands? 'I like the Original Mirrors, U2 and New Order in the new rash, and with the more decorative outfits, I think Richard Burgess is a genius, who's very clever, and I think he'll prove himself a brilliant film maker. He's got such a visual sense which he seems to sum up musically, so I like the bands he's involved with, like Landscape and Ultravox, and I like some of the pop bands that are around, like Duran Duran, who make great sounding records. But ultimately, I think I'll keep coming back to slightly more earthy things—I like odd dabbles in electronic music and stuff like that, but eventually, when it comes down to what I listen to in the car, at the moment it's very much U2 who sound a bit like certain early Who mixed with the Byrds mixed with the Beatles. It's difficult to explain, but it's just a sound that very much appeals to me. It's not that it's old fashioned, but it's the kind of music I relate to a lot at the moment, and I relate to the words as well. What's really difficult for me—and this is why people think I'm a pretentious old bugger when I say I like new bands—is that I've got an incredibly wide taste, and while all this new stuff is happening, which I sincerely enjoy, I still listen to all the old stuff, and also to jazz and classical music. I don't even mind middle of the road music, although I'm not saying I listen to it, because I was brought up on it with my dad playing in a dance band, and it doesn't offend me to hear Frank Sinatra or Ella Fitzgerald, or even Max Bygraves—they're the easiest people in the world to take the piss out of when they're doing their scat singing, but it doesn't offend or annoy me.'

So did any of these disparate influences play a part in the 1981 Who album, *Face Dances*? 'That was a very peculiar album, one of the most peculiar we've made—I think we've got a real job ahead of us to re-establish a direction, and the Who might really go back to square one for the next record. I'll probably continue in the direction that *Face Dances* established after *Empty Glass,* but which it didn't really follow through properly, on my next (solo) album, and try to get that out of my system, but I think the next Who album will be much more basic guitar/bass/drums and much simpler songs.'

At the time this interview was conducted, Pete was preparing to start recording his next solo LP, which eventually turned out to be *Chinese Eyes.* This was what he said about the album some months before it was released: 'It won't be anything like *Face Dances,* at least superficially, and not much like *Empty Glass,* I don't think. I'm still concerned with the art, the craft of writing, essentially, but I'm making incredible departures at the moment. Let me just say that when I played the demos to the record company in New York, they all went into shock, and they wanted me to go straight to a psychiatrist and have him play me AC/DC records, which are selling very well in America. So it's about as far from heavy metal as you can get, but I don't want to say too much, because I don't really know yet. I've written about twenty-five songs which I think are possible for the album—that's a single album, by the way, and you need fifty songs for a double . . .'

Although Pete Townshend is not a frequent player on other people's records, some of his sessions have been with interesting people, such as David Bowie, on the latter's 1980 LP, *Scary Monsters.* 'He didn't let me do much, but we really enjoy one another's company, and we see each other so rarely and I think he really invited me over for a natter. I saw him in New York when I went over there to play my new stuff to the record company, and we went out on two occasions—I like him because he's very intelligent, but he's also very relaxed and easy company, not the glamorous distant figure some of his fans imagine him to be. He took me to this Japanese restaurant, and I went into shock when he ordered the food in Japanese!' Other session credits include those for Billy Nicholls and Mike Heron; one of Heron's solo LPs has backing on one track provided by 'Tommy & the Bijoux'.

Two other involvements were on an Yvonne Elliman LP, and on the sound track for the film *Mahoney's Last Stand* . . . 'With Yvonne Elliman, I was just invited to play because she was covering one of my songs (in fact, "I Can't Explain"), and I didn't mind, although I don't think I added anything new. *Mahoney's Last Stand* was just showing up in the studio to see Ronnie Lane, and him saying "Pick up a guitar and play". It's the uncredited work that I've done on Rolling Stones' albums that's really interesting—I'll write a book about that one day, but I'm not going to say any more about it now, because it was uncredited for a reason.'

Finally we asked Pete Townshend, after this fractured and incomplete journey through his past, how long did he reckon he'd carry on writing songs and playing music? 'I don't really know how long I'll be in a group, but I suppose I'll always have to play with other musicians, unless I become a Stevie Winwood type. But I've worked at home on my own for so long, played the drums and the bass and anything else I can get my hands on, so now I enjoy playing with other good musicians, particularly as I can now command probably the best musicians in the world to play with, command them and pay them! In the rock frame, in the way I've been working for a long time, I think on my next album I'll have already started to change direction, to move away from the Who fans' conception of what rock'n'roll is about. I've changed my stance in the past several times, with great success, so I feel I could possibly do it again without too much trouble. I did it once on *Tommy* and once on our third album, *The Who Sell Out,* and those were radical musical departures for the band, away from the traditional sound that we still produce, but sometimes to get that needle a little bit off centre, you have to go a long way to left or right—it might feel very awkward to you, but from the outside, it can often look like very little is happening. So I want to create some major changes in the way I work now—not because I'm particularly worried about age, but I do think it's very difficult to age creatively. Some people look young forever, like Cliff Richard—I've looked forty since I was nineteen! But to age creatively with dignity is really difficult in heavy metal full frontal rock, because you can end up looking a complete prat, whereas in classical music or jazz, you can age with dignity. I think to some extent it's the high critique which surrounds rock and is always trying to bring it back down to earth, yet at the same time, by definition, high critique means it's worthy of high critique, and therefore must be art. It's difficult to live with the schizophrenia of being in the rock business, but I'm determined to find a route, perhaps less as a musician and performer and more as a writer. I'm going to have to concentrate on what I have to give, and try to develop it, hopefully in the company of a lot of other people and musicians that I enjoy playing with and being with, and to have it appreciated by some audience somewhere. Whether it's going to be as big as the audience I've enjoyed in the past, I don't really care anymore.'

WHO'S BACK

Charles M. Young | July 1989 | *Musician* **(US)**

If he remembered it, Townshend's comment in an interview earlier in this book about Mick Jagger's potential for self-parody must have seemed, by 1989, a bitter joke.

The Kenney Jones lineup of the Who made just two albums, *Face Dances* (March 1981) and *It's Hard* (September 1982). The public were as unimpressed by them as Roger Daltrey was by Jones's drumming. In 1982, the fractious, directionless band embarked on a farewell tour, which bequeathed a November 1984 live album pointedly titled *Who's Last*.

Then they changed their collective mind. In 1989, the Who were touring again, with Simon Phillips on drums in place of Jones. For many critics and long-term fans, the whole affair was grisly, whether it be because of the lack of attendant new recordings, the presence of corporate sponsorship (then novel), the frank admission that the venture was motivated by money, or the fact that Townshend's hearing problems resulted in a lowered stage volume and the guitarist having to restrict his playing to rhythm work performed inside a Perspex booth. The keynote line of "My Generation"—"Hope I die before I get old"—had always been a hostage to fortune, but never had the juxtaposition between then and now been more painful.

The controversy enveloping the tour seems to infect this *Musician* feature, in which Townshend is extraordinarily prickly and the whole band painfully honest even by their standards, with current personnel, Keith Moon, and Moon's ill-starred successor all coming in for what the British call "stick."

Note: for "Kenny Jones" read "Kenney Jones" —Ed.

MY TAKE on Pete Townshend is that he's extremely sensitive and chronically overwhelmed by his own emotions, so overwhelmed that anyone who is not overwhelmed by the same emotion at the same time makes no sense to him. And when a new emotion passes over him, his last emotion makes no sense to him either. Since he doesn't suffer fools lightly, and since no one in the world makes sense, most of all himself, the world is probably pretty lonely as well as overwhelming. No wonder he spent all that time practicing guitar drunk with the headphones on. He was going to shove those emotions right back down his ear canal, and made himself nearly deaf in the process.

Townshend has a new album out called *The Iron Man*, based on a fairy tale of the same name by England's poet laureate, Ted Hughes. It is the story of a little boy named Hogarth who encounters the Iron Man, a giant who wanders the countryside eating anything made of metal. Despite his instinct for proper ecology, the Iron Man is hated and feared until he defeats a destructive dragon the size of Australia. It's a delightful read, makes more sense than *Tommy* and has given Townshend a focus for his creativity. It has also cost him a lot of time and money. The songs are very strong work by a very talented guy. He wants *The Iron Man* to be successful, and he's doing a big tour to support it.

The band he's touring with is called the Who. Two of them, Roger Daltrey and John Entwistle, actually played in the original Who, whose twenty-fifth anniversary (counting from when Keith Moon joined the band) is this year. Announced at a press conference in New York's Radio City Music Hall, the Who tour promises to be highly lucrative: 30-40 football stadiums selling out with 60-80,000 people paying $23 and up to hear them. Figure in T-shirt and memorabilia sales, and it is difficult to see how the Who would gross less than a hundred million dollars. A few days after the last of these interviews, Budweiser was announced as sponsor of the band's New York shows, and several more stadium dates were added as tickets moved fast.

MUSICIAN: *You said at your press conference the other day that you were still looking for a corporate sponsor for your tour?*

TOWNSHEND: I can't speak for everyone in the group. But I feel and my manager feels that sponsorship is at a watershed. Great things are happening because of sponsorship. You might not agree. But the topping off of money allows you to look very differently at the profitability of tours. It might be the thing that allows people in rock to get away from playing stadiums, although it's the number of people corporations can hit in stadiums that makes sponsorship a viable prospect.

MUSICIAN: *If you got enough money from a sponsor, you would take this tour to smaller venues?*

TOWNSHEND: I think if you had enough money from a sponsor, you could afford to do some kind of show and reach the same number of people but not in stadiums. In other words, do high quality, subsidized-price videos of a show or a series of paid previews. If people want a stadium show, it can be arranged. But anyone who wants to go to a stadium seems to me to have a problem. Sponsors can make it possible to avoid compromise by the fact that arenas are designed for sport, not acoustics. Music just helps these places stay in the black. The other possibility is using sponsorship as per the Madonna video to make a personal statement in a very artistic way about something that you passionately believe. I don't know if that video is a masterpiece or an aberration. I don't know. But I do know it was a very, very dangerous thing. Was it Pepsi or Coke that sponsored it?

MUSICIAN: *It was Pepsi, and they withdrew their sponsorship.*

TOWNSHEND: Good. Doesn't matter as long as she made the video in her way.

MUSICIAN: *Madonna has enough money to make that video on her own.*

TOWNSHEND: You don't know anything about Madonna's money! You haven't got a clue! I haven't, and I'm sure I know her better than you do. In any case, the American film and record industry is based on the premise that you don't ever spend your own money. Well, there are people who have.

MUSICIAN: *Would you sell a song out of the Who catalogue for a commercial?*

TOWNSHEND: I've done it. Hundreds of times.

MUSICIAN: *If someone came to you and wanted "My Generation" for a shoe commercial?*

TOWNSHEND: Shoes? Depends on the subject. It's my legal property, my right to do what I like with it. You might not like it. You might feel it's your property. . .

MUSICIAN: *Not my legal property. . .*

TOWNSHEND: It's not your moral property either. It's just not your property. What's your property is your response. And the truth is, the advertisers have already made fortunes out of your response. They've used that response on a daily basis by advertising on radio and dictating what the playlist is going to be. If you respond in a positive way to a song like "My Generation" or "Baba O'Riley" or "Won't Get Fooled Again" because you listen to AOR and then go out like a turkey and buy fucking Odorono, then they've got you. But most of all, they've got me, because it's my career that's suffering. Because the other 400 songs I've written don't ever get heard. I can't deal with it. I go to a sponsor and say, "Give me the money to do what I want to do." The public are already in the vise-like grip of advertising agencies' reductive demographic practices, reducing my career down to eight songs as AOR radio reproduces it. If somebody offers me the right price and I think it's worth doing, I'll sell the song. I've done it many times.

MUSICIAN: *Aren't you contributing to the vise-like grip Madison Avenue has?*

TOWNSHEND: It's already been done! What's the difference? There's further damage to be done? Why shouldn't I benefit the same way that you do? It's my fucking work!

MUSICIAN: *How do I benefit from it?*

TOWNSHEND: You benefit from it because it's part of your society. If you want to change society, change it. It's not my job. I'm a songwriter. It's what I do for a living. Your article isn't worth shit without the advertisers who advertise in *Musician*. It wouldn't be here except for advertisers.

MUSICIAN: *I don't make much money. You're in a privileged position in society. You're expected to tell the truth.*

TOWNSHEND: Bullshit! Bullshit! I'm not expected to do anything. Nobody is going to tell me what to do. Nobody is even going to ask me what to do. If anybody doesn't like it, that's their problem. It's my work. If someone doesn't like it, I can't help it.

MUSICIAN: *I'm not saying I don't like it. Your songs meant an enormous amount to me when I was growing up. Still do. Take it from another angle: When I listen to "I Heard It Through the Grapevine," surely one of the great rock songs, I don't want to think about the dancing raisins. I feel that's Madison Avenue stepping on a part of my memory that I don't want them having access to. The many associations I have with that song are violated and overpowered by a commercial image. I resent it.*

TOWNSHEND: You obviously watch too much fucking television.

MUSICIAN: *Actually, I don't watch that much. But when I do, the dancing raisins are there.*

TOWNSHEND: Your memory is violated by dancing raisins? Are you crazy? Is your perception of "I Heard It Through the Grapevine" so shallow that it's violated by dancing raisins? I feel strongly about this, because I've had to consider every single song I've had a bid on. For a long time there were certain things I wouldn't let go. Someone wanted "Magic Bus," and I thought, "Okay, that's a fun song. People won't mind." Then somebody comes along and wants "My Generation" to sell laxative pills. You know, "Dah dah dah, my constipation." They seriously think you're going to give them the song. And you think, "Well, let's play with the motherfuckers." And you say, "Okay, you can have the song for 16 million dollars, 'cause that's what the hatred of every Who fan in the world is worth to me."

You have to realize there's a price to what I've done in my life. The price has been established by what people have already given me by buying my work. The ethics are absolutely clear in my mind. It's my decision. It's my right. I've been outraged by certain ads that were absolutely despicable. And you are outraged by the dancing raisins. Maybe what we should do, the pair of us, is get a couple of machine guns and machine gun the lot of them. Is it really that serious?

MUSICIAN: *I'm not willing to machine gun people.*

TOWNSHEND: What are you willing to do? I'll do it with you. I do think advertising has an enormous responsibility. And they've fucked a lot of things. I just think it's better to have advertising at the front end of a project. So if there is any question about a song being associated with a product, it's there from the beginning so the public can relate to it directly. The interesting thing about tour sponsorship is you have to deal with the promoters who have already sold the venue to a beer company. Often the deal is already done, and the promoter wants his sponsor, not yours. If you want to go to heaven saying, "It's all right, because I didn't get a dollar from it," I say take it a step further. Would the event have happened at all without sponsorship? Would you be paying by a reduction in your performance fee? Better to know what you're doing. Better to take the money. Better to let the artist deal with the moral issues. Better to let the artist influence the advertisers and agencies involved.

MUSICIAN: *What are your feelings about tour sponsorship?*

ENTWISTLE: I've got no objection to someone sponsoring us unless the product is something I don't believe in. It definitely helps the tour, makes the show better. I don't see why anyone should have a go at us for being sponsored when you've got football heroes sponsoring sportswear. Why shouldn't we have a sponsor like Coke or beer or cigarettes? Especially if the company is willing to give money to charity on top of what we get, it'll make someone else happy besides us. I haven't got much of a conscience, I suppose. I can think up really good reasons for doing things wrong. I live much easier that way.

MUSICIAN: *The Who meant so much to me growing up that I hate to see a product put in front of it. The meaning changes. The songs had such integrity.*

ENTWISTLE: Our sponsoring goes way back. We were really hunting for money in the '60s to finance our guitar smashing. We did ads for

Great Shakes and Coke. "Coke after Coke after. . ." We did a lot of little commercials on *Who Sell Out*. We insisted that in the Schlitz commercial from the 1982 tour, at no point did it say we drank Schlitz beer. I've never drunk a glass of beer in my life. I had a sip once as a kid, and it was shit. But if someone wants me to sponsor Remy Martin, I'll jump on it. I feel I still have my integrity. When I tour, it costs me money, and I don't give a fuck if it comes from Schlitz. It enables me to play.

MUSICIAN: *You're looking for a new tour sponsor?*

DALTREY: No, we're not looking for one. We're not doing this tour for the money.

MUSICIAN: *John and Pete seemed pretty clear that they were doing it for the money.*

DALTREY: I'm not. Which isn't to say the money won't be useful. I'm doing this for me, to put a lot of things to rest, because I thought the way the Who ended felt like unfinished business. It was a rotten way to end, that 1982 tour.

MUSICIAN: *Why was it rotten?*

DALTREY: The tour wasn't rotten. The way the band ended was rotten. Just petered out, for want of a better word. [*laughs*] I want the experience of singing those old Who songs again. It's my passion. I love those songs. I love the band—not socially, but the chemistry when we work. It's the inside of the personality coming out, not all these electronic condiments. I just want to sing songs that I love with people that I love.

MUSICIAN: *Not socially?*

DALTREY: Our social lives are very separate. We only get together to work, so the chemistry isn't wasted on anything else. That's what made it great. It's still unbelievable how great it is. The show will be very demanding, but it's going to give me opportunity to sing because of the lowered stage volume. Before, all I could do was shout above the din. I'm singing better than ever now. No doubt about it. And I just sing. I'm not good at vocal tricks. You don't need that with the Who. I heard the

W.A.S.P. version of "Can You See the Real Me" and it was just like the Who except for the metal vibrato vocal. I can't do that. If I'd been able to do that, the Who would not have had the same urgency, the same power.

MUSICIAN: *How did you feel about the Schlitz sponsorship in '82?*

DALTREY: It was great. I enjoy a drink. Nothing wrong with a beer. It paid for our plane. We did very well out of it. When we start this tour and people are printing the gate money, they look at the top line and they forget the expenses. When you get down to what's left after you cart around a stage and a 14-piece band, expenses are horrendous. Sponsorship *is* important. But I'm not doing this tour for the money, so I don't care if we have one or not. I live my life very simply now. I don't need all that money. I got another job to pay the rent. When the Who finished, it taught me a lesson. You can spend your whole life chasing that money, but it's not important. It's the freedom to do what you want to do. Aside from poor people who are fighting just to put food in their mouths, almost all of us have that freedom to do what we want.

I did go through a period where I regretted all that money we lost. 'Cause we lost millions, and we lost the bloody lot of it because we were crazy. But who cares? I'm still alive. I worked in Hungary last year, and it really taught me a lesson. The people are very poor there, but they still have a wonderful quality of community that we've lost here because of our stupid materialism. So I've changed. I'm different now.

MUSICIAN: *Could you describe that process of transformation?*

DALTREY: I'm not through it yet. I went through a period of a few years where I questioned my whole being. It was getting my life into balance. The end of the Who was terrifying. Now there was going to be nothing! But it wasn't true. A whole new life and career opened up for me. I've done so much living in the past seven years that I wasn't allowed in the Who. I'm a working actor now. I don't need this. *The Threepenny Opera* and *The Beggar's Opera*—that's the stuff I've been doing, and I love it. But if the Who want to do anything, I'm available because I'm a Who fan. I have my new life now, and I have this thing that I loved more than anything, and I can do it again. I'd do this tour for nothing! Better not tell John that. He'll want my share. But John hasn't got another career. He's got the Who, and he's got his own band that he takes on the road. His life is completely music.

MUSICIAN: *At the press conference, Roger had to repeat most of the questions for you. It was quite frightening. Aren't you afraid of losing more of your hearing? Did the others have to persuade you to do this tour?*

TOWNSHEND: No, it wasn't about persuasion. No one has nagged me about doing this tour. John and Roger and my manager have all said, "What we're most concerned with is your health, your well-being, your happiness." To be 100 percent honest, the first thing that made me think about touring was the money. The commercial force behind such a venture is fantastic. I started to think what it would mean to have so much money that I would never have to have to make records at all. But around Christmas I decided I couldn't face doing it in spite of the fabulous sums of money involved. I said, "No, I want out." I thought what I'd be doing this year was put out my solo album, do a week of interviews, make the videos and go sailing.

Then I came to New York for the Rock & Roll Hall of Fame ceremony. I saw the Soul Stirrers onstage, and this 86-year-old guy was onstage talking about music, and I realized that this undeniable American art form of rock 'n' roll had given me a reason for being, a focus, a destiny, a past, a present and a future. And I thought, "If these guys want to honor the Who next year, if the audience wants to come to our twenty-fifth anniversary party, who am I to stand in the way? Just so they know in advance that the music isn't going to be quite what they think it's going to be, then I'll go." Despite the fact that the news flashes all said Pete Townshend was going to play guitar like John Denver [Townshend's own line at the press conference] and he couldn't hear a word being said, the show in Boston sold out in two hours. I know the problem I face will compromise the show a little, but it's a problem that's technically easy to deal with, and it's important to show people that we're dealing with it. So many people have come up to me and said, "You know, I have the same problem that you do. I'm a DJ."

I say the problem is earphones. That's where my problem started. It was not loud guitar onstage rock 'n' roll style. It's very important to make this point. It was EARPHONES! EARPHONES! EARPHONES! It was going home after gigs, to my own studio, and playing guitar through the earphones. My sound was an electric sound. You couldn't reproduce it on an acoustic guitar. It had to be with earphones. Obviously I couldn't have a Marshall stack in my living room and practice with the babies upstairs. I used earphones for 20 years. That's what caused the damage. It's not helped now with loud music in performances, but I don't see any difficulty doing stadium shows when the sound is kept deliberately quiet onstage. It's also a different situation when your head is clear and you're not drunk. Wearing earphones when you're drunk can increase damage by a factor of 10, I think. Some of the muscles that operate the eardrum are disabled by alcohol.

———————

MUSICIAN: *I'm a little mystified by what Pete will actually be doing onstage.*

ENTWISTLE: I think everyone is mystified by what Pete will be doing, including Pete. We won't know until we start rehearsing. There will be a loud side of the stage and a quiet side of the stage. The quiet side will be the vocalists, some percussion and Pete. The loud side will be keyboards, the other guitarist, the horns and me. As long as Pete is protected from that, it should be workable. The acoustic guitars will go straight through the monitors, but Pete will do some electric guitar toward the end. There are amplifiers now where you can get the sound of a stack and it's almost inaudible. Gallien-Krueger do one. The Yamaha SPX, you can turn the distortion up and the volume down and it sounds like a Marshall stack on the other side of New York. Through the P.A. it would sound exactly like a Marshall stack. We're going to keep all our options open.

MUSICIAN: *His hearing loss is terrifying.*

ENTWISTLE: Most of our hearing damage didn't come from guitar. It came from P.A.s feeding back and headphones in the studio. I've got a slight whistle in this ear that goes off depending on how high I am in the world. I come down from where I live at 700 feet above sea level to Thames level for a business meeting, it starts whistling. For the first two hours I can't hear a damn word they're saying.

MUSICIAN: *Did it take much convincing to get Pete to agree to tour?*

ENTWISTLE: I believed in my heart he'd come around to thinking about touring again. He's inclined to change his mind quite a few times. Often in the same sentence. It was on and off, on and off. Maybe. Yes. No. Personally, I'm a much different person since the Who broke up. I'm more confident about my playing, my music, myself. I didn't want to get involved in the old Who power struggles again. The balance of power was always shifting backwards and forwards with me in the middle. When Keith died, I lost a lot of power because he and I always got together and agreed on things in advance. So that was 50 percent of the band wanting to do what we wanted to do. When Kenny Jones joined he didn't voice opinions, so I'd have to sit there while Pete and Roger mulled and changed their minds a few hundred times. Eventually they always came around to what I wanted to do anyway. The power structure has been distorted by the media from day one. No way I could be as powerful as Pete. He was the one with the gift of gab. It was a bit depressing when people would come up and say, "You're the best bass player in the world," and I was at the bottom of the pecking order in the band.

MUSICIAN: *Pete said at the press conference he wouldn't be playing much guitar. What is he going to do?*

DALTREY: He's just playing games. He'll be playing guitar. We're just trying to tell people it won't be the same. There will be elements that will be the same, but they will be getting more, not less, with this set. We'll still have the fire in "Won't Get Fooled Again," but on the other songs the color will be much greater. I intend to play acoustic guitar on some numbers with Pete playing the piano. We don't intend to generate that wall of sound from the stage anymore, mainly because of Pete's ears, but also because it's so self-defeating in the end. The music can't grow once you hit those noise levels. We'd be playing by rote instead of playing with what's left of our ears. We've all lost the top end of our hearing. It's part of the hazards of the job. But it's a nightmare for Pete. He's got tinnitus—not only is your hearing damaged, it's replaced by another noise. That's the worst part.

MUSICIAN: *Hogarth's fascination and fear and admiration of the Iron Man reminded me of my own relationship to the Who when I was a boy. There you were, this anarchic force for liberation lumbering through the countryside, living proof it was possible to escape middle-class repression.*

TOWNSHEND: I like that, but it didn't occur to me. I identify very much with Hogarth myself. I think it's quite simply a fairy story about the fear and deprivation of children. On a more polite note, it's about the moment when a child balances those symbols of fear and smashes them against one another and grows up. I have to remind myself sometimes that I'm a big, strong man. We're all big people with nothing to be afraid of. We're the masters of this planet and nothing should frighten us except our own actions and their consequences, our carelessness, the possibility that we are our own undoing.

MUSICIAN: *Child abuse runs through the media in waves of hysteria here. Yet 75 percent of the American people believe it's fine to spank children in school. This country has a long history of assaulting smaller people to make them do our bidding.*

TOWNSHEND: They're trying to pass an act of Parliament to stop spanking their children at home in Britain. Canada has been a leader in stopping domestic violence as well. But the thing about brutality is that it's valuable when we're united against a common enemy. We can drain ourselves of all emotion and kill. We should be mobilizing all this brutality we have to clean up all this shit we've created. As the sergeant said in Stanley Kubrick's *Full Metal Jacket*, "We are living in shit." People of conscience on this planet *have got to be prepared to be brutal.* It does no good being nice about it: "Please don't do that crack. Please don't beat your kids. Please don't shoot one another." We're dealing with dogs— *rabid, fighting dogs.* I'm not suggesting brutal policing. The people who care have got to be prepared to die for the cause. We've had wars and expected young people to go off and die in some far-off country. I'm surprised people aren't prepared to expect some of their young men and young women to die for the cause right here and now. Pollution, addiction, poverty—all these things are political issues and have to be dealt with in a political way. If you vote, vote with a big cross. Make a nick in your hand and vote with your blood. I feel that passionate about the way the world is going at this moment. It's urgent, and there is too much waffle. That factory where they're planning to build 500 million fluorocarbon refrigerators for the Chinese population—let's nuke it. Or buy them 500 million refrigerators. LET'S DO SOMETHING! Let's do something about those guys cutting down the rain forest. THEY'RE KILLING US!

MUSICIAN: *Are you working on a solo project these days?*

ENTWISTLE: I have a band that's changed members three times. And the album has been recorded three times because we weren't satisfied with a lot of the songs. We tried to get a deal for the band, but the day we were scheduled to sign the contract, the people at the company were arrested by the FBI for fraud. So no deal. Start from scratch. Again. The four songs that I wrote for the group album I'm going to remix and put on my solo album. But I won't be working on it for another year, because I'm not going back to England right away after this tour. I'm going to write a book about all the funny things that happened to the Who. After reading all these books by different people who thought they knew the Who, I've come to the conclusion that I never existed.

MUSICIAN: *You feel the various band biographers missed the humor along with your contribution?*

ENTWISTLE: Yeah. No humor in any of them. At all. All my fond memories of the Who are the silly things that happened. I haven't got any fond memories of working on albums or photo sessions. My memories are the fun we had on the road. As far as I'm concerned, the thing that made the Who a legend is the road work we did. It certainly wasn't the albums. They didn't sell particularly well. We didn't have hit singles. It was the way we performed those songs onstage. People grew to love them because of the show. None of the books talk about any performances, or why it ticked onstage. Why would 100,000 people come to our show and not buy the record?

MUSICIAN: *Care to share a fond memory of a concert before your book comes out?*

ENTWISTLE: I very rarely lose my temper. I let things bottle up and then something small or silly will be the last straw and I'll blow my top and everyone will run away and hide. Roger had been yelling at me all tour in 1974 to turn down. So I'd turn down and I'd be quite happy playing like that. And then Pete would scream from the other side of the stage, "I can't hear you! Turn up!" So I'd turn up, thinking, "What the fuck is this." For three weeks Roger would yell at me to turn down, and four seconds later Pete would yell at me to turn up. Finally we were in Houston, Texas, and Roger screamed in the microphone, "TURN DOWN!"

I thought, "I don't mind you screaming at me to turn down, but I don't need you to scream at me in front of the bloody audience." So I smashed the head off the bass, threw it in front of him and said, "You play the fuckin' thing!" He just stood there, with the song halfway through. I walked to the back of the amplifiers and they'd taken the fuckin' stairs away. I was in a bad enough temper that I jumped off the back of the stage. And it was 12 feet high. It felt like my spine came out the top of my head. But it was Chinese water torture out there: "TURN DOWN!" "TURN UP!"

MUSICIAN: *Do you approve of John's literary project?*

TOWNSHEND: I'll believe the book when I see it. I don't think any of these people know how hard it is. Very easy to start a book, very hard to finish. But it would be great if he does it, a research job like that. I coached Dave Marsh through his book on the Who and I published it in the U.K. And I coached Richard Barnes through his book on the Who. The reason I was happy with even the bad stuff about me was I was involved. Roger and John were just not available at that level to those authors. If they want to tell the story their way, they'll have to sit down and tell it. Very hard thing to do. I've contemplated a book on rock 'n' roll through my eyes. I can't imagine it being less than 150,000 words. The great thing about John is his sense of humor. If he writes down all the interesting anecdotes, whether they're true or not, it will be a wonderful story. What's fun about history is often the distortions. John is good at that. He remembers the stories and lets them evolve.

MUSICIAN: *Did John smash his bass in Houston?*

DALTREY: Yes, that's right. That's what I mean about the problem with volume. There was Pete, all the way up, only hearing himself. And there was John playing four times as loud as he needs to be to hear himself. It was a *Catch-22* situation. With the singer in the middle. A complete nightmare. You can't sing, you just shout. I'm a good shouter, but it gets very boring.

MUSICIAN: *I was quite moved by your chapter in* The Courage to Change *by Dennis Wholey, the harrowing description of your withdrawal from alcohol and other drugs.*

TOWNSHEND: He's an old friend of mine and we did an interview. I was quite happy with the way it turned out. I'd been in psychotherapy and he got me the only week that I decided I was going to quit. I was very disillusioned that week—it was year three, or something. And then I went back and finished off. I never did AA or NA.

MUSICIAN: *You're still sober?*

TOWNSHEND: Oh sure. I just wish the consequences hadn't been so fucking hard for the third parties involved.

MUSICIAN: *But you kept your family together.*

TOWNSHEND: With . . . with . . . with . . . with help from them and a certain amount of loss. There are advantages and disadvantages to the life I've led. The kids have financial security but there was a time when they suffered a certain amount of fear and deprivation as a direct result of my behavior. We try to talk about it regularly. Awful, awful thing to contemplate. You don't want to hurt anyone in your life but when you do . . . At least my old lady knew I was in a rock 'n' roll band when we got married. She knew I was an asshole. It's not like that with kids. They're born and they're subjected to all this shit. I've never beaten them up, but I've sure as hell scared the shit out of them when I was arguing with my wife, or even with myself. I think when I was a kid and my parents would argue, it really scarred me. Interestingly, it gave me a deeper love for them when they were together and it gave me a fantastic creative force. It brought forth a type of writing which everyone around the world loves and identifies with if they're interested in rock 'n' roll. I suppose that every family has some element of fear and threat written into its constitution for the children. I'm not saying it has to stop. Maybe it should be that children have to be aware of discipline and power, because in life, however big and tough you are, there is some wall you can't kick your way through. It's good to know that. No harm in that wall being your parents or something they represent. But there should never be fear, not abstract fear.

MUSICIAN: *Back on the subject of* The Iron Man, *if you're putting out a solo album, why not do a solo tour?*

TOWNSHEND: Because the odds are different. As a solo artist I get fantastic fulfillment from my work in the studio and the writing. Maybe 25 years from 1979, which is when I consider I made my first solo album, I'll decide to have a party and then I'll be faced with all these issues again. The chemistry, the presence of John and Roger as performers and friends, has inspired me to take a chance.

The thing I'm most anxious about is having a solo album out. John and Roger appear on it, but it's my album. I'll be performing songs from it, I'll be talking about it. We left no stone unturned in our discussions beforehand. They both said it doesn't bother them. Whether it still won't bother them after a few three-and-a-half-hour shows, I don't know. Depends on how much attention it gets, I suppose. I don't think I could tour solo. This Who tour is great for me. I worked so long on *Iron Man* and I don't want it to just slide into ignominy because the single isn't a hit or the video doesn't work on MTV. If the Who out there on the road lets people know I'm alive, it may be just the last little fillip to give me the hit I need.

MUSICIAN: *How did Arthur Brown's "Fire" get on the record?*

TOWNSHEND: When I first put the collection together, there seemed to be a hole in the fire scene. I said to my manager that the trouble with fire songs is that it's all been said. As recently as Bruce Springsteen, "You can't find a flame without a spark." You go back in history and the fire clichés make you want to vomit. I said the best song is just "Fire, fire, fire, fire/You're going to burn." And Bill [Curbishley] said what a great idea. I said, "No, I didn't mean the actual song." But I sat down and thought that it wouldn't hurt. I used "Eyesight to the Blind" by Sonny Boy Williamson on *Tommy.* Then I got a letter from Arthur in Texas. He's running a small commune there and leading a very simple life and I thought let's go for it. He wrote to me asking if I could help get him some money through publishing. I wrote back and said I've got a better idea. We'll put "Fire" on the album and pray for a hit.

MUSICIAN: *You want to do a theatrical production of* The Iron Man?

TOWNSHEND: That's right. I'm keen to do it. I've written a whole musical—20 songs and a score. I want to see it tested in the theater, get it into workshop as soon as possible. And if it develops, get it funded and out there.

MUSICIAN: *Twenty songs? Why a single album and not a double album? You can't follow the plot by what's on the album.*

TOWNSHEND: For financial reasons. I got a nice deal from Atlantic in the States and Virgin worldwide, but I had to contract all the different singers on was the record and I spent two years in the studio. It cost me a lot of money. I couldn't afford a double album because neither company was willing to pay me a double album rate. They would have put it out, but I wasn't willing to risk my own money. It would have taken another six months and another $200,000. John Lee Hooker would have sung five or six songs as opposed to two, and there would have been an enormous amount of detail work. I was working with six singers at once, all of whom were getting £600 a day. The money was just disappearing.

My aim is to change the music we hear in musical theater, not to take musicals to stadiums. I'd like to produce music for people who don't want to go to stadiums anymore. I enjoyed *Les Misérables,* and I enjoyed *The Phantom of the Opera.* Everything was great about them except the music was very old-fashioned. More than old-fashioned. Half of it was crap. The problem with Broadway is that no one in rock has paid any attention to it.

MUSICIAN: *At the press conference the other day, you described Keith Moon as sad. Why?*

TOWNSHEND: He was sad in that way of people who are looking for love and don't take the direct approach until it's too late. He started by trying to make people laugh, and he ended by making them cry. He had the sadness of the comic.

MUSICIAN: *He seemed to have the Sid Vicious disease of trying to live up to his legend.*

TOWNSHEND: He died fucking around with drugs and alcohol. Not in a nihilistic sense. He died fucking around. He'd lost perspective. He was not drinking at the time he died, he took an overdose of a drug to prevent seizures during alcoholic withdrawal. He took eight of the pills. He was thinking, "I'm a good boy, I've quit drinking, if one of these is good for me, eight will be better." It was like a sick joke it should happen.

He once took eight elephant tranquilizers in San Francisco and survived. Couldn't move, couldn't play. He was in a wheelchair for two days. I have a Super-8 film of when we brought him off the plane in a wheelchair. The doctor from the Free Clinic says, "His heart is only beating once every 30 seconds! He's clinically dead!" And Keith says [*mumbles*], "Fuck off." That is not apocryphal. I have it on film.

It was sad, because he had alienated so many people around him by his obstinate clinging to his image. That was a good analogy to Sid Vicious. About halfway through the recording of *Who Are You,* he was showing up late and not playing very well and I got into this mood: "I'm not taking any more of his shit." So I rang him up and told him to get the fuck down here. He came running down, babbling excuses. I got him behind the drums and he could not keep the song together. He couldn't play. He'd obviously been out the night before to some club. He'd put his work second. Again. But before I could say anything, he went [*imitates chaotic drum solo*]. "See?" he said. "I'm still the best Keith Moon-type drummer in the world."

There was nobody to top him doing that. But unless you wanted that, you were fucked. It happened that on that song, we didn't want that. Keith wrestling himself. He was funny, but he was capable of so much more. He was such a wonderful drummer, not just an ape-shit drummer. But he had reduced himself to that in the eyes of the world and in his own eyes. A couple of days after that, he started to call me up just to say good night and I love you. He did that about 10 times, and you could tell he was crying a little bit. He'd say, "You do believe me, don't you?" I'd say, "Yes, but you're still an asshole."

I helped him get a flat in London because he was broke after his stay in California. Nobody would buy his house in California, so I helped him get back on his feet by getting this flat. And a couple of days later he died in it. He couldn't live with the new character he was.

MUSICIAN: *Moving to a different part of the world and taking your problem with you is a classic alcoholic behavior pattern.*

TOWNSHEND: For a long time he wasn't treated as an alcoholic. A friend from AA came in to talk to Keith once, worked with him for two or three weeks. He said Keith was a heavy drinker with a strange emotional makeup. Then he said *I* was an alcoholic.

I wondered how he'd worked that out, because I hadn't had a drink in three or four weeks. I went back in the studio and I said to Glyn Johns, "Do you believe it? Keith's been coming in here every morning for weeks vomiting on the mixing desk, taking pills for this and that, and I'm supporting Keith by not drinking, and I could use a drink, but I haven't had a drink, and this guy thinks I'm alcoholic." Glyn kind of looked at me. Keith's driver was there, and I took him outside, and I asked, "I haven't had anything to drink, have I?" He said, "No, no." I said, "Listen, you don't have to defend my position. Have I had anything to drink?" "Not apart from when you go home." "What do you mean?"

"Well, every night after work you go off to the bar and drink a bottle of vodka. Everyone thought you were just not drinking while you were working. At the end of the session, you drink a bottle of vodka like water." And I suddenly remembered what I'd been doing. I was drinking alcoholically, but I didn't deal with it until several years later.

MUSICIAN: *How would the history of the Who be different if after* Who's Next *you'd all just quit drinking?*

TOWNSHEND: If I'd quit drinking, I would have quit the band.

MUSICIAN: *The only way you could tolerate being in the Who was by drinking too much?*

TOWNSHEND: Yeah . . . Ultimately . . . Might be unfair to the band . . . When I was in psychotherapy, the thing I talked about mostly was the two years or 18 months that I spent away from my parents when I was about five to seven years old. I lived with my grandmother. My parents were probably splitting up. I don't know. I'm afraid to bring up the subject with my mother, for fear I'll strangle her.

MUSICIAN: *Was there a similar incident in Keith's background?*

TOWNSHEND: Probably, but we'll never know. His father was an extremely nice man. My father was a wonderful man. The marriage looked normal. But who knows? My young parents were probably having difficulty staying married. My father was a touring musician, my mother had to stop being a singer to bring me up. They wanted to protect me from their arguments, so they sent me to live with my grandmother, who adored me. That's quite a normal situation. Doesn't amount to child abuse. My reaction was very repressive, I suppose. My grandmother was very strict and old-fashioned. It might be that Keith had a similar thing. The most interesting aspect about Keith was the excellence of his mind, the rapidity of his memory. You often find this with drummers, that they have the most extraordinary memories. It's an extension of their work. Maybe their memories are centered in a different part of the brain, because they have to remember long musical phrases as pure data. It's almost binary. They must know exactly where they are in a song at any given time. The best drummers have the best memories.

MUSICIAN: *Would you mind telling the story about the waterbed?*

TOWNSHEND: Keith heard this Danish hotel had one suite with a water-bed, and he kept ringing them to make sure he got that particular suite: "I want to try some sexual experiments. Naughty Copenhagen, here I come. It will hold the weight of five or six female bodies, won't it?" So we were having coffee in his room, and I said how great it would be if we could get the mattress—it was 4000 gallons—in the lift and send it down to flood the lobby. Of course it wouldn't move, but Keith tried to lever it out of the frame, and it burst. The water was a foot high, flooding out into the hallway and down several floors. At first it was "Ha! Ha! Ha!" Then, "Ha. . . ha . . . ha . . . ooooh, this is going to cost hundreds of thousands of pounds! What are we going to do?" The destruction was unbelievable.

"Don't worry, Pete. I'll handle this," Keith says, and he rings the desk. "Hello, I want to talk to the manager. I have a suitcase here full of the most expensive stage clothes, designed by Hardy Amis, tailor to the Queen. Yes, yes, and they have just been engulfed by 4000 gallons of water from this leaking waterbed. Not only do I demand immediate replacement of my clothing, but also a room on the top floor, straight away!" And the manager came running upstairs, "Oh my God! I'm sorry! I'm sorry!" Keith claimed it had burst when we all sat on the bed, and he *had* called several times beforehand to make sure it would hold a large number of bodies. The guy bought it, and we never had to pay.

MUSICIAN: *You agree with Pete's assessment that Keith was basically sad?*

ENTWISTLE: Yeah, I did a drawing of Keith from a photograph once. I was just trying to transfer the photograph but somehow in the process I changed his eyes, so now I've got this portrait of Keith and when you look in his eyes, they're almost in tears. Really weird. I've only just hung it up in my house, because I couldn't face looking at it.

I had the closest relationship with Keith. I hid a lot of my emotions when he died. It just didn't sink in, or I stopped myself from thinking about it, so it was like it never happened. I feel really bad about it because I haven't even spoken to his mother for a long time. Now it's so late in the day I'm ashamed to even talk to her about it. My protection for myself was to forget about it. It worked for a while but . . . it's weird, weird. I would have been a lot more devastated had he not spent those three years in California. I got used to him not being around. Had he died before he went to California, I don't know what I would have done.

He never seemed to be able to get offstage. He always had to be Keith Moon. He was playing the part of Keith Moon, because he couldn't remember what it was like to be normal. The only time he was normal was before two in the afternoon. After two, he became the alter ego.

MUSICIAN: *That's when he started to drink?*

ENTWISTLE: At some point he must have realized he was an alcoholic. He only needed one beer and he was gone. The alcohol seemed to stay in his body and all he needed was to top it off. But he didn't get falling-down drunk. He got obnoxious drunk. I wrote that song "Dr. Jekyll and Mr. Hyde" about him. He was Dr. Jekyll until two in the afternoon and then Mr. Hyde for the rest of the day. He'd say something to really hurt you, and then he wouldn't remember having said it the next day. That was the sad part about Keith.

Other drummers would try to work out what he did, but the problem with Keith was, he didn't know. All he knew was that he played differently from everyone else. All his tom-toms were tuned to the same note, probably because if he missed one, he ended up hitting one that sounded the same. And they all sounded like rattling biscuit tins. Instead of starting a drum break with his left hand, he'd always start it with his right, and he always played fast, so no one would notice he was slightly out of beat. It always sounded like a kit falling downstairs.

MUSICIAN: *Was it fun for you as a bass player?*

ENTWISTLE: It was fun if I was on top of it. If I was having problems with my sound, it'd be a nightmare. That was one problem too many, because I *always* had a problem with Keith. A lot of the time I'd just carry on playing with my left hand and sort of pull the cymbal to one side to see what his bass drum foot was doing, so I could get back to the beat. He would often come out of his drum break on a different beat than I had. But it helped me in my playing style a lot. And I helped him, 'cause he knew no matter how crazy his drums got, my bass would still be there. I could always hold the band together while playing some flashy licks myself. If I went off on a tangent, he'd suddenly get the message and take off with me. When we came out of it together, we sounded like a couple of geniuses, but if we came out separately—oooooh!

I think the thing that really screwed him up was when his chauffeur died. He was attacked outside this club by a bunch of guys and the chauffeur got out to have a go at them. They knocked him down and they were kicking him and he crawled under the car to escape. All Keith saw was that they were hammering at the car, so he drove off. They got down the road and the chauffeur was still under the car, dead. It had a much deeper effect on him than he ever let on.

DALTREY: Keith had the comedian's disease of trying to make people laugh all the time. But inside he was incredibly unhappy. It was inevitable that we lost Keith along the way, if you'd known the way he lived. He had nine lives in the short time he was here.

MUSICIAN: *Was his unhappiness a result of his alcoholism?*

DALTREY: No, the alcoholism was a result of the unhappiness. I never met anyone like Keith Moon. He had so much energy, so much drive. And if he wasn't channeling it through his drums he had no place to put it. And he had this desperation to be loved, really loved by the people he cared about. If he didn't get it all the time, if he wasn't shown it all the time, he would do more and more things to get it. A lot of the serious self-destruction happened after his marriage split up in '73 or '74. There was a definite change for the worse at that point.

MUSICIAN: *Do you have a favorite Keith Moon prank?*

DALTREY: It was a joke Keith and I played on John in Seattle. We turned Keith into John Entwistle—gave him a Fu Manchu moustache, dyed his hair, got the clothes just right. And Keith spent the whole evening walking one pace behind John. He mimicked him perfectly.

MUSICIAN: *You seem to be aging pretty well. Got any secrets?*

ENTWISTLE: If I restricted myself to England, I'd feel 15 years older than I am. I like the rock 'n' roll lifestyle because I've got the constitution to do it, which is why I was nicknamed the Ox. I can drink or leave it alone. I can stay out late as long as I pay back the sleep. As long as I feel okay, I plan to play into my 50s and 60s. If people want to hear me, I'll play. I don't care if it's fun or not. I can't do anything else. I'm a bass player. My biggest kick is playing, and fighting to stay ahead of all the other bass players. I don't lead the same life as Pete and Roger. I've got a girlfriend who's 11 years younger. I still go to clubs and get drunk. I enjoy doing naughty things. I enjoy living in hotels.

I look in the mirror and think, "Oh shit, I used to look better than this." But when I look at old photographs I think, "No, I didn't." I was a 210-pound Rasputin imitation at one point. The rock 'n' roll fatty. I look better and I feel better than I ever did. I want to live to be an eccentric old man.

MUSICIAN: *Why is Kenny Jones no longer your drummer?*

ENTWISTLE: It got to the point that there wouldn't have been a Who with Kenny Jones. That was around the time of Live Aid. Roger would not have come back to the Who if Kenny were here. I guess I was his closest friend in the band, but the fact is, you can only take friendship so far.

MUSICIAN: *The differences were personal or artistic?*

ENTWISTLE: Artistic. Kenny had already been working with other musicians—Paul Rodgers, specifically. And he got tired of waiting to get back together. We just separated. The oldest contingent of the Who was me, Roger and Pete. So we remain the Who.

MUSICIAN: *You feel Kenny Jones didn't fit in?*

DALTREY: I just never thought he was the right drummer for the Who. From Day One. I thought it totally unbalanced the way John plays bass. His bass playing evolved out of the chaotic way that Keith played the drums, while Kenny was simplicity itself. I never said that Kenny was a bad drummer or that we didn't get on socially.

MUSICIAN: *Your new drummer, Simon Phillips, can get that chaotic feel?*

DALTREY: Well, especially the imagination. That's the root of it. Being capable. Kenny was not capable of doing any more than he did. What he did was very good. But when you put him with a bass player of John's stature, who can play so much, who can move rhythms so fast, the drummer has to do more than boom chi chi boom. At first John couldn't see it. He finally saw it at a concert where Kenny was playing with another band. Then he got what I'd been trying to tell him. Kenny's simplicity was stifling. It was the same every night. Night after night. I'd be thinking, "ARGGGHHH!!!" But I'm not saying Kenny's a shit. It has nothing to do with that.

MUSICIAN: *John and Roger both seem to feel that Kenny was not the right drummer for the Who.*

TOWNSHEND: I think John and Roger are full of shit on that issue. What were they talking about?

MUSICIAN: *They both said they liked him personally but . . .*

TOWNSHEND: He wasn't Keith Moon?

MUSICIAN: *He was too simple and unimaginative. Keith could pick up a song in ways that Kenny couldn't.*

TOWNSHEND: The Who post-Keith was a different band. Kenny was very important in that band. And if you reduce Kenny's role to simply not responding to the spaces that Keith would have filled up, it's a kind of nonsense argument. I don't accept it as a valid basis to criticize Kenny. "Kenny was a nice guy but . . ." is not the right way to go about a subject as sensitive as that. Kenny was brought into the band probably more at my behest, so I'm quite defensive about it. I felt we should not try to replace Keith, not go down the same dynamic road. If they're still thinking that way, maybe I'm going to have some trouble down the road this trip.

The problem I've always had is that different people have different preconceptions about what the Who is. To me the Who is a banner headline. If you called the Who "Rock Will Define Itself," I think that would be what we're trying to do. It isn't the name of a familiar group of musicians, because once Keith died, that was dead. It's become a kind of ideology—a sense of personal emancipation as opposed to political or economic emancipation. We who are in the Who should know that it's impossible to invoke that other kind of music without Keith.

So I felt the band without Keith was a new band. Kenny was a drummer I'd worked with in the past. I liked him for his simplicity and directness and for the similarity of our backgrounds. He came up at the same time and had had a similar success. He was one of the few British drummers who could fill Keith's shoes, and it was courageous of him to do so. Roger really resisted Kenny being brought in as a quarter member—that was the other thing. He wanted Kenny on salary. I said, "I'm not ready for that. It means we're still running the Who. It's like we're on a pilgrimage to find Keith. To be really unpleasant about it, I'm kind of glad Keith is gone. He was a pain in the ass. The band wasn't functioning. This is a chance to do something new." I tried to get them thinking that way.

But Kenny doesn't actually deserve my solidarity here, because he's given me an extremely hard time lately. Firstly about our not going on the road for so long. And he said I denied him the opportunity to make a good Who album. When I broke the deal with Warner Bros., he felt we were just revving up to make a great album. And he became mesmerized by the Who in a worse way than anyone I've come across. I said to him that I wanted to work with Roger and I think there will be difficulties, but it's not my battle. You've got to sort yourself out with Roger. Got to convince him you can do the job. Nothing seemed to get done. One day Kenny's wife, or girlfriend, or whatever she was, rang me up and she said, "Listen, he's not going to wait while you fuck around anymore. He's going to get this band together with Paul Rodgers," and he went ahead and did it. And lots of other stuff that isn't fit to print.

I feel very sad about it because I think Kenny would be capable of performing well on this tour. But what we can do with Simon is probably a lot more ambitious than anything we could do with Kenny. I don't want to dwell on it too much. Kenny enabled me to get through an important period is musical life, and if John and Roger don't feel the same there's nothing I can do to change that. I feel greatly indebted to Kenny. I think Kenny should understand that. I think Roger and John should understand that, too.

MUSICIAN: *You said before that if you had quit drinking in the early '70s, you would have quit the band. What's different now that you're not drinking? There's obviously still conflict.*

TOWNSHEND: What conflict?

MUSICIAN: *Over Kenny.*

TOWNSHEND: That is not a conflict. Kenny isn't here. I chose the new drummer. You could go down the rest of the band and I think you'll find that I chose most of them. In fact, I chose the whole fucking lot of them. There's no conflict. This is my band. The only potential conflict is based on how John and Roger feel about working in that environment and calling it the Who. Maybe they would prefer going out as a four-piece and I had a stack and we thrash away like we did in the '60s. I don't know what's on their minds. They're not entirely honest with me all the time. They treat me like a lunatic sometimes.

My reasons for wanting a larger band are technical, really. With a larger number of musicians you can keep the stage sound level a lot lower. When dealing with a club-size band, it needs to be loud to be rich harmonically. That's how the sound began, how heavy metal began, and was refined by bands like Led Zeppelin and went downhill from there.

But there are no conflicts today. I told John and Roger that I can't make their dream come truc. It would be like making Nureyev dance at his eightieth birthday party. John and Roger accept it. You can't make a conflict out of their regret. They've been fantastically supportive. I know the show won't be what old Who fans want, but it's all they're going to get, and it might be very, very good if we do it in the right way.

MUSICIAN: *On the subject of metal, Jimi Hendrix is usually given most of the credit for popularizing the Marshall stack, but the Who first used one. Correct?*

TOWNSHEND: I don't give a shit.

MUSICIAN: *Well, didn't Hendrix take a lot of your act?*

TOWNSHEND: He was a fucking genius. He could have stolen my wife and I would have been happy about it. I had a very reverent attitude toward him. He could make you *see* what he was playing. Without acid. He was a cosmic player. But I don't think he took us very seriously. If anyone copied the Who, it was Noel Redding. He was a stone John Entwistle freak. Noel Redding was also a complete nonentity. Compared to Hendrix, so am I. Maybe not John, though. He's quite an extraordinary rock virtuoso. Do we really care about the Marshall stack? John should be remembered for his innovations in the upper frequencies of the bass, the way he worked in a three-piece with essentially a rhythm guitarist—which is what I am—to replace lead licks. And working with a drummer as voluble and crazy as Keith. And all the technical things he's done with the bass and bass strings.

MUSICIAN: *What should you be remembered for?*

TOWNSHEND: I don't know. I suppose I don't really give a shit.

MUSICIAN: *Well, thanks for your time. I know you're flying back to England tonight.*

TOWNSHEND: No, I'm staying over one more night. I'm meeting with Coca Cola tomorrow.

WHO M I?

JOHN Entwistle on the bass: "Since the last time I played with the Who, I've changed absolutely everything, except the basic idea of sound splitting. All I have to do is press a footswitch and the whole thing changes. I couldn't find one amplifier manufacturer who made all I wanted, so it starts with a t.c. electronics digital delay that controls all the outboard stuff. The Yamaha SPX1000 gives me a lot more effects and splits into a stereo chorus. I've got a Gallien-Krueger 2000 CPL preamp, which I use to get a beefy overdrive. I've got the top sound, the distorted trebly guitar sound, coming out of four 12s and 16 fives in stereo. That goes into two Trace Elliot 500W power amps. I've got a Trace Elliot computer preamp for the bottom end, or I can use a t.c. graphic EQ, whichever I favor at the time, going through four 15s. All the speakers are Fanes in A.S.S. English cabinets.

"I've designed a new bass guitar for Warwick called a Buzzard, a big, weird-shaped bass, similar in dimension to the Explorer basses I was using. But now it's shaped like a flying buzzard. It reminds me of the Queen of Hearts in *Alice in Wonderland* playing croquet with a flamingo." **Pete Townshend** was not definite, but expected to play Takamine semi-acoustics and Fender's Eric Clapton model Stratocaster "because they're good all-'round guitars." No Marshall stacks this time—to save his hearing, Townshend will play direct through the P.A.

"IT'S LIKE CLIMBING
MOUNT EVEREST": ROGER DALTREY

Sean Egan | January 2002 | Previously unpublished in this form

Despite Moon's death, the poor quality of their eighties albums, and their lack of new product, the public were perennially happy to see the Who in concert. With Ringo Starr's son Zak Starkey on drumming duties, there were Who tours in 1996–1997, 1999, and 2000, with proceeds often going to charity.

This Roger Daltrey interview was conducted in January 2002 when the band was about to embark on a series of live dates, partly to promote the Teenage Cancer Trust charity. This is the first publication of the verbatim transcript. —Ed.

What is the Who's involvement with the Teenage Cancer Trust charity?

We've been involved in them for years because the charity was started by my own doctor and his wife. So it's something we've been aware of for years and when we started getting back to work two years ago, I said to Pete, "Rather than do loads of diverse charities, why don't we focus on one?" We picked on this one because it's got attainable targets. It's not open-ended. It obviously needs to raise money in the future but it's got a target that is attainable and it's something that unlike most things these days we [Britain] lead the world in.

Have any of your relatives been stricken by the disease?

Not as teenagers, no. I lost a lot of family with cancer, just like most families I'm sure.

How does cancer specifically adversely affect teenagers?

I think the problem with teenagers is because they're very visible in themselves, the way they dress and people tend to notice them a lot in that respect, but they tend to suffer in silence because they bottle things up so much and the problem does get overlooked. [It's] very easy to get people to feel sorry for young children and as people get older obviously, but teenagers seem to be the ones stuck in the middle. They're neither here nor there. If they get cancer they're either put in a ward with young children with bunnies on the wall or stuck in with old people dying of the disease. Now that is completely unsatisfactory. They're dealing with enough problems in their life without having the disease. Going through adolescence is incredibly traumatic—as we all remember!

What are those attainable targets you speak of?

What we're after is twenty units around the country which will, at the moment, cover the numbers of teenagers [who get cancer]. It is epidemic. The number of teenagers that get cancer now, it was one in 360 boys and one in 420 girls. They haven't released new figures but according to the people on the units, it seems to be getting worse. So you could say that in every secondary school in this country, in any given year, there'll be one of each gender with cancer. That's pretty high statistics. The trust also funds the staff in those units. So again that's a fixed cost and our budget for the next five years is £25 million. The evidence is that if teenagers go into a unit there is on average an up to 15 percent improvement rate on the success of the same treatment [in a normal ward], which is quite astonishing. It's because of the environment and the support they give each other. So for a very small input it's an incredible outcome.

You're starting your new tour with warm-up gigs—do the Who really need to warm up these days?

Oh yeah, we do! No matter what you do—you can sing around the house, you can rehearse—it's not like being on a stage. The Who's a weird band. It's to do with energy and things that happen in the spur of the moment. A lot of what we play is actually made up on the night.

The song's the framework for a lot of other things that happen. So we do need to warm up.

Who's going to be drumming with you?

Zak Starkey.

Is he a good drummer?

One of the best in the business, in my opinion.

Can anybody replace Keith Moon?

No, of course you can't. You can replace the technical or the musical side of the drumming although it'll never be the same, he was totally unique. Moon was much, much more than just one of the best rock drummers ever. He was an enormous personality. He's always missed and can never be replaced.

When Keith died, I've always thought that he could only have been replaced by either Ginger Baker or Mitch Mitchell.

I think Mitch had already kind of moved on from that kind of drumming. And he wasn't the powerhouse that Moon was. He was more of a technician.

What got the Who the reputation as the best live band in the world?

I think we just are a great live band. I think there's so much of what the Who are that just doesn't come across on a record, never has. There's an enormity of the Who that is very difficult to capture on record. I think if you watch the DVD of the Teenage Cancer Trust concert with surround sound you get some idea of the power of it. Maybe it's getting better 'cause I must admit when I saw the New York concert that we did [for victims of the World Trade Center attack], albeit a very short stab, the Who kind of blasted out of the screen to me. It's very difficult to watch yourself in the first place, but it's big—and there's only four of us.

But in the 1970s on albums like Who's Next, you began to sound as grand in the studio as you were live.

Yeah, but it's not the same as when you're there! There's another ingredient that just doesn't transfer to records. I think we're coming better now.

It seems to me that we went through a period where we were adding more and more and more, and now we're stripping down and taking things away. We're getting back to more of what the Who really are and that in some ways gives it more strength. Less is more.

Live work is all very well but it's been twenty years since the last Who studio album. Will there be another?

That's down to whether we feel we could ever make one good enough. It's down to whether Pete will ever record anybody else's material and whether he can ever write anything that he feels would be worth releasing. But we're gonna try. We are trying. We haven't given up. But who knows? We'll be the judge of whether it's good enough.

Has Pete got a mental block about writing for the Who?

I think there's a lot of fear there. I think there's a fear of failure and "Can I do that anymore?"

When you split up in the early 1980s, he said the songs he was writing didn't sound like Who songs and the Who couldn't really change their style, therefore you had to split up . . .

I don't think Pete ever wrote Who songs. He wrote Pete Townshend songs that the Who then recorded and made them Who songs. And if he could only see it that he writes Pete Townshend songs and sometimes the Who record them, then I think he wouldn't have the same hang-ups about it.

Perhaps Pete might have a mental block because as his songs became more personal and autobiographical down the years, it began to seem more and more strange that they were coming out of your mouth.

It's irrelevant. It's like someone writing a book, a work of fiction. A lot of writers write themselves into a book through another person. It's whether he's got a problem with that. I think it's whether we ever sold his songs well, and I think we did. I see it much more simpler than he does.

I assume you discuss this face-to-face?

Of course we do. I just don't have the same hang-ups and I won't have because I haven't been through the same thing. I do appreciate how painful some of the areas that he wrote those songs from must have been for him but I'll always stand up the fact that I feel the Who did Pete Townshend songs a lot of justice.

Maybe a way round that is for Pete to just write ten pop songs like on *A Quick One*?

It's easy to say that. It's whether he feels he can do it.

So what likelihood is there that we'll get another Who studio album?

Fifty-fifty. We're going to go in the studio and we will do something. It's whether we enjoy ourselves and we feel that what we've actually recorded is worth releasing. I think we'll have to have an adjudicator on that! We will know in our bones whether it's any good or not.

The Who's back catalog had been remastered and reissued very impressively and conscientiously.

Well we try. And you are dealing in an area really that is controlled by the industry, not really by us, but we try and keep as much value in there as we can.

There's one slight problem with the generous number of bonus tracks you put on CDs in that they destroy the original sequencing of an album. For instance, we're used to *Who's Next* climaxing with "Won't Get Fooled Again" and now it ends with an array of miscellaneous bonus tracks.

The climax of "Won't Get Fooled Again" went out with the CD. The running order of albums disappeared with the coming of the CD so I don't think that's relevant anymore. Running order used to be important. It's not anymore—unfortunately. Another art form lost.

Are you planning on any solo records?

If the Who don't do anything, I might do something. I don't know. I just like to sing. I'm a jobbing actor. I go out and sing in all kinds of stuff and I have fun. I'm extremely lucky. But I've written a load of songs. I might put them into an album. I've written a load of songs for the Who.

You've often said you find it really hard to write songs . . .

I still don't find it easy. The musical side of it is not as easy for me as it is for Pete, but lyrically I'm okay.

You play guitar these days as well, don't you?

I play more guitar onstage than I used to, yeah.

Do you think Pete would write songs for any solo album you do?

Well he has in the past. He wrote "After the Fire" for me, and if he ever did I'd only be too pleased to do them if it was a good song.

What can you tell me about the Who's forthcoming American tour?

Basically what we're trying to do this year is to stay in shape, because every time we have eighteen months off and then have to come back and do gigs it's like climbing Mount Everest, so the idea is just to try and do enough shows so that we maintain a peak so that if ever anybody asks us to do a benefit that we feel we want to do, we haven't got this great big ladder to climb. We space our work out now: every time we do something for ourselves, we do something for charity. That's how we like to work. But obviously you can't put it down for eighteen months and just pick it up and expect it to come back immediately. It has up to now, but we're getting older.

What about going on the road for several months?

No, I wouldn't want to go on the road. I couldn't do it. The ideal thing for me is to do thirty, forty, fifty shows a year so that we're always in peak condition. Voices aren't like guitars—you can't change the vocal chords like a set of guitar strings.

Is your voice changing as you get older?

Well obviously it is. Some of those high notes that I used to be able to just soar up to, now it's not quite as easy. I get criticized for wearing out but I'm entitled to wear out—I'm getting up there [in age]. But I think in some ways I'm a better singer today. I think one of the problems I've got is I'm singing songs that we became famous for twenty, thirty years ago. I think if we did do [new] stuff, I think people would suddenly think: "Fucking hell—Daltrey *is* a good singer."

Your voice changed so much between *Tommy* and *Who's Next*.

That was to do with trying to find a voice. I'd been a soul singer. I'd been James Brown, Howlin' Wolf—I sang all this black music. And when I was presented with these first Townshend songs, I just didn't know what voice to give them. It was a complete mystery to me, that whole period: "Where do I find the voice to these songs?" I found them very difficult to sing, even though they're very, very simple songs. *Tommy* was the making of that. *Tommy* was the thing that did it.

***Tommy* has taken on a life of its own, with four or five different versions now available, including the one on the new deluxe *Live at Leeds*. Do you have a preference for any of them?**

I never listen to 'em! I'd like to get a DVD done of it one day. I'd like the Who to actually play it all the way through and film it.

Do you think the quality of *Who's Next* made you the best band in the world in 1971?

No, you never feel that. You go on just being what you are. You never believe all that shit. I just think we're a very good rock and roll band.

What do you think about the way the Rolling Stones have persevered?

They've got a good attitude to it: it's only rock and roll but they like it. And I love that about them.

"ANY CUNT CAN BE AN ENTERTAINER": PETE TOWNSHEND

Sean Egan | 2003 | Previously unpublished in this form

In June 2002, John Entwistle died. The Quiet One had gone colorfully, expiring of a cocaine-induced heart attack while in the company of a stripper.

There was further trauma awaiting the Who. In 2003, Pete Townshend was cautioned over his accessing indecent images online in a wrongheaded attempt to highlight child abuse. While the case unfolded, he decided on a moratorium of media interviews. This July 2003 interview was his first for several months. It was mostly concerned with the recent release of the deluxe version of *Who's Next* and the *Lifehouse* project that bequeathed the original version of that album, but took in a range of other subjects.

The interview is here presented verbatim in English for the first time.

Note that Townshend, who had once dismissed it as best forgotten, is now acknowledging *Who's Next* to be a classic. —Ed.

One of the biggest mysteries about the story of the Who is that in 1966 you asked Eddie Phillips of the band the Creation to join the Who as a second guitarist. Is this rumor true?

I don't have a clear memory of it but I have enough of a memory of it to know that it's true. I can't remember what was going on at the time—because of course a lot of the time I would have been doing amphetamines and so would he and we probably went and hung out together a few times. We loved the band. They were the best support band that we had at the Marquee, although the Move did a couple of supports for us and they were pretty hot at the time as well. But the Creation had a much purer audience contact than even we had at the time, because they brought their audience with them I think.

But what role could he have filled in the Who, being a virtuoso guitarist who sometimes played guitar with a violin bow?

I think he would have fitted in very well because if you go back to that period and you listen to live recordings, I couldn't play and he could, and I really wanted to concentrate on my role as a writer and a power-chord man and I thought that the way that he played would fit in really, really beautifully with my power chords. I often did play with other musicians: Eric [Clapton] or Stephen Stills or Leslie West. The person I always wanted to play with was Jimi Hendrix. Just to think if they had me playing rhythm behind them. Fucking hell, how extraordinary that would be, and I think that's where it came from.

I once spoke to a studio engineer who said that at that time you really felt threatened by other guitarists and, for instance, you walked out of the studio when Jimi Hendrix walked in on a Who session once. Is that unfair?

Yeah, it is. I may have had a bit of low self-esteem in that department, but I knew what I was good at. No, when Jimi came to meet the Who at IBC [Studios], I spent an hour with him telling him what amplifiers to buy, so on the contrary I didn't walk out and I remember that he was the one who seemed in awe of me at the time—a situation that was going to rapidly change within a couple of weeks. But when we first met, he was very shy. Well, he was always shy. But [his manager] Chas Chandler brought him to IBC. I think we may have been recording early draft tracks for *Tommy*. He wanted to know what kind of amps to use and I'd asked him what he'd been using. I think he'd been using a small Fender amp. And I said, "Listen, mate, you need big amps"—I'd never heard him play—"You need one of these Marshalls and one of these Hiwatts and stick them together and pick the one that you like and then buy another three of them."

I think the first time that I saw him was at Blaises in London and there he was with his twin stacks and I regretted giving him the advice because he used feedback in the most extraordinary way. No, I was a great proponent of Syd Barrett. I took Eric Clapton to see Syd Barrett for the first time. I was always a big fan of other guitar players that were more in my area as well. I loved Dave Davies from the Kinks and always thought he was hugely underrated.

I can see that happening but I can also see that it was a bit of a pipe dream. You can see also that if you look at Who chronology that it's quite possible that, around the time that this happened, the Who were in disarray. You remember that story about Keith and John wanting to leave the Who to form a band with Jimmy Page and call it Led Zeppelin? That may have been happening at the same time, so I may have been cooking up a new band. There were a couple of players that I really liked from Pete Meaden's band called the Vagabonds: Phil Chen on bass I think I probably would have imagined, and so it goes. So I may have been trying to make an alternative band, seeing trouble ahead or something. But I remember the Creation was one of the only bands other than the Vagabonds that I would get there early enough to watch . . . In fact, once the Creation did do a set after we'd finished. I can't remember what happened. Keith got ill or something and we stopped, we only played fifteen minutes and they came on again.

Turning to Who's Next, we all know it started as a concept album called Lifehouse. It seems that the Lifehouse project was never viewed with much enthusiasm or even understood by any of the Who. Was this an annoying period for you because of that?

Variously on and off, it depends. There's been a lot of revisionism really, looking back by everybody involved. Me, Roger, and everybody that's been involved in it has looked at it in different ways. There were huge misunderstandings between me and the Who's managers about the way the piece was going to be funded and all that, and we were riding on the back of a hugely successful concept album which was actually very dodgy in premise which was Tommy, and that had done very well so in actual fact I almost had a carte blanche from everybody around me to do whatever I wanted. In a sense, the concept behind Lifehouse was another kind of Tommy, like a mechanical device, a way of creating a device that would work to show how we become disconnected and unaware of the spiritual mechanics that go on in day-to-day life. I had done a similar thing with *Tommy*.

In *Tommy* I used the device of a child being smitten deaf, dumb, and blind by witnessing a violent trauma, and in *Lifehouse* I used a similar device again: an individual plunged into a life of virtual reality fed by something like the Internet, suspended in a kind of parallel life in virtual animation, experiencing totally phony lifestyles. It was very simple, I believed. Certainly as naive as *Tommy* in basis but a very simple story, and although it predated William Gibson's first book about the matrix, a lot of writing had already been done about the future of the Internet, about the way the computers would link people together, that data would be exchanged. Although the first two computers weren't linked together until after I'd scratched out the story for *Lifehouse*, they were working on it. It was all going on and it had been going on for quite some time and the only reason I knew about all this—and I've certainly never claimed to have really been a visionary in imagining it—was because I'd been taught about it at art school. Harold Cohen, who was one of the teachers there, is still doing computer art. He built that robot that paints pictures. A couple of the other people—Roy Ascott in particular—were really smart about how computers would change the way people were entertained and the way that that entertainment could be used to subvert their lives.

But the story itself was very, very simple and I actually think everybody in the band did get it. I think what happened was I took it a step too far. I wrote a very, very simple narrative which is a very basic film script—I'd never written a film script—but then I tried to do a kind of theatre workshop version of it. I wanted to do a bit of the film to show everybody around me that you could make music using computers that reflected a limited number of facets of an individual's personality. And it was that bit that went astray because what happened was that Frank Dunlop, who was my writing partner at the time at the Young Vic [theatre], was approached by Kit Lambert—the Who's manager—and told in a heroin haze that we weren't really working on *Lifehouse* at all, we were working on *Tommy*. And Frank Dunlop—bless his heart, who's still a terrific friend of mine—held a press conference, and of course it completely threw me because I couldn't really quite work out why he was holding a press conference, and also the idea of the workshop based on the *Lifehouse* story had not been finalized. And it was at that point when the members of the band lost faith in the idea because a whole bunch of journalists took people like Roger and Keith aside and said to them, "You know Pete's mad. This will never work."

One of the story strands of *Lifehouse* is said to be the universal chord, which is an aggregation of the individual chords produced by every human being.

That's simply a fictional idea. It does have of course a metaphysical and to some extent some scientific basis. The universe resonates. It's well known and there's quite a lot of writing about that. It resonates in a way that produces measurable vibrations. But further to that there's been lots of writing over the years about the music of the spheres, about the fact that individuals have electronic resonances running inside them and all this is now bog standard accepted information. When I was working on *Lifehouse*, we were kind of at the leading edge. The thing about the universal chord—that was actually something to do with the Moody Blues. It had nothing to do with the Who's *Lifehouse*. Absolutely nothing to do with it. What I talked about in my script was a man who goes mad, who starts to work with people and produce pieces of music and actually starts to affect them spiritually and a kind of *Tommy* figure again. I called him "Bobby." Perhaps not very smart but that's what I called him. What he did was, he started to have an effect on the people around him and as a result started to become carried away. And started to aspire to the idea that he could bring everybody together. I don't know whether Roger's going to like this but you may have seen some of Roger's interviews over the years about everything to do with rock and roll, to do with my relationship, to do with Keith Moon. If I was a rock bible puncher . . . I stopped doing it as a quite young man. Roger continues to do it to this day. It was based on the fact that as a group we had one area on which we all agreed and that was that something extraordinary and magical happened when a really great band properly tried to reflect the feelings of the assembled audience. Now that sounds pompous but it's simple.

In other words, you don't go up there and do a Freddie Mercury—not that there's anything wrong with that—you go up there and you try to perform in such a way that you channel the audience's feelings, energies, frustrations—and the Who were brilliant at that.

And the interesting thing is the Who played at all three of the major festivals of the era—Monterey, Woodstock, and the Isle of Wight. Was that what partly inspired that feeling?

It may well have been what made me feel that such a pompous idea [was viable]. I think *Lifehouse* is far more pretentious in aim than really *Tommy* ever was. *Tommy* is much more of a sociological document about the family postwar. *Lifehouse* is science fiction and based on the promise of the home computer, which we all knew was coming but we didn't know when. So going and playing those big festivals—some of which we played a very important part in—yeah. I can remember for example after playing the Isle of Wight, one of the guys from the Moody Blues coming [over]—we'd just played *Tommy*—saying, "This is it, you've really, really cracked it." I said, "Oh you liked it, did you?" He said, "No, what I thought was extraordinary is there was a point at which the audience seemed to forget themselves." And so what he was claiming for that performance was something more than a musical event. He was claiming something that was a meditative event or something. And I think you have to go back and talk to people about what happened at those great Who performances to get a measure of the impact that we had at the time as a live band and the loyalty that we've managed to hang on to over the years, particularly with respect to the music from *Lifehouse*.

How far were you into recording *Lifehouse* before you realized that it wasn't going to work as a rock opera and that you were going to have to put it out as a conventional album?

I think it was almost immediately after the concerts at the Young Vic. That's as far as we got. When we did the three concerts at the Young Vic—one of which was recorded—they were meant to be workshops, so the first couple of days I don't think we even played a normal concert, but when those concerts happened, we'd already been waiting maybe six months for money to fund the work at the Young Vic, which was going to include, by the way, a foundation sum. Which is partly why to this day the Young Vic isn't properly finished, because I'd told the principals of the Young Vic—who at that time included Laurence Olivier—that because the Who was going to make this big movie there, we would be able to make a big donation and they could finish off their scenery dock. And if you go the Young Vic, there's a great big hole where they were going to have a conventional proscenium scenery dock at the back of their building and we were supposed to pay for it.

What actually happened was that I'd been six months before that concert to see people in the States with Kit Lambert and Pete Kameron, who was his producer, and we got a promise from them of $2 million based on a scrappy little document that I'd written about *Lifehouse* (probably though more based on the success of *Tommy* at the time). I'd come back to London and immediately gone off with this imaginary money and started to talk to computer programmers, to emeritus musicians and composers. I started with Karlheinz Stockhausen and I worked downwards. That's what actually happened. I actually met him and talked to him about my idea. He was not impressed, but I met him. After about three or four months we started to run out of money. It was only about ten years ago that Chris Stamp explained to me what had happened. When *Tommy* was finished as an album, Kit Lambert had written a very simple film script based on the *Tommy* story which he wanted to make into a film. He'd gone to Universal, he'd got an agreement in principle to make the film himself. He was an unknown director but he'd got an agreement to make the film and apparently—I don't remember this—but I'd blocked him doing that. I'd read the script, I said, "Listen it's very nice but I don't want you to become a film director, I want you to continue to support me in my writing and be the Who's manager." So I as the copyright holder blocked his first attempt to make a film. So what he did is he immediately after my meeting with the bigwigs at Universal went back in and, unbeknown even to Pete Kameron, said, "You know, Pete Townshend's mad and what this is about is the film of *Tommy* but this is just his new version of it." Now in a sense, what Kit said is true because *Lifehouse* was just an extrapolation of the central idea of *Tommy*, which is that we are all spiritual beings locked in a human body and spiritual people living a human existence and it was just another way to tell the same story.

After all the hard work behind *Lifehouse*, the best songs were cherry-picked for the album *Who's Next* and put on the album with no regard to the *Lifehouse* narrative. How did you feel about that?

Well there was a fantastic sense of relief. I didn't feel happy or unhappy. I just felt fantastically relieved. There was a finer moment which was when Kit Lambert finally reached out to me after the Young Vic sessions, which were abortive. All we got out of the Young Vic sessions was a bunch of Who songs played again. I'd done a lot of going round in the hall talking to people, but at the end we just gave up and played a show. Kit Lambert reached out and said, "Listen I'm in New York in the wonderful new Record Plant studios. Why don't you come over and we'll record some of the tracks and maybe we can hock something together?" I arrived in New York and I was really elated because I wanted Kit back. I really felt that I needed him as a creative mentor and that I was getting lost and that something had fundamentally gone wrong and I'd mismanaged everything. Because I didn't know that he had engineered this problem. And when I got there I found that he was far from being my friend. He'd set himself up as my enemy. He was calling me by my surname rather than my first name and it was very, very painful. Then I discovered that he was a six-month heroin addict. We went into the studio. We only did about five days and it was good fun but Kit was very, very uneven and he was trying to produce two albums at once. He was trying to do a follow-up album to the first Labelle album, which had been a big success for him, in one studio while producing us down the road. He got Felix Pappalardi in to help out. I don't intend to blame Kit Lambert for the failure of the whole thing. It probably would never have happened—because it's certainly never happened since, despite all my best efforts! It's never really happened in the way that I imagined it could happen. But you know today I still feel that if somebody gave me a couple of million dollars, I could do a little workshop which would demonstrate this very simple premise, that if you take basic data from somebody you could produce a piece of music. I think it's self-evident in a modern technological world.

That might be possible, but on the other hand you're an entertainer and the music you've got to produce has got to be easy on the ear. So it seems like you've got this scientific idea which is not necessarily an artistic idea.

Well I think it is artistic. I am an artist but I came from that hothouse art-school background that David Bowie shared, that Brian Eno shared. We did the same ground course with Roy Ascott and his whole premise was to lift our heads off and put them back on again at a different angle. It's not so much about science but about metaphysics and about what it does, what the artist's function is. You have to remember too that I met [painter, performance artist, and creator of auto-destructive art] Gustav Metzger, whose most recent action was to boycott all art as being bourgeois. I am not proud of the fact that I'm an entertainer. I'm proud of the fact that I'm an artist. Any cunt can be an entertainer. To be an artist and an entertainer is very, very difficult, and also to do good work as an artist is very difficult. When I'm an entertainer, this is probably why sometimes I appear to have little kind of regard for the process. I don't hold it up particularly large because when all I have to do is jump up and down, smash a guitar, play a few power chords, and there it is, it's done, it makes the audience look as though that's all they really want. It's for the girl from the Yeah Yeah Yeah's to have a sulk and pull up her blouse. It's not that's simple. There's a lot more going on. I think in the background of even my earlier, more innocent bits of writing there was the fact that I really had my brain turned inside out at art school . . . Harold Cohen was such a big personality. I digress for a second: I can remember him shouting at me and going, "Townshend, you're such a fucking stupid boy!" like an old-time schoolteacher. I remember going up to him once and saying to him, "I wish you wouldn't fucking humiliate me." Because these were classrooms full of the most incredibly beautiful, intelligent, smart, and sexy women. And he said, "Yes, but you know why I'm doing it, don't you?" I was expecting him to say something like "Because you like it."

He said, "You're the only one in the room who's got any chance of understanding all this shit. Concentrate."

Were you surprised that despite the phenomenon that *Tommy* had been, *Who's Next* was almost immediately recognized as the Who's definitive album and masterpiece?

No. I learnt a valuable lesson. I learnt that *Tommy*, with only the best songs taken off it and released, probably would have enjoyed the same success. In other words, we would have got respect as a band that played great music and not necessarily as a band that were great entertainers and were full of great ideas. What's very interesting was that *Who's Next* was gladly accepted because it didn't seem to suffer from the hysteria that pulled at me and obviously made it very difficult for me to be a proper functioning member of the Who. On the one hand I didn't want to be a puppet entertainer smashing guitars every night, and on the other hand I was really tortured by this idea that I had to find some great artistic premise which would make my work more important. When the album came out, I felt fantastic 'cause one of the great things about it was that because we'd recorded it with Glyn Johns, it just sounded so great. It was one of the first records the Who had made that to me sounded good. I don't know that it particularly captured the Who's sound. "Won't Get Fooled Again" did.

We worked in Olympic Studios, where of course I'd worked hundreds of times and been hundreds of times watching the Stones at work, watching the [Small] Faces at work, and Glyn Johns had always been a friend of mine and done a lot of solo work as well, but the Who had never worked there really. At that time the studio was at its peak. It was a great big room—nearly a hundred-foot-high ceiling, like an old film stage. Beautiful Helios desk. Well run. The guy that was the chief engineer there, Keith Grant, was and is still an inspired guy in the way he set up the monitoring. And Glyn was at his most effective in that room. Also, because we'd done so much rehearsing on the material—both at the Young Vic and then in New York with Kit—we went in and we just kind of played it, so it had that immediacy as well. I was really proud of it—proud of the way it sounded and also proud of the fact that although it was being perceived as a very straightforward album, I knew that there was a bit of depth there if you wanted to look. Subsequently, of course, I've spent a lot of time trying to encourage people to look more deeply into *Lifehouse*. It's become a tradition among Who fans to nod their heads to me and say, "Okay Pete, if you say so, we'll go and have a look." That has meant a huge amount to me because I put so much energy into it. And I do feel it was a great lost idea.

You've been quoted as saying that with hindsight the Who were not crucially important like the Beatles and the Stones, but when this album came out, the Beatles were gone, Bob Dylan seemed in a decline, and the Stones that year put out *Sticky Fingers*, which is a good album but not as good as *Who's Next*. So this was one juncture when the Who probably were the most important artists in the world. Were you conscious of that in any way at that time?

I'd never claim that title for myself. It's something that's lazily claimed by whoever has got whichever band on sale at any particular time. The rock industry is competitive but it's not that kind of competition. I don't know what I said in the past about that but I think really probably what I'm talking about is hierarchy. There was a hierarchy and if you start your honoration by saying, "Listen, I was influenced by Big Bill Bronzy, Pete Seeger, Louis Armstrong and Ella Fitzgerald and the Basie Band or something, and then when I heard Elvis and Bill Haley, something changed . . ." What you're talking about is performers who had an extraordinary superficial [allure]. They were the front men for an industry of music for two generations, actually, which emerged in its new form in rock 'n' roll in the mid-sixties, in a number of different guises. If you draw Dylan's line, you go back through the Hudson River trips and all that stuff. So it's a completely different journey but we all landed in the same place.

In actual fact, the Rolling Stones, looking like a bunch of reprobate tramps, used to walk past the [art] college on their way up to the Ealing Club to do their concerts and I never had the fucking courage to go and see them play then. It was very much like the Sex Pistols had arrived. It was really subversive [and] they hadn't quite got their band together but a couple of times I saw them in the streets and it was like seeing Martians. So as far as I was concerned the Rolling Stones were part of that mysterious legacy of faces, people who were making it possible for me to move away from art college and become a working musician and a writer. It's a legacy really, I think. The same applies in a slightly different way to the Beatles, probably the year before. I was trying to decide whether it was cool to be at art college but still have a Beatle haircut. Torn in two different directions. They were an incredibly important band. There was a fantastic article last year about the Kinks [and] it was incredible to realize that people are starting to understand how vital was that [period]. The chronology is so compressed up. Maybe six months or a year, a huge number of different things happened.

Do the bonus tracks on the deluxe version of *Who's Next* dilute the power of the original concept, especially the way it used to climax with "Won't Get Fooled Again"?

As I was never that pumped up about the idea of the album as an organic entity I suppose it doesn't bother me much at all. I think anybody that goes out and buys the deluxe package will expect to get some of the background. For years, the way that I used to address the background of all the work that I was doing was through long elongated interviews with the press which I no longer do. So to some extent these packages do help to bring in dispassionate journalism and collection of collateral outtakes to give background really.

If what you're saying is that there needs to be an original album in the package standing alone, one of the problems with that is we're in a time shift here. The album is a classic. It's been blurred by a hundred different exigencies. One has been the fact that I've propped up my publishing company on the sale of a lot of the songs on *Who's Next* to commercial companies and been decried left, right, and center for doing so. [There has been] a lot of exploitation of that music so I don't know that it will ever stand clean and clear the way that it did when it first came out. Which I think was an illusion. It wasn't clean and clear. It was born of a lot of muddiness, a lot of ambition, a lot of pompousness, pretentiousness, artistic arrogance to some extent. But also I think behind it there was a lot of simple joy that we had as musicians in the performing process. At the time, as well as playing big festivals, we were still playing universities here and there, so [we had] that sense that we were in contact with people that really understood that this music was growing. I don't think rock music had really folded down and become the kind of REM-type bible study class that it's now become, or on the other hand the kind of silly teenage "If you get in my way, I'll squirt at you" thing that we get from the *Kerrang!* bands.

How far were you into recording the Who album you were making before John Entwistle died?

I'd written a couple of songs. That's not strictly true: I'd pulled a couple of songs from the pile that I had. Roger had written three—or, again, he'd submitted three. John had refused to give us any material for reasons of his own but we were trying to persuade him to give us some material and we were in rehearsal at my studio in Twickenham and we filmed the whole thing. We ran through one of Roger's songs called "Certified Rose" and we ran through one of my songs called "Good Looking Boy," and that was as far as we got because two, three weeks later we were in L.A. waiting [to] tour and found that John had died.

But subsequent to that, before Christmas [2002], I decided to produce some backing tracks for Roger, who was hoping to write lyrics over them, and that's something that we're still in the business of looking at. God, I read something that [Roger] said recently where he sounded incredibly upbeat and positive but also possibly in some denial about how the songwriting process works, but he seems to be determined to get me back into a studio and to push me to making what he would call a Who album with him, and I'm in no mood really to turn away from his friendship. He's been such a fantastic support to me in my recent troubles. So we'll probably go into the studio later this year and try and scratch some material out.

Does the fact that John died when you were recording the first Who album for twenty years make you regret the fact that you declined to do a Who studio album in that period?

No. You have to realize that what made me stop making Who albums is very much the same thing that happened to Led Zeppelin. Somebody in the band died. And unlike them I was very slow to get the message. We made another two albums that we probably shouldn't have made. *It's Hard* and *Face Dances* contained really good material for a solo album but they weren't classic Who songs. And by "classic Who songs" maybe I'm putting my foot in it there 'cause I don't know what a classic Who song is, but I think it's a fairly stereotyped piece of work now. So I don't think there were missed opportunities.

I think what's going on now, it seems to me to be a bit simpler. John actually was afraid I think of having all the material that he'd produced with his partner Steve Luongo, who is the drummer and keyboard player in his touring band, having it kind of sifted through, having the best stuff taken to use for a Who album and nonetheless compared either to the best work that I was doing or having it frigged around by Roger and just didn't want to do it. So we wouldn't have got a balanced Who album at the time anyway without an incredible amount of strategic commit-ment—almost political commitment—to doing an album that was a third my songs, a third Roger's songs, and a third John's songs, which—to be absolutely brutally frank about this—that is not what I would call a Who album. I have written all this stuff over the years.

I get the impression that Roger was happy for any new album to be comprised completely of Pete Townshend songs but felt you weren't willing to give those songs to a Who project?

No, I think what was clear was that Roger couldn't do what he wanted to do, which is he couldn't be the Who without me in the band. When I left the band in 1982, I did give John and Roger and Kenney Jones the right to use the Who name without me being involved, and I even at the time offered to write songs for it. What I didn't want to do—it's a bit Brian Wilson I suppose—but didn't want to be seen to be lugging my body round the world in the aftermath of the Cincinnati disaster, which I really felt we hadn't dealt with emotionally. I'm not sure that we have to this day, so it had a massive impact on me and hurled me from being a heavy drinker into much worse circumstances, and I had an enormous problem with it. I had a real problem with the way that I handled it and I really did believe that it was something to do with Who fans, something to do with the kind of promoters that we were working with, something to do with the way that we were being managed and fundamentally to do with the kind of music that we had started to play in the early eighties, which was kind of post punk, old-guard rock and roll, which is that "We can do what the fuck we like" kind of arrogance. I'm not saying we were responsible—I'm not saying that any one faction was responsible—but I was certainly not responsible for handling it properly. So in real terms Roger had the opportunity to carry the Who on and to perform my songs. What he wanted was he wanted nothing to change and I understand why but everything *had* changed and there was no way of arguing with that. Everything had changed massively and I was deeply disturbed by it.

Will there be any more Pete Townshend solo albums?

I've got no idea. I've got no drive to do solo albums. I'm not even sure that if Roger and I do an album together that it should be called the Who. What Roger said in one of his recent interviews was that I write a song and then he comes in and turns it into a Who song. That's paraphrasing cruelly I think but that's what he said. Well I've never experienced that process. I think what made one of my songs a Who song was simply that I wrote it for a very clear brief. The Who, for a writer, presented a very, very clear brief. I used to sit down and I used to think, "This is exactly what the band needs today." Today I don't get that clear brief. What I get is an incredibly special, wonderful, corny friendship that I have with Roger that after all those years of thinking of him merely as the school bully, I love him so much that tears come into my eyes when I think about him. That friendship I hope will drive something between us that will produce good music, but Roger and I as an old pals act don't offer the kind of clear brief to a songwriter that the Who used to.

The Who had such an incredibly clear audience brief as well: our audience was 80 percent male, they were fantasists, dreamers, they were football hooligans, they were romantic, they were idle pursuers of metaphysical dreamland, they were apolitical—they were an extraordinary bunch of people. Some of them were blue collar but some of them weren't, and in a sense, sitting and writing a song like "Won't Get Fooled

Again" today would be a very dangerous thing to do. To say, "Listen, I don't fucking care. I don't care about what the politicians say, just don't come and talk to me about politics"—you couldn't write that today.

When did you start writing to brief?

I wrote to the brief from the very, very first song that I wrote for the Who, which was "I Can't Explain." And I never ever wrote solo songs, I only wrote songs. The songs from [solo album *All the Best Cowboys Have*] *Chinese Eyes*, a couple of those songs were written knowing that they wouldn't be recorded by the Who, but by that time I was in a kind of habit pattern of writing. I wrote with the Who's audience, I suppose, in my mind.

How far have you progressed with your autobiography?

You know, I may well not do that now but I'm about a third of the way through. What happened to me is that I was writing my autobiography—this is back in 1996—and I was loving it and I got to the part where I leave art school. I have my big conversations with Harold Cohen and he calls me a drip and then off I go with my guitar and I join the Who. And I started to get incredibly depressed! Clinically depressed. I started to think, "Oh fuck, I've got to sit here for two years writing about the Who. I want to put it behind me." So I couldn't do it. And then circumstances recently made me feel that people really need to know who I actually am and not who they think I am and the only way that they'll have a chance of understanding that is if I dispassionately write my life story.

Because for example, when I left the Who in '82, I devoted myself almost exclusively—apart from a little bit of Faber & Faber editing on the side—to charity work. People know that I do it but they don't know the extent to which I've done it and they don't know the extent to which I've been successful, or in certain areas failed, in the work that I've done. So I think rather than shouting that simple fact from the housetops and looking like I'm trying to defend myself in some way—looking like an apologist—I should just lay it out.

So I'm thinking about getting back to what I call the morning program: sitting down with a piece of paper and picking it up. But I haven't yet got to that point. It was only the other day that I spoke to Roger and he told me that he wasn't available now 'til the middle of October so what occurred to me is that what might be better for me to do would be to take the summer months and just whip up some backing tracks and see what happens. 'Cause Roger's not a drummer or a bass player. We can't sit in a studio and jam. So it might be nice to just whip up some backing tracks and I can have a lot of fun with that. Do all kind of different things and add them to the backing tracks that I've already got that I'm going to send to him in case he wants to write lyrics for them and see where that goes.

I don't know whether I care whether we call this the Who or not. I think to some extent—and I'm only speaking for myself, Roger will really not subscribe to this, we've never completely agreed and it's never really done us any harm—but I don't know that he and I on a stage, whatever we call ourselves, can avoid the fact that we in some illusionary way bring down the mysterious mantle of the Who around us. It will always happen. So we might as well call it the Who. It will look like something to do with the Who simply because Roger and I have inherited this mantle, but whether or not it will truly be that Roger and I are picking [up] that rather wonky, twisted tradition of writing songs and making albums that ended with *It's Hard* back in 1982, that's the question. Do we really want to do that?

More people know of you now than ever before because of recent allegations about you accessing child pornography Internet sites. For that reason, is it not important that you do put out your autobiography to explain and clear the air?

Lot of assumptions there really. What can I say? I feel as though I live in a village. If the loud voice of the general population are going to judge anybody on the front page of the [British tabloid] *Daily Mirror*, or snide quips made by Howard Stern on the radio or of the diary opinions of [right-wing journalist] Lynda Lee-Potter when she gets up on a bad day, if that's what they want to do then they can do it, but those people have no connection to me. They're not a part of my orbit. I have no influence over them and they have no influence over me.

The people that I really care about are the people who have reached out to me in these troubles, and those are friends, fans, family, and strangers who feel they know me through my work and if I do sit down to write my autobiography for the reasons that you've suggested, it would only be to make them look good, because they're the people that are standing up now defending my good name.

Presumably the recent exposure has had a detrimental effect on you despite the support of people around you?

No, it doesn't, because I'm innocent. I know I'm innocent and apart from the first day when I heard the news when I was quite shaky, and made quite a shaky statement I think, I've been absolutely certain that this is not about me.

Do you think politics were behind the police investigation?

I don't think there's any conspiracy. I think my intentions—anybody that has read the material that's freely available and still is available on my website; there's not a lot of it but it's there—will know that I was trying to whip up hysteria. [*Laughs.*] There is a measure of the kind of rock 'n' roll arrogance that I still carry in my dotage that made me think I'd have no trouble with it. I really thought of myself as a professional researcher who worked to help victims, not a guitar-smashing rock star. But the old rock-star arrogance carried me into very dangerous water. But I should say no more really because I think what's actually happened here is that I have been silenced. On this issue—the issue that I was so passionate about, which was the subversion of the Internet, which I saw coming thirty years before the Internet itself was even fucking invented, I could see trouble ahead that would have dire psychological manifestations for the future of everybody really—here I am—I can't really say a thing.

My *Lifehouse* horror story, as it became—because I did two further drafts of the original draft—it became more and more a horror story as I started to look at what might happen when an uncensored liberated free flow of data from person to person, from home to home, from country to country, was subverted and taken over by, if you like, evil forces. The last two versions of *Lifehouse* are really pretty horrible. The version that

I published which went into the Radio 3 play—which was dismissed by most serious critics—ended up with a pirate event held at the Millennium Dome which somebody chose to blow up. I think the very nature of the Internet breeds a sense of conspiracy and I don't believe that I've been involved in the conspiracy. I think it's an incredibly touchy area—the sexual abuse of children—and it had been for a long time and it affects the whole of the psychological community of people working in care and the psycho-therapeutic communities and everything.

There's a fantastic book just been released by a guy called Richard McNally called *Remembering Trauma*, which is about the fact there is now a debate among psychologists as to whether or not if somebody has actually experienced a traumatic event, even as quite a young child, there's any chance that you might forget it. Most of the people that I've worked with who have childhood trauma remember every single sick detail only too well, but it does undermine my own personal theses that something in me is repressed and that that's what's driven me to work with and help the surviving victims of childhood sexual abuse. I don't know why I've been driven to do it. Although I can continue to fund treatment, I don't think this is something I can talk about anymore. I'm on a sex offenders list. And even that is not something I want to keep repeating because it's not something that people care that much about, particularly in America.

It's the first time I've talked to anybody at all about the case and the way it's been affected. I'm really earnestly keen to avoid looking arrogant. I don't want to look hypocritical. I have been rapped on the knuckles and I don't want to appear like I don't take this thing seriously, but I have to tell you that this has not destroyed me. So that said, it definitely has had a huge impact on me, so if I gave you the impression that it hasn't then that's nonsense. This is the first time I've spoken to anybody about it and I'm going to try to avoid talking about it in future.

GENERATION TERRORISTS

Simon Garfield | September 2006 | *Observer Music Monthly* **(UK)**

John Entwistle's death occurred on the eve of the American leg of the Who's latest tour. Given the circumstances of his demise, it was feared tour insurers might refuse to pay out. A replacement was therefore hastily found and the shows went ahead as planned.

Surprisingly for some, the Who did not cease work once those commitments had been fulfilled. They have performed concerts every year since 2004, establishing a new regular rhythm section in Starkey and bassist Pino Palladino. Recording work, however, was something they steered clear of.

In May 2004, though, came a new Who single in the shape of the Elvis Presley tribute "Real Good Looking Boy." Two years and five months later came *Endless Wire*, their first studio album in almost a quarter of a century.

This feature about the album and their current activities appeared in the monthly music supplement that the *Observer* was then producing. It makes reference to that famous Who *Observer* magazine feature of forty years previously.

Note: for "Howling Wolf" read "Howlin' Wolf" —Ed.

About three years ago, Pete Townshend and Roger Daltrey had a conversation that went something like this.

Daltrey: 'Whatever you do, Pete, I'll support you!'

Townshend: 'Great, because I've got this idea that I want to do this musical in Las Vegas called *The Boy Who Heard Music.*'

Daltrey: 'Where?'

Townshend: 'Las Vegas.'

Daltrey: 'I'm not going there.'

Townshend: 'But you said you would support me in whatever I want to do.'

Daltrey: 'Except Las Vegas.'

Townshend: 'But it's only in Las Vegas that we'd get the 200 million dollars that I'd need to make my exploding Mirror Door moment.'

Daltrey: 'Yes, but whatever else you want to do, I will completely support you.'

A short while later, Townshend gave him some early chapters of his novella about three kids in a band.

Townshend: 'Well, could you read the story, because I want to write some songs about it?'

Daltrey (after reading it): 'It's the same old shit, isn't it? Come up with something new!'

Townshend: 'But this is it. *This is me.* I only have one story, one thesis. I'm a cracked record, and it's going to go round and round and round until I die.'

Such, at least, is Townshend's recollection of the conversation. He had endured these sorts of dispiriting exchanges with Daltrey before, and decided to press on regardless. One of the first songs he wrote was called 'In the Ether', which, like many of his compositions, appears to be about spiritual awakening and the expiation of pain. Townshend considers it, without question, one of the best things he has ever done, proclaiming, 'I am writing better Stephen Sondheim songs than even Stephen Sondheim is writing!' Initially, Daltrey was less convinced. 'I played it to Roger,' Townshend recalls, 'and about a month passed. In the end, I got on the phone and said, "So, what did you think?"'

Daltrey: 'It's a bit music-theatre. Maybe if you didn't have piano but just had guitar . . ."'

Townshend: 'Yeah, and maybe if it was three guitars and was rock'n'roll and sounded like "Young Man Blues" it would be OK.' And then Townshend put the phone down. 'I was really, really hurt,' he says.

But three years later, and 25 years since the last one, we have a new studio album by the Who. *Endless Wire* contains 19 tracks, 10 of them comprising what Townshend calls a 'full-length mini-opera' entitled *Wire & Glass*. Its creator is 61. He looks his age as he walks into his recording studio in Richmond at the end of August with the latest mix of the CD in a bag over his shoulder, but he looks good with it, not excessively ravaged, grey in a dignified way. He puts the CD into the mixing desk, and Daltrey's voice fills the air: 'Are we breathing out/ Or breathing in/ Are we leaving life/ Or moving in/ Exploding out/ Imploding in/ Ingrained in good/ Or stained in sin.' It sounds like they've never been away.

'In the Ether' soon follows, as do several love songs, several songs of yearning, and several very angry songs.

The angriest is called 'A Man in a Purple Dress', an attack on the trappings of organised religion written after watching Mel Gibson's *The Passion of the Christ*. 'It is the idea that men need to dress up in order to represent God that appals me,' Townshend explains. 'If I wanted to be as insane as to attempt to represent God, I'd just go ahead and do it; I wouldn't dress up like a drag queen.'

The song 'Mirror Door' imagines a place where legendary musicians gather after their death to drink and discuss the value of their work. Elvis and Buddy Holly are mentioned, alongside Howling Wolf and Doris Day. It was only after the recording was finished that someone mentioned to Townshend that Doris Day was still alive. 'I was absolutely convinced she was dead,' he admits. 'But I went to the internet and there she was—a fucking happening website!'

When the album is over, Townshend offers me tea in an upstairs room overlooking pleasure boats and rowers on the Thames. It is time for something he does better than almost any rock star of any age—the analysis of his craft, the opening of a vein in the process of confession. It is hard to imagine that anyone has thought deeper about their role in popular music, or produced such honest appraisals of triumphs and failures. It is no surprise that Townshend's most enduring work— *Tommy* and *Quadrophenia*—arrived in the form of a concept. From his art-school education and finely crafted emergence as a mod, right through to his new mini-opera, the music has never quite been enough without a story, and the stories aim to be both universally appealing and intricately personal. Sometimes they hit and sometimes they don't, but precisely why this should be is something that Townshend is still struggling to comprehend. As Roger Daltrey told me a few days later:

'He always needs a bigger vision, but some of his narratives are just so difficult to understand. He's talking about the ethereal and the spiritual, and it's very difficult to write that stuff down.'

Townshend's personal story is equally complex, and frequently auto-destructive. When he used to smash guitars on stage it was only part-publicity stunt; he really was raging against something he couldn't explain. These days, after years of therapy and creative output, he has found a more eloquent expression for his joys and torments.

'The dream that is at the heart of the Who's work is a dream that I think Roger and I have realised,' he says. 'That dream is . . . It's like the Stones at Twickenham. They're a pub band, but they're up there in front on many thousands of people, and what happens is quite extraordinary. Even though I understand they didn't play their best ever concert at Twickenham, a bunch of people I know who were there say, "It didn't matter. What matters is that we were there together." As artists, we can affect gatherings of people. People lose themselves, and in the moment of losing themselves they then find themselves. They find a commonality, an innocence, and a sense of being which, I suppose, is close to a meditative state. When they walk away from it, they look back and think something special happened.'

Townshend refers to his current band as Who2, not so much to separate it from the band that existed before drummer Keith Moon died in 1978 and bassist John Entwistle died in 2002, but more to reflect a state of mind. Townshend, and probably Daltrey as well, have come to recognise that rock bands have a certain natural life, and their survival beyond that depends on an acceptance that its most creative and famous days may be over, and should be celebrated. I mentioned that the Who I saw play a couple of years ago at the Forum and Royal Albert Hall—in which the mesmerising power of Daltrey's singing and Townshend's playing seemed unprecedented for a couple of guys approaching their sixties—reflected a remarkable rejuvenation of spirit, but he questioned my interpretation.

'It's not a rejuvenation at all, because we really don't have that in us. I think it is a rebranding, a recognition that the old Who brand is inviolable. It's just inviolable. There's almost nothing you can do with it. This was my problem in the Eighties—the brand was just so powerful.

Who fans didn't like the last couple of albums that we made, *It's Hard* and *Face Dances*—and they weren't made lightly, they were struggled over—but they just didn't fit the model of the brand. So I sensed that what Roger and I should do was honour the brand, honour the history, honour the classicism. We should respect the fact of what we did, and accept our knighthood. And just live with it. And then the knighthood ties us to charity work. Anything that we do now has to be seen in context of that, but we can also draw a line and make a new start.'

The Who have just embarked on the second leg of a world tour. The live band has expanded to a six-piece—Townshend's brother Simon on second guitar, Pino Palladino on bass, John 'Rabbit' Bundrick on keyboards and Zak Starkey on drums—and nothing has pleased Townshend more than the reaction to recent shows from younger musicians. The Fratellis and Oasis enthused backstage, but approval from Paul Weller meant the most. 'If that cynical guy thinks it's OK . . .' Townshend reasons. 'He was always very stern with me. You know, "Don't go back, don't ever go back, you're going back, I would never go back . . ." I would just say, "Listen, I don't know if I could ever do what I did again." I sit and look at "My Generation" and "Won't Get Fooled Again" and I think, "How can I do that again?"'

You mean, you felt you can never better that?

'Yes, it was intuitive. And being intuitive is fucking difficult.'

I wondered how it was possible that the Who today looks less old than it did 20 years ago. 'Yes, something has happened,' Townshend says. 'People don't mind if you're old, as long as you're content. What's unbearable is somebody who's old and won't let the past go.'

I had first met Townshend in 1985, not long after he had begun working at the publishers Faber & Faber. He helped me with a book I was writing about exploitation in the music industry. The Who had signed some disastrous early deals, and Townshend told me one reason for this: 'Every major contract that I've signed, I think, has been done in a dressing room, or I've signed it when I was drunk . . . Can you imagine actually trying to sit down in the middle of a tour and explain a very complex bit of tax law to somebody as stoned as Keith and I used to be most of the time, or as thick as Roger used to make himself out to be?'

He says he went to work at Faber because he 'needed some dignity'. He liked the idea of regular employment without pressure to deliver solo albums to a shrugging audience, and he offered a creative service to writers and photographers who wanted to tell their stories. His job coincided with the longest fallow period of the Who, from 1982-89, a period in which Townshend told everyone the group was no longer relevant. 'There were two real reasons I stopped the band when I did,' he says. 'One was that I blamed the rock industry for the death of Keith, of Brian Jones, of Jimi, for the death of 11 kids at Cincinnati at one of our shows. I felt that we hadn't looked after our own, and there was something wrong with our business.

'But I also felt we'd worn out the form. Punk had shaken everything, but what followed was computers and Linn drums and Heaven 17 and Scritti Politti. Interesting music, but quite manufactured and complex, and much less of the blood. I felt that my role in that world was over. And I would get these regular visits from Roger saying, "I want to do this, I want to do that," and I would say, "Listen, it's over. Fuck off." Well, I wouldn't say fuck off, but "I'm not your man". Watching him pretending to be who he was . . . it was all just pathetic. I had very little sympathy for him. I thought he should really go back and be a builder. A woman said to me the other day, "But he couldn't let it go." I said, "Well, why not?" "Because he was fucking gorgeous!" I said, "Is that really what it's all about?" and she said, "There aren't very many gorgeous men in the world."

'Looking back now,' he adds, 'it does seem very cold of me to have brought down such a heavy door. John Entwistle was very resentful as well. What happened with John was that he'd got used to living high, and his money supply was cut off. In the end, when Roger came to me and said, "Listen we've got to help John, let's try to train him to live less high," and we couldn't do that. And as we trained him to live less high, he died. He didn't want to live less high. He preferred to be dead, in a sense.'

He thinks of another reason he broke up the band. 'I didn't want to be in fucking pain all the time. I didn't want to be so disdainful or so intellectual or so arrogant. I didn't want to be doing interviews with people saying [moany voice] "What's it like being old, and you said you wanted to die before you got old." I remember thinking, "Are these people *vegetables* or something?"'

Did drugs have much to do with the break-up?

'No. I drifted into drugs immediately after Keith's death in 1978. By 1981, I was fairly full-blown. It's certainly not a period I regret—I had quite a wonderful time. The only thing I regret is that the dabbling with drugs meant that I stopped drinking. I was a very, very functional drinker. I used to love alcohol. I didn't love being drunk, but I loved drinking. Drifting into cocaine, because everyone else in the world was doing it except me, and then finding that all that really did was increase the amount that I drank—I think that did create what toppled me physically. My real descent into extreme narcotics like heroin was a bit like that Pete Doherty thing that he's elongated into a life story now. I was trying to stop drinking, thinking, "Well, if I stop drinking I can use this, and if I use this then I can use that, and that's prescribed, and that's not prescribed . . ." and in the end you're thinking, "I can't deal with this—please help."'

What are you thinking when you see Pete Doherty self-destruct?

'He's such an intelligent man. I completely understand, I just understand.'

In the past few years, Townshend has been writing his autobiography, but it is a slow process. In effect he has been working on it since the mid-Sixties, dutifully keeping old receipts and correspondence and many photographs in the hope that they would one day become revealing. And so they are. Townshend mentions one photo in particular by his friend Colin Jones, an iconic image of the Who posed in front of a Union flag at the time of 'My Generation'. Townshend is in the front in a Union Jack blazer. 'With this fish-eye lens, it made my already quite prominent nose look massive. You can see if you look at it that I'm crying, because Chris Stamp [the band's co-manager] and Colin Jones were making me ugly rather than beautiful, and taking my worst feature, which I now regard as my best feature, and exaggerating it'

The book, which Townshend is writing chronologically, has now reached 1970, and he has shown early drafts to Stephen Page, the chief executive of Faber, and Jann Wenner at *Rolling Stone*. It is called *Pete Townshend: Who He*. He says he is blessed with a good memory, but he found a peculiar gap. 'I went to my mum and said, "Weirdly enough, I can remember from 13 months up to four-and-a-half, but then from four-and-a half to six-and-a-half, I can't remember anything."'

His mother, now in her mid-eighties, said there was a reason for this. Townshend was born in May 1945, a few days after VE Day. His mother was keen to celebrate victory by singing with his father, a saxophonist in the RAF dance band the Squadronaires, and she would follow him around the world. 'So my early years were a mixture of unbelievable glamour and unbelievable shock at being dumped with my grandmother,' Townshend says. His grandmother lived in Westgate, on the Kent coast. 'She turned out to be clinically insane and very abusive, and sexually abusive, or possibly something going on around her that was sexually abusive—this loon grandmother who walked around naked under her fur coat and tried to shag bus conductors.'

His mother's recent revelations filled in the years Townshend had blanked out. 'As she was telling me, I fell in love with my mum again, because she came out of it looking terrible, but she had the courage [to tell me]. And though it was shocking, it was the making of me as an artist.'

For as long as he can remember, Townshend has been intrigued by the components that make rock music both so effective and so destructive, and he has made compelling connections.

'It's because of this denial that anything ever happened to us during the war. We're worse than the Germans, worse than the fascists. There's all this echoing damage going on. I began talking to people, and found that, almost universally, people who had been evacuated had been unbelievably traumatised. But they had been refused the option of any mention of the trauma. Because what had actually happened was victory, peace, 'you're lucky'. I believe that when rock'n'roll came along, it had to happen. It sounds pretentious, and I never set out do it, but *Tommy* was an allegory of the postwar British condition.'

In January 2003, Townshend became suddenly aware that his life had taken a dramatic new turn: he recognised himself in a newspaper report as the 'famous rock star' the police were about to question as part of an investigation into child pornography.

'There were two things that went through my mind,' he says. 'One was that I don't deserve to be on the front of any tabloid newspaper. And two, this is gross hypocrisy that I'm obviously going to be sacrificed. So for a moment I thought there's just no point trying to continue. Luckily, Rachel [the musician Rachel Fuller, his partner since 1998] was next to me when I read the paper. I turned to her and said, "Fuck, this is the end," and she said "No, it isn't. Let's go and make a few phone calls . . ."'

'After a while I did actually realise that it wasn't going to have the sort of massive effect that I feared. But my first fear was that I was going to be framed. On the basis of the evidence and my immediate admission—I coughed up straightaway that I had used a credit card to access a web-site, as part of research—it would be then assumed, "Ah, we've got your number," and they would then feel inclined to frame me. They took 14 computers from my house, all of my CDs, all of my DVDs, and I was away from the house at the time so I couldn't [ask] myself, "Do I have a porn DVD under the bed?" In the four months that followed I just had to cross my fingers and hope. I was frightened. And when there was no evidence found, it was all over.'

Except, of course, it may never be over. Despite his admission of misjudgment, and the fact that he was never charged, such associations are hard to shake off.

'I see it a bit like surviving cancer,' he says. 'Like a life-changing positive experience. God, the arrogance of me! I looked at myself and I thought, "Fucking hell, Pete, what did you think was going to happen?" And the fact that I had deliberately kept all my charity work secret . . .'

He remembers when he first came across an image in 1998. 'I was researching to give money to an orphanage in Russia. I put these words in: Russian . . . orphanages . . . and then I thought "boys", so I put boys in, and this horrible porno picture came up of a child being buggered. The conceit of me! I was thinking, "I'm going to be the one to stop this . . ." When I told Johnny Cusack, the actor, this story in the autumn of 2003, he said, "I think I know the picture you're talking about. Pete, it's Photoshop, it's not even real." I said, "Well, the damage is done. I saw myself. I saw myself." It probably never happened to me, but I saw myself and I saw millions of kids like me.

'I suppose it's true to say that it could have had a much worse effect had Roger not been so profoundly and powerfully behind me. My lawyers and I decided that I shouldn't speak. So Roger spoke for me, and he was such a powerful voice. I remember Bill Nighy saying to me, "Fucking hell, everyone could use a friend like that." Because the fact is that Roger didn't know what was going to happen.'

I wondered how his relationship with Daltrey had changed over the years.

'You know, it's survived. My marriage to my wife has not survived, and my marriage to Roger has survived, and it might be that only one of them could. I think you can only do one thing. I remember saying to [my wife] Karen, "I was a pop star when you met me," as though that would expiate the problem. The problem for her wasn't me going away [on tour]. She often used to say to me, "Goodbye, don't come back, just send a cheque . . ." She just wanted me to be who she believed I was when I was home, and to be less affected by the ravages of the industry I was in. When I started to bring the ravages of my work home with me, it became harder and harder. She would go to me, "But it was great playing, was it?" And I would go, "No, it was fucking miserable." "But you're selling records, aren't you?" And I'd say, "Yeah, but it's a load of shit." And she'd say, "Well, why are you doing it then?" "Because I have to."

Things have improved. He is still not divorced (complex property issues), but he is contemplating the matter again now that their third child is 16. He says that Rachel Fuller would like him to be divorced, and when I ask whether he plans to have children with her (she is considerably younger than him), he says they haven't talked about it. He adds: 'And as we don't have sex at all, it's not a problem.'

At the end of our interview, Townshend drives me to Richmond station in his small black Volkswagen Lupo. He also owns a Ferrari, but he gets a lot less hassle in the Lupo. On the way, he mentions the paucity of rehearsal time before the American tour, and the recent American anti-terrorism law that prohibits live webcasting. As he pulls up at the station he turns his face into the car, away from a pedestrian who has just begun to recognise him from his youth.

A week later, Roger Daltrey picks me up at Stonegate station in East Sussex in a new black Mercedes, and as he drives the short distance to his 400-acre estate he talks of how proud he is of Pete and the new album, and what a terrible time it is to be a farmer.

Wealthy rock musicians are traditionally assumed to inhabit baronial mansions, and Daltrey really does. 'It's 1610,' he says. 'It's coming up for its birthday.' He says that he bought the place 35 years ago for the magnificent view, but he's had a separate career just trying to maintain it. 'I lose money every year,' he says as he looks out onto his grazing cattle and freshwater fisheries. 'I have to go on bleeding tour just to pay for it.'

We settle in the lounge, while his second wife, Heather, and a grandchild amuse each other in the kitchen. The conversation drifts to the coverage of rock music on television ('The sound's got better, but the visuals have got fucking awful! All that swooping, whooping . . .') and Live8 ('Absolutely appalling! All the things that Live8 was about in Africa, we did the same thing in Hyde Park—"them and us" with the Golden Circle [the privileged-access area at the front]. By the time we went on, the Golden Circle was exhausted, paralytic and asleep, and the real crowd at the back were going bananas').

At 62, Daltrey is stocky and exuberant. His golden locks have long been supplanted by a light brown crop. He says he is 'absolutely blind' without his blue-tinted granny glasses; he has considered laser treatment, but is frightened of error. He thinks he may have lost a few top notes over the years, but he is pleased how well his voice held up while recording the new material.

Not that he ever thought there would be new material. 'It's been a tortuous process,' he says. 'I thought, the idea was finished, this time last year. I thought, "Pete's got to let go of the Who." But the next thing I know Pete says, "I've done all the demos."'

Daltrey says he wrote six songs himself. 'None of them suitable, of course. I'll never be the songwriter Townshend is, I don't kid myself, but at least I came up with something. It's been a rough five years for us both, and how he's come through it, I don't fucking know.'

He told me he came through it because he had you and Rachel.

'I really love him. I do have to deal with the madness of some of his schemes. He's a technomaniac. I don't like the internet. I don't like the world he lives in. I don't think we've created a better society from the internet. Virtual relationships—I can't deal with that.'

I wondered whether the tension between the two of them—so evident and important onstage—was something they were keen to cultivate; not for the public image, but for their own creative wellbeing.

'Well, I feel very close to him,' Daltrey says. 'But we don't have to see each other all the time. It's a different closeness, and I really treasure it for that. The Who is the energy that exists between Pete and I, and that energy is increased by doing it separately. I don't care when people say we're not getting on—it's not fucking important All that matters is what exists onstage and in our music. In that music is our relationship, is our love. I have such a deep love and respect for him, and that goes through all of it. He forgives all my foibles, and I forgive all his, and underneath all that I love him dearly.'

Daltrey says that it is getting a little harder every year to sing the old material, but it has never been easy. 'With the Who and Pete's music, you cannot cheat it,' he says. 'You cannot go through the fucking motions, because the music is just so gut-wrenching. It's so different from most of the other stuff that's out there, and you're got to be incredibly courageous to even attempt to do it.' He adds that there is still nothing that gives him greater artistic satisfaction than performing Townshend's songs. 'I don't get paid for the singing—that's free. It's the schlepping I get paid for.'

I had heard that the impact of John Entwistle's death four years ago was particularly sustained for Daltrey. 'I got very depressed,' he says. 'Very, very: it was much more of a shock to me than I ever thought it would be. I thought I had learnt to deal with those sorts of things, with mum, dad. John was John—you could never change him, a real rock'n'roll character and a real rock lifestyle. I mean does it matter, the sudden ending with the line of coke and the hooker in Las Vegas—I mean, is it that bad at 57? What's the alternative? The alternative may be very slow and smelly, as George Orwell said. All I know is that I fucking miss him.'

Daltrey had opted out of that hard rock lifestyle a long time ago. 'I wanted to sing. I had to decide very early on, especially when his writing got into the *Tommy* era—this stuff needs some interpretation and it needs an awful lot of discipline. You can't do the other stuff as well.'

And so Daltrey's other stuff has taken a different course—most notably towards charity and film work. I had asked Townshend why he had produced everything on the new album except Daltrey's vocals, and he said that Daltrey had a studio technique 'which is really quite eccentric. It's intense and extraordinarily self-obsessed.' But what really gets to Townshend is the thought, 'God, does Roger actually believe that all he does is *sing*?'

He also spends much time organising charity concerts for the Teenage Cancer Trust, a project he says has kept him sane following Entwistle's death. He is also trying to get a film made about Keith Moon, with Mike Myers playing the drummer. It's hard to get it exactly right, Daltrey says, because he doesn't want it to be *Carry On Moon*, the story that everyone knows. 'If I've done anything, I've stopped a bad Keith Moon film from being made.'

I ask him how he will know when the Who really is over. 'Oh, it will give me up,' he says. 'I just won't be able to sing it.'

But this may not be for a while. 'Can you see us onstage in wheelchairs?' he asks.

Not really.

'Why not? It will still be us, still be the same music, and it's only the music that matters.'

You'd have troubling swinging your microphone lead.

'Not necessarily. Pete may have trouble with the guitars, I suppose. He does like to jump around. I'm not saying I want to be in a wheelchair, but it could happen.'

It would certainly be a novelty.

'It would! I would never rule it out.'

Daltrey then took the photographer and his publicist and me on a little tour of his grounds in his Land Rover. We passed a woman who keeps the hawks that keep his rabbits down. We passed several fishermen by the edge of the beautiful lakes which he had made. At a fishing lodge, we paused to pick sweet plums from a tree. 'Just think,' one of us said to Daltrey, 'those lakes that you built are now going to be part of the English landscape for ever.'

'Nah,' Daltrey said. 'Nothing lasts for ever. Nothing. We're just pushing dust around.'

AMAZING JOURNEY: ROGER DALTREY

Sean Egan | 2007 | Previously unpublished in this form

Roger Daltrey granted this interview to promote the 2007 Who DVD biography *Amazing Journey*—unabashed by the fact that he hadn't watched it.
This feature has never previously been published in this form. —Ed.

"I lived it so I don't really need to see it," says Roger Daltrey of *Amazing Journey*. "And if I watched it, I would only watch me—I wouldn't see the whole thing."

It's not often a journalist is tasked with interviewing a celebrity who is promoting a product he knows little about, but as *Amazing Journey* is the new DVD charting the career of the Who—something that Roger Daltrey does know something about, having fronted the British superstar band for forty-four years—it would be silly to pass up the chance of a rare audience with one of the titans of rock.

Amazing Journey—directed by Murray Lerner and Paul Crowder—is a product of its times, a four-hour home-entertainment extravaganza far removed from the previous Who film-biography *The Kids Are Alright*, a one-hundred-minute picture released in cinemas in 1979. There are other differences. "That was made by two fans," Daltrey says of *The Kids*. "We funded it, but basically that's just a series of clips. It's their artistic representation of the Who. This has got much more of a narrative line. We're executive producers on this because it's our archive that they use, but that's the extent of our input. I did one interview and a pick-up interview. I think Pete [Townshend] did one short one. I mainly had to do an interview because most of the film over the years of anybody talking from our band was all Pete. You have to let the filmmaker then do their job."

It's a note of interest that for a while the Who were themselves film-makers, diversifying in the late seventies into feature-film production. *McVicar*—a biopic of a notorious UK bank robber—and *Quadrophenia*—a film version of one of their concept albums—were highly worthy. However, those movie ambitions seemed to stall. "We lost the money, that's why," shrugs Daltrey. "We had to borrow money at such extortionate rates. When we made *Quadrophenia* and *McVicar*, they were two of about seven [British] films made in those years. We were just trying to be a one-man film industry and it was financially crippling."

Daltrey doubts that *McVicar* has even recouped its budget. "I think *Quadrophenia* has now. The people who lent the money have done very well out of it. It was hard to do. We raised the money on soundtrack stuff and all that and everything went in the pot to make the film. But at least we made two British films out of seven. That's pretty good."

The *Amazing Journey* narrative to which Daltrey refers begins with four Londoners who, unlike most band's members, never got on particularly well as people but whose extraordinary individual talents meshed so well that only the Beatles and the Rolling Stones could reasonably claim to dwarf them in artistic achievement and legend. Pete Townshend provided the crashing guitars and contrastingly literate songs, John Entwistle the unusually prominent and melodic bass lines, Keith Moon the thunderous, wide-span drumming, and Daltrey the booming vocals and sex-god image.

The DVD features some astonishingly early footage of this fearsome aggregation, filmed at the Railway Hotel, Wealdstone, in 1964 not only before the Who had a proper record contract but before they were even called the Who. "I'd lost it for thirty years and then someone called up our office and offered us to buy it," Daltrey reveals. "That was filmed by our first serious managers, Kit Lambert and Chris Stamp. When they saw the High Numbers, we were the band they wanted to discover. Everybody had done the Merseybeat to death. There was a new thing happening in London which was the mod scene and they were looking for something to reflect that."

For Daltrey, the intensity of the youth culture of modernism—which receives a nigh ten-minute examination as one of the DVD's bonus features—is something that kids of today would not understand: "Their world is so much wider than our was. Music was so important to us because it was such a gray world in a lot of ways. Music was our whole outlet. Now you've got DVDs and you've got all this stuff coming down the pipe constantly into your house and it's easily accessible. Everything we wanted out of life was hard to get."

The Railway Hotel footage is merely the cherry on the cake however, with the DVD boasting much concert footage never before aired. "Even a lot of our fanatics, as I call them, say there's so much they haven't seen," says Daltrey.

There is also of course more familiar Who footage, but often of such iconic status as to bear any number of repeated viewings, particularly in narrative context. Their American breakthrough at the 1967 Monterey Pop Festival, where they introduced the States to the auto-destructive stage act already familiar to British fans, is present and correct. Daltrey admits it was a shock how much bill-sharer Jimi Hendrix had pilfered from that stage act. "Mainly 'cause he did it so well! But fortunately we had the backup of the intelligence of Pete's songwriting. And in some ways maybe it was a good thing when you look back on it. You think, 'Well if it had only ever ended up on all the smashing and that had been totally ours and not spread out into other people like Jimi and dumped'—'cause I think he actually took it one step further and did it better in a lot of ways—maybe we wouldn't have gone off in that other direction of the quirky writing that Pete came up with."

Another clip whose omission would be unthinkable is the band's performance on *The Smothers Brothers Show* in September 1967, memorable not just for their powerful presentation but because the madcap Moon provided an unexpected finale by setting off a gunpowder explosion in a bass drum. "Absolute shock to all of us and it was much more dangerous than [people realize]," recalls Daltrey with a shudder. It was an incident which Townshend has claimed left his hearing permanently damaged. Daltrey: "It was a huge explosion. I literally disappear out of shot. It's because I'm blown off my feet."

Asked about such behavior on the part of "Moon the Loon," Daltrey says, "It never was a worry in the early days because he was like Superman. But then when he started to miss a few gigs and stopped bouncing, it got to be a worry."

Not long after those events, the perennially fractious Who were in danger of splitting up, with Moon and Entwistle talking of forming a new band and Townshend making overtures to other musicians. Amazingly, a time remembered so unhappily by his colleagues is one Daltrey seems to have spent in a sunny little bubble of optimism. "I could hear what was going on in the music and it was getting more and more solid all the time," he recalls. "That was the only thing I was interested in. I used to think, 'Moony playing drums with these other people? Dream on.' There weren't any other players that could play with Keith Moon other than Pete Townshend. The same with John Entwistle's bass. John Entwistle's bass would have swamped every other band. So it never, ever bothered me. Artistically we were still growing."

The triumphant culmination of that growth was *Tommy*, the 1969 release with which the band rewrote the rules of popular music. It was, if not the first, then certainly the most celebrated and influential "rock opera." Nineteen seventy-one's *Who's Next*, meanwhile, is widely considered one of the dozen greatest rock albums ever released.

These albums deservedly made the Who rich men. They were so well-off that they could—and did—retreat to their country piles and work ever more sporadically, something Daltrey found a bit of a mixed blessing. "I was raising a family so it was nice to have time. But you always miss that hurly-burly. But in some ways it probably stopped me ending up like Keith Moon and the other people we've lost, because it is such an easy industry to drown in."

Moon ended up fatally overdosing on anti-alcoholism pills in 1978 after a lifetime of physical abuse and stimulant use. Daltrey himself had long given up drugs. "Anything that would make the work suffer, then I left it alone," he says matter-of-factly.

The Who's response to the tragedy of Moon's death was to seek solace in work, recruiting old mod mate Kenney Jones to fill the vacant drum stool. Although he is interviewed for the main documentary, Jones—former drummer for the Small Faces and Faces—is not afforded the profile the four original members receive on disc two of the DVD. Daltrey's arms-length relationship to the project exonerates him from culpability in what some would assert to be an unfair omission, but the legend is that the Jones-era in Who history—which encompassed two albums—was not a happy period relations-wise and that this was mainly due to Daltrey's criticisms of the new setup. Daltrey: "Sadly, we boxed ourselves in in that period in so many things: in shock, grief, all those things that followed Keith's death. We just wanted to get out and play music and Kenney was a friend—and still is a friend—and it's very hard that people want to be divisive on it and say, 'Oh Daltrey says he's not a good drummer.' Actually, I've never, ever said that. Just not the right one and the right one was Keith Moon. Zak Starkey's got the same style. That's why Zak works."

Starkey now plays most live dates with the Who. Nonetheless, Daltrey says, "Zak's not a member of the Who. The Who is Pete Townshend and Roger Daltrey these days," a reference to the fact that Entwistle—Moon's partner in probably rock's greatest-ever rhythm section—died of a heart attack in 2002.

The once edgy—even sometimes violent—relationship between the impulsive Daltrey and the thoughtful Townshend has now, unexpectedly, mellowed into a genuine friendship. With regard to the chalk-and-cheese perception of the pair, Daltrey himself demurs. "It's like two magnets—they are the same, meeting on the wrong sides and they repel each other. I think we were very, very similar to each other."

However constituted, the Who continue to thrive. The duo augmented by hired hands remain a massive live attraction and released a decent studio album, *Endless Wire*, only last year.

For Daltrey, *Amazing Journey* is no capstone or epitaph. Though sixty-three, his enthusiasm for the Who is undiminished by jibes about he and Townshend failing to live up to the line "Hope I die before I get old!" that he boldly enunciated in arguably their most famous song,

"My Generation" (1965). Can the Who go on indefinitely? "Course it can," he asserts.

"As long as the artist feels that they've got something to put across, as long as that's not being cheated, there's no reason to stop."

KENNEY JONES, DRUMMER OF SMALL FACES, FACES WITH ROD STEWART AND THE WHO, LOOKS BACK (AND FORWARD)

Binky Philips | January 17, 2014; updated March 19, 2014 | *Huffington Post* (US)

By the time he joined the Who, Kenney (formerly Kenny) Jones had been responsible for many imperishable, virtuoso drumming performances, not least on the Small Faces' "Tin Soldier" and Rod Stewart's version of "(I Know) I'm Losing You." His appointment, therefore, as replacement for Keith Moon in the Who seemed reasonable, even logical. It famously, however, didn't work out, although it should not be forgotten that Jones subsequently played with the Who at Live Aid in 1985 and—to celebrate the group's Lifetime Achievement honor—at the British Phonographic Industry award ceremony in 1988.

Chart success in the nineties and noughties with near-supergroups the Law and the Jones Gang seemed to confirm the impression of a lucky charm attending Jones's career. Binky Philips took Jones on a journey back through that career.

Notes: for *"Here Comes the Nice"* read *"Here Come the Nice"*

for "C'mon Children" read "Come on Children"

for "from 1972 through 1982" read "from 1978 through 1982"

for *"Ogden's Nutgone Flake"* read *"Ogden's Nut Gone Flake"* —Ed.

A few weeks back, I interviewed Ian "Mac" McLagan, here on the *Huffington Post*, keyboardist for the Small Faces, Faces with Rod Stewart and

The Rolling Stones. The folks who set up the interview at Charly Records, have just released an incredible Small Faces' box set called *Here Comes The Nice*, available exclusively at Amazon, and were so happy with my "Mac" chat, that they decided I should have a go at his surviving Small Face brother, drummer Kenney Jones.

That was more than fine with me. These two men are undiluted heroes to me, members of one of rock's greatest bands of all time, Small Faces.

[Trans-Atlantic beeps and books . . . phone is now ringing].

Kenney: Hello there.

Binky: [slightly dazzled]: Hi. Ken, Uhhh, wow. Look, right up front, I'm not really a journalist, I'm a musician. Playing guitar 50 years this February.

Kenney: [laughs] Join the club.

Binky: Also, I have been a huge Small Faces fan since January 1967, very, very early for an American kid. Also, I'm a stone Who freak.

Kenney: Good to know, thanks very much.

Binky: I think we have in common that we didn't do it for the money.

Kenney: Absolutely not!

Binky: I say that because it's well known that the Small Faces never made money with either tough guy Don Arden as your manager, or wacky visionary Andrew Loog Oldham. Any comments on those two?

Kenney: They *were* total opposites, that's all I'll say.

Binky: Okay, then. I have to tell you. Kenney, as we move forward here, I believe the Small Faces belong in the pantheon of those shitty bands, The Beatles, The Stones, The Who, Led Zeppelin . . .

Kenney: Well, I might agree with you entirely [lots of giggles]. Really, I feel very fortunate to have grown up at the same time as The Beatles and The Stones, and guys like that. I feel very fortunate to have played with The Who, to have played with the Stones. But, Small Faces rule! There ya go.

Binky: Ha! Indeed! What I'd kinda like to do here, Ken, is a chronological order type of interview . . . but, before I do, I just wanna say, in the early

90s, I thought your band, The Law, with singer Paul Rodgers, had a killer killer cut with 'Layin' Down The Law.' Monster groove from you, sir.

Kenney: I came up with that title, 'Layin' Down The Law.' Gave it to Paul, and he put it together 'round that. Yeah, that song was nasty.

Binky: Okay, why the drums, Kenney? Why did you choose an instrument that takes five times longer to pack up than a guitar and amp?

Kenney: Uhhh . . . They run outta banjos, that's why.

Binky [thinking this is a Mumford joke]: Yeah, all right . . .

Kenney: When I was growing up with of bunch of friends in the East End of London, and sorta out of the blue one day, as he and I were washing a car, actually, one of my mates announced that we should form a Skiffle group. 'What's a Skiffle group?' My pal said, 'Well, you get a banjo, you get a tea chest or wash tub and broom handle and a piece of string and that's your bass, and then you get your Mum's washboard, and you get some thimbles from her sewing kit and stick 'em on the end of your fingers and scrape 'em up and down the washboard.' Well, I thought he'd gone mad [laughs]. He then said, 'Look, there's a Skiffle band on TV tonight, let's go and watch that.' It was Lonnie Donegan.

Binky: I *knew* that was coming!

Kenney: Yeah, he was playing the "Rock Island Line" and that's when I fell in love with the banjo.

Binky: Oh! [slightly stunned] You weren't joking about the banjo!

Kenney: Oh yeah, I just fell in love with the banjo. The very next day, I saw a banjo in a pawn shop next to Bethnal Green tube station. I realized I'd seen it before. It had been there awhile. So me and my mates went to get the banjo from that pawn shop the day after with no money in our pockets, just enthusiasm [more laughs]. When we got there, the banjo was gone. '*Where's the banjo?!*' I asked. 'Well, the guy paid us back and took it home, didn't he.' I said: 'Well, get it back!' Then, we had to leave and I was upset. So, a friend of mine said, 'Man, you're really disappointed. Look, I have a friend with a drum kit. I'll get him to bring it over this afternoon.' I was okay with that. The drum kit turned out to be a snare drum and a bass drum and two sticks and one of them was broken in half [laughs]. I spent that afternoon trying to glue it back together decades before superglue. It never worked. Anyway, so, I learned by bashin' around on that. That was my introduction to drums.

Binky: So, it really was . . .

Kenney [actually wistful]: Yes, it really was the banjo.

Binky: Yes, but, now you were a drummer. One of the things I always found incredibly exciting about your style was that you had kind of a rubbery looseness . . . I don't know quite how to put this any other way, but, as a British East End teenager, you were playing like a 45 year old black guy. How did the 18 year old you wind up with that style? Was it Hal Blaine in the Wrecking Crew or Tamla-Motown, Stax-Volt or . . . ?

Kenney: To be honest, I used to listen to [soul-jazz organist] Jimmy McGriff. Then, Booker T and the MGs with one of my favorite drummers, Al Jackson. He deserves every credit any drummer could ever have the credit for. He played slightly behind the beat. Just a natural. Al Jackson taught me that a drummer should know his place. In other words, you're the backbone and you push the feel.

Binky: I have long believed that Al Jackson came up with about 50 percent of every loose funky groove ever cut. I totally hear him in your playing . . . I recently listened to all the early Decca stuff the Small Faces did as well as three of the four discs, so far, in this amazing new *Here Comes The Nice* ultra-box set on Charly that you and Mac curated. I have to say, disc one with all your Immediate singles in their original mono-mixes, just utterly blew me away. And, no shit, your playing, in particular, Kenney, really jumps out. I don't mean in the mix. I mean you are one bad ass drummer, man.

Kenney: Thanks much. Yeah, they sound great.

Binky: You know, on that early Decca stuff, you go around the kit sounding a lot like Keith Moon. Yet, you had more 'soul' feel and your fills themselves were never cops. It's as if you two guys seemed to come up with those sorta 'falling down the stairs' shambling fills independently.

Kenney: No, I never tried to copy Keith at all. It just came naturally to me. If anything, I was really more the Al Jackson type. I was playing me and we were so damn young, and wound up so experimental. When I got confident enough to actually hit the tom toms, what they are actually for, well, at that point, I just played anything, y'know. Prior to the Small Faces, I did my first session at 15 or 16. I played on lots of other people's records. I didn't charge any money. I didn't care. I wanted to play. I ended up playing some big band stuff.

Binky: Really! Big bands?!

Kenney: Yeah . . . Whatever I learned, I brought with me. I loved playing orchestrally with those great big fills and staggered fills and big big moments and makin' 'em powerful. And I took that and put it into the Small Faces as I was improving as a drummer.

Binky: Well, early on, at least until Mac McLagan showed up for your second album, you were, to my ears, the true natural musician in the band . . . And I LOVE Steve Marriott and Ronnie Lane's playing. Let's talk about the Decca material a bit. To this day, almost 50 years later, I find 'C'mon Children' to be one of the most exciting moments ever put down on tape by anyone, in any genre. One of my personal Top Ten songs of all time, truly. The thing that blows me away about the Decca stuff is it sounds just utterly spontaneous, Kenney. They almost don't seem like songs, they seem like Captured Moments.

Kenney: Y'know what it was, we all had that charge, we cut them live. One of the great things about the Small Faces; we were very telepathic, we'd play with each other and just know what we were gonna do without 'learning' it.

Binky: That is exactly what it sounds like!

Kenney: Yeah, that's really it.

Binky: Love it! How many takes were you doing on those wild Decca cuts like "E Too D" or "You Need Lovin'?"

Kenney: We used to make an album in a day.

Binky: Ummmm, yep. One of the most striking things about Small Faces is the maturity, the artistic growth, between the raw Decca stuff and the first Immediate-released album, recorded and released within a year of your Decca debut. It was as if the Small Faces went from their *Please Please Me* album to their *Rubber Soul* within one fucking record.

Kenney: I'll tell you why. We'd been playing for awhile and really learning to write songs by the time we got to Immediate. Once there, we had unlimited studio time. We were in there all the time.

Binky: I have to say, I never understood why Steve and Ronnie always put down their own musicianship in interview after interview. They were both fantastic players.

Kenney: Oh, they could be very excited about even discovering another *NOTE*. [lots of laughter] As far as our sound, we were just very complementary to each other, we just played it all naturally.

Binky: Having listened to those Immediate singles in this box set, I was struck by something else, powerfully. There are so many moments in those songs, virtually every one a stone smash in the UK, folks, where I swear I hear bits of The Who's *Sell Out*, or *Something Else* by The Kinks, *Between The Buttons* by the Stones, maybe even some *Sgt. Pepper*. Like, your most monolithic colleagues/competitors would listen to a new Small Faces single and say, *'Ooo, that's nice. I'll have that, thanks.'* The chronology bears me out, I think.

Kenney: You know, you're right. Binky, I feel the same way. I love that Led Zeppelin and Robert Plant are the first to admit how heavily they were influenced by Small Faces.

Binky: Well, how could they not? They just **STOLE** shit from you guys.

Kenney: Well, yes, I know, but, it's a nice compliment.

Binky: I brought this next subject up with Mac a few weeks back and he thought it was very funny. But, one of the things that was a huge draw for me, even before I heard your music, and stuck with me, was that the Small Faces were easily the best dressed, coolest looking band, period. And I LOVED the way The Who dressed, too. But, you guys . . . class, elegance, forward thinking. So cohesive. You looked like a band. Did you, Kenney Jones, buy into the look, or was someone like, say, Ronnie, pushing you go along?

Kenney: Well, we really were all the same. Apart from learning how to play our instruments, we were all so young, just discovering clothes. I grew up in the East End. Remember, we were the first teenagers after World War Two, and I remember growing up in black and white. Really. Clothes were black, gray, and white. That's it. The minute we saw anything with color, we put it on. We made it up as we went along. We realized we were creating a look.

Binky: Can you conjure up a typical day in your life at the height of the Small Faces success? Mac told me Immediate had put the four of you in your own house . . .

Kenney: Yes, they did. I'd wake up in the morning, get in my Mini or my MGA [I wish you coulda heard the teenage pride when Kenney uttered that phrase] and drive over to Pimlico, which was where we had the house. I had the key to the door, my own room there. But, I never stayed there because I could never get any sleep. Everyone was always up all night, doing whatever they were doing. You know, I'd walk in, and there would be Paul McCartney hangin' out. Another day, it would be Mick Jagger. You'd be meeting lots of different people.

Binky: Mac told me that was where he first met Ronnie Wood.

Kenney: Yeah . . . That house was a musical experience. There were guitars just laying all over the place. You might indulge in hash in a cigarette, that sort of thing. And then, it would be time to go to the studio, put down whatever music we'd been working on at the house.

Binky: Sounds like a life in Hell!

Kenney [laughs]: It was *wonderful* . . . Not to mention the women.

Binky: Oh, let's not! [laughs] Back to the box set, finding all this material that you and Mac combed through, this must've been heavy, emotionally, for you guys. Can you give me an idea of what the greatest surprises were, and maybe the saddest moments for you?

Kenney: The greatest surprise was the amount of 'new' studio stuff, and times where you hear us to talking to each other . . . you can SMELL the damn studio. I mean, *you are there*. The saddest moments . . . Listening to this stuff, you just really really missed Ronnie and Steve. That's as simple as it gets. You just wanted to go back into that time, straight away. And, this box, well, I've been there again.

Binky: Do you have a 'mission statement' about this Small Faces *Here Comes The Nice* box set, Ken?

Kenney: [pause] Anyone who buys it will just be *delighted* with it. One of the nice things we've seen is interest from teens, the same age we were when we were starting out. It seems like every year, we get younger fans. You buy this set and you hear the energy, the truthfulness, that feel . . . The idea is to *enjoy the moment*.

Binky: Oh! Beautifully put. The Steve Marriott/Ronnie Lane songwriting partnership was one of the strangest I can think of. You had a mad fireball like Marriott, and with Ronnie, almost a holy man. What a combination. Oh, and I've been in bands long enough to know that you and Mac were contributing without credit.

Kenney: Oh yes! You've got that right.

Binky: I think Marriott/Lane might be the single most underrated songwriting team in the history of rock 'n' roll.

Kenney: Yeah, I think so. I think you're right. The great thing about their songs . . . I find something new in there with almost every listen. Shit, I go straight back to Memory Lane again, y'know. The thing I like about the Decca stuff leading into the Immediate stuff is how you can hear, as you said, the amount of learning we'd been doing.

Binky: Let's move up a decade . . . Anything you want to say about the Rod Stewart/Ronnie Wood Faces era? I saw you live with Rod and Ronnie three times and loved that band, too.

Kenney: I've got quite a lot of happy memories from the Faces. The good thing, we always got together whenever we could, over the years, have a drink, do a TV show, and we've been trying to get back together for years. But, I feel a lot of seriousness in the air now about a possible reunion. We've been talking to Ronnie and Rod's managers about a 2015 tour.

Binky: I gotta tell you, I'm *not* one for reunion tours. But, Faces, I would LOVE to see again. *Somehow*, I still like Roddie the Moddie.

Kenney: Yeah [chuckles].

Binky: So, Kenney, there are four very very important musicians in rock history that you had direct first-person contact and interaction with, all of whom are gone. Allow me to throw the four names at you, and if you would, give me a quick summary of your feelings or whatever you'd like to say . . .

Kenney: Okay.

Binky: First up, Steve Marriott . . .

Kenney: What can I say about Steve? [long pause . . . then very wistful] Such a small guy had the most powerful and soulful voice I've ever heard.

Binky: Amen! Ronnie Lane . . .

Kenney [suddenly really affected]: Ronnie Lane . . . was . . . the kindest . . . and my best friend from the onset, y'know. We started this together. That being . . . he's . . . he's . . . I . . . I . . . I miss him every day.

Binky: John Entwistle.

Kenney: Oh, John. God, I miss John. I loved John. Apart from doing things together in Small Faces and The Who, like that Australian tour, we used to do sessions together. John and I used to hang out, especially once I'd joined him in The Who, just all the time. My old drinking partner. I learned to lip-read from John. He'd played his bass so loud and yet he'd talk so quietly, [laughs] I had to lip-read him. I developed a really quick foot playing with John. All those triplets he'd do with his fingers, I had to do with my foot. I learned a lot from John.

Binky: You guys locked in beautifully, I remember. Lastly . . . Keith Moon.

Kenney: Oh, Keith . . . Keith . . . We used to hang out. He was lovely. Always willing to send anyone up, he'd never sent me up. He was just a great guy, a great drummer. Sadly missed, again. Wish he was back in The Who. I wish I'd never joined The Who. Wish he was here.

Binky: You just brought up that Australia tour. Mac and I talked about that, too. He told me a very funny Keith story that I'd never heard . . .

Kenney: What happened with me with Keith in Australia . . . We were in Melbourne. Keith called and said *'Come up to my room. I want to show what I've got.'* So, up I went, walked into his room, and . . . he had . . . oh, I dunno . . . 15 or 16 snare drums of all different sizes all lined up in a row. I said, *"Keith, what you gonna do with all them?!"* He sorta growled, *'I'll show what we're gonna do with all of them . . .'* He picked one up and threw it straight through the window. We were overlooking Melbourne High Street, at least 10, maybe 20 floors up, I dunno. We looked out the window and saw this snare drum fallin' to bits and rollin' down Melbourne High Street. We quickly ducked back from the window and acted like nothing had happened. That's how nuts he was, but, he was lovely. That said, he was wonderful wonderful drummer.

Binky [laughs]: Okay, I've never heard that one either, Kenney! Wow! Moon the TRUE Loon!

Kenney: Oh, yeah.

Binky: We've been doing it for the last five minutes, anyway . . . Do you mind if we delve into your ten year tenure with The Who, one of the top five most influential bands in rock history?

Kenney: I've got nothing to hide when it comes to The Who . . .

Binky: I'm gonna be a bit blunt. Sadly, your legacy with the band seems to be Roger kinda trashing your playing. I saw your first tour with The Who in 1979 and it was fucking brilliant, and I'm a Moon worshiper. Maybe my single all time favorite musician. Then, I saw the Shea Stadium show in '82 and, I have to say, both Pete and Roger seemed pretty sour. Was there real tension by then?

Kenney: Yeah, I think, by then, there was a bit. We were off to Toronto the next day for the world's first global simulcast. That was nerve-wracking, just thinking about it. I recall feeling like I had to Superglue my hands to the drumsticks that night. Roger just could never get used to the fact that he'd turn around and Keith wouldn't be there. And one of the things I didn't do was copy or emulate Keith Moon. I couldn't and I wouldn't. I could only play me. I mean, there were certain fills that were part of the arrangement, you could get near to the point. The arrangements really remained the same. We played within that structure. I could play with John, but, Roger would look for Keith and he wouldn't be there. I think it really upset him more than anything else. We toured for four years, from 1972 through 1982. Then, over the years, we got together to do different TV things, Live Aid, The Concert For Kampuchea, things like that. The time I had with The Who, especially in the later stages, was the best time I ever had with The Who without Keith Moon.

Binky: They were still The Who when you were with them, not The Who Revue.

Kenney: I was an equal member in every respect. They respected me, I respected them. And we went on like that. We had some good times together.

Binky: I feel I have to go here, Kenney, and I don't mean to get painful. But, how did you learn that Keith had died and how and when did The Who get in touch with you?

Kenney: [long long pause] It is very clear . . . very . . . vivid to me. I was with Keith Moon the night before he died. We were at Paul McCartney's party at The Pub in the Park before the Buddy Holly film. Normally, you have an after-party. But, they had a pre-party, too. I'd just gotten back from America that day. I'd been in the middle of forming a Trans-Atlantic band with Glyn Johns' help. I was sitting with Keith telling him about this new band while we were at a table with Paul and Linda McCartney, Paul's brother, Michael and David Frost.

Binky: David Frost?!

Kenney: I've got a picture of us somewhere . . . So, Keith, who I hadn't seen in awhile, started up about me being in America . . . *'But, Keith, what about you? How are you?'* He said, *'I'm good. I'm on these pills I have to take to keep me off drinking. I can't drink, otherwise I get violently sick. I haven't had a drink for about six months or so.'* Well, that was something! Anyway, so, then we went off to see the film. I think the film started at midnight. We got out of there about half past one in the morning. Keith and I said goodbye to each other and we both went home. I woke up the next morning and switched the TV on. The news was on and was announcing that 'rock star Keith Moon' had died from a drug overdose. His body had been found during the early hours of the morning. I said this is fuckin'. . . this is . . . This is crazy! This is wrong. It can't be. I was with him just a few hours ago. That . . . that's how I found out.

Binky: God, I've never known you were with him the very night before . . . Wow, Kenney . . . Well, Okay, so, Keith's gone . . .

Kenney: One thing I must say, although he was nuts to everybody else, whatever, Keith was *always* gracious to me.

Binky: That doesn't surprise me, Kenney. So, who from The Who actually called you to say, 'Hey, we need you playing drums with us.'?

Kenney: As I said, I'd been busy forming this band with Glyn, and about three months after Keith died I got a call from Bill Curbishley, The Who's manager . . . He said, *'Hey, Kenney, I'm gonna get straight to the point, The Who have had a meeting and they want you to join the band. I'll tell you their exact words were . . . "Won't you please going the band, we won't consider anybody else."* I said, *"Well, thanks for this compliment, but I've formed a band."* And then Bill said that Pete was coming by his office this afternoon and why don't I drop by and have a chat with Pete about this. I was happy to have a chat with my friend, Pete. I came 'round towards the end of the day and Pete and Bill and I sat around a couple of hours having a real laugh over mutual stuff from the past. Pete just turned around and said, *"Look, you've got to join the band. You're one of us. You're a Mod."* Stuff like that. He really got to me. You know, Pete had been a good friend for quite awhile. I'd worked with Pete prior to joining The Who. I'd been over to his house several times when he was working on demos and we wound up kinda working on each other's demos. We got to know each other pretty well from it. As you know, we met back in the 60s. When I was in the Small Faces, we toured with The Who all over England, Europe, Australia. I have the utmost admiration for Pete. He's a fine musician. I'm privileged to have worked with him. He's great. He and John. Working between Pete and John I was contending with two lead guitarists [laughs]. The only one playing a bass part was my bass drum [more laughs].

Binky: Oh, that's good! One of my favorite collaborations of yours with The Who is the Ken Russell's *Tommy* version of "Acid Queen". Your groove in that track is just incredible, Kenney.

Kenney: Thanks. Those *Tommy* were great sessions. I love the movie. I though it was great.

Binky: Yes. Ken Russell took the badly needed piss out of the whole deal and brought *Tommy* back to entertainment for me. Back to the moment you joined The Who, the announcement that you were Keith's replacement seemed like some kind of cosmic Zen symmetry to this rabid Who freak.

Kenney: The thing that convinced me . . . Pete said that yes, Keith was a nutcase and all that, and was a great stylist. But, now we, The Who, with me on drums, had a chance to actually do something completely different now. I said, *"Great. Then, I'll join the band on that note."* But, we never did anything completely different.

Binky: Yeah, well, by then, they were already a bit of a hit machine in their live shows. Once you joined, did you find The Who's recording methods different or unusual?

Kenney: It was pretty much along the same lines I was used to. But, when we did the first album, *Face Dances*, I was taken aback by their choice of Bill Szymczyk as the producer.

Binky: Me, too!

Kenney: I thought, Oh God, this ain't right. I mean, we had an edge to our sound. Bill was brought in and we ended up sounding like The Eagles.

Binky: Damn, you took that right out of my mouth, Kenney! For me, *It's Hard* is a far superior album, particularly the material and natural production. Do you have favorite cuts that you were part of on either or both albums?

Kenney: First, understand, I love Bill Szymczyk. He is a fantastic guy. I just always thought he was wrong producer for The Who.

Binky: I totally agree.

Kenney: My drums sounded like *pudding!*

Binky: Oy! Sticking with a food metaphor, it sounded to me like The Who, pureed.

Kenney: I do like the second album very well. Glyn Johns did that one. I'd worked with Glyn for years, y'know. As far as tracks, I like 'Eminence Front'. That was different. 'You Better, You Bet' is great. Funnily enough, I liked 'Athena'.

Binky: Ahhh, 'Athena', yes! I love 'Don't Let Go The Coat'. I also dug how Pete took the three most tired chords and created something really good with the title track, 'It's Hard'.

Kenney: Oh, and I really like 'Cry If You Want', too.

Binky: Okay, major ugly gear switch, and I really *do* hate to ask you about this, but, can you give me an idea what that Cincinnati tragedy where eleven kids died trying to get into a General Admission show was like for you and the band?

Kenney: Ahhhhh . . . to be honest, that was one of the darkest days of my life. I've joined the band. I've been in it for five minutes, and biggest tragedy on the planet that day happened. I just could not believe it. Those poor kids who died. I feel so sorry for their families. What people might not know was the band was taken back and questions by different lawyers, just layers of lawyers in the same room. I was questioned for at least two hours and half hours. Pete was questioned for over four hours. We had no idea.

Binky: I felt sick about it for the kids and the band for a long long time. Back to our chronology, things wound down. I'm hoping you and Roger get along.

Kenney: Yeah, we do, we do. I see him here and there and it's very . . . polite [chuckles].

Binky: Besides the possible Faces reunion in 2015, is there anything else you want to cover here?

Kenney: I have two projects in connection with the Small Faces that I want to get out of my system. Both dealing with our 1968 album, *Ogden's Nutgone Flake.*

Binky: Folks, *Ogden's* is, in my opinion, one of the Top 25 Albums ever recorded. Sorry, Ken, I needed to state that. Oh, and that round cover . . . So very very cool!

Kenney: Take your time. [chuckles]. One is the animation film of *Ogden's Nutgone* and I've done a classical version of *Ogden's* as well . . . I've had the album transcribed into a classical piece.

Binky: *WOW!* Damn, Kenney! What awesome ideas! An animated film and a classical rendition of one of the great rock albums of all time! I am so impressed! Wow, again! I have to say, you've laid at least 6 or 7 real revelations on me today. Is there anything we haven't covered?

Kenney: Well, yeah, we covered some ground today. I suppose all's well that ends well.

Binky: Man, Kenney Jones, I can't thank you enough for your time and righteous forthrightness.

Kenney: It's been a pleasure, Binky. Thank you.

LOOK WHO'S TALKING!

Adrian Deevoy | October 26, 2014 | *Mail on Sunday/Event* (UK)

In November 2014, the Who embarked on a three-continent fiftieth anniversary tour called The Who Hits 50! Although they perhaps wisely did not declare it to be the definitive end like they had the 1982 jaunt, Daltrey described it as "the beginning of the long goodbye." A compilation album, also called *The Who Hits 50!*, was released to coincide with the tour and contained a taster for a projected new album.

In this feature from the *Mail on Sunday*'s supplement *Event*, Townshend and Daltrey examine the Who's history from the perspective of their twilight years. What some Who fans will find most interesting is Daltrey's assertion that it was he who broke up the band in 1982 (and, furthermore, not over Kenney Jones's drumming) and Townshend's declaration "I hate performing and the Who and touring." —Ed.

The Queen Mother, God bless her, can't claim responsibility for many rock songs.

But she can take considerable credit for The Who's *My Generation*, the loudest, snottiest rock 'n' roll anthem of them all.

A howl of teenage angst that still reverberates through the music of U2, Oasis, Robbie Williams and even One Direction, the song takes pride of place on their latest release, *The Who Hits 50*, and is certain to feature in all its live and livid glory when they start their two-year 'Beginning Of The Long Goodbye' tour next month, celebrating The Who's half-century.

My Generation came kicking and screaming into the world in late 1964, when Pete Townshend, The Who's guitarist and principal songwriter, purchased an ancient Packard V12 hearse for £90 and parked it proudly outside his flat in Belgravia.

Fifty years later, Townshend picks up the story. 'I wasn't made to feel particularly welcome in that area,' he recalls. 'I thought they were snobs. I was an angry, cocky young man but I felt pushed around. The funny thing back then was that you didn't have to pay for parking, so I plonked it outside my place thinking it looked rather cool.'

Within days, the vehicle had vanished. A mysterious telephone call informed Townshend that the car had been impounded upon the request of the Queen Mother, as she had to pass it every day and it brought to mind her late husband King George VI's funeral 12 years earlier. Recovery would cost an extortionate £250, but the caller offered to pay this fee in exchange for ownership of the majestic motor.

Whether or not the enigmatic Royal representative ever really existed we'll never know. But Townshend resentfully agreed to the dubious deal then, suitably incensed, finished writing *My Generation* ('which I'd had brewing') and dedicated it to the Queen Mum.

'I saw her as a boring old lady who had nothing better to do than go around taking away teenagers' cars,' he says now. 'But I got a rather decent song out of it, so, cheers, Ma'am.'

The Queen Mother's regal reaction to the stuttering *sturm und drang* smash went unrecorded, but as The Who prepare for their Golden Jubilee jolly-up, singer Roger Daltrey CBE remains a big fan of her daughter's work.

'I think the Queen is remarkable,' Daltrey enthuses. 'She is fabulous but I feel for her. It must be very difficult for her. I can't understand people thinking she leads a life of luxury. She works her socks off. I'm hard-working, I don't stop, but she'd out-run me any day of the week. And she's 19 years older than me.'

The Who's busy main men, who run a £180 million business with a highly profitable two-year projection, have agreed to talk exclusively to *Event*, and talk they do. Roger Daltrey gives his longest interview in recent memory, the new 'Chatty Rog' amazing his management team.

After an exhaustive discussion, Pete Townshend offers *Event* a lift home in order to continue the conversation ('I'm enjoying this!') into the night.

The pair preferred to be interviewed separately on this occasion to avoid any unseemly squabbling – they don't want to cause a big sensation – but, as with their music, they complement each other perfectly. Daltrey: gutsy, down to earth. Townshend: poetic, head in the clouds.

To have them both salute The Who's 50th, with the only interview commemorating this significant birthday, is a rare treat.

Controversially, Townshend claims that the band have only technically been together for 33 years, as they effectively split as a touring and recording unit between 1982-99, but ignore the old grouch – The Who are 50. Let's all have a smashing time.

In the pantheon of great British rock groups of a certain vintage, The Beatles were bigger, the Rolling Stones sexier, The Kinks cooler, Pink Floyd more psychedelic and Led Zeppelin were bluesier. But The Who were tougher.

Sonically, psychologically and, when required, physically. Their incendiary live appearances had a blast-furnace intensity, the music juddering like a jet engine, the songs seething with violent intent. The Who elevated anger to an art form and produced hit after hit: *I Can't Explain, My Generation, Substitute, Pinball Wizard, Baba O'Riley, Won't Get Fooled Again, Who Are You?*

Onstage, the west London quartet would all but combust with rage. They were so furious with society that they wanted to die before they got old.

Two of them regrettably did. The band's famously eccentric drummer, Keith Moon, died from an overdose of clomethiazole, an alcohol-withdrawal drug, in 1978.

Their uniquely gifted bassist, John Entwistle, succumbed to a cocaine-induced heart attack in the company of a prostitute at the Las Vegas Hard Rock Hotel prior to The Who's 2002 US tour.

'I've lost a lot of friends to coke,' rues Daltrey. 'Horrible, horrible drug. I've never taken it, only at the dentist. Never done chemicals. I've seen too many wonderful people turn into absolute a***holes overnight. I used to stay away from it – everyone else would be up all night and I'd shut myself away but I was incredibly naive.'

The relationship between Townshend, the pontificating art-school progeny of professional musicians, and Daltrey, the street-fighting son of Shepherd's Bush, is a complex and contradictory one. 'A longstanding friendship that has turned into a bonded love, founded on a deeper understanding of each other's limitations,' is how Townshend puts it.

'I love him,' shrugs Daltrey. 'We're like brothers, I suppose.'

Both born to hold opinions and prepared to die defending them, it is remarkable that two such diametrically opposed souls have only come to blows once. 'Ironically, we were filming *Love Reign O'er Me* for the *Quadrophenia* movie,' chuckles Daltrey. 'Pete was very drunk and has come at me with a guitar, then he's tried to punch me so I ducked the punch and hit him. It was a very clean uppercut and it knocked him spark out. He still reckons that's what caused his bald spot.'

'I probably deserved to get knocked out,' sighs Townshend, tugging at the collar of a stylish black shirt. 'It wasn't a fight, I just stood there and let him hit me. What's interesting is that he could have killed me. I went out like a light. It took me a while to piece things back together. It was a hell of a punch. But it was the only one – there was too much respect there for it to happen again.'

Whereas Daltrey has been content to work on his country pile (an interviewer once arrived to find him shirtless and happily mixing cement), Townshend has, in his donnish way, generally enjoyed a party.

At a David Bowie after-show bash in London at the end of 1999, I joined Townshend, Mick Jagger, Bob Geldof and Bowie in a conversation about Chinese space travel and quality knitwear (it was winter and most of us were wearing what was comically referred to by the assembled Londoners as 'a larvely bit of cashmere'). 'I had a homoerotic crush on Mick Jagger when he was young and beautiful,' Townshend admits, although his autobiography puts it more robustly. 'It was fashionable at the time and it was something I was trying to foster.'

'Bowie's also very beautiful to look at and always has been,' he muses. 'When we did *Tommy* at the Royal Albert Hall in 1970 he came up to me afterwards and took hold of me and said, "This is what I want to be doing – spectacle and storytelling." And of course he went on to do it with *Ziggy Stardust.*'

Daltrey, who unlike Townshend doesn't appear to have a highly developed feminine side, eschews the luxurious leather sofas at The Who's Camden Town management office and squeezes into the cramped kitchen to chat. We perch upon steel chairs.

He left Holmshurst Manor in East Sussex early this morning, where he resides in 35-acre Jacobean splendour, and took the train to London to see hypnotist Paul McKenna, 'a brilliant man', about a TV show. Daltrey's teenage reminiscences are studded with 'horrible fights' and 'terrible behaviour'. Even at 70, you wouldn't want to take Daltrey on. Fit and compact, with a full head of hair, he cuts a foreboding figure in his fitted waistcoat and snug Levi's.

'I had a really bad fight with a very good friend of mine, which I've always regretted,' he frowns. 'I almost killed him. I could never back off from a fight. And I was a sheet metal worker, so I was strong. I had a pair of shoulders on me and my hands were like rocks. It was like being hit with a club hammer.'

In a brusque bark, he talks with refreshing candour about the Sixties. Woodstock was a 's***hole'. He 'got p***ed' with The Doors' Jim Morrison on Southern Comfort at the 1970 Isle Of Wight concert. Jimi Hendrix may have written *Foxy Lady* for Daltrey's wife-to-be Heather 'but she came home with me. There you go. How lucky was I?'

The couple married in 1971 and have had three children. Daltrey had one child from his four-year marriage to Jackie Rickman in 1964, another son was born in 1968 as a result of an affair with model Elisabeth Aronsson.

Townshend's 40-year marriage to Karen Astley, which bore three children, ended in 2009, although they had been separated for 15 years and have remained friends. He now lives with his long-time girlfriend, musician Rachel Fuller, 41. Both men are modestly bemused by their time as 'highly unlikely sex symbols', although Townshend concedes that in their pomp 'Roger looked like a god'. 'It's called youth, dear boy!' hoots Daltrey. 'But it was also confidence. My wife really liked my curly hair and previous to that I'd always straightened it. But she said it was beautiful and that gave me enormous self-belief.'

'Before that it was always there but was sort of squashed. Maybe I have built-in paranoia from being bullied. When I was young I'd broken my jaw and in proportion I had a very big chin and used to get terribly picked on. Young kids are cruel.

'But my whole look just seemed to come together. The look I was trying to create, particularly with *Tommy*, was a visual of a spirit.'

It was during this time of spiritual searching that Daltrey's jeans became so tight it looked as if they might cause him problems in later life.

'They caused me problems in my early life!' he laughs, like a Victorian circus master. 'But we wore them tight. It was like the Shakespearean codpiece, it was showing off the wares. Nothing's changed, it's just that now kids want to show off their a**es. Personally, I preferred to show off the front view.'

We witness the legendary Daltrey ire when his 1985 American Express advert is mentioned. Wasn't the tweedy gentleman rocker on his trout farm rather rubbing his fans' noses in it? 'What did they want me to say, I'm a pauper?' he huffs. 'I'm in one of the biggest rock 'n' roll bands in the world and yet I've got no money? Bulls***!'

Pete Townshend opens the grand front door to his Georgian house on the Richmond riverside grumbling about *The Great British Bake Off*. 'They were making bread with a ton of sugar and cherries in it,' tuts the tall, slim 69-year-old, immediately making tea and polite conversation. He exhales gently.

The subject of Townshend's arrest in 2003 for using his credit card to access a website containing indecent images of children in 1999 is not up for discussion this evening. Townshend addressed the matter in detail over 14 pages in his 2012 autobiography *Who I Am*. He was cautioned by police and cleared of all charges 11 years ago. In his book he wrote: 'Dozens of people spoke on my behalf but Roger was the most vocal, allowing himself to get angry about the absurdity of my arrest. Clearly his own future was at risk if I was convicted but he went further than he needed to on my behalf. His solidarity with me, his faith in me and his rage at the injustice against me is something I will never forget.' For Townshend this chapter of his life is now closed.

Earlier, Daltrey had rather abruptly said that he hadn't read Townshend's book, nor did he intend to. 'Why would I need to?' he asked, the distinctive jaw setting hard. 'It might interfere with our relationship. So, best not to. I've known him for over 50 years.'

The Thames glitters at the bottom of Townshend's garden; there is modern art on the walls that would make the Tate's curators twitch with envy and an acoustic guitar in the corner that costs more than most cars. The venerable rocker sits at a long table in his workroom – part mod prophet, part mad professor – steeples his hands thoughtfully and addresses tonight's first query: why on earth are The Who touring again?

'I'm sort of asking myself the same question,' he laughs. 'It seemed like a good idea about six months ago but I hate performing and The Who and touring. But I'm innately good at it, I don't find it hard. I feel empowered on stage – not possessed as has been suggested.

'We tour because we can. I'm still very fit. I wouldn't be complaining at my age if I had Alzheimer's. My dad died when he was 69. I feel very lucky to be alive and well.'

Townshend's anecdotes are much like his extended guitar solos on The Who's peerless 1970 *Live At Leeds* album, riffing on a theme before moving into more mind-bending territory. He is, however, nakedly honest. 'I'm a rock star,' he says. 'Exalted one minute, brought down the next, under constant examination. You have no rights, but you can also do things that no one else can do. You can get at a table at The Ivy, if that's what you want.

'When you hit 70, which I almost have, it's nice to have a luxurious life, but it's not about money. Time is the most valuable commodity now.'

The Who have been a proudly apolitical band throughout their long career although, in the Camden kitchen, Daltrey says that *Won't Get Fooled Again,* replete with its primal scream of discontent, 'is a political song to me at the moment'.

'I try not to support any political party because as an artist I don't think you should. But I would dearly love to get out of Europe. I wouldn't vote Ukip because I don't think they're going to get us out, although I think Nigel Farage is very clever. I don't dislike him.'

'I've always been centrist,' grimaces Townshend. 'But as I get older I start to value the past and traditions. A more conservative view of British life, island life.'

'I don't think I'll ever forgive Labour for the state they left us in,' Daltrey glowers, looking as if he is about to spit. 'If Margaret Thatcher hadn't got in, then we would have had to have left the country. We struggled to stay here throughout the Seventies. We were the only band that didn't leave. Tax was 83 per cent. If the Tories hadn't won I'd have gone to America like everyone else did. I'd have been a really, really, really rich man now.

'But I'm not a Tory.'

Daltrey, a millionaire many times over, drains his mug, and warms to his theme. 'We're employing an ever-cheaper workforce, which can only drive the people at the bottom in this country further down the ladder. I'm not anti-immigrant or anti-immigration. I'm an immigrant! I don't blame the people who came over – it's not the people, it's the politics. But it's pulling our country down and that's not the answer. Keep us where we are and pull them up. It's destroying ambition. They brought five million people into this country and we can't get into our hospitals now.'

His rant, in a roundabout way, brings up the sore subject of The Who's own health issues.

Working at high volume and relying on high-risk stagecraft has taken its toll on both founder Who members. Townshend still uses his trademark 'wind-milling' guitar technique, while Daltrey continues to recklessly swing his microphone around the stage.

As a result, the guitarist is partially deaf, ('my hearing "rolls off" at the high end') and his right hand is 'a mess, the wrist is only connected to the hand by cartilage.' Meanwhile, Daltrey complains of 'flat feet and arthritis' and in 1996 almost lost an eye when he 'got clumped in the face by a mike stand'.

Yet these ailments are small fry compared to Townshend having once actually died. 'That's what they say, if that indeed was death,' he muses philosophically of his collapse in a nightclub during the early Eighties.

'I don't know what I'd taken or been given. I certainly know I was turning blue. Is that a heroin overdose? Maybe. But apparently I died for a while. They had to inject adrenaline directly into my heart then take me to hospital and beat me back to life.'

'For a brief period I hung out with the The Sex Pistols,' Townshend remembers fondly. 'Steve Jones and Paul Cook once carried me down to a girl's place down by the river and when they got me there I was in a bit of a stupor, but as soon as they'd gone I woke up and had a three-hour sex session with a pretty girl. So I couldn't have been that bad.'

'Pete's drinking had got very bad by '82,' Daltrey contends. 'That's why I stopped the band. Two bottles of brandy a day and who knows what else. It was going to kill him. And I didn't want to kill Pete Townshend.

'So I went to see him, tell him I love him. Why are you doing this to yourself? It wasn't pretty but he listened and went into rehab the next day. I think we still all had a lot of guilt about not saving Keith.'

Daltrey confesses that his last physical fight had been with Moon in 1965. The bright blue eyes switch to full beam as he recounts the incident. 'Keith hit me with a tambourine; we got into a proper punch-up and I got thrown out of the band,' he recounts. 'I had flushed the band's purple hearts, speed pills, down the toilet – not on a drug principle but on a music principle. I was on probation with The Who after that, but they stopped taking the drugs onstage, for a while at least. Keith still took the occasional monkey tranquiliser. But he should never have gone for me.'

When the news about Moon's demise broke in 1978, Townshend phoned Daltrey, who simply said, 'He's done it.'

Remind Roger that Keith was just 32 when he died and he shudders. 'My son is 32 now,' he says quietly. 'But in truth you couldn't imagine Keith Moon becoming an old man, he just burned too brightly.'

'As that four-piece,' says Townshend, 'me, Roger, John and Keith, we were the best rock band on the planet. *Were...*' he mutters to himself.

In 2006, The Who received an unanticipated reboot when Townshend, a fan of grumpy detective Kurt Wallander, agreed to his song *Who Are You?* being used for the TV drama series *CSI*. 'I knew it would help me financially,' says the Ferrari-fancying artist reputed to be worth £40 million. 'Because every time it's on you get about 300 quid.

'I also think it helped The Who, because we were coming off the radar at that point and it re-established us in people's minds.' Townshend could therefore afford to be magnanimous last year when it was noted that One Direction's *Best Song Ever* bore suspicious similarities to The Who's *Baba O'Riley*. 'It wasn't important enough to get excited about,' he sniffs. 'I could hear a bit of The Who in it, but so what? Considering the stuff we ripped off over the years, it doesn't really matter.'

Daltrey is less keen on the young pop pretenders. 'Here we are with the world in the state it is in and we've got One Direction,' he scowls. 'Where are the artists writing with any real sense of angst and purpose? There are no movements at the moment: we had mod and then there was punk, but it's so hard to start a movement now. Unless it's ISIS.'

The sun has long since set on the river and in the fading light Pete Townshend remembers his friend John Entwistle. It is a moving eulogy, which concludes in Townshend revealing that his miniature Yorkshire terrier was named Wistle after his beloved mate and mentor. Townshend tugs at his collar again.

We move on. A movie about Keith Moon is still in development, although the process has been so protracted that Robert Downey Jr, originally earmarked for the part, is 'too old now', according to Daltrey, for the lead role. Meanwhile, The Who have tentatively started work on their 12th studio album. But will they be emulating their devoted Who disciples U2 and 'give away' their music?

'I don't think that was such a great mistake,' says Townshend evenly. 'What Bono said is very true: it was a moment of grandiosity and arrogance mixed with generosity. That kind of sums him up. He gets very bad press and we all know why: he is a megalomaniacal man but that's what makes him a singer in such a big band.'

Townshend turns on a lamp, strokes his silver beard and once again ponders The Who turning 50.

'I still really like *My Generation*,' he smiles, returning to his Queen Mother-indebted classic. 'The meaning has changed over the years but it says, "Don't tell me what to do", which I love. It's still f****** anarchic'

CREDITS

"The Making of The Who" by John Heilpern. First published in the *Observer*, March 20, 1966. © 1966, John Heilpern. Reprinted by permission of the author.

"Miles Interviews Pete Townshend" by Miles. First published in the *International Times*, February 13, 1967. © 1967, Barry Miles. Reprinted by permission of the author.

"Pete Talks about Tommy Part One" by Miles. First published in the *International Times*, May 23, 1969. © 1969, Barry Miles. Reprinted by permission of the author.

"Pete Talks about Tommy Part Two" by Miles. First published in the *International Times*, June 13, 1969. © 1969, Barry Miles. Reprinted by permission of the author.

"A Talk with Pete Townshend" by Jonathan Cott. First published in *Rolling Stone*, May 14, 1970. © 1970, Jonathan Cott. Reprinted by permission of Jonathan Cott and *Rolling Stone*.

"The Who Puts The Bomp or They Won't Get Fooled Again" by John Swenson. First published in *Crawdaddy*, December 5, 1971. © 1970, John Swenson. Reprinted by permission of the author.

"Chatting with Pete Townshend Part One" by Connor McKnight and John Tobler. First published in *Zigzag*, approx. February 1972. © 1972, Connor McKnight and John Tobler. Reprinted by permission.

"Chatting with Pete Townshend Part Two" by Connor McKnight and John Tobler. First published in *Zigzag*, July 1974. © 1974, Connor McKnight and John Tobler. Reprinted by permission.

"Chatting with Pete Townshend Part Three" by Connor McKnight and John Tobler. First published in *Zigzag*, August 1974. © 1974, Connor McKnight and John Tobler. Reprinted by permission.

"Who's Still Who" by John Lawless. First published in the *Observer*, March 19, 1972. © 1972, John Lawless. Reprinted by permission of the author.

"Four-Way Pete" by Charles Shaar Murray. First published in *New Musical Express*, October 27, 1973. © Time Inc. (UK) Ltd. Reprinted by permission of the publisher.

ABOUT THE CONTRIBUTORS

One of the grandees of British music journalism, **Roy Carr** made his name at IPC, working for *New Musical Express, Melody Maker, Vox,* and *Uncut*. He is credited with pioneering the concept of the cover-mount CD. Among his many books are entries in the Illustrated Record series on the Beatles, the Rolling Stones, David Bowie, and Elvis Presley.

Jonathan Cott has been an editor and writer for *Rolling Stone* magazine since its inception. He is the author of *Days That I'll Remember: Spending Time with John Lennon and Yoko Ono* and *Dinner with Lenny: The Last Long Interview with Leonard Bernstein*. He is the editor of *Bob Dylan: The Essential Interviews*.

Adrian Deevoy is a London-based journalist who works for *GQ*, the *Guardian,* and the *Mail on Sunday*. He is the only writer of his generation to have conducted extensive interviews with Bob Dylan, Prince, Freddie Mercury, Madonna, and Daevid Allen of Gong.

Sean Egan is a writer specializing in arts and entertainment. His two dozen books include works on the Rolling Stones, the Beatles, *Coronation Street,* Tarzan, James Bond, William Goldman, and Manchester United.

Simon Garfield is the author or editor of seventeen books of nonfiction, and a contributor to the *Observer, Intelligent Life,* and *Esquire*.

Stuart Grundy was a producer and executive producer with BBC Radio One for twenty-five years, writing, producing, and presenting numerous music documentaries and documentary series. He has contributed articles to magazines and books and cowritten two books with John Tobler.

John Heilpern had just joined the *London Observer* when, at age twenty-three, he wrote "The Making of The Who." He is the author of the official biography of the iconic British playwright John Osborne, *The Many Lives of John Osborne* (Knopf). *How Good Is David Mamet, Anyway?* (Routledge) is a collection of his profiles and theater criticism.

While studying journalism in London in the 1960s, **John Lawless** staged a concert at his college for the High Numbers. His early career included the night newsdesk at the *Times*, covering archaeology for the *Observer*, and exclusive picture-stories for the *Sunday Times*. Having his own weekly pop-music column resulted in him writing a cover feature on the Who for the *Observer*. He has since reported from sixty countries for the likes of the *Financial Times*, the *Economist*, *BusinessWeek*, and the *Sunday Times*, and has edited several international business magazines. He's not sure what happened to the High Numbers.

Australian **Connor McKnight** worked for IBM before moving into music journalism. He was editor of *Zigzag* and music editor of *Time Out*. He is credited with writing the only major article about Nick Drake published during Drake's lifetime.

Greil Marcus is the author of *The History of Rock 'n' Roll in Ten Songs* (2014), *Lipstick Traces* (1989), *Mystery Train* (1975), and other books. He is a contributing editor for *Rolling Stone, Artforum*, and *Oxford American*. He lives in Oakland, California.

Barry Miles was the co-owner of Indica Books and Gallery, and in 1966 cofounded the *International Times* (*IT*), Europe's first underground newspaper. He was label manager of Zapple, the experimental offshoot of the Beatles' Apple Records. He went on to freelance for the *NME*, edit *Time Out*, and work as editor for Omnibus Press before becoming an author. Among his many books is *Many Years from Now*, the authorized biography of Paul McCartney.

Charles Shaar Murray's journalistic career got off to an explosive start: the 1970 "Schoolkids Issue" of underground paper *Oz* in which he made his print debut led to an obscenity trial for its editors. He joined the *NME* in 1972 and went on to become a founder contributor of *Q* and *Mojo* magazines. His writing has also appeared in the *Evening Standard, Guitarist,* the *Guardian,* the *Independent,* the *Independent on Sunday,* the *Observer, MacUser, New Statesman, Prospect, Vogue,* and the *Word.* He is the author of the award-winning *Crosstown Traffic: Jimi Hendrix and Post-War Pop.*

Eamonn Percival was born in Cheshire but moved to London when a teenager. He considered a career in the priesthood but eventually became a journalist who combined his writing with guitar roles in bands such as Eve, Tapestry, Jimmy James and the Vagabonds, and the Nashville Teens. He was editor of *CB Citizen's Band* magazine. He died in 2001 of jaw cancer, aged fifty.

New Yorker **Binky Philips** was permanently ruined by seeing the Beatles on *The Ed Sullivan Show.* Over the last four decades, he has been performing, writing, and recording with the Planets. He has run record stores, an indie record label, and spent twenty-five years in radio promotion and artist management. *My Life in the Ghost of Planets,* his memoir of his musical youth and adulthood, was published by Rhino in 2012. On June 7, 1970, Pete Townshend threw him his guitar at the end of the Who's matinee at the Metropolitan Opera House.

Steve Rosen has been writing about the denizens of the rock 'n' roll world for the past forty years. During this period, his work has appeared in a myriad of publications including *Guitar Player, Guitar World, Guitarist, Rolling Stone, Playboy, Creem, Circus, Musician, Classic Rock, Q, Mojo,* and a host of others.

Tony Stewart was deputy editor of *New Musical Express,* editor of *Sounds,* creator and launch editor of *Select,* and managing editor of *Rage!* After leaving music journalism, he spent twenty-one years as an entertainment journalist and newspaper executive at the *Daily Mirror.*

John Swenson has been writing about popular music since 1967. Over that time, he has been published in virtually every popular music magazine of note. He also worked as editor of *Crawdaddy, Rolling Stone, Circus, Rock World, OffBeat,* and jazze.com. He has published fourteen books including biographies of Bill Haley, the Who, Stevie Wonder, and the Eagles, and coedited the original *Rolling Stone Record Guide* with Dave Marsh. He is also a sports writer, covering ice hockey and horseracing.

After working in accountancy, insurance, and banking by day and writing for *Zigzag* by night, **John Tobler** joined CBS Records in 1974, where he became ABBA's first UK press officer. He would later write ABBA's official biography and the sleevenotes to their multimillion-selling compilation *ABBA Gold*. In 1976, he started freelance work at BBC Radio One, interviewing dozens of acts, including the Eagles and the Sex Pistols. He runs the small independent Road Goes On Forever record label.

Charles M. Young, the son of a Wisconsin Presbyterian minister, joined the staff of *Rolling Stone* in 1976 after winning the magazine's first national college writing competition. He proceeded to make his name by covering the New Wavers of the CBGB's scene. He later worked for *Musician* and *Playboy*. In his later years, his writing increasingly focused on politics. He died in 2014, aged sixty-three, after a battle with a brain tumor.

INDEX

All song and album titles are by the Who unless otherwise attributed.

"Accidents" (Thunderclap Newman), 39, 44, 115, 117

"Acid Queen, The," 25, 377

Ad Lib discothèque, 8

"After the Fire" (Roger Daltrey), 324

Aitken, Jonathan, 157

Alexandra Palace, 279

All the Best Cowboys Have Chinese Eyes album (Pete Townshend), 287, 341

Altamont Speedway Free Festival, 40, 52, 97, 254–255

Altham, Keith, 149

"Amazing Journey," 140

Amazing Journey film, 359–364

Amazon, 366

American Express, 385

Amnesty International, 283

"Anarchy in the U.K." (Sex Pistols), 253

Anderson, Jon, 186

"Anyway, Anyhow, Anywhere," 8, 269–270

Arden, Don, 366

Aronsson, Elisabeth, 384

Arthur discothèque, 11

Ascott, Roy, 329, 334

Assembled Multitude, 118

Astley, Karen, 354, 384

"Athena," 378

Atlantic Records, 306

Baba, Meher, 33–34, 39, 40, 43, 48, 55–56, 84, 96, 99, 101, 128, 138–139, 227, 228, 233, 253, 274, 275, 279, 280

"Baba O'Riley," 71, 74, 76, 110, 246, 275, 293, 382, 389

"Baby Don't You Do It," 142

Back Pages, 227–228, 230–231

Backtracks, 119

Baker, Ginger, 321

"Bald-Headed Woman," 124

Band, the, 35, 100

Banks, Peter, 186

"Barbara Ann" (Beach Boys), 158

Barnes, Richard, 303

Barrett, Syd, 278–279, 328

Barrett, Wild Willie, 215

Basho, Robbie, 279

Beach Boys, 158

Beat Goes On, The album, (Vanilla Fudge), 36, 184

Beatles, the, 3, 10, 27–28, 41, 42, 45, 48, 71, 90, 96–97, 100, 122, 155, 156–157, 158, 184, 185, 186, 336, 337, 360, 370, 382

Beck, Jeff, 104–105, 181, 184, 268

Beck's Bolero (Jeff Beck), 104–105

Bee Gees, 28, 120

Beggars Banquet album (the Rolling Stones), 48

Beggar's Opera, The film, 297

"Begin the Beguine" (Cole Porter), 40

"Behind Blue Eyes," 70, 110, 141

Berlin Opera House, 152

Bernstein, Leonard, 152
Berry, Chuck, 28, 29, 96, 142–143, 176, 180
"Best Song Ever" (One Direction), 388–389
Bethnal, 224
Bickford, Bob, 5–6
Birch, Lionel, 55
Black, Cilla, 157
Black Sabbath, ix
Blackburn, Tony, 130
Blake, Peter, 266
Blood, Sweat & Tears, 140
"Blue Red and Grey," 225
"Bodies" (Sex Pistols), 253
Bono, 389
Bonzo Dog Doo-Dah Band, 76, 84
"Boris the Spider," 62, 125, 183, 206
Bowie, David, 165, 182, 287, 334, 383
Boy Who Heard Music, The, 345–347
Boyfriend, 7
Brighton Pier, 169
British Phonographic Industry, 365
Brown, Arthur, 115, 133–134, 306
"Brown Sugar" (the Rolling Stones), 98, 99
Bruce, Jack, 211
Budweiser, 291–292
Bundrick, John "Rabbit," 245, 275–276, 349
Burgess, Richard, 286
Butler, Anya, 9
Butler, Tony, 245

Cage, John, 279
Camel, 185
Captain and Me, The album (the Doobie
      Brothers), 165
Captain Fantastic and the Brown Dirt Cowboy
      album (Elton John), 196
Cardboard, Richard, 116
Carr, Allan, 251
Carr, Roy, 174–189, 192
Carry On Moon, 357
"Certified Rose," 338
Chandler, Chas, 327
Charles, Ray, 267
Charly Records, 365–366
Chen, Phil, 328
Chicago Seven, 284
"Christmas," 118
"Circles," 122–123
"Clampdown" (the Clash), 253

Clapton, Eric, 28, 97, 113, 265, 268, 278, 327, 328
Clash, the, 224–225, 232, 247, 252, 253
Cobham, Billy, 240
"Cobwebs and Strange," 66
Cochran, Eddie, 158, 211
Cohen, Allen, 40
Cohen, Harold, 329, 334–335, 341
Cole, Peter, 50
Concert for Kampuchea, 375
Covent Garden, 129
Cook, Paul, 215–216, 388
Cooper, Alice, 170, 182
Cott, Jonathan, 38–57
Courage to Change, The, 304
"Cousin Kevin," 25–26
Crane, Vince, 134
Crawdaddy, x, 58–94
Cream, 120, 149
Creation, the, 326–327
Creedence Clearwater Revival, 53
Crowder, Paul, 359
"Cry If You Want," 378
CSI, 388
Curbishley, Bill, 222–223, 233, 306
Cusack, John, 354

"Daddy Rolling Stone," 124
Daily Express, 50
Daily Mail, 5, 233
Daily Mirror, 342
Daltrey, Heather, 355, 384
Daltrey, Roger, vii, 70, 71–72, 88–90, 153–154,
      157, 161, 190–191, 202, 203, 221, 291,
      303, 313, 316, 319–325, 338–340, 342,
      345–348, 355, 358, 359–364, 378, 380,
      381–382
   acting, 174, 178, 197, 202, 241, 297–298, 323
   charity work, 319–320
   corporate sponsorship, 296–298
   drugs and alcohol, 362, 382, 388
   fame, 190–191, 233, 272
   fashion, 7, 158, 216
   getting old, 176, 324, 355
   guitars, homemade, 104
   John Entwistle, about, 192, 194, 199, 356–357
   Keith Moon, 192, 199, 201, 312–314, 321,
      330, 362, 388
   Kenney Jones, about, 313–314, 380

live performance, viii, 4, 60, 79, 87–89, 143, 144, 183, 202, 247, 313–314, 320–322, 324, 361, 374
musical influences, 267
nickname, 61
Pete Townshend, about, 86–88, 192–194, 196, 198–198, 200–201, 216, 298, 300–301, 304, 322–323, 324, 354, 356, 383, 385, 388
Pete Townshend on, 79, 84, 121, 179, 221, 225–226, 250, 251, 258, 265, 281, 383–385, 386
politics, 387, 389
relationships with the press, x, 86
rock music, thoughts about, 200–201, 330, 355
solo albums, 190–191, 196, 323, 324
Tommy, 325, 357, 385
touring, 86, 88–90, 223, 296, 320, 324
Who's Next, 109, 321, 325, 328–329
Davies, Dave, 184, 328
Davies, Ray, 135, 180
Day, Doris, 347
"Day of Silence," 40
Dead Kennedys, 283
Debussy, Claude, 117
Decca, 120, 369–370, 372
American, 5, 6–7, 10–11
British, 9, 10
Dennis, Dave, 5
Denver, John, 298
Detours, the, 190, 204, 265, 266–267, 277
Deevoy, Adrian, 380–389
Diddley, Bo, 28, 29
"Disguises," 112, 286
"Dogs," 185
Doherty, Pete, 351
"Dr. Jimmy and Mister Jim," 163, 172, 276
Donegan, Lonnie, 367
Donovan, 41
"Don't Let Go the Coat," 378
Doobie Brothers, the, 165
Doors, the, 384
Double O Charity, 284–285
Downey, Robert Jr., 389
"Drowned," 183
Dudes and Dolls, the, 10
Dunlop, Frank, 329
Duran Duran, 286

Dylan, Bob, 45, 96, 97, 107–108, 219, 221–222, 246, 274, 336

"E Too D" (Small Faces), 369
Ealing Club, 132, 336
Eddy, Duane, 211
Electric Ladyland, 119
Electric Light Orchestra, 220
Elizabeth II, 381
Elliman, Yvonne, 288
Emerson, Keith, 168
Emerson, Lake & Palmer, 185, 220
"Eminence Front," 378
Endless Wire, 345, 347, 363
Empty Glass album (Pete Townshend), 244, 245, 248–249, 285
Eno, Brian, 334

Entwistle, John, 61–69, 83, 92, 93, 94, 155, 161, 203–213, 291, 298, 311–312, 316, 317, 328, 350–351, 362, 377
aging, 313
audience, 303
bass, home-made, 104, 204–205
bass style, vii, 206–207, 208–209–210, 313–314, 317–318
biography, 303–304
compositions, 25–26, 49, 62–67, 210, 218, 272
corporate sponsorship, 295–296
death, 326, 338–339, 345, 348, 351, 356–357, 363, 382
fashion, 7
instruments/instrumentation, 67, 204–208, 210–212–213, 264–265, 271
Keith Moon, about, 310–312
Keith Moon on, 236–237, 239
live performance, vii–viii, 4, 60, 183, 208, 210, 247, 299–300, 304, 374
musical influences, 211, 213
nickname, 61
Pete Townshend on, 80, 84, 178, 179, 183, 388, 389
practicing, 211–212
Quadrophenia, 163, 167–168, 209, 213, 281
rock journalism, 302–303
Roger Daltrey on, 192, 194, 199, 356–357

solo albums, 61, 70, 80, 84, 86–87, 125, 204, 302

Tommy, 25–26, 37, 61, 65–67, 153, 209

touring, 154, 223, 300

Epstein, Brian, 97, 157

Essex Music, 123

"Everyone Else," 109

"Eyesight to the Blind," 25, 306

Faber & Faber, 341, 349–350, 352

Face Dances album, 286–287, 290, 339, 349, 377

Faces, the, 149, 244, 365, 379

Fahey, John, 117, 279

Fairfield Hall, 144

Faith, Adam, 241

Farr, Rikki, 274

Festival Hall, 75

"Fiddle About," 26, 66–67

Fillmore, 80–81, 143

"Fire," (Arthur Brown), 306

"5.15," 163

Fly Posters Association, The, 4

"Fortune Teller," 49

Four Seasons, the, 36

Fox, Jim, 67

"Foxy Lady" (Jimi Hendrix), 384

Frost, David, 251, 375

Full Metal Jacket film, 301

Fuller, Rachel, 353–354, 356, 384

Fury, Billy, 241

Garfield, Simon, 345–358

Geesin, Ron, 40, 145–146

Geldof, Bob, 383

George VI, 381

"Get Back" (the Beatles), 28

"Getting in Tune," 70, 109, 110, 141

Gibson, Mel, 347

Gibson, William, 329

Glamour Magazine, 11

Glitter, Gary, 187

"Glow Girl," 128

"Going Home" (the Rolling Stones), 98

"Going Mobile," 74, 110

Goldhawk Club, 105–106

Goldhawk Record company, 191

Graham, Bill, 31, 81

Graham, Larry, 211

Grant, Keith, 335

Grateful Dead, 53, 255

Green, Richard, 7

Greenfield, Lloyd, 9, 11

Grundy, Stuart, 263–289

"Guitar and Pen," 218, 229

Guitar Greats, The, 263–289

Guitar Player, 203–213

Hafiz, 249

Hair musical, 121

Hammersmith Odeon, 222, 284

Happy Goday, 10

Happy Jack album, 58, 61–62, 82, 85, 92

"Happy Jack," 104, 185

Hard Rock Hotel, 382

Harper, Roy, 280

Harrison, George, 155, 157

Havens, Richie, 52

"Hawker, The," 25

"Heaven and Hell," 49, 62–64, 125

Heaven 17, 350

Hells Angels, 96, 97–98

Helpern, John, 1–11

"Helpless Dancer," 163

Hendrix, Jimi, 28, 81, 97, 113, 120, 127, 143, 149, 265, 277, 317, 327–328, 350, 361, 384

Herd, the, 145

Here Come the Nice (Small Faces), 366, 368, 371–372

Herman's Hermits, 81, 102, 154

Heron, Mike, 104, 287

High Numbers, the, 2–3, 155, 267–268, 360

Hitler, Adolf, 130

Hodenfield, Jan, 38

Hoffman, Abbie, 40, 52, 54, 107, 284

Hogg, Quintin, 123

Hollingsworth, Roy, 148–149

Holly, Buddy, 9, 347

"Hollywood Dream" (Thunderclap Newman), 114, 115

Hooker, John Lee, 265, 270–271, 306

Hopkins, Nicky, 124, 139–140, 275, 279

"However Much I Booze," 225

Howlin' Wolf, 267, 347

Huffington Post, 365–379

Hughes, Ted, 291

"Hullabaloo," 9–10

Hynde, Chrissie, 253

IBC, 115, 327

"I Am an Animal," 249
"I Am the Sea," 160
"I Believe in Everything," 64
"I Can't Reach You," 139
"I Can See for Miles," 42, 185, 272–273, 276
"I Can't Explain," 5–6, 49, 123–124, 135, 153, 246, 269, 288, 341, 382
"I Don't Even Know Myself," 39, 41, 247
"I Don't Know" (Thunderclap Newman), 115
"(I Know) I'm Losing You" (Rod Stewart), 365
"I'm a Boy," viii, 151, 154, 231
"I'm Free," 30, 129
"I'm One," 160
"I'm the Face," 267–268
Iggy and the Stooges, 166
"Imaginary Man," 192
In the City album (the Jam), 220
"In the Ether," 346, 347
Incredible String Band, 41
International Musician and Recording World, 235–243
International Times, x, 12–37
Iron Man, The album (Pete Townshend), 291, 301, 305–307
"Is It in My Head," 163
Isle of Wight festivals, 144, 150, 274
"It's Hard," 378
It's Hard album, 290, 339, 342, 349, 377
"It's Not True," 121
Ivy League, 124, 135

Jackson, Ziggy, 4
Jagger, Mick, 50, 97–98, 132, 142, 166, 177–178, 180, 187, 220, 269, 290, 371, 383
Jam, the, 220–221, 224, 285–286
James Gang, 145, 274
Jefferson Airplane, 53
Jenkins, Gordon, 184
John, Elton, 140–141, 196, 220, 225
Johns, Glyn, ix, 68, 97, 109, 110–111, 114, 122, 132, 142, 224, 279, 280, 282, 308–309, 335, 375–376, 378
Johnson, Wilko, 265
"Join My Gang" (Hair soundtrack), 121
"Joker James," 129
Jones, Brian, 39, 45, 50, 132
    death, 50–51, 350
Jones, Colin, 1, 351–352

Jones, Elvin, 240
Jones, Kenney, 246, 247, 290, 313–316, 363, 365–379, 380
    instrumentation, 367–368
    joining the Who, 376–377
    Keith Moon, 362–363, 375–376
    musical influences, 367–368
Jones, Philly Joe, 240
Jones, Steve, 215, 388
Jones Gang, 365
Joplin, Janis, 81

Kameron, Pete, 332
Keen, John "Speedy," 113–114
Kell, Peter Vernon, 266
Kerrang! magazine, 338
Khan, Imrat, 109
"Kids Are Alright, The," 163
Kids Are Alright, The film, 223, 227, 241, 245, 359
King, B. B., 266, 272
King, Dave, 119–120
King, Kay, 11
King, Martin Luther, Jr., 80, 154
Kinks, the, 47, 124, 135, 151, 180, 328, 337, 370, 382
Klein, Allen, 122, 214–215
Kooper, Al, 140–141
Krupa, Gene, 240
Kubrick, Stanley, 301

Lambert, Constant, 2, 129, 157
Lambert, Kit, 1, 2, 3–6, 7, 8, 48, 83, 95, 97, 105, 112, 118, 120, 126, 129–130, 141, 151, 157, 226, 267, 335, 360
    drug use, 329, 333
    production work, 37, 109, 111, 121, 270, 278, 279, 281
    script for Tommy, 20, 82, 332
Lancing and Trinity College, 2
Landscape, 286
Lane, Ronnie, 96, 105, 280, 282, 288, 369, 372–373
"Last Time, The," (the Rolling Stones), 171
Law, the, 365, 367
Lawless, John, 151–159
"Layin' Down the Law" (the Law), 367
"Lazy Fat People" (the Barron Knights), 121–122
Leary, Timothy, 42

Led Zeppelin, ix, 149, 316, 328, 338–339, 370, 382
Lee-Potter, Lynda, 342
"Legal Matter, A," 122
Lennon, John, 155, 156
Lerner, Murray, 359
"Let My Love Open the Door," 249, 285
"Let's See Action," 139
Lewis, Edward, 9, 10, 11
Lifehouse project, ix, 109, 139, 141, 149, 229, 241, 279–280, 326, 328–330, 336, 343
    narrative, 330–331, 333–334
    recording, 331–333
Lindsay-Hogg, Mike, 241
"Listening to You I Get the Music," 129, 131
Lisztomania film, 196–198, 199
"Little Is Enough, A," 248–249, 285
Live Aid, 313, 365, 375
Live at Leeds album, ix, 39, 49–50, 111, 128–129, 152
Live8, 355
Locke, Patricia, 9
London Coliseum, 146, 152
London Symphony Orchestra, 28
"Love Ain't for Keeping," 70, 141
"Love Man, The," 40
"Love Me Do" (the Beatles), 156
"Love, Reign o'er Me," ix, 160
Luongo, Steve, 339
Lydon, John, 246
Lynyrd Skynyrd, 222

Mad Dog album (John Entwistle), 204
Madison Square Garden, 59, 183, 193
Madonna, 292
"Magic Bus," 49, 294
Mahal, Taj, 132
Maharishi (Mahesh Yogi), 31
Mahler, Gustav, 30
Mahoney's Last Stand film, 288
Mail on Sunday/Event, The, 380–389
"Man in a Purple Dress, A," 347
Mansfield, Mike, 241
Marcus, Greil, 244–262
Marquee Club, 4, 5, 6, 16, 250–251
Marriott, Steve, 105, 177, 369, 372–373
Marsh, Dave, 303
Martin, Derek, 124
Mayfair Ballroom, 127

McCartney, Linda, 375
McCartney, Michael, 375
McCartney, Paul, 10, 155, 156–157, 158, 211, 284, 371, 375
McCulloch, Jimmy, 113
McInnerney, Mike, 27
McKenna, Paul, 384
McKinnon, Mike, 138
McKnight, Connor, 95–150
McLagan, Ian "Mac," 365, 368, 369, 372
McLaren, Malcolm, 232
McNally, Richard, 344
McViar, 360
Meaden, Peter, 160, 267–268, 328
Meaty Beaty Big and Bouncy album, 173
Melody Maker, 137–139, 151
Metzger, Gustav, 13, 334
Middlesex Youth Orchestra, 4
Miles, Barry, 12–37
Mitchell, Mitch, 321
"Mirror Door," 347
mods, 106, 155, 158, 160–161, 187–188, 216, 285, 376
    Quadrophenia and, 161–163, 168–169
    Shepherd's Bush, 6, 105
Monterey Pop Festival, 101, 145, 245, 275, 361
Moody Blues, the, 229, 330

Moon, Keith, vii, 81, 84, 91–94, 134, 154–155, 158, 161, 174, 179, 192, 199, 201, 204, 235–243, 267, 290, 330, 357, 365, 373–374
    chauffeur's death, 52, 312
    death, 235, 244–245, 246, 248, 275, 283, 300, 308, 315, 319, 321, 348, 350, 351, 362–363, 375–376, 382, 388
    depression, 307–309, 310–313
    drugs and alcohol, 48, 51, 101, 102–103, 105, 178, 307–309, 311, 350, 376
    drum kit, 235–240
    electronic instruments and music, 235–236
    fashion, 7
    headphones, 92–93
    health, 238–239
    John Entwistle, about, 236–237, 239
    Kenney Jones on, 362–363, 375–376
    Pete Townshend on, 102–104, 120–121, 129, 168–169, 172, 178, 234, 276, 281, 307–310, 314–315, 317, 321, 328, 388

live performance, viii, 4, 60, 79, 92, 103–104, 129, 145, 147, 183, 209, 240–242, 242–243, 271
musical influences, 240
nickname, 61
parents, 4–5
pranks, 102–103, 310, 312, 361–362
production work, 104–105
rehearsal time, 238
style, 237–238, 240–242, 368–369, 375
That'll Be the Day film, 168–169
Tommy, 21, 37, 92, 93, 94, 239
touring, 93–94, 223, 242
Morrison, Jim, 31, 384
Mothers of Invention, the, 27
Murray, Charles Shaar, 160–173
"Murray the K" Easter Show, 59
Music Echo, 6
Music from Big Pink (the Band), 100
"Music Must Change," 218
Musician, 290–318
"My Generation," viii, ix, 2, 8–9, 10, 15, 16, 43, 46, 49, 54, 135, 154, 158, 163, 165, 175, 179, 183, 212, 222, 230, 232, 269–270, 275, 290, 293, 349, 351–352, 363–364, 382, 389
inspiration for, 380–381
"My Size," 62
"My Wife," 64, 84, 207, 257
Myths and Legends of King Arthur and the Knights of the Round Table, The (Rick Wakeman), 184

National Front, 231, 233, 259
New Musical Express, x, 6
interviews with Pete Townshend, 160–189, 192–193, 196, 200, 214–234
interview with Roger Daltrey, 190–202
"New Song," 229
"New Speedway Boogie" (the Grateful Dead), 255
New Order, 286
New Wave, 218–220, 230–231
Newman, Andy "Thunderclap," 113, 115–117
Nicholls, Billy, 280, 287
Nighy, Bill, 354
"Normal Day for Brian, a Man Who Died Every Day, A," 39, 51

"Note, The," 110
"Number 29 (External Youth)," 63, 68

Oakland Coliseum Arena, 245
Oasis, 380
Observer, x, 1–11, 151–159
Observer Music Monthly, 345–358
Odds & Sods, 174, 177, 281
Odessey and Oracle album (the Zombies), 36
Ogdens' Nut Gone Flake album (Small Faces), 105, 177, 379
"Old Cornmill" (Thunderclap Newman), 115
Old Grey Whistle Test, The television show, 176
Oldham, Andrew Loog, 8, 122, 366
Oldman, Edward, 122
Olympic Studios, 121, 335
On the Air, 245, 256
One Direction, 388–389
100 Faces, the, 4, 6
"Open the Door Homer" (Thunderclap Newman), 114–115
Orchid Ballroom, 146
Original Mirrors, the, 272, 286
Orwell, George, 357
Otway, John, 215
Oval, the, 145, 148–149
"Overture," 118, 140
Ox, The, 178, 208–209

Page, Jimmy, 124, 135, 181, 328
Page, Stephen, 352
Palladino, Pino, 345, 349
Pappalardi, Felix, 141–142, 333
Parker, Charlie, 270
Passion of the Christ, The film, 347
Passion Play, A album (Jethro Tull), 184
Pepsi, 292
Percival, Eamonn, 235–243
Perrin, Les, 50
Pete Townshend: Who He, 352
Pete Townshend's Back Pages, 217
Phillips, Binky, 365–379
Phillips, Eddie, 326–327
Phillips, Simon, 290, 314, 315–316
"Pick Me Up (Big Chicken)," 62
"Pick Up My Guitar and Play," 109
"Pictures of Lily," viii, 247
PiL, 246
Pin-Ups album (David Bowie), 165

"Pinball Wizard," 26, 37, 40, 382
Pink Floyd, 113, 185, 278–279, 382
Plant, Robert, 370
Platz, David, 6
Please Please Me album (the Beatles), 158, 370
Poe, Edgar Allan, 18
Polydor, 120, 190–191, 200
Pop, Iggy, 166
Pop Art, 7–8
Porter, Cole, 40
Presley, Elvis, 345, 347
Pretenders, the, 253
Pridden, Bob, 136
Procol Harum, 34–36
"Punk and the Godfather, The," 174, 188
Punk movement, 283, 350
Purcell, Henry, 30
"Pure and Easy," 70, 109, 141

"Quadrophenia," 171,
Quadrophenia album, ix, 160–173, 192, 209, 213, 247, 347
    artwork, 164
    film, 241, 245, 259–260, 262, 360
    narrative, 161–162, 167–173
    Pete Townshend on, 164–165, 167–173, 226, 259–260, 272, 276, 281, 282
    post-production work, 170–171
Quick One, A, album, 15, 58, 85, 111, 323
Quiver, 146

Radio London, 5
Radio 3, 344
"Rael," 128, 129
Railway Hotel, 360–361
Railway Tavern, 2, 11
Rainbow, the, 146
Ramport recording studio, 281
Reaction Records, 120–121
Ready Steady Go, television show, 5–6, 7, 241
Ready Steady Who EP, 111–112
"Real Good Looking Boy," 338, 345
"Real Me, The," 160, 161, 163, 168, 297
Record Mirror, 7
Record Plant studios, 141–142, 333
Redding, Noel, 317
Reed, Jimmy, 133, 265
Remembering Trauma, 344
"Revolution" (Thunderclap Newman), 114

Richard, Cliff, 288
Richard/Richards, Keith, 52, 132–133, 158, 277
Richmond Organization, 10
Rickman, Jackie, 154, 384
Ride a Rock Horse album (Roger Daltrey), 190–191, 199
Rigor Mortis Sets In album (John Entwistle), 204
Riley, Terry, 279
Riverfront Coliseum, 244–245, 246, 250, 254–258, 339–340, 350, 378
Robert James Hairdressers, 3
"Rock, The," 168, 171
Rock & Roll Hall of Fame, 298
Rock Against Racism concert, 284
Rock and Roll Circus film, 55, 132
"Rock Around the Clock" (Thunderclap Newman), 116
Rock Farm, 125
Rockestra concert, 284
Roddam, Franc, 259, 262
Rodgers, Paul, 313, 315, 367
Rolling Stone, x, 38–57, 132, 138–139, 244–262, 352
Rolling Stones, the, 8, 28, 41, 45, 47, 48, 51, 55, 59, 78, 96, 98–99, 106, 122, 132–133, 142, 143, 151, 158, 171, 220, 246, 269, 277, 288, 325, 336–337, 348, 360, 365, 382
Roman, Murray, 134
Rosen, Steve, 203–213
Rotten, Johnny. *See* Lydon, John
Rough Mix (Pete Townshend and Ronnie Lane), 282
Rough Trade, 258–259
Royal Albert Hall, 142–143, 274, 348, 383
Royal Theatre, Copenhagen, 152
Rubber Soul album (the Beatles), 370
"Run, Run, Run," 16
Russell, Bertrand, 269
Russell, Ethan, 164
Russell, Ken, 178, 197, 377

Sadler's Wells Theatre, 129, 152
Sgt. Pepper's Lonely Hearts Club Band album (the Beatles), 48, 156–157, 184, 185
St. Mary's Ballroom, 133, 277
Salkin, Marty, 10
"Sally Simpson," 24, 31, 129, 140, 144
Sampson, Anthony, 1
Sampson, Sally, 1

Sandon, Doug, 155
Santana, Carlos, 53
Saturday Night Fever film, 221
Scary Monsters album (David Bowie), 287
Scene, the, 158
Schlitz, 296
Scritti Politti, 350
Seaman, Dick, 114, 116
Sebastian, John, 100
"See Me, Feel Me," 118, 129, 131, 276
"See My Friends," 135
"Seeker, The," 40, 41, 42–43, 247
"Sensation," 27
Sex Pistols, 215–216, 232, 253, 283, 336, 388
Shadows, the, 264
"Shaking All Over," 49, 54
Shankar, Ravi, 145
"She Loves You" (the Beatles), 158
Shepperton Studios, 227, 235, 241
"Sheraton Gibson," 280
Shine on Brightly album (Procol Harum), 34–35
Sinclair, John, 284
Sky, 283
Sly and the Family Stone, 54, 144
Small Faces, 17, 105–106, 155, 244, 335,
    365–366, 369–371, 376, 379
"Smash the Mirror," 26
Smash Your Head Against the Wall album (John
    Entwistle), 61, 204
Smith, Jimmy, 267
Smith, Patti, 228
Smothers Brothers Show, The, 361–362
Snow Goose, The (Camel), 185
"So Much Love," 140
"Something in the Air" (Thunderclap Newman),
    112, 114, 278
Sondheim, Stephen, 346
"Song Is Over, The," 74–75, 76–77, 109–110, 141
Soul Stirrers, 298
Souster, Tim, 279
Southern TV, 6
Springsteen, Bruce, 268, 269, 272, 306
Squadronaires, the, 352
"Squeeze Box," ix
Stamp, Chris, 1, 2, 118, 120, 126, 151, 157,
    214–215, 226, 259, 332, 352, 360
    promotional campaigns, 5, 6, 7, 8, 9–11
Stamp, Terence, 2, 10, 95, 157
Stanshall, Viv, 84, 104

Starkey, Zak, 319, 321, 345, 349, 363
Starr, Ringo, 47, 155, 157, 319
States Opera House, 152
Stern, Howard, 342
Stewart, Rod, 106, 220, 365, 373
Stewart, Tony, 190–202, 214–234
Sticky Fingers album (the Rolling Stones), 336
Stigwood, Robert, 8, 120, 121
Stills, Stephen, 327
Stockhausen, Karlheinz, 18, 332
Stone, Sly, 144
Stormy Petrel, 116
Strauss, Johann, 29
Stray Cats, the, 279
Studio 2,000, 5
"Substitute," viii, 49, 120–121, 122, 154, 246,
    275, 382
"Summertime Blues" (Eddie Cochran), 49, 54,
    158
Sunday Telegraph, 55–57
Sweet, 166
Swenson, John, 58–94
Szymczyk, Bill, 377–378

Takoma, 279
Talking Heads, 283
Talmy, Shel, 5, 15, 112, 120, 121, 122–124, 135
Taylor, Mick, 51, 97
"Ted End," 62–63
Teenage Cancer Trust Charity, 319–320, 321,
    357
That'll Be the Day film, 168
"That's for Me," 6
Thatcher, Margaret, 387
Theatres des Champs-Elysées, 152
"There's a Fortune in Those Hills," 39
Threepenny Opera, The film, 297
Thunderclap Newman, 39, 44, 96, 112–117, 278
"Tin Soldier" (Small Faces), 365
Tobler, John, 95–150, 263–289
Tommy album, viii–ix, 39, 92, 93, 94, 125–126,
    152, 161, 184, 197, 239, 246, 273, 281,
    323, 347, 362
    audience, 45, 47, 54, 268, 289, 331
    Dream Sequence, 23–24
    ending, 31–33
    EP, 117–119
    film based on, 82, 125, 174, 179, 251,
        281–282, 332, 377

John Entwistle on, 25–26, 37, 61, 65–67, 153, 209
live performances of, 21–22, 40, 41, 54, 59, 60, 66, 72, 144, 146, 148, 185, 284
musical influences on, 27–31
narrative and structure, 23–27, 32–34, 45–46, 130–131, 152, 172, 329
Pete Townshend on, 19–37, 45, 47–48, 72, 111, 117–119, 128–131, 140, 148, 153, 160, 172, 185, 251, 273, 274–276, 288, 306, 329, 332–333, 335, 353, 383
Roger Daltrey on, 325, 357, 385
time spent making, 22
"Tommy Can You Hear Me," 26
Top of the Pops, television show, 6, 130, 175, 241
Tork, Peter, 100
Torme, Mel, 184
Townshend, Karen. *See* Astley, Karen
Townshend, Pete, 92, 93, 95–150, 158, 161, 192, 196, 203, 214–234, 244–262, 290, 303, 317, 322, 324, 326–348, 360, 362, 376–377, 380–382
  art school, 13–14, 100, 106, 116, 185, 266, 341, 347
  autobiography, 341–343, 351–352, 385–386
  "Birdman, The," 4, 158
  Brian Jones' death, 50–51
  child abuse, 301, 309, 326, 343–344, 352
  child pornography case, 342–343, 353–355, 385
  childhood, 264, 266, 309, 343–344, 352
  corporate sponsorship/commercials, 291–295, 317
  drugs and alcohol, 53, 55–57, 79, 99–102, 125, 138–139, 166, 188, 215–216, 216–217, 227, 233, 249, 275, 279, 290–291, 299, 304–305, 308–309, 350–351, 387–388
  early influences, 264
  electronic instruments and music, 16, 70–74, 96, 126–128, 186, 268–269, 279
  family and marriage, 102–103, 154, 248–249, 250, 304–305, 353, 384
  feedback, 3, 16, 184, 270–271, 328
  film projects, 69–70, 75, 82, 94, 157
  getting old, 175–176, 182–183, 192–193, 217–220, 225–227, 230–234, 249–250, 272, 276, 288, 386
  guitar playing, 180–181, 212–213, 265, 277, 280

guitars, 277–278, 318
hearing issues, 298–301, 304, 318, 362, 387
John Entwistle, about 80, 84, 178, 179, 183, 388, 389
Keith Moon, about, 102–104, 120–121, 129, 168–169, 172, 178, 234, 276, 281, 307–310, 314–315, 317, 321, 328, 388
Kenney Jones, 314–316
Lifehouse, ix, 109, 139, 141, 149, 229, 241, 279, 328–334, 336, 343
live performance, 4, 12–18, 58–59, 60, 72–73 75–76, 79–80, 94, 144–145, 147, 158, 181, 188, 224, 247, 268, 271–272, 277, 342
making of the Who, 1–11
Meher Baba, 39–40, 43, 48, 55–56, 84, 99, 101, 128, 138–139, 227, 228, 233, 253, 274–275, 279, 280
Melody Maker column, 137–139
musical influences, 264–266, 286–287
parents, 263, 266, 286, 309, 352, 386
patronage of other musicians, 273–274, 278
physical appearance, viii, 1, 351–352
politics, 130, 230–233, 259–260, 284–285, 302
production work, 39–40, 95, 170–171
Quadrophenia, 164–165, 167–173, 226, 259–260, 272, 276, 281, 282
rock, thoughts about, ix–x, 46–47, 77–79, 165–166, 182–183, 187–188, 218–222, 227–228, 230–232, 252–253–254
rock journalists, thoughts about, 165–166, 171
Roger Daltrey, about, 79, 84, 121, 179, 221, 225–226, 250, 251, 258, 265, 281, 383–385, 386
solo albums, 244–245, 248–249, 285–287, 290–291, 301, 305–306, 339, 340–341, 349, 377–378
songwriting royalties, 6
Thunderclap Newman, 113–117, 278
Tommy, 19–37, 45, 47–48, 72, 111, 117–119, 128–131, 140, 148, 153, 160, 172, 185, 251, 273, 274 276, 288, 306, 329, 332–333, 335, 353, 383
touring, 69–70, 223, 255–256, 272, 276, 278, 298, 305–306, 386
Who's Next, 70, 72–74, 108–110, 119–120, 139, 141, 173, 279, 328–329, 333–338
Woodstock, 52–55
youth culture, 187–188, 258–262

Townshend, Simon, 245, 255–256, 349
Track Records, 95, 115, 117, 119–120, 134
Traffic, 145
Travis, Geoff, 258–259
Travolta, John, 221
Tremeloes, the, 145
"Trick of the Light," 218
Tull, Jethro, 132, 184
2 I's Coffee Bar, The, 5
2001: A Space Odyssey film, 29

UFO Club, 278
U2, 286, 380, 389
Ultravox, 286
Uncle Meat album (the Mothers of Invention), 27, 29
"Under My Thumb" (the Rolling Stones), 171
"Underture," 129, 140
Universal Pictures, 332
Untamed, the, 121

Vagabonds, the, 328
Vanilla Fudge, 35, 36, 184
Vicious, Sid, 261, 307
Vigoda, Joe, 10
Virgin Records, 286, 306
"Voodoo Chile," 119

W.A.S.P., 297
W.M.C.A., 10
W.N.E.W., 10
Wagner, Richard, 30
Wakeman, Rick, 184
Walsh, Joe, 273–274, 279
Warner Bros., 315
Waters, Muddy, 124
Waters, Roger, 278
Watford Trade Hall, 2
Watts, Charlie, 48
"Waltz for a Pig," 95, 123
"We're Not Gonna Take It," 30, 129–130
Weberman, A. J., 107–108
Webster, Martin, 259
Welch, Chris, 240
"Welcome," 31–32
Weller, Paul, 221, 230, 285–286
Wembley Arena, 196, 221
Wenner, Jann, 138–139, 352
West, Leslie, 141, 327

"What Are We Doing Here," 63, 67
"What Kind of People Are They," 63–64
"When I Think" (Thunderclap Newman), 1115
"Whiskey Man," 61
Whistle Rhymes album (John Entwistle), 204
White Hart, the, 267
Who, the, 194
   American Decca contract, 5, 6–7, 10–11
   audiences/fans, 79–81, 88–90, 93–94, 143,
      146–150, 146–150, 158, 181, 183, 186–
      187, 192, 221, 222, 225, 227, 230, 242,
      245–247, 250–251, 254–255, 257–258,
      337–338, 340–341
   back catalog, 323
   benefit concerts, 41, 283–284, 319–320, 321,
      365, 375
   breaking up, 80, 86, 105, 121, 141, 158,
      178–179, 196–197, 202, 215, 328, 362,
      380, 382
   comeback, 69–70
   commercials, music used in, 292–293
   concert tragedies, 80–81, 244–245, 246, 250,
      254–258, 339–340, 350, 378
   corporate sponsorship, 290, 291–298
   demos, 124–125
   DJs and 9–11
   early bookings, 3–4
   expenses and finances, 6–7, 8–9, 12, 14–15,
      52–55, 123–124, 153–154, 226, 241, 277,
      281–282, 291–292, 295–298, 306, 332,
      360
   fashion, 3, 7, 155, 158, 370–371
   films about, 6, 8, 10, 55, 83, 86, 223, 241,
      359–364
   group dynamics, 72
   legal issues, 122–124, 195–197, 226, 257
   name changes, 3
   opera tours, 54–55
   photo sessions, 3
   production on records, 47–48, 120–121,
      123–124, 141
   publicity campaigns, 6, 8–11
   relationships with the press, x
   sound, 157–158
   standards, 177–178
   support acts, 142–146
   tours, vii, 8, 102, 145–146, 154, 221–223,
      305–306, 345, 349, 380, 381–382
"Who Are You," ix, 216, 218, 388

Who Are You album, 214, 217, 218, 222, 229, 235, 246, 275, 283, 307–308, 382

Who by Numbers album, ix, 191–192, 214, 218, 220, 225–226, 230, 281, 285

Who Came First album (Pete Townshend), 280

Who Hits 50! album, 380

Who I Am, 385–386

Who Orchestra, The, 123

Who Sell Out, The album, 19, 85, 139, 288, 296

Who 2, 348

Who's Last album, 290

Who's Next album, ix, 58, 60, 85, 139, 192, 213, 325, 326, 362

   artwork for, 119–120

   deluxe version, 337–338

   Pete Townshend on, 70, 72–74, 108–110, 119–120, 139, 141, 173, 279, 328–329, 333–338

   Roger Daltrey on, 109, 321, 325, 328–329

Wholey, Dennis, 304

Williams, John, 283

Williams, Robbie, 380

Williamson, Sonny Boy, 25, 306

Wilson, Brian, 28

Winwood, Steve, 145

Wire & Glass, 347

"Won't Get Fooled Again," ix, 70, 73, 87–88, 93, 94, 110, 130, 141, 218, 230, 275, 283, 293, 300, 323, 335, 337, 340–341, 349, 382, 386

Wood, Ronnie, 371

Woodstock film, 82–83, 273

Woodstock festival, 52–55, 82–83, 144, 274, 284, 384

Woolf, John "Wiggy," 136–137

World Trade Center attack, 321

Wright, Angus, 6

Wright, Tom, 42–43

Yardbirds, the, 268

Yes, 185–186

"You Better, You Bet," 378

"You Need Lovin'" (Small Faces), 369

"You Really Got Me" (the Kinks), 135

"You're Mine," 63, 67–68

Young, Charles M., 290–318

Young, Neil, 113, 279

"Young Man Blues," 49, 346

Young Vic, 125, 126–127, 137, 142, 331–332, 335

Youth Club, 2

Zappa, Frank, 27–29, 168

The Rise and Fall of Ziggy Stardust and the Spiders from Mars album (David Bowie), 161, 383

Zigzag, x, 95–150

Zombies, the, 36